# PRAISE FOR THE FIRST EDITION OF "INFANTS & TODDLERS"

*"In search of direction to their latest parenting dilemma, many parents head to their local bookstore only to end up further frustrated and confused as they gaze over the hundreds of titles available. Now parents can search quickly and effectively through some of the best resources available, identify a title or resource that will meet their needs, saving them time, money, and possibly their sanity. . . . a great gift for any new parent, a gift that they will use for years to come."*

Jerri Wolfe PhD
Parent Education Consultant, Boise, Idaho

*". . . we found this guide to be exciting, comprehensive, and hands-on practical for all who take on the most important job of parenting. It's organized, concise, and a great tool for any parent searching through the vast amount of literature for everyday help."*

Deborah Rosen
President, Organization For Parent Education, Seattle, Washington

*". . . an indispensable guide for parents and professionals working with families that includes reviews of parenting books and websites, a clear rating system for materials, and a well-organized format in which to find answers. . . . captures some of the best information about parenting young children and catalogs it in a manner that is user-friendly. The resource rating system will help parents decide where to spend their time and money."*

Debbie Reilly
Parents As Teachers Coordinator, Clayton School Stanley Center, Clayton, Missouri

*"A wonderfully useful resource for parents seeking to find their way in the multitude of advice available through books, tapes, videos, and the Internet. The detailed descriptions of each source of information gives parents an overview from which they can begin their search of how they want to nurture and guide their children."*

Harriet Heath, PhD
Haverford, Pennsylvania

*". . . will help parents and parents-to-be make sense of some of the mountain of materials that beckon from bookstore and library shelves. Visual codes help quickly determine format, age group, and audience for each entry. The indexes plus appendixes listing parent support organizations round out this useful work."*

Library Journal
January, 1999

*"Parenting is the toughest job there is. Most new parents know they need help and well-tested counsel, they just aren't sure where to find it. . . . now there's a way to really get connected—Infants & Toddlers: The Best Resources to Help You Parent."*

Portland Family Magazine
December, 1998

# INFANTS & TODDLERS

---

## The Best Resources To Help You Parent

**Second Edition**

*Julie Soto, MS*

*Editor*

A Resource Pathways Guidebook

Seattle, Washington

Published by Resource Pathways, Inc.
22525 S.E. 64th Place, Suite 253
Issaquah, WA  98027

*Editor:*   Julie Soto, MS

*Managing Editor:*
        Lisle Steelsmith, MA

*Associate Editors and Researchers:*
        Kathie Jackson Anderson,
        Lucy Campos, Jill K. Nixon

*Book Design and Production:*
        Sandra Harner and Kelly Rush
        Laing Communications Inc., Redmond, WA

*Printing:*   Hignell Book Printing, Winnipeg, Manitoba, Canada

*Publisher's Cataloging-in-Publication*

Infants & toddlers : the best resources to help you
        parent / Julie Soto, editor. -- 2nd ed.
            p. cm.
            Includes bibliographical references and
        indexes.
            LCCN: 99-60551
            ISBN: 1-892148-10-2

            1. Child care--Bibliography.  2. Parenting--
        Bibliography.   I. Soto, Julie.  II. Resource
        Pathways (Firm)  III. Title: Infants and toddlers

        Z7164.C5I64 1999              016.649'12
                        QBI99-405

Printed in Canada.

# CONTENTS

## III. Special Resources For Specific Purposes 317

## IV. Helpful Organizations 323

# INTRODUCTION

I

# INFANTS & TODDLERS: THE BEST RESOURCES TO HELP YOU PARENT

**"The Fine Art Of Parenting"**

*"Life affords no greater responsibility, no greater privilege, than the raising of the next generation"*

—C. Everett Koop

Those tiny hands and solemn stares, those all-mighty cries and smiles that tug at your heart . . . these are all signals that you have become a parent. But what does it really mean to "become a parent?" In basic terms, it means you have taken on the task of caring for and raising a child to become a contributing member of adult society. It also means that you have embarked on a journey whose destination is not clearly defined; you'll experience days full of new challenges and insights, ending with nights of wonderment and on occasion, exhaustion.

Parenting today is, in many ways, characterized by the same challenges and solutions parents have always faced. Nonetheless, parenting today is dramatically different than it was just a generation ago. For example, new research in infant and child development emphasizes the importance of effective parenting in the first three years. These findings, along with the new "methods" to handle various parenting situations, require that new decisions be made by new and prospective parents. This new body of knowledge, coupled with societal changes, lifestyle trends, and the evolving roles of men and women, means that some issues facing new families are more complex than they have ever been before.

With close to 75 percent of men and women returning to work shortly after the birth of their baby, new parents are rightly concerned whether or not their baby's caretaker is truly qualified to offer their child quality care. Working parents need information and advice to help them make informed decisions on care for their baby or child in their absence. Additionally, trying to juggle careers and home life can often create anxiety for working parents. This is compounded by guilt they impose on themselves or that others impose on them for placing their child in someone else's care.

On the other hand, some parents choose to take a leave of absence from their job or career and stay home to be the primary caretaker of their child. Not only are family finances impacted, but responsibilities shift for each parent, and confusion can set in as new roles are defined. Stay-at-home parents, too, need information, support, and ideas to make this transition easier and help them use available time and money effectively.

With time at a premium and budgets constrained, parents today want to make wise choices, whether it be the furniture they buy to outfit their nursery, the childcare provider they hire to care for their baby or child, or the way they structure their "spare" time with their child. But no matter what their circumstances are, whether one parent is staying at home with the children or both parents are working, one thing remains constant—parents want the best information available. In short, they want answers to their questions and they want practical, concise guidance that can be digested quickly.

# THE PURPOSE OF THIS GUIDEBOOK

Our purpose in creating this guidebook is to identify the best resources to help you as you parent your baby or child. We have divided our resource reviews into four topical chapters to help you find what you need quickly.

- **"Caring for Your Child"**—Many parents wish they had an "owner's manual" to accompany their child's birth and many of these resources are included in this section. Some focus on the more general aspects of baby and child care, while others highlight specific concerns such as breastfeeding, choosing a caregiver, coping with a baby's crying and finding ways to soothe a baby, buying equipment and supplies, feeding a baby or toddler, and helping a baby or child go to sleep.

- **"Understanding Your Child's Growth And Learning"**— Children grow and as they do, parents find they face new challenges. Sometimes a child may follow a parent's request, while at other times a child's temper tantrums, aggression, whining, or that formidable "no!" can all add up to making a parent question their resolve and esteem. Resources we have identified in this chapter aim at helping parents understand their child's development in general terms, and then specifically as it applies to their child's behavior and discipline, selection of activities, and toilet training.

- **"Strengthening Your Family"**—Parenthood brings about many changes especially in terms of each person's perception of their role within the family. Fathers and mothers strive to create a sense of family while transitioning from their previous role as a couple. Women may get caught up in the "Superwoman" myth while men may seek to understand the strong emotional changes their tiny baby has induced. Many families make this transition smoothly while others struggle. Issues arise such as clarifying family values and morals, deciding upon a parenting style to suit both partners, and combining work and family life. Added to this confusion are the adjustments an older sibling may encounter while a new baby is being introduced into the family, and parents' time and attention are now at a premium. Resources in this chapter focus on ways to successfully adapt to fatherhood, motherhood, and a new sibling. Also provided are avenues for parents to connect to other parents for support and advice.

- **"All-Inclusive Overviews About Parenting"**—The resources in this chapter address the broad scope of issues parents will encounter while raising their baby or young child, from changing their diaper to changing their behavior. Many of these tomes offer general perspectives which can, of course, be further supplemented with resources more specifically focused. Several resources are websites which not only present basic information on virtually all aspects of parenting a child, but also offer forums for parents to converse through the Internet and learn from the "true experts"—other parents.

# How This Guidebook Is Organized

This guidebook is designed to help you as you parent your baby or young child. In it, we have:

- Identified the key issues you'll face from the moment your child is born through their toddler years.

- Provided detailed full-page reviews of over 280 resources so you can identify those best suited to your interests and needs.

- Created an extensive table of contents, multiple indices, and a comprehensive list of support organizations to serve as clear "pathways" to the most useful resources for each key issue.

Following this introduction, you will find we have divided the guidebook into four sections:

- **Resource Reviews**—the heart of the book, with full-page reviews of resources from a variety of media. These reviews are organized according to the topical chapters described earlier. Each chapter begins with background information and advice on the topic with the resource reviews following. These reviews include a fact-filled description, an evaluation section, "ease-of-use" and "overall" ratings, background on authors, and publishing and purchasing information. Our full-page reviews are hierarchically arranged according to Overall Rating (1–4 Stars) within each topical chapter, and the best resources (4 Stars) are always listed first. Each follows the same format making it easy to do cross-comparisons to find the resource that best meets your family's needs.

- **Special Resources For Specific Purposes**—short descriptions of 12 outstanding resources that we find especially useful in specific parenting situations. Use this chapter to gain support and advice for such concerns as parenting an only child, parenting twins or multiples, or parenting a strong-willed child. Other recommended resources here offer parenting advice according to Christian perspectives, the latest in brain research, and other areas. In any case, we encourage you to also refer to the full-page reviews of these resources as presented in and cross-referenced to the topical chapters.

- **Helpful Organizations**—a comprehensive directory with up-to-date contact and background information on more than 60 organizations offering parental support, education, and referrals.

- **Indices**—six resource indices arranged alphabetically by title, author, publisher, media type, subject, and age group (which is further subdivided according to the guidebook's chapters). Resources are also arranged by Overall Rating within the subject, media type, and age group indices to help you get to the information you need quickly.

## How We Develop Our Reviews and Recommendations

Our editors and researchers have identified virtually all available sources of consumer-oriented information focused on parenting infants and toddlers, including books, Internet resources, videotapes, audio cassettes, and CD-ROMs.

We have created a concise, one-page review of each resource. Each review contains information about the resource (author, publisher, number of pages, and edition copyright date), describes its content and focus, evaluates its quality, style, scope, and effectiveness, and summarizes our findings in an **Overall Rating** and an **Ease-of-Use Rating**. We also provide prices and "where to find or buy" information for each resource.

Our Star Rating system is defined as follows:

| FOUR STAR RATING SYSTEM |
| --- |
| ★★★★  Highly recommended—top quality at a fair price! |
| ★★★  Well done—a good resource, but not outstanding. |
| ★★  Worth considering—check the description. |
| ★  Your time and money are better spent elsewhere. |

We have put a great deal of time and effort into reviewing and evaluating these resources. Here is how the process works:

- **Printed Material**: We read the book cover to cover, identify the author's focus, and make a judgment about how the contents are best applied. Our judgment about the relative quality of each book is based upon readability, organization, breadth and depth, and style. We make every effort to ensure that the latest editions of books are reviewed, and that no out-of-print resources are included.

- Internet Websites & Online Services: We review all websites and online services that have significant original material related to the subject of parenting babies and toddlers. Our reviews consider the site's graphic and navigation design, as well as the usefulness of material provided relative to that available in other media. We revisit sites frequently to stay abreast of revisions and improvements.

  We include the current "address" (URL) of the homepage or a specific page within a website to facilitate direct access on the Internet. Of course, the World Wide Web is a dynamic place, and many URLs will change over time. If you find that an address is outdated, we recommend that you simply delete the last expression in the address and hit the "Enter" or "Return" key again.

This procedure will point your browser to a file "further up" in the website's file directory. In most cases, you will return to the website's homepage (indicated by the phrase ending in ".com," ".edu," ".gov," etc.). From there, you can find your way back to the specific information or page you were looking for.

- **CD-ROMs:** We carefully review all facets of each CD-ROM, including all branches and multimedia options, and thoroughly test software applications available on disk. Our reviews include judgments about the "cost/benefit" of multimedia additions, as well as the product's usefulness relative to the same offering in other media. We also note technical problems in loading or using programs provided.

- / **Videotapes and Audio Cassettes:** We evaluate each product's content, visual and audio quality, and usefulness relative to print, electronic, and Internet offerings.

## Note:

We do not review high-cost CD-ROM based products or videotapes sold primarily to professionals with costs that are out of reach for most families.

Because our mission is to help you find your way through this "forest" of information and take control of the issue at hand, we also make carefully considered recommendations on which resources will best serve your needs. Only 25 percent of the resources we review are recommended. We base our recommendations on the resource's value, relative to alternatives in the same media and against all available sources regardless of media.

**Recommended resources** can be found directly following each chapter's introduction and are noted by the following icon:

**"Recommended For:"**

Additionally, resources that are recommended as **"Special Resources for Specific Purposes"** are noted with the following icon:

**"Special Resource For:"**

## Conventions Used

Throughout this guidebook and our reviews, we have adopted the convention of using certain terms which are defined as follows:

- **Infants**—children from birth to the age at which they are walking (about one year of age)

- **Toddlers**—children from the time they are walking (about one year of age) to age three

- **Parent or Parents**—refers to biological parents, stepparents, adoptive parents, foster parents, or any other guardians responsible for the care and safety of a child

- **Child care**—the act of providing for the health and development of a baby or child

- **Childcare**—care provided by another person or persons during the parents' absence

- **Caregiver**—those who provide care for a child during the parents' absence

# RESOURCE
# REVIEWS

II

# CHAPTER ONE—CARING FOR YOUR CHILD

"How can they send us home from the hospital without an owners' manual?" New parents are naturally concerned they won't know how to take care of this new member of their family. They get countless "words of wisdom" from others trying to help. In trying to solve this mystery, parents may venture into a bookstore or a library in search of that elusive complete "how-to manual" only to be overwhelmed at the number of resources available. Where do parents start?

The good news is that there are lots of "owners' manuals" out there, waiting for someone to "drive" them home and be "parked" next to a parent's reading chair. The bad news is that many of them barely meet parents' needs, or fail to answer their questions in a concise and readily digested manner. Recommendations on child care seem to be constantly changing and come from all directions—the medical community, researchers and educators, politicians, and parents.

Prospective parents may find it hard to understand why taking care of a new baby should be so difficult. But as soon as their newborn baby starts crying, parents generally start panicking, and the louder the cry, the stronger the panic: "What do we do now? Are we doing something wrong?" New and prospective parents are hungry for answers to such questions as:

- How do I choose a health care provider? How will I know when to call?
- If I'm going to return to work, I will need to find a caregiver; what are my options? How do I make the right choice?
- Should I breastfeed my baby or use a bottle? How will I know if my baby is getting enough nourishment?
- What things do I need to have for my baby? What furniture, what equipment, what clothing, what toys work best?
- My baby is crying! What's wrong? Is she sick, hurt, hungry, too hot, too cold?
- Is my baby sleeping too much, or perhaps too little?
- How and when do I bathe my new baby?
- How do I hold him? Is there such thing as holding a baby too much?

Parents of older babies and young children also have concerns, but their concerns differ. They focus on their child's daily habits—eating, sleeping, hygiene, and dental care—along with whether or not their child is "normal" in terms of their physical development. As their child begins to explore his or her environment, parents also worry about poisons and injuries. They want easily accessed information on how to take care of minor cuts and scrapes, along with how to handle major emergency situations.

Taking care of children requires that we understand the choices to be made in a wide variety of issues. Some issues, such as breastfeeding, choosing a caregiver, and buying baby equipment and supplies, typically involve decisions often made during one's pregnancy, or shortly after childbirth. Other decisions, such as handling and soothing baby's crying, feeding baby, and helping baby sleep, are often made after parents and their newborn get settled in, or as baby grows older.

In the paragraphs that follow are some of the general and specific issues parents will encounter as they take care of their baby. Following this introduction are our recommendations for resources that can help parents deal with each of these concerns.

## General Overviews

During the course of our research, we have reviewed "all-inclusive" resources designed to help new parents survive those first few days, weeks, months, and years as they learn to take care of their new baby and child. These resources detail a child's general development along with suggestions of how parents can promote those milestones in growth. The "how-tos" of caring for, cleaning, diapering, and feeding a newborn are explained, as well as the basics for how to deal with a child's illnesses, hygiene, comforting, sleep issues, feeding decisions, and more. Parents will find tips on how to deal with anxious moments, along with how to decide when to enlist the help of their baby's doctor.

Our recommendations for all-inclusive guides include those resources whose recommendations are up-to-date, those that include numerous how-to photographs or illustrations, and those who present an objective parenting style so parents can decide important issues for themselves. Any one of these recommended guides will be a worthwhile companion to any new mother or father as they struggle to learn the fine art of parenting.

Although all-inclusive guides do a tremendous service by presenting much information in one convenient package, they often cannot offer in-depth information in any one area. Whenever you find you need help in a specific area, check out the recommendations we have made for the following topics:

- Breastfeeding
- Choosing A Caregiver
- Crying & Soothing

- Equipment & Supplies
- Feeding
- Sleep

# Breastfeeding

Recent scientific studies and findings emphasize the benefits involved with breastfeeding a baby and child. Some studies suggest that infants who have been breastfed have less chance of developing allergies, cancer, and other serious illnesses later on in life; others suggest that breastfeeding may even be good for a baby's brain development, their interpersonal relationships, and their ability to comfort others and themselves. Breastfeeding satisfies a baby's inherent need to suck for comfort and security, and contributes to a gentle introduction into their new world.

Some women may have already decided while they were pregnant that they want to breastfeed their baby. Others may be unsure whether or not they want to nurse their baby, or how long they will do it. Many prospective mothers want to nurse their infants but also know they will be returning to their jobs. Finally, how does a father fit into the picture? Without information to support him, a father may feel left out of the bond growing between mother and baby. It is imperative that fathers understand the nature and benefits of breastfeeding and how their support for a mother's decision to breastfeed is important.

The resources that we recommend can help you decide whether or not breastfeeding will be right for you. We have included a number of resources that will answer your questions from "How do I get started breastfeeding my baby?" to "How do I wean my child?" Many are written by lactation consultants specializing in breastfeeding. Many of these resources address special situations, such as returning to work while your baby is still young and breastfeeding, breastfeeding an adopted baby, how to breastfeed while your baby is in intensive care or if she or he has a handicap, how to nurse a toddler, and even how to breastfeed twins or multiples! These resources offer the support and information new fathers and mothers need to make breastfeeding a positive experience for the whole family.

# Choosing A Caregiver

Many parents have concluded they will need childcare at some point, while others may still be weighing this decision as they research their choices. Options for parents to choose from can range from one-on-one care in a parent's home, to a facility that houses children from infancy to school age. If parents wish to have in-home care, they can hire a nanny, a student from another country (commonly known as an "au pair"), or solicit help from another parent or relative. Parents who wish a home-like setting (but not necessarily their own home) may consider a family home center in which children of varying ages are cared for by one or more childcare workers. Another option is, of course, larger childcare centers. Finally, some employers address parents' needs for childcare and include a workplace childcare center for their employees' children, sometimes subsidized by the organization.

Regardless of which choice parents eventually make, there are a number of issues to keep in mind during their decision process. As parents search for quality care, the resources we recommend will help parents weigh the pros and cons of the various childcare situations and settings that are available. These resources offer application forms, ideas for interview questions, forms for screening applicants, tips on how to conduct criminal record checks, tax information, descriptions of your responsibilities as an employer, agreement contracts, and more. They also offer advice and support to help parents and children through this transition. We also refer parents to some resources listed in Chapter Four "All-Inclusive Overviews About Parenting"; several resources present philosophical discussions about childcare issues. Be sure to read the full-page review of any resource you select to be sure it covers all the facets of this decision that pertain to your family's needs.

## Crying & Soothing

"Why does my baby keep crying? What's wrong?" It is rare to find a baby that doesn't cry, because instinctively babies know that is their primary way of communicating their needs. This distress signal is designed by nature so that parents can't ignore it. Responding to a baby's cries, figuring out what they need, and finding ways to soothe them can be a tiresome yet rewarding proposition. Babies cry for many reasons, and their cries have definite meanings (pain, diapers need changing, bored, hungry, and so on). And then there is "colic," for which scientists and doctors have yet to find a definitive cause. Babies with colic typically cry continually for more than three hours a day on more than three days within a week. Colic often begins a few weeks after birth and continues until the baby is about three months old. Knowing these bouts of crying will end at some juncture, however, doesn't help alleviate parents' frustrations and exhaustion. "What can we do to help our baby (and us) through this?"

Fortunately, several resources focus on a baby's primary means of communicating, their cries. These resources explain the importance of responding to a baby's cries, along with what the different cries sound like and what they mean. You will find tips on how to survive a "colic phase" that makes your baby miserable and fussy. If you are breastfeeding, many of these resources offer nursing tips that can help if your baby is fussy at the breast. These resources also briefly address the disadvantages and advantages of methods suggested by several "sleep trainers" that believe in a step-by-step process of letting babies cry themselves to sleep (for more in-depth information on the subject of nighttime waking/crying look to other recommended resources in the section following entitled "Sleeping").

## Equipment & Supplies

Many parents are faced with tight budgets, yet innumerable equipment and supplies are suggested by well-meaning friends. Which ones are really necessary, which ones will last, and for how long? If parents have ventured into the baby supply section of any store, they may find their choices overwhelming. Fortunately, there are resources available to help you make some sound decisions. We have listed some resources that can not only tell you what you REALLY need, but also compare one manufacturer's product with another. Some offer advice on how to find items for free or for a relatively inexpensive price. Some resources also include information about relative safety, pricing information, and manufacturer contact information.

Check out a few of our recommendations. Whether you are shopping for your new baby, a friend's shower present, or your future grandchild, chances are these resources will save you money.

## Feeding

"When do I start my baby on solids?" Surprisingly, this simple question has become a hot topic. In the past, it was suggested that babies would sleep better at night if they were fed solids as soon as possible. However, recent studies have shown that this may not be the case. Experts now suggest that, because of babies' immature digestive systems, parents should delay starting their baby on solids until they are four to six months old and certain readiness signs begin to appear, such as interest in what parents are eating, attempts to grab others' food, lessening of the tongue-thrust reaction (whereby food is projected back out), and more. Some suggest that starting as late as possible helps combat certain food allergies and digestive problems.

Once parents begin to give their baby solids, they can choose between manufactured baby food and homemade. Recently, nutritionists have publicized the extent to which manufactured baby foods contain additives and fillers, and conversely stressed the ease by which parents can make and store their own more nutritive food. To address this need, authors with backgrounds in cooking have compiled baby food recipes along with basic nutritional needs of babies, tips on how to prepare food, and ways to make and store large quantities. Other authors have followed suit and explored recipes to get toddlers and preschoolers (often known for their discriminating or "picky" eating habits) to try healthy snacks, main courses, desserts, and more.

Cookbooks involve a personal adventure since not everyone's tastes are the same. We've tried to recommend those resources that offer recipes that not only use fairly common household ingredients, but are also nutritious for growing bodies and are easily prepared. After all, feeding your child is important, but spending all day on a recipe as likely to be met with a "yum" as it is with a "yuck" may not be a good idea!

## Sleep

"Should I let my baby cry it out or should I pick her up and help her go back to sleep?" Who would have thought that the gentle act of helping a child go to sleep would create such controversy? "Sleep trainers" suggest that a baby's cries (or a child's) should be ignored for progressive periods of time each night, with the parents responding only after the timer goes off; this way, trainers say, babies will learn to soothe themselves. This approach has been rejected by those who believe in responding to all of baby's cries, simply because a baby needs to know that their needs are important and that the parents are there to help them. Sleep trainers stress that these "attached" parents will keep their child dependent and wear themselves out unnecessarily by constantly responding to baby's cries. To this, "attachment parenting" proponents reply that a baby IS dependent and adults need to change their sleep habits temporarily instead of insisting babies and children do so prematurely. One camp says that it won't do babies any harm to cry by themselves, while the other camp says that babies will learn that when they cry, it does not matter. To add to this confusion, other child experts argue the advantages of the "family bed" or "shared sleep" whereby parents and baby (or child) share the same bed with one another. To judge any method, parents need to look closely at the method's basis in objective research, and assess how well the method supports their own beliefs.

We have recommended those resources that we believe are backed by solid research and reflect undisputed facts about the developmental stages of babies and young children. Be sure to read the full-page review of any resource that we recommend to be sure it will meet your needs and answer specific questions you may have. To help focus your search for answers, we have divided our recommendations into these seven categories:

In addition, we recommend that parents also refer to our recommendations in Chapter Four—"All-Inclusive Overviews About Parenting." These resources present general discussions of child care along with other parenting concerns.

Think of parenting in terms of traveling a long distance by car. As you are driving, you will encounter advertising and conflicting information, quick decisions to be made, and destinations that change. But with the best "owners' manual" and a couple of detailed maps by your side, you can develop the confidence and skills to take care of any adjustments and emergencies along the way. Although being a parent is the most difficult job you will ever take, your journey is one whose destinations will bring you smiles, laughter, and joy.

*"A hundred years from now . . . it will not matter what my bank account was, the sort of house I lived in, or the kind of car I drove . . . but the world may be different because I was important in the life of a child."*

—Kathy Davis

## General Overviews

# BABY BASICS (VIDEOTAPE)
## The Complete Video Guide For New And Expectant Parents

**Recommended For:**
Taking Care Of Your Child

**Special Resource For:**
The how-tos of infant care and development (using a videotape)

## Description:

Focusing on the care and development of newborns and infants, this 110 minute videotape is divided into eight "chapters"; an accompanying booklet lists all subtopics. Combining professional advice and sample footage of four new families, this video takes parents through their newborn's life from birth onward. Chapters One and Two discuss "the newborn at birth" along with postpartum care of the mother. Chapter Three describes the newborn and new parents' first days at home with details about emotional adaptations, changes in the newborn, reflexes, development, signs of overstimulation, sleep states, and swaddling. "Daily Care" in Chapter Four offers information about bathing, diapering, dressing, circumcision and umbilical care, and more. Chapter Five includes breastfeeding how-tos (positions, problems, expression, storage) and bottlefeeding information. Chapter Six focuses on "Health and Safety" (check-ups, immunizations, illnesses, and more). Chapter Seven discusses babies' cries and sleep patterns, while Chapter Eight describes babies' growth and development.

## Evaluation:

The price tag is not exactly cheap, but this is the closest new parents will get to having a visual owners' manual to baby care. It will be like having a child health care provider/mother/close friend on hand offering advice and information every step of the way as a new parent struggles "on the job." The footage is excellent with real life demonstrations in every case. The companion booklet is very well-thought out suggesting that parents start their VCR counter on "O," view the tape, and then record the counter number next to each subtopic listed in the booklet. This will make for quick easy access for busy new parents who haven't the time to scan through the tape's two hours looking for the information they need later. The advice is up-to-date (despite its listed copyright date), and compiled from health care professionals, child development specialists, educators, and parents. The segment on breastfeeding in particular was outstanding offering advice and support for a subject that most often is best learned visually but not often presented in that form. This video is a must whether as a gift for new parents, the focus of a parent education class, or to help train a childcare provider.

## Where To Find/Buy:

Bookstores, libraries, videotape dealers, or order direct by calling Vida Health Communications at (800) 524-1013 or AMR at (877) 99VIDEO. Orders can also be taken online by AMR at http://www.amr1.com.

★★★★

**Overall Rating**
★★★★
Outstandingly comprehensive and illustrative, a must-have for any new parents

**Design, Ease Of Use**
★★★★
Companion booklet lists all "chapter" subtopics; real-life demos; concise and interesting

1–4 Stars

**Publisher:**
Vida Health Communications

**Edition:**
1987

**Price:**
$39.98

**Media:**
Videotape

**Principal Subject:**
Taking Care Of Your Child

**Secondary Subject:**
General Overview

**Age Group:**
Infants (0–1)

**★★★★**

### Overall Rating
★★★★
Excellent resource combining sight and sound for first-time or prospective parents

### Design, Ease Of Use
★★★★
Visually pleasing art backdrops, inspiring quotes, & video clips; navigation a breeze

1–4 Stars

### Publisher:
PARENTING/Time Publishing Ventures

### Edition:
1996

### Price:
$34.95

### Media:
CD-ROM

### Principal Subject:
Taking Care Of Your Child

### Secondary Subject:
General Overview

### Age Group:
Infants (0–1)

## General Overviews

# YOUR PREGNANCY, YOUR NEWBORN
## The Complete Guide For Expectant And New Mothers

### Recommended For:
Taking Care Of Your Child

### Special Resource For:
The how-tos of infant care and development (using CD-ROM)

### Description:
For Mac (3.1+, 68040/33+), Windows/DOS (3.1+, 5.0+; 486/66+). Created by the editors of *PARENTING* magazine, this CD-ROM is divided into five main sections. The first three focus on pregnancy with information on how to plan for pregnancy (work, exercise, health, etc.), a month-by-month description of pregnancy (baby development, changes in the mother, doctor relations), and labor & delivery (options, pain relief). Section Four highlights the newborn. Subtopic discussions include: the newborn's appearance, warning signs, senses, reflexes, communication, bonding, breastfeeding, bottlefeeding, and more. Section Five offers parents advice for "Life With Baby." Mom's needs, dad's needs, and baby's needs (feeding, sleeping, bathing, crying, etc.) are outlined. Also provided are baby health and safety tips from immunizations to first aid to car and home safety. A discussion of childcare options and issues is also given. An interactive pregnancy calendar is available, as well as an index and gift registry (Fisher-Price items).

### Evaluation:
This is a must for prospective parents. Although it comes with a pretty high price tag, it will prove valuable for calming the fears of new parents-to-be as they gain confidence in their parenting. Combining visually stunning backdrops, realtime video clips, and audio advice from experts, this CD-ROM fills a need not addressed elsewhere. Numerous experts and parents from *PARENTING* are made available to parents offering their advice about maternity leave rights, birth and delivery, the older mom's experience, exercise, breastfeeding, choosing childcare, and more. Two areas which lack depth, however, deal with how to start breastfeeding and how to administer first aid. For both of these areas, video clips would have been an asset. This resources is more expensive than most print resources, but it will satisfy the needs of many parents.

### Where To Find/Buy:
Bookstores or computer software stores.

## General Overviews

# BABYSENSE
## A Practical And Supportive Guide To Baby Care

**Recommended For:**
Taking Care Of Your Child

### Description:

In its second edition, this well-known guide to baby care includes updated information about breast- vs. bottle-feeding, child care, the adjustment to motherhood, and more. In the introduction, the author states, "I spent a lot of time . . . working out solutions to problems that had been worked out before by countless other parents." The book's basis is that "parents are the ultimate experts" on baby care. Written for the first-time mother separated from extended family networks, this guide includes common-sense advice her mother would give her in a warm, personable tone. The first section of six discusses newborns, feeding (breast, bottle, solids), and such "comfort" matters as interpreting the baby's crying, colic, sleep, bathing, and clothing. The next two parts discuss coping with motherhood and childcare. The last section contains a hodgepodge of "practical matters," from traveling with your baby to childproofing your house, health care, and "playing and learning." Interspersed throughout are anecdotes and tips from real mothers, forming, as the author puts it, "the backbone of the material in this book."

### Evaluation:

New mothers looking for a single book offering excellent information about baby care with warmth and support will appreciate this resource. It is wonderfully written, presenting practical how-tos clearly and effectively. It offers both breadth and depth, running the gamut of baby care issues from getting to know one's newborn to a recipe for home-made playdough. Recent SIDS findings are not included, so information on newborn sleeping positions is inaccurate; also, some breastfeeding guidance is outdated. Most readers will appreciate the author's belief that parents are the real experts on their baby's care, avoiding professional opinions that leave parents feeling "inadequate and imperiled." Readers will find lots of helpful tips from real mothers, as well as a memorable account of the author's own 12-hour day with her firstborn. Useful drawings show everything from positions to nurse and burp babies to the safest ways to hold a baby during bath time. In an age when a first-time mother may not have someone to show her how to swaddle a baby or reassure her when she feels she has reached the end of her tether, this book makes a heroic attempt to give both practical advice and a sense of community to mothers.

### Where To Find/Buy:

Bookstores and libraries.

---

**Overall Rating**
★★★
An excellent, sensitive, and "human" guide to baby care; needs updating regarding SIDS

**Design, Ease Of Use**
★★★★
Wide pages, personable tone makes reading enjoyable; many chapters use Q & A format

1–4 Stars

**Author:**
Frances Wells Burck
Frances Wells Burck is the author of another book on parenting, *Mothers Talking: Sharing the Secret.* She lives outside New York City with her husband and three daughters.

**Publisher:**
St. Martin's Press

**Edition:**
2nd (1991)

**Price:**
$16.95

**Pages/Run Time:**
313

**ISBN:**
0312050569

**Media:**
Book

**Principal Subject:**
Taking Care Of Your Child

**Secondary Subject:**
General Overview

**Age Group:**
Infants (0–1)

★★★

**Overall Rating**
★★★
Thorough, basic information on hundreds of health topics

**Design, Ease Of Use**
★★★
Search engine and clear subtitles make finding topics easy

1–4 Stars

**Author:**
This site is sponsored by the American Academy of Family Physicians, one of the largest medical associations in the U.S.

**Media:**
Internet

**Principal Subject:**
Taking Care Of Your Child

**Secondary Subject:**
General Overview

**Age Group:**
Infants & Toddlers (0–3)

General Overviews

# AMERICAN ACADEMY OF FAMILY PHYSICIANS

**Description:**
This site is provided by the American Academy of Family Physicians, one of the largest medical associations in the U.S. It includes information about a broad range of medical issues handled by family physicians. The group's mission is to promote and maintain "high standards for family physicians—the doctors who specialize in you," according to the site's homepage. Four major headings can be accessed on the site's homepage: "Healthy Living," "Common Conditions/ Diseases/Disorders," "Treatments," and "The Body." A search engine helps viewers locate specific health information, or visitors can quickly click through subcategories to reach topics such as "Newborns, Infants and Children's Health," "Pregnancy," "Women's Health" (all located under the heading "Healthy Living"), and "Female Reproductive System" (located under the heading "The Body").

**Evaluation:**
The extensive bank of information presented here is compiled and maintained by the American Academy of Family Physicians. Sections offer information about every imaginable health topic, and a search engine and clear site layout makes information easy to find. The information presented is parent-friendly, void of unnecessary medical jargon, and the explanations are clear, complete, and easy to understand. The "Newborns, Infants and Children's Health" section lists dozens of topics, from "Runny Nose in Children" (which provides an interesting explanation of runny noses) and "Pets and Parasites" to "Checking Your Child's Hearing" and "Taking Care of Twins." The information provided is mainstream medical advice, well-grounded in tradition. This isn't the site to investigate the latest medical or alternative treatments, but it is a comforting place for parents who just need to know what to do about pinworms or earaches or runny noses.

**Where To Find/Buy:**
On the Internet at http://www.aafp.org/patientinfo/

**General Overviews**

# BABY MANEUVERS

★★★

## Description:

The author, a veteran traveler prior to being a parent, aims to provide reassurance and information to parents about the logistics of toting supplies and traveling anywhere with young children. Fourteen chapters make up this 224-page guide which is divided into three main parts to gradually ease parents into maneuvering around with their child—The Crawling Maneuvers (chapters two through four), The Walking Maneuvers (chapters five through ten), and Advanced Baby Maneuvers (chapters 11–14). Chapter topics include dealing with: bodily functions on the road (breastfeeding, diapers, etc.), eating out, day trips (errands, grocery store, zoo, etc.), types of travel (by foot, car, boat, train, bus), what to pack in a day pack, air travel, types of vacation lodgings, outdoor adventures, traveling alone with a child, work travel with a baby, and overseas travel. Each chapter begins with bulleted points that summarize what will be covered. A page-by-page listing of the book's contents is included in the table of contents. Two appendices (odds and ends, resources) and an index complete the book. Lutz's tips are included throughout in colored block insets.

## Evaluation:

No other book deals quite as thoroughly with this subject as this one, almost exhaustively, does. Whether parents are beginning "baby maneuvers" or already feel confident with baby on outings, they will be sure to find advice in this book that they've never come across before. The author's tone is very friendly; her humor is delightful and sure to receive a knowing chuckle from her audience—"the supermarket can be fun, or a trip through a chamber of horrors." A principal problem with this book, however, is that it is often difficult for the reader to maneuver through its content. Each chapter is broken into too many subheadings causing one to oftentimes become confused and/or exhausted. All that aside, this guide would make an unusual baby shower gift or perhaps a wonderful read prior to a family's first vacation together.

## Where To Find/Buy:

Bookstores and libraries.

**Overall Rating**
★★★
Advice from a seasoned traveler on how to parent a child while on the road with them

**Design, Ease Of Use**
★★
Humorous and engaging, but numerous subheadings within chapters halt navigation

1–4 Stars

**Author:**
Ericka Lutz

Lutz writes fiction and non-fiction and travels extensively with her daughter, now four years old. Her writings have been published in books, magazines, and periodicals nationwide including *Parents' Press*, *Chicago Baby*, and the anthology, "Child of Mine."

**Publisher:**
Alpha Books (Macmillan General Reference/Simon and Schuster Macmillan)

**Edition:**
1997

**Price:**
$14.95

**Pages/Run Time:**
224

**ISBN:**
0028617320

**Media:**
Book

**Principal Subject:**
Taking Care Of Your Child

**Secondary Subject:**
General Overview

**Age Group:**
Infants & Toddlers (0–3)

II. Caring For Your Child

★★★

**Overall Rating**
★★★
Vast amount of concise information on topics from pregnancy to baby's first year

**Design, Ease Of Use**
★★
Cumbersome subtopic list (often 100+) can be difficult to access, but worth the search

1–4 Stars

**Media:**
Internet

**Principal Subject:**
Taking Care Of Your Child

**Secondary Subject:**
General Overview

**Age Group:**
Infants (0–1)

## General Overviews

# BABYCENTER
## Complete Pregnancy & Baby Information

### Description:

Launched in November 1997, this site offers many areas of parenting information from "preconception" to "baby." Other options available at the homepage include daily "Features" that address issues such as infertility, eating during pregnancy, nannies, and spanking. Another option includes "Popular Areas" with subtopics such as "The Dads Page," "Ask the Experts," "Pregnancy Calendar," "Find a Health Provider," and more. Experts in "Ask the Experts" include 19 different professionals and their biographies, from pediatricians (Brazelton and Dixon) and lactation consultants to clinical psychiatrists and midwives. Previously asked questions are summarized, along with the particular expert that responded, in a list format. There are numerous polls throughout the site on various topics regarding pregnancy and childcare. "BabyCenter Community" offers a visitor opportunities to participate in the website through its bulletin boards, chats, "Great Debates" and "Community Update." Online shopping is available as well.

### Evaluation:

At first (and second and third) glance, this site is an assault on the senses. The numerous commercial advertisements and disorganized layout make an initial visit seem daunting. The homepage merits a quick glance for interesting, daily updated features, but if one is looking for specific information, skip the homepage and go directly to the Site Index or the Table of Contents. Once one learns to navigate the maze, valuable and concise information can be found. For example, a parent seeking information on a baby's development also will be given links to related topics, other sources (websites and print references) and other parents. Some subtopics ("baby sleeping through the night") also reference bulletin boards on the same topic ("babies and sleep") and "great debates" ("baby sleeps alone vs. the family bed"), offering pros and cons on an issue, experts' advice, and more. The only area needing some help is in the access of these articles. Parents will need to read through a rather unwieldy list of titles (often 100+), although a search can be conducted. The sheer volume of information can take a significant amount of time, but it is well worth it.

### Where To Find/Buy:

On the Internet at the URL: http://www.babycenter.com

## General Overviews

# BABYCARE FOR BEGINNERS

★★

### Description:

This 96-page book's spiral-bound, cardboard-stand format allows it to open upright on a changing surface, table, or bath leaving parents' hands free as they take care of their baby. Offering numerous step-by-step color photographs on each page with additional information on the flipside (once it is standing upright), this baby care guide is divided into ten parts of how-tos with an additional four-page illustrated first aid section (choking, CPR, etc.), a detailed table of contents, and an index. Instructional tips and photographs for taking care of baby include: handling, carrying, soothing, feeding, diaper changing, dressing, sleeping, cleaning/bathing, daily care routines, and signs of illness. Photographs within the ten parts include specific instructions for breastfeeding (positioning, pumping/expressing), bottlefeeding (sterilizing, mixing, feeding), getting baby into a sling or other type of carrier, cutting nails, brushing teeth, cleaning a girl, cleaning a boy, and more.

### Evaluation:

New parents who have very little access to others' help and hands will appreciate this book's format and how-to instructions. Although some topics are treated lightly (signs of illness, amusing your baby, soothing your crying baby, etc.) and some suggestions are not advised for safety reasons (carrot sticks for an infant), most of the photographs are detailed enough to guarantee parents confidence and success. The format and information in this baby care guide will be most helpful for parents of newborns, but less so for parents of older babies. These parents will need to look to other resources for additional information and suggestions surrounding the topics of feeding solids, playing with their baby, bathing in the tub, etc. Although the user of this resource may enjoy a format which frees up an extra set of hands while conducting certain baby care tasks, other resources can be easily found which also address the how-tos of newborn care along with tips for continued care throughout their first year.

### Where To Find/Buy:

Bookstores and libraries.

**Overall Rating**
★★
Offering step-by-step photos to help parents learn to take care of their newborn baby

**Design, Ease Of Use**
★★★★
Large color photographs, bold headings; vertical standing format, spiral bound

1–4 Stars

**Author:**
Dr. Frances Williams

**Publisher:**
Carroll & Brown Limited (Harper Perennial/ HarperCollins Publishers)

**Edition:**
1996

**Price:**
$16.95

**Pages/Run Time:**
96

**ISBN:**
0062731041

**Media:**
Book

**Principal Subject:**
Taking Care Of Your Child

**Secondary Subject:**
General Overview

**Age Group:**
Infants (0–1)

★★

## Overall Rating
★★
Fun treatment of old wives' tales using fact (and opinion); good for shower present

## Design, Ease Of Use
★★★
Layout and design attractive

1–4 Stars

## Author:
Colleen Davis Gardephe & Steve Ettlinger

Gardephe is a writer and editor specializing in parenting topics. Her articles have appeared in many magazines (*Woman's Day, Parenting, American Baby, Healthy Kids*). Ettlinger is an author specializing in popular reference books.

## Publisher:
Chronicle Books

## Edition:
1993

## Price:
$9.95

## Pages/Run Time:
95

## ISBN:
0811802426

## Media:
Book

## Principal Subject:
Taking Care Of Your Child

## Secondary Subject:
General Overview

## Age Group:
Infants (0–1)

**General Overviews**

# DON'T PICK UP THE BABY OR YOU'LL SPOIL THE CHILD
And Other Old Wives' Tales About Pregnancy And Parenting

## Description:
As mentioned in the foreword, the advice expectant mothers are given is well-meant, but certain sayings have passed from generation to generation and can "mislead a woman at a time when she is trying to be . . . careful about everything she does." This book is intended for those times when "everyone starts telling you what to do . . . what to expect . . . spewing out old superstitions and homespun wisdom with the certainty of a prophet." This little (7" x 7") 95-page book is broken into two parts that list myths and sayings about pregnancy and parenting. Each part is further divided into common threads. Part One—about pregnancy—includes myths about determining your baby's sex, labor and delivery, health or looks of the mother and baby-to-be, and "myths that need no response" ("If you conceived in the morning, you'll have a boy"). The second part—about parenting—includes myths about feeding, sleeping, discipline, development, breastfeeding, bottlefeeding, and more. Each "old wives' tale" is highlighted and then a paragraph follows which debunks, explains, or extends the myth using input from the authors and a "panel of physicians."

## Evaluation:
Exaggerations and superstitions abound in this little book. It's fun and it's easy to read; its format is friendly and its illustrations lend an informal, sweet touch. Much of the authors' advice accompanying the "old wives' tales" is sound, based upon facts. Some, however, is based on opinion with little basis in facts, e.g. "around seven months, however, babies can start to manipulate their parents." New parents need to be careful using this little book as a source of real information to help get through pregnancy or to obtain suggestions about parenting. Rather, it should be used in strictly for fun by a newly pregnant couple, passed around at a baby shower, or given to those who constantly offer well-intended, but misinformed, advice. On the other hand, if a couple were to use this as their principal reference point, they would have a source that does have some solid facts, but also contains opinions that taint its solidarity. And if they heed ALL the advice contained within, they will find themselves swimming in yet another sea of tales.

## Where To Find/Buy:
Bookstores and libraries.

**General Overviews**

# THE KIDZ ARE PEOPLE TOO PAGE

★ ★

## Description:

Pregnancy, childbirth, breastfeeding, and infant care are some of the major topics at this website created by a Christian mother. Her site's focus is that "children should be treated with respect, too." The homepage to this site includes a Table of Contents to the entire site. Each topic includes links to other sites offering further information. Pregnancy links include those offering general overviews, nutrition, low tech ways to conceive, etc. Also included are essays and brochures detailing an unborn child's right to life and sites offering alternatives to abortions. "Childbirth" offers birth stories and invites users of the site to submit their own stories. Links at this topic include Advice on Childbirth, Birth Stories, Siblings at Birth, Birth Links, and more. Areas linked under "Infant Care" include diapering, weaning your baby, understanding your baby's cries, the family bed, and more. "Breastfeeding" offers highlights of "why breast is best," along with links to articles supporting that choice; also included are tips on starting solids, nursing toddlers, etc. Excerpts from the Bible are offered to support the site's focus and beliefs.

## Evaluation:

Several distinctive approaches to parenting have evolved and steer many current parenting practices. One approach, "attachment parenting," believes in heeding the baby's every cry, sharing sleep with one's baby, breastfeeding, etc. A contrasting approach (termed by some "detachment parenting") believes that a baby needs to be taught to be independent, cry it out, learn to sleep by himself/herself, etc. This site takes both elements into account. In doing so, it uses quotes from the Bible, couples this guidance with the author's own experiences and attitudes, and supplies additional informational sources. The tone of the website is loving and joyful. The author offers her Christian background as a basis for her parenting methods, without being preachy. The best part of this site is that the homepage is a table of contents for the entire site. There are not many graphics, which can make a website boring and dry. However, with this site, the lack of graphics makes it easy to read and navigate. The site is positive, well-organized, and straightforward in its approach. Visitors wishing forums or chats will need to go elsewhere.

## Where To Find/Buy:

On the Internet at the URL: http://www.geocities.com/Heartland/8148

**Overall Rating**
★ ★
Offers Christian parenting perspectives without being fanatical

**Design, Ease Of Use**
★ ★ ★
Straightforward, succinct; few graphics; numerous links to get more information

1–4 Stars

**Media:**
Internet

**Principal Subject:**
Taking Care Of Your Child

**Secondary Subject:**
General Overview

**Age Group:**
Infants (0–1)

★★

**Overall Rating**
★★
Best used for parenting classes to introduce newborn care; incomplete for home use

**Design, Ease Of Use**
★★★
Well-organized and laid-out with numbered highlights on screen, segment headings

1–4 Stars

**Publisher:**
Creative Outlook

**Edition:**
1995

**Price:**
$29.98

**Media:**
Videotape

**Principal Subject:**
Taking Care Of Your Child

**Secondary Subject:**
General Overview

**Age Group:**
Infants (0–1)

**General Overviews**

# PARENT'S OWNER'S MANUAL: NEWBORN
Volume 1: A Child Care Series

**Description:**

Creative Outlook's goal is to "ease your transition into parenting and enhance your comfort level in this new role." To that end, they have broken this 55 minute videotape into various segments: baby furniture (essentials), different ways of holding and picking up a baby, what to do when baby cries, using a pacifier, swaddling, feeding (breastfeeding, bottlefeeding), burping, diapering (pros and cons of cloth/disposables, how-tos), buying the layette (safety and comfort constraints), dressing, bathing (sponge bath, infant bath), sleeping (how-tos, sleep positions), nail trimming, "the medicine box" (essential supplies, medical aids), playtime, and packing the diaper bag for outings. Each segment includes live footage taken of parents as they illustrate the narrator's dialogue. In many cases, numbered highlights appear on the screen to isolate main points. Freeze frame techniques are also used to capture highlights in various segments.

**Evaluation:**

Parents who are visual learners and work best with live hands-on instructions may appreciate this tape. Others will do better to invest their money in other resources that offer more in-depth information about the same topics. Although this tape's intent is applaudable, once parents have seen it a few times, they'll wonder why they invested time and money in it at all. This tape's primary value would be in its use for new parents-to-be perhaps as a follow up for a parenting class on newborn care. For home use, however, its possibilities are limited. Viewers will also note subtle biases: the discrepancy between the details given for bottlefeeding compared to those for breastfeeding, advice to increase response time to baby's cries, and advice on training a baby to sleep on its own. Additionally, sleep positions described do not reflect new SIDS research. Parents will find that this videotape is not a complete "owner's manual" but is better used as a catalyst for seeking other sources offering more in-depth information and advice.

**Where To Find/Buy:**

Bookstores, libraries, videotape dealers, or order direct by calling Creative Outlook at (800) 97-KIDS-1 or AMR at (877) 99VIDEO. Orders can also be taken online by AMR at http://www.amr1.com.

**General Overviews**

# BABY: AN OWNER'S MANUAL

★ ★

### Description:

This book was written by an experienced pediatrician, and a first-time mother, and consists of "some fast answers to questions we know you're going to ask, addressing the issues that are common to virtually all new parents." It is intended to be used as a source of quick, accessible information, easy "to grab in the middle of the night." Although there is no table of contents, questions and answers are arranged in roughly chronological groupings, from taking the baby home from the hospital to bottlefeeding, breastfeeding, setting up a feeding schedule, and dealing with diaper rash, colic, and crying spells. The book progresses to questions dealing with choosing daycare, weight gain, teething, starting on solid foods, fevers and colds, childproofing your house, discipline, and maintaining balance in one's own life.

### Evaluation:

This pediatrician takes a decidedly and unapologetically old-fashioned approach to baby-rearing. The advice given is sensible, succinct, and often humorous, obviously drawing on his experience in answering questions of anxious mothers ("Question: Can his umbilical cord come untied? Answer: I have this vision of an umbilical cord coming untied and a baby flying around the room backward, deflating like a balloon . . ."). Dr. Zukow, a self-described "parent advocate," believes that parents who "get back into their routines as quickly as possible are generally rewarded with more easy-going and independent kids as they grow." Thus, parents will find advice about setting up feeding schedules, getting your baby to sleep through the night, and so forth. Also stressed is the parents' right to make choices, unpressured by current trends (such as deciding whether to feed baby with a bottle or breastfeed). Altogether, this resource will be helpful to those who subscribe to Zukow's parenting style.

### Where To Find/Buy:

Bookstores and libraries.

---

**Overall Rating**
★★
Advice and support with a light, often humorous touch

**Design, Ease Of Use**
★★
No table of contents, roughly listed chronologically; index helps; easy Q & A format

1–4 Stars

**Author:**
Bud Zukow, MD and Nancy Sayles Kaneshiro

Zukow is Chairman Emeritus of the Dept. of Pediatrics at Encino/Tarzana Regional Medical Center in Tarzana, CA, where he is also in private practice. He is the author of a previous book on parenting. Kaneshiro is the mother of Ian, a patient of Dr. Zukow's.

**Publisher:**
Kensington Books

**Edition:**
1996

**Price:**
$14.00

**Pages/Run Time:**
226

**ISBN:**
1575660555

**Media:**
Book

**Principal Subject:**
Taking Care Of Your Child

**Secondary Subject:**
General Overview

**Age Group:**
Infants (0–1)

★★

**Overall Rating**
★★
A generally useful list of practical and monetary concerns during your baby's first year

**Design, Ease Of Use**
★★
Eclectic gathering of topics with some uneven treatment; "necessity checklist" a plus

1–4 Stars

**Author:**
Anne K. Blocker, RD

The author has taught prenatal nutrition and counseled on gestational diabetes, maternal nutrition, infant feeding, and breastfeeding for over 10 years. She is also the mother of three children.

**Publisher:**
Chronimed Publishing

**Edition:**
1997

**Price:**
$12.95

**Pages/Run Time:**
295

**ISBN:**
1565610903

**Media:**
Book

**Principal Subject:**
Taking Care Of Your Child

**Secondary Subject:**
General Overview

**Age Group:**
Infants (0–1)

## General Overviews

# BABY BASICS (PRINT)
A Guide For New Parents

**Description:**
To quote: "It's common knowledge that babies cost a bundle. That's . . . what this book is all about—keeping the bundle from becoming the national debt by simplifying baby care." This is a guide to the practicalities of baby care. The 15 chapters of this 295-page book focus on identifying one's options, ways to save family money, and understanding health and safety issues for such areas as medical care, health insurance, traveling with baby, and babyproofing one's home. Other chapters focus on other investments such as choosing maternity clothes, buying nursery furniture, selecting baby clothes, diapers, and toys. Additional tips are offered in areas such as feeding the baby, choosing childcare, weighing decisions about returning to work, and investing in one's future (financial matters). Each chapter introduces its topic which is accompanied by a "necessity checklist" of things to do/buy, and includes tips on safe use, what to consider when buying an item, smart shopping tips, and "budget helpers," as well as a list of further reading, catalog resources, support groups and organizations, and more.

**Evaluation:**
The author provides a rather eclectic array of topics related to baby care in her book, all of which seem to revolve around issues of decision-making, finance and budgeting, and safety. Reading through this book should give one a grasp of many of the practical aspects involving raising a baby. What it lacks is overall coherence. Is this book about safety or budgeting or health/nutrition? At times the book makes up for this lack of coherence with a good chapter, e.g. "Baby's Basic Wardrobe," a chapter which provides in-depth information about buying clothing a few sizes ahead to save money as your baby grows, safety tips such as avoiding drawstrings and arm/leg bands, laundry tips, etc. Also useful are the chapters on travel safety, baby proofing your home, and childcare. But other chapters, such as those on feeding and health, really include only the basics and do not offer the depth of advice that other resources do. Overall, this book might best be used to introduce some practical concerns while identifying those that need to be researched further with the help of other resources.

**Where To Find/Buy:**
Bookstores and libraries, or order direct by calling (800) 338-2232.

**General Overviews**

# YOUR NEWBORN BABY WITH JOAN LUNDEN
## Everything You Need To Know

### Description:

Narrated by *Good Morning America's* Joan Lunden and featuring her family pediatrician, Dr. Jeffrey Brown, this 60 minute videotape outlines topics concerning newborn infant care. Eleven segments are introduced by cartoon vignettes with a corresponding icon in the lower right hand corner also displayed on the videotape jacket. These icons are designed to be used with search/scan features of VCRs to locate information. Topics included in the discussions are: choosing your baby's doctor, decisions to think about before birth (breastfeeding, rooming-in, circumcision, etc.), preparing for baby (equipment, layette, packing for the hospital), "the magic moment" (hospital birth), newborn appearances and senses, feeding your baby (breastfeeding, bottlefeeding), diapering and caring for baby's bottom, bathing, how to deal with baby's cries, what to expect for baby's sleep, and when to call your baby's doctor. The guidelines in this 1985 videotape are based on recommendations from the American Academy of Pediatrics.

### Evaluation:

Parents viewing this videotape will have the uncanny sense they are viewing episodes from Good Morning America. Produced in an interview format either with prospective mothers, the featured pediatrician, or parents of newborns, Lunden interjects her personal experiences along with professional advice. These short, concise segments may appeal to some, but most new parents will find the topics are treated too lightly to be of much value. Some sections are done well including the segments on the how-tos of breastfeeding (endorsed by La Leche League), when to call your doctor, and how to prepare for baby's arrival (includes what to pack for the hospital). However, due to the video's outdated copyright, some advice is currently considered to be unacceptable practice (putting a baby to sleep on their stomach), unnecessary (sterilizing bottles with a sterilizing device), or missing (how to deal with colic). The tape has an attractive sticker price, but parents will find their money better spent on more useful and up-to-date resources.

### Where To Find/Buy:

Bookstores, libraries, videotape dealers, or order direct by calling Library Video Company at (800) 843-3620, through FAX at (610) 645-4040, or online at http://www.libraryvideo.com. It can also be ordered through AMR at (877) 99VIDEO, or online at http://www.amr1.com.

---

**Overall Rating**
★
Info far too concise to be of much practical use; some info currently not recommended

**Design, Ease Of Use**
★★★★
Short interview-type vignettes; icons for accessibility; recaps at end of each segment

1–4 Stars

**Publisher:**
J2 Communications/Ripps Communication

**Edition:**
1985

**Price:**
$9.98

**Pages/Run Time:**
60 minutes

**Media:**
Videotape

**Principal Subject:**
Taking Care Of Your Child

**Secondary Subject:**
General Overview

**Age Group:**
Infants (0–1)

## General Overviews

**Overall Rating**

★

Good for a chat, making
a card or getting a recipe;
information is dry, largely
unusable

**Design, Ease Of Use**

★★

Categories are mostly vague;
no site map is available;
graphics slow down navigation

1–4 Stars

**Media:**
Internet

**Principal Subject:**
Taking Care Of Your Child

**Secondary Subject:**
General Overview

**Age Group:**
Infants (0–1)

# THE BABYNET

**Description:**

Here parents will find 31 category selections, plus contests and links to catalogues. Several options revolve around baby products, stores, and manufacturers. Alphabetical lists give contact information (phone, address). Another option contains an extensive list of product recall notices. At this site, one can create a birth announcement and greeting card, or participate in games and contests. Baby shower ideas are provided, along with rhymes and songs to sing with your baby. BabyNet offers chat rooms and bulletin board forums; topics for the bulletin board include parenting forums, "expectant clubs" (choose the month you're due), and labor and pregnancy issues. The department "Tender Loving Care" offers information on the following: prenatal care (pregnancy, Chinese birth chart), newborn care (breastfeeding, why babies cry), health issues (ear infections), help for parents (product recalls, safety issues, babysitting) and more.

**Evaluation:**

This site contains a little of everything, but not a lot of anything. It is true that most of its options offer visitors some lighthearted material, which tired parents certainly will enjoy. One can come here to chat, make a card, print out a recipe, even enter a contest. But it contains little more than that. The information packed into "Tender Loving Care" is cumbersome and dry, with few graphics to help one digest information. Titles to some of the departments are vague or misleading. For example, "Freebies" leads one to believe it is a resource for finding free or discounted product information; it actually is a solicitation to enter a contest. Also, it is difficult to know what you are jumping into when entering the department "Splash"; visitors, it turns out, are invited to tell their stories about where they were when their water broke. Extensive links to child-related products, stores, and manufacturers are the sole unexpected delight, but also lend a feeling of commercialism to this site. Parents with the time to follow the links will find unusual and delightful baby and child items. Where else would you find heart-shaped adhesive bandages? Still, those whose primary purpose for visiting isn't shopping will find their online time more wisely spent elsewhere.

**Where To Find/Buy:**

On the Internet at the URL: http://www.thebabynet.com

**General Overviews**

# PARENTS' PAGE

### Description:

Parents' Place is the creation of Lewis Wasserman, an Orlando pediatrician. Its goal is to be a "source of friendly advice and helpful hints," and it was last updated in early 1997. It offers the full text of Wasserman's The Baby Booklet, which contains answers to frequently asked questions about newborns. Also at this site is a number of lists, including resources for parents, websites for children and teens, a reading and reference list, a selection of doctor jokes, and access to The Parents' Letter, an email newsletter.

### Evaluation:

This is a pleasant enough small site with a good heart. However, it evidently has not been updated since early 1997 and contains very little basic information—and no frills—by today's web standards. It primarily provides access to the doctor's booklet on newborns and other miscellaneous information about the doctor himself. This site doesn't offer much in terms of substance, but it doesn't pretend to.

### Where To Find/Buy:

On the Internet using the URL: http://members.aol.com/allianceMD/lw.html

---

**Overall Rating**

★

Limited information; not updated since 1997

**Design, Ease Of Use**

★★

Few frills; guided tour and a small site means visitors can't get lost

1–4 Stars

**Author:**

Lewis Wasserman, MD

Wasserman is a pediatrician with a practice in Orlando, Florida.

**Publisher:**

Lewis Wasserman, MD

**Media:**

Internet

**Principal Subject:**

Taking Care Of Your Child

**Secondary Subject:**

General Overview

**Age Group:**

Infants (0–1)

**Overall Rating**

★

A variety of info is available but not easily accessed

**Design, Ease Of Use**

★

Topics arranged alphabetically in cumbersome list, no graphics, inactive discussions

1–4 Stars

**Media:**
Internet

**Principal Subject:**
Taking Care Of Your Child

**Secondary Subject:**
General Overview

**Age Group:**
Toddlers (1–3)

General Overviews

# DAILY PARENT

**Description:**

This site offers a list of articles regarding many subjects pertinent to parenting. At the homepage, a visitor must choose a topic that is listed under one of four "channels," which include "Family," "Pregnancy," "Health," and "Education and Development." That chosen topic leads to a list of articles which discuss various related parenting issues. The articles are written by various authors with the Scripps Howard News Service, and all topics and issues are organized alphabetically. A visitor also can submit comments, and read others' comments and responses regarding that issue. Topics listed under the "Family Channel" include auto safety, family finances, nutrition, summer camps, and more. "Health Channel" topics include allergies, exercise, menopause, and stress. Bedwetting, childcare, back to school, self-esteem, and other issues are listed under the "Education and Development Channel." Finally, the "Pregnancy Channel" covers issues such as premature babies, birth, and postpartum depression.

**Evaluation:**

The visitor to this site can only be amazed when accessing its lengthy topic list. The information offered in the articles provides good, direct advice, along with examples of real-life situations and suggested ways of using that advice. But that is where the excitement ends. First of all, the list of topics is cumbersome and awkward. It needs to be better organized into smaller distinct categories (such as "Child Health Concerns," "Discipline Problems," etc.). Also, the discussion forums seem nicely laid-out at first glance, but upon further research one discovers that the chats are relatively inactive compared to other sites. One must also question the source of the information. Little information is given regarding the expertise of the authors of these articles. Some information doesn't pertain to parenting. For example, information in the "Health Channel" includes discussions of menopause and breast cancer. Also, some areas pertinent to new moms' needs are minimal. For example, "breastfeeding" contain two articles both of which address how to breastfeed upon returning to work. In short, this site's problem can be summed up with one word: scattered. One can certainly find clearer routes to information at other sites.

**Where To Find/Buy:**
On the Internet at the URL: http://www.dailyparent.com/

# BREASTFEEDING YOUR BABY

**★★★★**

**Recommended For:**
Taking Care Of Your Child

## Description:

There are eight major sections in this 160-page book. The first section outlines the benefits of breastfeeding, how pregnancy can change your breast shape, and problem-solving tips for various breast types (large, small, inverted nipple, breast surgery). The second section discusses the first days of breastfeeding including topics such as nursing positions, latching on, sucking rhythms, nursing at night, and clothing suggestions for mother and baby. The physiological process of breastfeeding is addressed in the next section along with suggestions on how to take care of yourself to ensure a good milk supply, and more. Section Four offers help for possible problems, such as engorgement, sore and cracked nipples, mastitis, and other deterrents to nursing. The next four sections highlight: learning about your baby's needs (the sleepy baby, the excited baby, etc.), the baby with special needs (jaundice, handicaps, etc.), the family's dynamics (baby, siblings, parents), and "security and adventure" (older baby, sex, traveling, weaning, and returning to work). A reference section, support organization contact information, and an index are given.

## Evaluation:

This is clearly a beautiful, well-written book. Numerous color and black and white photographs are provided on virtually every page with clear, concise captions that fully explain and illustrate each topic. Step-by-step instructions, bulleted notations, and bold subheadings also add to this book's ease of use. This guide does an excellent job of covering all aspects of breastfeeding in a progressive, matter-of-fact format. Not just concerned with the basics and how-tos, this resource also covers other issues, such as time management, what to do if you are thinking of giving up breastfeeding, how to deal with babies with special needs, how to nurse the older baby, and more. Topics are presented knowledgeably, with constant reassurance and advice on the most frequently encountered aspects of breastfeeding. Additional resources will be needed to support nursing mothers planning to return to work; minimal advice is given here. But for those women who want a companion to support them in their decision to breastfeed, this is the book that will guide them each step of the way.

## Where To Find/Buy:

Bookstores and libraries.

**Overall Rating**
★★★★
Complete, supportive & affirming guide sure to be a companion to every nursing mother

**Design, Ease Of Use**
★★★★
A guide with style; user friendly and intelligently formatted; numerous color photos

1–4 Stars

**Author:**
Sheila Kitzinger

Sheila Kitzinger, a childbirth educator, has written over 16 books on pregnancy, birth, and childcare.

**Publisher:**
Dorling Kindersley (Alfred A. Knopf/Random House)

**Edition:**
(6th) 1997

**Price:**
$20.00

**Pages/Run Time:**
160

**ISBN:**
0679724338

**Media:**
Book

**Principal Subject:**
Taking Care Of Your Child

**Secondary Subject:**
Breastfeeding

**Age Group:**
Infants (0–1)

II. Caring For Your Child

★★★★

**Overall Rating**
★★★★
Honest, informative, supportive evaluation and practice of breastfeeding

**Design, Ease Of Use**
★★★★
Well organized, easily referenced with bold print and index, clearly communicated

1–4 Stars

**Author:**
Marianne Neifert, MD

A pediatrician and lactation specialist (20+ years experience), Neifert lectures to health professionals nationwide about breastfeeding, serves on the Health Advisory Council of La Leche League International, and started one of the first U.S. breastfeeding referral centers.

**Publisher:**
Plume (Penguin Putnam)

**Edition:**
1998

**Price:**
$14.95

**Pages/Run Time:**
470

**ISBN:**
0452279909

**Media:**
Book

**Principal Subject:**
Taking Care Of Your Child

**Secondary Subject:**
Breastfeeding

**Age Group:**
Infants (0–1)

**Breastfeeding**

# DR. MOM'S GUIDE TO BREASTFEEDING

**Recommended For:**
Taking Care Of Your Child

**Description:**
This 470-page book begins with an introduction by Neifert where she tells of her long (20 year) history of breastfeeding experience, and research. In the remainder of the book, Neifert sets out to offer "a blueprint for attaining your breastfeeding goals, a practical guide to help you achieve the success you desire and deserve so you can one day look back on your breastfeeding experience with infinite pride and satisfaction." First, the reader is educated about the choice to breastfeed: "Why Breastfeed?" "Preparation for Breastfeeding—Before the Baby Arrives," and "How Milk Is Made and Released." Then, a broad overview of the breastfeeding experience is given with special attention to techniques, what to expect (including myths and facts), nutrition, problems with insufficient milk, and special situations (returning to work, twins, etc.). In the last chapter, weaning is described, both literally and emotionally; additional information is provided on nursing the older baby. At the back of the book, there is an index and a seven page "Breastfeeding Resource List."

**Evaluation:**
Neifert's introduction captures the reader's trust. Readers will benefit from Neifert's attitude, knowledge, and experience. Her dual role as both a breastfeeding mom and a professional breastfeeding expert is conveyed throughout the text. The factual teachings in this book strongly encourage the choice to breastfeed, while the compassionate delivery offers further support for that choice. Throughout her research and work, breastfeeding problems that must be solved, instead become problems that can be prevented. Although breastfeeding is a natural process, the possible obstacles to breastfeeding are so numerous (originating from a mother, an infant, and/or their cultural environment) and as such are outlined here. However, Neifert acknowledges both the benefits and possible challenges to breastfeeding, offering new mothers a prevailing "I can do it" attitude. Consequently, inexperienced and experienced breastfeeding mothers will benefit from the information contained in this book. This comprehensive book is worth reading from cover to cover and may be easily revisited due to its helpful organizational elements.

**Where To Find/Buy:**
Bookstores and libraries.

**Breastfeeding**

# SO THAT'S WHAT THEY'RE FOR!
## Breastfeeding Basics

★★★★

**Recommended For:**
Taking Care Of Your Child

### Description:

This 15 chapter book on breastfeeding basics is divided into three parts: "The Learning Curve," "Mine Didn't Come with a Manual," and "Everything Else You Wanted to Know but were Too Tired to Ask." Tamaro taps from a large pool of breastfeeding-related resources, as documented in her list of references. She also uses many breastfeeding anecdotes from her own life, as well as from many others she has interviewed. The book begins in Part One with background on social influences on breastfeeding and the debate between breastfeeding and formula feeding. Part Two launches into how to prepare for baby and breastfeeding, and the how-tos and early days and weeks of breastfeeding. Topics include nursing apparel, your stay at the hospital, the anatomy of the breast, and common questions and mistakes. Part Three addresses the many breastfeeding-related concerns after mom has become a pro at breastfeeding. Among the many subjects discussed are starting baby on solids, air travel, mom's diet and exercise, breast pumps, storing breastmilk, returning to work, and sex after baby. The book is lightly illustrated. Related resources are provided at the back of the book.

### Evaluation:

Taking a humorous approach, this resource offers all the fundamentals on why and how to breastfeed along with discussing physiological and social problems. Many anecdotes are provided, adding light entertainment value. These diversions are a nice complement to merely offering factual information, giving readers added humor at a time when many new tired parents struggle to laugh. Tamaro's breastfeeding-related tales range from teaching a mother gorilla how to breastfeed to a father who squirted an elderly man with his wife's breastmilk in an airport. Her writing style is casual and conversational, as she interlaces personal stories as well as others' stories with facts. A well-rounded list of related resources includes contact information for lactation consultants, pump manufacturers, drug information, and milk banks. Tamaro also presents information on some subjects other resources ignore or treat lightly, such as breastfeeding multiples, adoptive children, babies with Down syndrome, and more; a chapter is dedicated to helping fathers feel involved. This informative guide is easy and fast reading, and well worth having on your bookshelf.

### Where To Find/Buy:

Bookstores, libraries, or order direct by calling (800) 872-5627, or in Massachusetts call (781) 767-8100.

**Overall Rating**
★★★★
An excellent resource on breastfeeding

**Design, Ease Of Use**
★★★★
Easy to read; conversational and humorous writing style

1–4 Stars

**Author:**
Janet Tamaro

Janet Tamaro became a certified lactation educator after her first daughter was born. She is a television correspondent, reporter, and author. She has worked for ABC News, Fox, and KingWorld Productions.

**Publisher:**
Adams Media

**Edition:**
2nd (1998)

**Price:**
$10.95

**Pages/Run Time:**
304

**ISBN:**
1580620418

**Media:**
Book

**Principal Subject:**
Taking Care Of Your Child

**Secondary Subject:**
Breastfeeding

**Age Group:**
Infants (0–1)

**★★★★**

**Overall Rating**
★★★★
Excellent, practical information that is concise and easy to read

**Design, Ease Of Use**
★★★
Well-organized chapters; helpful lists, charts, and illustrations

1–4 Stars

**Author:**
Diane Mason and Diane Ingersoll

Diane Mason is a freelance journalist, television producer and reporter, and former editor and publisher. She specializes in articles about women, and has co–authored two other books. Diane Ingersoll was a hospital social worker who counseled breastfeeding mothers.

**Publisher:**
St. Martin's Griffin

**Edition:**
2nd (1997)

**Price:**
$11.95

**Pages/Run Time:**
216

**ISBN:**
0312154860

**Media:**
Book

**Principal Subject:**
Taking Care Of Your Child

**Secondary Subject:**
Breastfeeding

**Age Group:**
Infants (0–1)

**Breastfeeding**

# BREASTFEEDING AND THE WORKING MOTHER

**Recommended For:**
Taking Care Of Your Child

**Description:**
The 11 chapters in this book include: "Why Breastfeed?" which focuses on the history of breastfeeding along with its advantages (bonding, nutrition, getting back into shape); "Breastfeeding Basics"; "Problems, Health, and Special Situations"; "Meals on Wheels" (manually expressing milk, breast pumps, how and when to pump breast milk); "Back to Work-Your Plan" (timing, caregivers); "Under Way" (work and breastfeeding alternatives); "Women in Unusual Job Situations" (single parent, self-employed, coal miner); "Weaning"; "Special Tips for Fathers"; "Sex and the Breastfeeding Woman" (breasts and sex, contraceptives); and "Your (Legal) Right to Breastfeed" (case history, legal rights, finding an attorney). In each chapter, the authors address a number of issues or problems related to the chapter topic. Explanations are brief, and a number of suggestions are offered to deal with each issue.

**Evaluation:**
Sometimes the best idea begins as a quest. In this case, it is the authors' urge to come to the aid of working mothers who breastfeed. "The working mother doesn't have time to read a stack of books on the subject, nor does she have time to wade through a tome," author Ingersoll says. "The book I envisioned would hit all of the important questions about breastfeeding, offer lots of practical advice and experiences . . . and be short and to the point." The authors achieve all of their goals in this book. When discussing problems, they touch only briefly on why the problem may occur before offering a list of solutions. The Chapter "Under Way" offers six work-breastfeeding scenarios, along with their corresponding problems and solutions. Throughout the book, the authors relate stories about a variety of women and their situations, along with suggestions. The situations presented are common ones with which many women can relate finding not only advice but a sense that they are not alone in their experiences. This book would be a wonderful addition to the library of any breastfeeding mother, whether or not she is working. It is a very supportive book to any mother who is going back to work, offering practical advice in a simple, easy-to-read format.

**Where To Find/Buy:**
Bookstores, libraries, or order direct by contacting Publishers Book & Audio, P.O. Box 070059, Staten Island, NY 10307.

**Breastfeeding**

# MOTHERING YOUR NURSING TODDLER

**★★★★**

### Recommended For:
Taking Care Of Your Child

### Special Resource For:
Support and advice for parents who continue to nurse their child beyond one year

**Overall Rating**
★★★★
Compassionate, supportive advice for those who breastfeed beyond baby's first year

**Design, Ease Of Use**
★★★
A detailed table of contents would help; subchapter headings good; easily read

1–4 Stars

## Description:
Bumgarner believes that "young children need the calming and reassuring effects of sucking . . .(and) the very best place for this sucking to take place is in mother's arms, at her breast, where it is entirely natural and complete." She further states that the ensuing suckling plays an enormous part in a child's ability to mature and grow up without the need for alternatives (pacifiers, thumbs, blankets, etc.) that are difficult to rid from the child's life. Her book describes the continued breastfeeding relationship between mother and child, focusing on the child's development and his consequent natural desire to wean once his sucking need has been met. Divided into four parts, Part One discusses the "whys" of nursing a toddler from the perspectives of both mother and child. Part Two then offers the "hows" of nursing with advice on marriage, night nursing, mother's health, and more. Part Three highlights a toddler's development year by year (age four and beyond) and their accompanying nursing needs. Various ways to approach weaning are offered in Part Four (natural, time-honored/time-worn, etc.).

**Author:**
Norma Jane Bumgarner
Bumgarner has been very active in La Leche League for 14 years and is a frequent contributor to La Leche League publications and a speaker at LLLI conferences. She has three sons and a daughter, three of which nursed well past their first birthdays.

**Publisher:**
La Leche League International

**Edition:**
1982

**Price:**
$8.95

**Pages/Run Time:**
208

**ISBN:**
0912500123

**Media:**
Book

## Evaluation:
This is the bible for those mother-child relationships that have consciously or unconsciously decided to continue breastfeeding past their child's first birthday. At this point in time, many mothers often get discouraged, have little or no support, and often become misinformed about the nature of breastfeeding. These are the mothers who will benefit most from reading this book. Bumgarner does an excellent job of shedding light on why nursing is not only beneficial for a child's development but can also help foster the independence that child is seeking. Mothers will learn that breastfeeding is not just for nourishment, but helps satisfy a child's basic needs while the child learns to satisfy these needs himself. When nursing mothers doubt that weaning will ever occur, Bumgarner offers support, guidance, and reassurance to help mothers focus on the positive aspects of their relationship with their child while they breastfeed. No other book addresses these concerns quite succinctly, or with complete compassion and honesty. This is a must-have for those beginning to nurse or those continuing to nurse their child.

**Principal Subject:**
Taking Care Of Your Child

**Secondary Subject:**
Breastfeeding

**Age Group:**
Toddlers (1–3)

## Where To Find/Buy:
Bookstores and libraries.

★★★★

## Overall Rating
★★★★
Full explanations of how to continue breastfeeding upon returning to work

## Design, Ease Of Use
★★
More details in table of contents would help; flows well but must be read cover to cover

1–4 Stars

## Author:
Gale Pryor

Pryor, a graduate of Cornell University, is the co-author with her mother, Karen, of the highly respected *Nursing Your Baby*. She lives outside of Boston with her husband and her two children, both of whom she breastfed while working full-time.

## Publisher:
The Harvard Common Press

## Edition:
1997

## Price:
$9.95

## Pages/Run Time:
184

## ISBN:
1558321179

## Media:
Book

## Principal Subject:
Taking Care Of Your Child

## Secondary Subject:
Breastfeeding

## Age Group:
Infants (0–1)

Breastfeeding

# NURSING MOTHER, WORKING MOTHER
The Essential Guide For Breastfeeding And Staying Close To Your Baby After You Return To Work

## Recommended For:
Taking Care Of Your Child

## Special Resource For:
Nursing mothers who want to continue breastfeeding when they return to work

## Description:
This 184-page book extends a section of the author's book, *Nursing Your Baby*. Divided into seven chapters, this guide focuses on the needs of the woman who wishes to continue breastfeeding when she returns to work. Pryor's preface and Chapter One offer a treatise on the importance of forming an attached relationship between baby and mother; beliefs of current society are challenged here (encouraging the baby to be "independent," i.e., letting baby cry it out, sleep separately, not room-in after birth, etc.). She then details why breastfeeding is important for both mother and baby along with "breastfeeding basics." The next three chapters are dedicated to enjoying maternity leave and adjusting to baby, getting ready to go back to work (getting necessary supplies/equipment, reconnecting with coworkers, finding care), and returning to work (dealing with fatigue, pumping and storing milk at work, business travel, baby's illness, and more). Chapter Seven is a plea to help change negative attitudes in the workplace concerning motherhood. Resources, a sample proposal for a pumping space at work, and an index are given.

## Evaluation:
If read from cover to cover, this guide offers working women answers to just about every breastfeeding question they can think of, except how to choose childcare. Parents will need to look to other resources for that information. Sometimes distracting, but always interesting, are Pryor's strong opinions, mostly backed by research. The message she threads throughout the book is that women need to take more initiative about their role in the workplace as they tackle new motherhood. She believes that women and children suffer because women feel they must ignore motherhood while working and vice versa. To that end, she has included numerous strategies and offers welcome tips for those who choose to go back to work and continue breastfeeding. The chapter on "Your Return to the Outside World" is especially useful offering advice from how to deal with leakage at work, to taking baby on business trips, to what to do when baby gets sick. No other guide is available that focuses solely on this subject. Every prospective mother who plans to breastfeed and eventually return to work needs to read this resource before her child is born.

## Where To Find/Buy:
Bookstores and libraries.

**Breastfeeding**

# BESTFEEDING
Getting Breastfeeding Right For You

★★★

## Description:

This guide to breastfeeding, accompanied by photos and drawings, presents the "mechanics" of breastfeeding and cultural and emotional issues. The authors state that "breastfeeding is not always easy for women who live in societies where it is hidden, and we don't get a chance to learn how to do it." Thus, this book focuses on convincing mothers that breastfeeding is really "bestfeeding," and gives ways to overcome cultural/social resistance and emotional/physical obstacles. The first part offers a rationale for breastfeeding. The next three parts deal with: becoming familiar with positioning, posture, support, and latching on; learning to express and store breast milk, diet; what to do for babies with special needs; how to deal with too much or little milk flow, sore nipples, and fussy/dissatisfied babies. Cultural factors are discussed, including a look at harmful "modern myths." Closing sections include case studies of women with specific problems, and a "storyboard" detailing the basics of breastfeeding in English and Spanish with drawings. Also included are lists of other resources (groups, books) offering help and support.

## Evaluation:

If you are considering or have chosen to breastfeed, this is one of many good resources to help you. This book includes a strong message about the importance and superiority of breastfeeding, and it will help women overcome many of the problems that arise when they make the effort to breastfeed their babies. It focuses on the mechanics of positioning (of both mother and baby) which is often the real source of a myriad of problems including sore nipples, too much or too little milk flow, and a fussy baby. Invaluable illustrations and photos show correct and incorrect positions, and how a baby should properly latch on to the breast. This book also focuses on the emotional aspects of breastfeeding since successful breastfeeding depends on a relaxed, confident mother as well. Overall this is an excellent guide for mothers who plan to breastfeed.

## Where To Find/Buy:

Bookstores and libraries, or order direct by calling (800) 841-BOOK.

**Overall Rating**
★★★
A sensitive and instructive guide to successful breastfeeding

**Design, Ease Of Use**
★★★★
Well written, with numerous and very helpful photos and drawings

1–4 Stars

**Author:**
Mary Renfrew, Chloe Fisher, and Suzanne Arms

Renfrew is a midwife who earned a doctorate for her research in breastfeeding. Fisher has over 30 years' experience as a community midwife. Arms has been a teacher, mother, and photographer, as well as an author of other books on women, childbirth, and adoption. Maggie Conroy is an artist and illustrator, with experience also as an art therapist.

**Publisher:**
Celestial Arts Publishing

**Edition:**
1990

**Price:**
$14.95

**Pages/Run Time:**
225

**ISBN:**
0890875715

**Media:**
Book

**Principal Subject:**
Taking Care Of Your Child

**Secondary Subject:**
Breastfeeding

**Age Group:**
Infants (0–1)

★★★

**Overall Rating**
★★★
Contains much of the
necessary basic information
for breastfeeding

**Design, Ease Of Use**
★★★★
Logical order and easy reading;
succinct and concise; includes
resource list and photos

1–4 Stars

**Author:**
Gwen Gotsch

Gotsch has written and edited
numerous books, articles, and
pamphlets on breastfeeding and
parenting. She was also editor of
"Breastfeeding Abstracts," La Leche
League's newsletter for health
professionals, and she is an
accredited LLLI Leader.

**Publisher:**
La Leche League International

**Edition:**
1993

**Price:**
$8.95

**Pages/Run Time:**
116

**ISBN:**
0912500425

**Media:**
Book

**Principal Subject:**
Taking Care Of Your Child

**Secondary Subject:**
Breastfeeding

**Age Group:**
Infants (0–1)

**Breastfeeding**

# BREASTFEEDING
Pure & Simple

**Description:**
This six chapter, 116-page book discusses the whys and hows of
breastfeeding. Included in Chapter One are background information,
benefits of breastfeeding, and a short section about La Leche League.
Chapter Two discusses preparation, including breast and nipple care,
selecting a health care provider for baby, and lifestyle changes after
baby comes. Chapter Three highlights topics such as breastfeeding
the newborn, breastfeeding positions, frequency, and breastfeeding
after a Caesarean. How to deal with breastfeeding difficulties is
covered in Chapter Four. Advice is offered about sore nipples,
sleepy babies, breast infections, and more. Chapter Five describes
the growth of a baby and daily life with a breastfed baby. Also
outlined are ways to return to normal life, deal with social criticism,
and ways mothers and fathers can take care of themselves (diet,
drugs, smoking, medications) and deal with new feelings. Chapter
Six—"Looking Ahead"—focuses on babies' changing behavior as
they get teeth, eat solid food, and grow; also discussed are issues
such as how to return to work, breastfeed, supplement, and wean.
A list of resources is also provided.

**Evaluation:**
*Breastfeeding Pure & Simple* is a very good information source
for mothers who plan to breastfeed or are in the early days of
breastfeeding. It does well in filling the needs and allaying the
concerns of parents new to breastfeeding. It also provides
encouragement to those who may have had problems or are in
doubt about breastfeeding. This book answers common questions
that parents-to-be and new parents may have about breastfeeding.
The book progresses in an easy-to-follow, logical order: from getting
ready before baby is born, to breastfeeding the new baby, and various
aspects of life after breastfeeding has been established (parents' sex
life, going out with baby, and more). This resource is also good to
have on hand if problems related to breastfeeding arise. For example,
help is given on what to do if baby is not nursing well, what to do
in the event of a breast infection, and how to handle baby's biting
while nursing. Also given is good advice on how to express and store
breast milk which is useful for mothers returning to work. This book
is succinct and concise, but no information is provided for those
mothers having multiple births or breastfeeding an older and
younger baby.

**Where To Find/Buy:**
Bookstores and libraries.

**Breastfeeding**

# BREASTFEEDING AND NATURAL CHILD SPACING
## How Natural Mothering Spaces Babies

★★★

## Description:

This 208-page, 17 chapter book is built around "complete" and "total" breastfeeding as a means of natural infertility and a way to space babies naturally. That is, a strict adherence must be made to giving no water, juice, solid foods, or pacifier to a baby during the first six months at least. Many other details on "complete" and "total" breastfeeding are given. "Natural mothering" (in general, freely responding to baby's needs) is also a theme of this book. In addition to describing how breastfeeding can be used to space babies, the basics on breastfeeding (why, how, frequency, benefits of), and much more are also discussed. Chapters include "Your Baby's Sucking Needs," "New Light on Night Feedings," "Stepping Out with Baby," "Weaning and the Return of Fertility," "The First Six Months," "Nursing the Older Child," "Sex and the Lactating Mother," "Personal Experiences," and "Natural Family Planning." Two appendices ("A Postscript to Husbands" and "Personal Research"), an index, and a "Mini-catalog" listing related resources are provided at the back of the book.

## Evaluation:

If the reader can get over some of the relatively dated feel of Kippley's style, advice, and even the book's physical design, the reward will be much solid and substantive information. *Breastfeeding And Natural Child Spacing* covers a well-rounded, wide range of topics related to breastfeeding and "total breastfeeding." Many personal experiences of the author and others give diversified viewpoints. The author uses many of these personal experiences, through their successes and failures, to help fully illustrate the strict definition of "total breastfeeding." In Chapter 13, "Disappointments with Ecological Breastfeeding," Kippley also gives fair treatment to the alternative view of breastfeeding as a means of natural infertility. This is a complete book on educating couples on how to space babies through breastfeeding. However, if a parent is interested only in breastfeeding for its nutritional and emotional value for their baby or needs basic information on breastfeeding, this is still a worthwhile book to read.

## Where To Find/Buy:

Bookstores, libraries, order direct by calling (800) 745-1184, in Ohio call (513) 471-2000, or send a FAX request at (513) 557-2449.

**Overall Rating**
★★★
Complete book on spacing children naturally; contains good general breastfeeding info

**Design, Ease Of Use**
★★★
The writing is clear and easy to understand; graphics would be nice addition

1–4 Stars

**Author:**
Sheila Kippley

Sheila Kippley became interested in breastfeeding following the birth of her first child. She started a La Leche League group in Canada and, as a result of many questions she received about breastfeeding and its relationship to child spacing, she began collecting material to help mothers and eventually wrote *Breastfeeding And Natural Child Spacing*. In 1971 she and her husband founded The Couple to Couple League, which helps couples learn the art of natural family planning.

**Publisher:**
The Couple to Couple League International

**Edition:**
2nd (1989)

**Pages/Run Time:**
208

**ISBN:**
0960103686

**Media:**
Book

**Principal Subject:**
Taking Care Of Your Child

**Secondary Subject:**
Breastfeeding

**Age Group:**
Infants (0–1)

★★★

**Overall Rating**
★★★
An experienced, relaxed and personal support resource for breastfeeding

**Design, Ease Of Use**
★★★
Clear, easy to read; inserts are poorly positioned and occasionally confusing

1–4 Stars

**Author:**
Janis Graham

Janis Graham is the author of *Your Pregnancy Companion*. She also writes articles on health and fitness that have been published by *Family Circle, Self, McCall's* and *Working Mother*.

**Publisher:**
Pocket Books
(Simon & Schuster)

**Edition:**
1993

**Price:**
$10.00

**Pages/Run Time:**
211

**ISBN:**
0671749633

**Media:**
Book

**Principal Subject:**
Taking Care Of Your Child

**Secondary Subject:**
Breastfeeding

**Age Group:**
Infants (0–1)

**Breastfeeding**

# BREASTFEEDING SECRETS & SOLUTIONS
Fast, Reliable Answers To The Questions Mothers Really Ask

**Description:**
This 211-page book takes the experienced mother approach to provide a modern woman's perspective on the issues and challenges a first-time mother will encounter when choosing to breastfeed her baby. Common questions that occur during pregnancy are fielded first, then each successive stage is addressed, from how to hold the baby for comfort and healthy posture, to how to prevent soreness, diet and nutrition information, milk supply concerns, and food allergies. The later chapters of the book deal with related issues, including those of a working mother maintaining a breastfeeding schedule, concerns about food supplements, and solid foods and weaning. The author also summarizes family and behavioral issues that can occur with older babies and second children. The author cites resources such as the American Association of Pediatrics, La Leche League International, and the International Childbirth Education Association. Additional resources are listed for women with special needs such as mothers of multiples, mothers of babies with Down Syndrome, cleft lips and /or palates, and mothers of adopted babies.

**Evaluation:**
This is a useful book on preparing to breastfeed, and is supportive of the practice regardless of lifestyle. The writing style is clear, relaxed, and personal. Information is presented informally and made relevant by a light intermingling of personal experience. The author is a mother herself (still in the process of nursing her second child), which gives the book an informed, balanced and experienced perspective. She avoids sermonizing and assists mothers with choosing the best course through the maze of "Dos & Don'ts" that are offered by well-meaning relatives, friends, and conservative medical professionals. Of use to the first-time mother in particular, the book is still useful during additional breastfeeding experiences due to its insightful and informative approach to the problems, issues and concerns that can arise from differences between one child and the next. To the woman who is not surrounded by other mothers who can share their experience, this book will be a welcome companion.

**Where To Find/Buy:**
Bookstores and libraries.

**Breastfeeding**

# MILK, MONEY, AND MADNESS
The Culture And Politics Of Breastfeeding

## Description:

The aim of this book, written by a science writer and a former advisor to UNICEF and WHO, is to "bring alive the history, the culture, the biology, and the politics of breastfeeding so women can appreciate the contribution of breastfeeding to the survival of our species." As the authors state, this is not a how-to book but rather a why-to book. They also do not intend the book to be a "tirade" against formula but instead to balance the scales, "to make informed choice a reality." Within the 256 pages of this three section, six chapter book, you'll be exposed to breastfeeding beliefs and practices around the world past and present, a comparison of breastmilk with formula/artificial feeding, and the relationships between formula manufacturers/promoters, politics, and economics throughout the years. Seven appendices offer the following information: organizations working to promote breastfeeding, reading and resource lists, infant formula recalls (1982–1994), boycott information (Nestle and American Home Products), breastfeeding legislation (as of June 1995), and more.

## Evaluation:

Not for the faint-of-heart, this book doesn't mince words. Intimidating at first due to the amount of information, data, and historical accounts contained within, this book nonetheless packs a powerful punch you can't avoid. The authors' expose of formula manufacturers' tactics to push their products upon the medical profession, arguments used to convince lower economic groups and developing countries to not breastfeed, and the rates of infant mortality, especially in the U.S., as a result will leave you angry. Although pregnant women, unsure of whether or not they should breastfeed, will be better able to make informed decisions after reading this book, breastfeeding mothers will also find it useful as they deal with criticism for continuing to breastfeed after society's "approved" nursing period. We recommend this book primarily for professionals and hospitals who are bombarded with enticing freebies from formula manufacturers, yet must struggle to offer an unbiased opinion to new or prospective mothers. You'll be frightened, but you'll become enlightened.

## Where To Find/Buy:

Bookstores and libraries.

---

**Overall Rating**
★★★
Excellent "why-to"—best for medical professionals & those who need supportive data

**Design, Ease Of Use**
★★★
Table of contents lists all chapter contents, good graphics, reads much like a textbook

---

1–4 Stars

**Author:**
Naomi Baumslag, MD, MPH and Dia L. Michels

Baumslag is Clinical Professor of Pediatrics at Georgetown University Medical School in Washington, DC, and president of the Women's International Public Health Network (Bethesda, MD). Michels is a science writer. Both are published authors and frequent lecturers.

**Publisher:**
Bergin & Garvey

**Edition:**
1995

**Price:**
$26.95

**Pages/Run Time:**
256

**ISBN:**
0897894073

**Media:**
Book

---

**Principal Subject:**
Taking Care Of Your Child

**Secondary Subject:**
Breastfeeding

**Age Group:**
Infants (0–1)

★★★

**Overall Rating**
★★★
Original content, a welcomed "Lighter Side" offers humorous relief to nursing moms

**Design, Ease Of Use**
★★
Beautiful images; site map would help since info can seem scattered, unorganized

1–4 Stars

**Media:**
Internet

**Principal Subject:**
Taking Care Of Your Child

**Secondary Subject:**
Breastfeeding

**Age Group:**
Infants (0–1)

Breastfeeding

# BREASTFEEDING.COM
The #1 site for breastfeeding information, support and attitude

**Description:**

The purpose of this site is to "support breastfeeding women and to provide information on nursing to anyone (including fathers) who want to know more." Sections listed on the homepage include: "All About," "Lighter Side," "Advocacy," "Reading," "Help Me," "Shopping," and a directory of lactation consultants. "All About" lists many articles that address how a prospective mother can prepare for nursing prior to the birth of her child, information on why a mother should breastfeed, positioning, and common myths and their realities. "The Lighter Side" takes a humorous look at breastfeeding by offering a gallery of cartoons and photos, funny stories, and a comic history of breastfeeding. Articles on the infant food industry, legislation, breastfeeding in public, and many more topics are included in the "Advocacy" section. "The Reading Room" is a place to purchase breastfeeding and parenting books, find online articles, and links to magazines and journals. A shopping area is also included at this site.

**Evaluation:**

This site is a joyous, exciting, and fun promotion of breastfeeding for expectant and nursing parents. Many photos and illustrations are used to identify articles, without cluttering the layout. The video clips and art gallery are not to be missed. One of the most exciting and novel parts of this website is the Lighter Side which takes a humorous look at breastfeeding, without ridicule, stating, "No matter what the trouble, the day goes easier with a little humor." Essays include, "Pumping at 35,000 feet," "Bird's eye view," "Stop the exploitation of dairy cows," and "Express Yourself." Another bonus of this site is its inclusion of beautiful photos and artwork depicting breastfeeding images, provided throughout the site, but especially contained within the Art Gallery. Actual information may seem scattered and unorganized; be sure to link with the article titles contained within "All About." This section—and its intended purpose—would be better served if it were retitled; visitors may be misled thinking this section defines the website's mission and background. Overall though, this site provides definite value to prospective mothers and those who are currently nursing.

**Where To Find/Buy:**

On the Internet at the URL: http://www.breastfeeding.com/

**Breastfeeding**

# THE NURSING MOTHER'S COMPANION

★★★

### Description:

Huggins, a maternity and newborn nurse and founder of a breastfeeding clinic, has written this book "to provide mothers with a practical guide for easy reference throughout the nursing period." The seven chapters of her 240-page guide focus on breastfeeding and deal with the following topics: preparation during pregnancy, the first week, special mothers (mothers with diabetes/epilepsy/herpes/thyroid conditions, nursing after breast surgery, nursing an adopted baby, and more), and special babies (premature, twins, birth defect, etc.); four chapters specifically focus on baby's needs the first two months, from two to six months, and needs of the older baby and toddler. Following each of these special chapters are "survival guides." The cover page of each of these guides lists its contents. These sections are intended to be a "quick yet thorough reference for almost any problem you or your baby may encounter." The end of the book includes three appendices listing resources for nursing mothers, charts to determine baby's milk needs during the first six weeks, and a listing of drugs and whether or not they are safe while breastfeeding your baby.

### Evaluation:

Mothers-to-be and nursing mothers will find this reference guide useful, practical and up-to-date. Of special interest are the sections on dealing with "special mothers" and "special babies"—situations not often covered in many breastfeeding guides. Also of use are the survival guides, helpful for busy mothers who need suggestions quickly. The appendices of resources and drug effects is something every hospital should give mothers upon their departure. Chapters focusing on nursing the older baby and toddler offer many reassurances in dealing with disapproval from others. The only unnecessary item is the appendix for determining the baby's milk needs. Breast milk can only be measured if it's expressed into a bottle. Since bottles are not suggested until AFTER six weeks (due to nipple confusion), this section seems unclear. The chapters focusing on preparing during pregnancy and breastfeeding the first week are good, and old advice about breast preparation is dispelled—"nipple 'toughening' maneuvers . . . brisk rubbing," etc. This is a helpful resource.

### Where To Find/Buy:

Bookstores and libraries.

**Overall Rating**
★★★
Terrific for the beginning nurser, may be intimidating for the unsure mother-to-be

**Design, Ease Of Use**
★★
Table of contents dense; each chapter lists contents separately on chapter cover page

1–4 Stars

**Author:**
Kathleen Huggins, RN, MS
Huggins has been a maternity and newborn nurse and is founder of a breasfeeding clinic and telephone counseling service.

**Publisher:**
Harvard Common Press

**Edition:**
3rd (1995)

**Price:**
$11.95

**Pages/Run Time:**
240

**ISBN:**
1558321055

**Media:**
Book

**Principal Subject:**
Taking Care Of Your Child

**Secondary Subject:**
Breastfeeding

**Age Group:**
Infants (0–1)

## ★★★

### Overall Rating
★★★

Great tips on integrating breastfeeding into your life, including working moms

### Design, Ease Of Use
★★

Small type, rather dense style; more illustrations would help breastfeeding discussion

1–4 Stars

### Author:
Karen Pryor and Gale Pryor

Karen Pryor is a writer and a biologist specializing in behavior and learning. Her daughter, Gale Pryor, is a freelance writer and collaborated on this while nursing her own first child and working full-time.

### Publisher:
Simon & Schuster
(Pocket Books)

### Edition:
3rd (1991)

### Price:
$6.99

### Pages/Run Time:
416

### ISBN:
0671745484

### Media:
Book

### Principal Subject:
Taking Care Of Your Child

### Secondary Subject:
Breastfeeding

### Age Group:
Infants (0–1)

**Breastfeeding**

# NURSING YOUR BABY

### Description:
Written by a mother-daughter writing team, this 416-page book's third edition includes updated information "reflecting changes since the sixties." Part One discusses the facts behind human lactation. Included in this part are descriptions of how the breasts function, how the baby functions (body and behavior), the positive benefits of human milk, how breastfeeding strengthens the mother-baby bond, and the "politics of breastfeeding" (lack of support, the marketing of formula to medical professionals, etc.). In Part Two, a "mother-to-mother, month-by-month practical guide" is provided for breastfeeding newborns to toddlers. You'll find tips on selecting a hospital and doctor (obstetrician, pediatrician) that support breastfeeding. You'll find suggestions on first and subsequent nursings including positioning, relaxation tips, dealing with home stresses, and problem-solving; "confidence builders" are also included for dealing with others' criticisms. The final two chapters focus on breastfeeding for working mothers (24 pages) and nursing an older baby. An appendix lists sources of breastfeeding information and supplies.

### Evaluation:
The only complaint we find with this resource on breastfeeding is the way the information is presented. The table of contents at times is vague, the headings within the chapters impersonal, the writing style dense, the type compact, and not enough illustrations (we counted 6 total). But, if you're ambitious and can wade through it, this is a great book on breastfeeding at a great price. Especially useful are the week-to-week and then month-by-month advice that reflect the changes you and your baby go through. No other book addresses the evolution of the breastfeeding relationship quite so thoroughly. We also appreciated the effort that went into the section for "The Working Mother: How Breastfeeding Can Help." Practical input such as getting yourself and your baby ready to go back to work (from four weeks onward), how to express, pump, and store milk, realistic points to consider (fatigue, stress, leaking, etc.), and more are highlighted. The book's strong supportive dialog, its discussion of how breastfeeding changes as your baby develops, and its suggestions for working mothers makes this book a good choice for women considering breastfeeding.

### Where To Find/Buy:
Bookstores and libraries.

**Breastfeeding**

# PROMOM, INC.
Promotion Of Mother's Milk, Inc.

★★★

## Description:

This website, now encompassing a different website formerly known as "The Breastfeeding Advocacy Page," contains information on two aspects of breastfeeding. The first is the educational component of how and why to breastfeed. Included in this category is a list of ten things expectant parents should know about breastfeeding, 101 reasons to breastfeed, along with tips on how to return to work and continue breastfeeding. Other issues include taking medication while breastfeeding, the risks of breastfeeding, breastfeeding a toddler, monitoring milk intake, and others. The second aspect of the website is the advocacy of breastfeeding in the United States. Website authors are "dedicated to seeing breastfeeding become the number one choice of infant nourishment in the U.S." This site addresses the remaining cultural taboos concerning breastfeeding. Links to resources regarding laws that protect public breastfeeding are included. Other advocacy topics include the importance of breastfeeding, why breastfeeding rates are low, and how to support breastfeeding as an individual, employer, or organization. The "Interactive" link takes visitors to message boards, chat rooms and opportunities to sign up for a mailing list.

## Evaluation:

The message of this website is straightforward—breastfeeding is the best thing one can do for one's child and oneself, and support systems abound to make it easier. Surprisingly, actual how-to information is scarce at this website. However, mothers can find links and contact information here for help with breastfeeding. The site's format could be better organized to reflect its two focuses—dealing with the how-tos and promoting advocacy in support of breastfeeding. "Features" offers articles on reasons to breastfeed, opportunities to become an activist in support of breastfeeding in our society, and various essays. The articles detailing a perceived cultural prejudice against breastfeeding may be useful in arousing some parents to take action; a number of letters to companies and media outlets taking various advocacy positions are included. There is a lack of graphics at this website which would do much to soften the text's edges. Parents searching for basic information on breastfeeding will use this site primarily as a jumping-off point to other collections of links. For parents who have experienced the frustration of breastfeeding in American society and want to do something about it, this site is the place to go.

## Where To Find/Buy:

On the Internet at the URL: http://www.promom.org/

---

**Overall Rating**
★★★
Great website for advocacy of breastfeeding, less useful for actual how-to information

**Design, Ease Of Use**
★★
Straightforward navigation, information is minimal, graphics would be an added asset

1–4 Stars

**Media:**
Internet

**Principal Subject:**
Taking Care Of Your Child

**Secondary Subject:**
Breastfeeding

**Age Group:**
Infants (0–1)

★★★

## Overall Rating
★★★

A great deal of information, much of it conveyed through anecdotes

## Design, Ease Of Use
★★

Clear, well-illustrated, and organized; anecdotal sidebars distract from text

1–4 Stars

## Author:
La Leche League International

La Leche League International started 35 years ago when seven women, committed to breastfeeding at a time when most babies were bottlefed, met to provide information and encouragement to breastfeeding mothers. Currently there are 3000+ groups worldwide.

## Publisher:
Penguin Books USA (Plume)

## Edition:
5th (1991)

## Price:
$13.95

## Pages/Run Time:
446

## ISBN:
0452266238

## Media:
Book

## Principal Subject:
Taking Care Of Your Child

## Secondary Subject:
Breastfeeding

## Age Group:
Infants (0–1)

**Breastfeeding**

# THE WOMANLY ART OF BREASTFEEDING
La Leche League International

## Description:
*The Womanly Art of Breastfeeding* is an acknowledgment of the 9,000+ active Leaders in the U.S., Canada, and 43 other countries who contributed to this work. This 446-page book begins with "Planning to Breastfeed" with a chapter each focusing on the "whys" of breastfeeding, the "hows" of planning before birth, and ways to gather support networks. Part Two, "The Early Months," covers ways to adapt to breastfeeding, stating that it is 10 percent technique and 90 percent attitude. Many basic issues on child and mother care are addressed, like latching-on, engorgement, the family bed, breastfeeding in public, and more. Part Three discusses issues related to "Going Back to Work," and Part Four addresses "Life as a Family" with tips on how fathers can get involved, how to manage home duties, other children, etc. Part Five—"As Your Baby Grows"—addresses solid food, weaning, and discipline as "loving guidance." Part Six discusses "special situations" (C-sections, multiple births, premature babies, etc.) and how to breastfeed. Part Seven highlights advantages of "why breast is best" and Part Eight commemorates LLL's 35th anniversary.

## Evaluation:
This book contains useful information and is touted as the "bible of breast feeding." Although this revised edition includes updated information about the benefits of breastfeeding, some extension of the section for working mothers would enhance the book. The 16 pages that are included on how to juggle breastfeeding and working seems far too light a treatment of the topic. The reality for most women is that they do return to work; more logistical tips, information on their rights on the job, resources that are available, and information on skills that could help combine work and breastfeeding would be useful. For the first-time mother all the anecdotes may provide the support she needs; to others they distract from the facts buried in the text. But, for most women with busy lives this book will seem to drag on and on. There are other resources on the market which address the same issues in a more succinct fashion.

## Where To Find/Buy:
Bookstores and libraries.

**Breastfeeding**

# MEDELA
## Welcome To Breastfeeding Solutions And Medela, Inc.

★★

### Description:

Medela "has been providing superior-quality breastpumps and breastfeeding accessories to nursing mothers" since 1979. The homepage features the benefits of breastfeeding, how to breastfeed, choosing a breastpump, common problems and solutions, working and breastfeeding, board certified lactation consultants, and related links. A list of company products, prices, and where resources can be purchased is also available. "How To Breastfeed" offers an article written by Dr. William Sears and Martha Sears, R.N., detailing techniques and positions, complete with blackline drawings and color photographs. Information about collecting, storing, and freezing milk also is provided, along with information on how to use various breastpumps. "Problems and Solutions" offers remedies for various breastfeeding problems (breast engorgement, breast infections, sore nipples, flat/inverted nipples, and more). "Working and Breastfeeding" focuses on creating employer awareness of a nursing mother's needs and desires, selecting a caregiver who supports the desire to breastfeed, and helpful hints for combining work and breastfeeding.

### Evaluation:

Good, basic information can be found here to get a mother through most problems and questions she'll encounter concerning breastfeeding. Some visitors, however, will find themselves annoyed at the constant thread of commercialism apparent at this site. Its mission is clear—to sell Medela products. While the information is pertinent and ample to steer mothers through the difficulties of breastfeeding, many will find the product promotion intrusive. For example, "How to Breastfeed" offers the message "to help make breastfeeding an easy and pleasant process, Medela offers a variety of resources to give you expert instruction and helpful information." On the other hand, if a woman already uses and/or likes Medela products and/or she can ignore the "propaganda," she will obtain good information here on breastfeeding.

### Where To Find/Buy:

On the Internet at the URL: http://www.medela.com/

**Overall Rating**
★★
Good information, but a strong commercial tone promoting this company's products

**Design, Ease Of Use**
★★★
Well-organized site layout with color photos, blackline drawings

1–4 Stars

**Publisher:**
Medela, Inc.

**Media:**
Internet

**Principal Subject:**
Taking Care Of Your Child

**Secondary Subject:**
Breastfeeding

**Age Group:**
Infants (0–1)

II. Caring For Your Child

★★

## Overall Rating
★★
Practical advice, but little to no support for early weaning

## Design, Ease Of Use
★★★
Chapters divided according to age; easy to read, good organization

1–4 Stars

## Author:
Kathleen Huggins, RN, MS and Linda Ziedrich

Kathleen Huggins, RN, MS, is a certified lactation consultant and the author of *The Nursing Mother's Companion*. Linda Ziedrich is an editor of parenting books.

## Publisher:
The Harvard Common Press

## Edition:
1994

## Price:
$10.95

## Pages/Run Time:
196

## ISBN:
1558320652

## Media:
Book

## Principal Subject:
Taking Care Of Your Child

## Secondary Subject:
Breastfeeding

## Age Group:
Infants & Toddlers (0–3)

**Breastfeeding**

# THE NURSING MOTHER'S GUIDE TO WEANING

## Description:
This book is divided into five chapters highlighting ways to wean a child at various ages. Chapter One gives a history and background of "The Western Way of Nursing and Weaning." It also discusses the hazards of formula feeding. Chapters Two through Five each discuss possible reasons and ways to wean a child at specific ages. For example, Chapter Two discusses weaning a child before four months of age; reasons to wean include breastfeeding difficulties, returning to work, pressure from family, and negative feelings. Chapter Three focuses on "Weaning Your Four- to Twelve-Month Old." Reasons to wean at this age include biting, neglected siblings, getting sleep, and another pregnancy; the section on how to wean discusses gradual versus abrupt weaning and formula feeding. Weaning a one- or two-year-old is the focus of Chapter Four. Topics discussed include nursing in public, the night waker, and the aggressive toddler. Chapter Five addresses weaning the child over the age of three, including discussions of continual nursing, dealing with negative reactions from others, and accusations of child abuse. Finally the author discusses life after weaning.

## Evaluation:
If a person has an inherent interest in all of the historical facts about weaning, then Chapter One would be particularly interesting. The authors state that weaning has evolved in our culture to connote a child being torn away from its mother. They continue by pointing out that throughout history weaning has instead indicated a fulfillment in a child who is ready to move forward with his life and learning. In the first section of all the chapters then, the authors try to convince the mother not to stop breastfeeding. For example, in the chapter about weaning the three-year-old, the authors state, "nursing still has important benefits for the child past three. Nursing still soothes after upsets and injuries, comforts during illness and makes getting to sleep easier." The chapters provide useful information on how to deal with barriers to breastfeeding. And the second half of the chapters offer valuable and thorough information on how to wean, such as what formula to choose, how to store milk, how much to feed, and a variety of other questions a weaning mother would ask. They are not, however, at all supportive or reassuring to those mothers who decide to stop breastfeeding, for whatever reason.

## Where To Find/Buy:
Bookstores and libraries.

**Breastfeeding**

# LA LECHE LEAGUE INTERNATIONAL

★★

### Description:

La Leche League International (LLLI), "an international, nonprofit, nonsectarian organization dedicated to providing education, information, support, and encouragement to women who want to breastfeed," offers many features at their homepage. Pertinent to new moms' needs are the topics of "Breastfeeding Information from LLLI Periodicals," "Frequently Asked Questions about Breastfeeding," and "Breastfeeding Help Form." Also available are LLLI's conference, meetings, and chatroom schedules. LLLI's periodicals contain selected breastfeeding topics including 100+ articles dealing with subjects such as "Breastfeeding Multiple Babies and Tandem Breastfeeding," "Common Breastfeeding Concerns," "Working and Breastfeeding," and more. Each subject area lists how many articles can be found within it. Answers to "Frequently Asked Questions" are found within general topic headings (varying from newborn needs to special situations—nursing an adopted baby, tandem nursing, etc.). Breastfeeding support is available through LLLI's online help form; answers to questions will be sent by email "within one week."

### Evaluation:

La Leche League's reputation and proactive stance in the breastfeeding arena are well-known. One would then visit this site with great expectation that this is the site for all there is to know about breastfeeding. Those expectations would be too high. This site is not the be-all and end-all regarding breastfeeding. To illustrate: in the article "Preparing to Breastfeed," the only advice given to an expectant mother is to attend a local La Leche League meeting prior to childbirth. That's it. New moms may find their questions answered within the "FAQ" section, although this area lacks the graphics necessary to illustrate key points; for example, in answering the question of how to position a baby at one's breast, it is difficult to translate words into actions without visual aids. The online help forum is useful unless one needs immediate advice. In summary, La Leche League meetings generally are excellent sites for obtaining information about breastfeeding; the website, however, is not, and one needs to check other sites for information and help.

### Where To Find/Buy:

On the Internet at the URL: http://www.lalecheleague.org/

**Overall Rating**
★★
Disappointingly meager information from a well-respected breastfeeding advocacy group

**Design, Ease Of Use**
★★
Difficult to find the real information; no graphics, no illustrations

1–4 Stars

**Publisher:**
La Leche League International

**Media:**
Internet

**Principal Subject:**
Taking Care Of Your Child

**Secondary Subject:**
Breastfeeding

**Age Group:**
Infants (0–1)

★★★★

## Overall Rating
★★★★
Information is clear and well-organized—lots of useful lists, charts, and other tools

## Design, Ease Of Use
★★★★
Chapter topics listed on the contents page; sidebar tips and blocks of highlights

1–4 Stars

## Author:
Peggy Robin

Peggy Robin is the author of four books, including *How to Be a Successful Fertility Patient, Bottle-feeding Without Guilt*, and *Outwitting Toddlers*. She lives in Washington, DC with her family—and a nanny.

## Publisher:
Quill (William Morrow and Company)

## Edition:
1998

## Price:
$14.00

## Pages/Run Time:
214

## ISBN:
0688162142

## Media:
Book

## Principal Subject:
Taking Care Of Your Child

## Secondary Subject:
Choosing A Caregiver

## Age Group:
Infants & Toddlers (0–3)

**Choosing A Caregiver**

# THE SAFE NANNY HANDBOOK
Everything You Need To Know To Have Peace Of Mind When Your Child Is In Someone Else's Care

**Recommended For:**
Taking Care Of Your Child

**Special Resource For:**
Choosing a nanny as caregiver of your baby

## Description:
The author of this book bases her information on her own experience, surveys, and interviews. The structure of the book and what it will cover are addressed in the first chapter. The pros and cons of using a nanny, as well as issues such as money and living arrangements, are addressed in Chapter Two. Chapters Three through Five discuss a wide range of topics regarding the hiring process, such as hiring through an agency, hiring independently, and more. Stages of interviewing are highlighted including meeting face-to-face, meeting the children, reference checking, and the driving test. Making a choice and negotiating an offer, as well as how to fire a nanny are also discussed in these chapters. Maintaining the nanny relationship, training the nanny, and solving common problems that may arise are addressed in Chapters Six through Eight. The last chapter wraps up the information given in the book. It also relates the nanny experience from the nanny's perspective. Sample live-in and employment agreements are included for reference. Finally, a resource guide for finding more information on tax, insurance, safety, and babyproofing products is also provided.

## Evaluation:
Unfortunately, this author begins with the tragic case of the British au pair accused of the manslaughter of one of the children in her charge. Not the most positive beginning. She further goes on to list what the parents of the child should have done differently to keep the child safe and alive. While this is a vital message, it could have been addressed in a much more tasteful manner. Beyond this negative beginning, this book is quite helpful to those considering hiring a nanny. Because nannies are often considered the Rolls Royce of childcare options, this book's audience may be quite limited. For those, however, who are considering hiring a nanny, then the book offers many helpful tools to decide on whether nanny care is their best option and, if so, how to go about finding and keeping a suitable nanny. There are many charts and tables used for comparisons, quizzes to evaluate true needs, and sidebars on related information. The author's tone is an asset to this book. The information is straightforward and clear. All the background, history, and statistical information is located only in a few places as identified in the Contents. Readers can skip it if they are not interested. The tips are specific and easy to use, making this book a definite necessity during any nanny search.

## Where To Find/Buy:
Bookstores and libraries.

**Choosing A Caregiver**

# THE UNOFFICIAL GUIDE™ TO CHILDCARE

★★★★

**Recommended For:**
Taking Care Of Your Child

## Description:

Douglas writes this book as part of the publisher's Unofficial Guide series which include "books that deliver critical, unbiased information that other books can't or won't reveal." This book, which is reviewed by the Unofficial Panel of official experts, goes into detail about aspects of finding childcare, specifically the two types of childcare—in-home and out-of the home. Parts One through Four examine statistics, pros and cons of the different types of care, places to find childcare, costs, and how to deal with problems that may arise. Parts Five and Six address special situations, such as single parents, special needs children, and breastfeeding while working. Part Seven discusses reducing the stress of being a working parent by choosing alternative working arrangements and taking advantage of special childcare services and programs. Special sidebar features on each page are entitled "Timesaver," "Moneysaver," "Watch Out!," "Bright Idea," "Quote," or "Unofficially. . . ." A glossary, reading list, list of resources, and list of childcare interview questions are also included.

## Evaluation:

The author promises to reveal insider information about the childcare industry. While none of the information could be considered "secret," it effectively offers the accumulated wisdom of someone who has been involved with the childcare industry. In addition to the when, where, who, and how of childcare options, the book covers a broad range of topics: the tax ramifications of hiring childcare, employer tax and employment obligations, protection against allegations of sexual harassment or child abuse, and handling confrontations or other problems that could arise. Douglas also provides an excellent list of questions for interviewing either potential in-home caregivers or out-of-home caregivers. The first half of the book deals with the "average" daycare need situation—one or more children in a family with two working parents. Equally insightful are the individual chapters that deal with special situations such as single parents and special needs children. Stating that "our country is in the midst of a childcare crisis," the author believes that childcare overall is lacking and what exists is either too expensive or of a dangerously low quality. Fortunately, with the advice and guidance of this tome, a parent has an improved chance to find the best possible care for his or her child.

## Where To Find/Buy:

Bookstores, libraries, or order direct by calling (800) 428-5331.

**Overall Rating**
★★★★
The most complete, up-to-date information available

**Design, Ease Of Use**
★★★★
Well-defined sections, chapters, headings and table of contents

1–4 Stars

**Author:**
Ann Douglas

Ann Douglas is a Canadian journalist who has written for *The Chicago Tribune, Cottage Life*, and *Canadian Living*. She has also authored other books on parenting and history, and is a contributing writer and columnist to websites, TV programs, and radio programs.

**Publisher:**
Macmillan (Simon and Schuster)

**Edition:**
1998

**Price:**
$15.95

**Pages/Run Time:**
546

**ISBN:**
0028624572

**Media:**
Book

**Principal Subject:**
Taking Care Of Your Child

**Secondary Subject:**
Choosing A Caregiver

**Age Group:**
Infants & Toddlers (0–3)

★★★★

**Overall Rating**
★★★★
Presents a reassuring but informative study of the various child care options

**Design, Ease Of Use**
★★★
Needs bolder headings, there's a tendency to get lost; excellent checklists & forms given

1–4 Stars

**Author:**
Eva Cochran and Mon Cochran

Mon Cochran is a member of the governing board of NAEYC and was a professor of early child development and family studies at Cornell University for 25 years. Eva Cochran is a former director of the Day Care and Child Development Council in New York.

**Publisher:**
Houghton Mifflin

**Edition:**
1997

**Price:**
$14.00

**Pages/Run Time:**
355

**ISBN:**
0395822874

**Media:**
Book

**Principal Subject:**
Taking Care Of Your Child

**Secondary Subject:**
Choosing A Caregiver

**Age Group:**
Infants & Toddlers (0–3)

**Choosing A Caregiver**

# CHILD CARE THAT WORKS
A Parent's Guide To Finding Quality Child Care

**Recommended For:**
Taking Care Of Your Child

**Description:**
Divided into six parts with 19 chapters, this 355-page book highlights various options and considerations to "help you locate and organize child care arrangements that satisfy you and support the healthy development of your child during your absence." Part One offers an overview of the available options using several examples to illustrate the look and feel of quality care. Six chapters are included in Part Two and deal separately with various types of care (family and group family childcare, center care, part-day programs, care in your home, school age childcare, and "creative alternatives"), how to find them, and what to look for. Possible emotional reactions to childcare, both from the standpoint of the child and the parent, are illustrated in Part Three. Part Four outlines various ways to build a partnership with a caregiver, and Part Five focuses on how much to pay for a caregiver's services as well as tax information. In Part Six, the authors invite readers to become advocates and work toward improving childcare conditions. Nine appendices are provided including organization and referral agency contacts, checklists and childcare forms, and more.

**Evaluation:**
The strength in this book lies in its continual thread of support for those parents who must choose childcare for their children. Unlike many books on this topic, it combines an emotional and informational approach when discussing the various choices available. In terms of the emotional side, it refutes the myths parents generate internally when they must place their child in the care of others and their feelings of guilt and anxiety in doing so. Also, many of the other resources on this subject mention, but don't devote much effort to, the importance of building a partnership with a caregiver. This one does a nice job of this. Careproviders get equal time here; for example, although parents may complain about the high rate for quality care, the effects of low compensation for a careprovider's services unfairly leads careproviders to a lower quality of life. The sample forms this resource provides are also a plus. Parents looking for a book on quality care will find this to be a quality book.

**Where To Find/Buy:**
Bookstores and libraries.

**Choosing A Caregiver**

# THE COMPLETE NANNY GUIDE
Solutions To Parents' Questions About Hiring And Keeping An In-Home Caregiver

**★★★★**

**Recommended For:**
Taking Care Of Your Child

### Description:
This 154-page guide, written by the founder of a childcare agency, seeks to help parents find and keep a reliable nanny. It provides "all the information you need to hire in-home help and will save you the labor and cost of enlisting a child care placement agency." The book contains 12 chapters. Subjects discussed include in-home care versus daycare; finding the right kind of person; costs; conducting interviews and screening applicants; keeping a nanny; filing taxes, Social Security, and payroll programs; using a placement agency; and current laws. In addition, Chapter 11 deals with finding a nanny for children with special needs. There are seven appendices. These contain a listing of U.S. nanny training schools, sample employment applications, checklists for screening applicants, a criminal background release form, tax and government forms, and more. A listing of childcare placement agencies and services in the United States is also given. There is no index.

### Evaluation:
This is a well researched book with good, sound, up-to-date information. The author's experiences gained from owning a placement agency adds strength to this book. She offers a detailed outline of the standard procedures a nanny placement agency uses when screening household help for families. Her suggestions on securing and keeping a nanny along with her presentation of hard facts and laws on hiring in-home help makes this book credible. Questions are answered succinctly in a progressive, logical manner. Additional sources of information for parents are noted where appropriate in each chapter. Using this book as a guide, parents will be able to successfully sort out the best way to obtain childcare for their specific family's needs. Unique to this resource is the wealth of forms provided by the author. This affords parents the opportunity to familiarize themselves with these forms before beginning the hiring process. Parents looking to add a nanny to their family will find this guide to be very informative and necessary.

### Where To Find/Buy:
Bookstores and libraries.

**Overall Rating**
★★★★
Good information presented in a step-by-step format with many helpful employee forms

**Design, Ease Of Use**
★★★
Descriptive chapter titles, an index would also help; blocks of highlighted text useful

1–4 Stars

**Author:**
Cora Hilton Thomas
Cora Hilton Thomas is the founder and owner of Mother's Helpmates, a childcare placement agency. The mother of three, she lives and works in Brandon, Florida.

**Publisher:**
Avon Books (Hearst Corporation)

**Edition:**
1995

**Price:**
$10.00

**Pages/Run Time:**
154

**ISBN:**
0380782286

**Media:**
Book

**Principal Subject:**
Taking Care Of Your Child

**Secondary Subject:**
Choosing A Caregiver

**Age Group:**
Infants & Toddlers (0–3)

**Choosing A Caregiver**

★★★

**Overall Rating**
★★★
Information is concise, to the point, even if a bit dry

**Design, Ease Of Use**
★★★★
Lots of suggestions, checklists, worksheets, rating systems, referrals, and more

1–4 Stars

**Author:**
Stevanne Auerbach, PhD

Stevanne Auerbach received a PhD in child psychology and has given seminars for working parents in conjunction with many large corporations. She also has written extensively on many aspects of parenting.

**Publisher:**
Barron's Educational Series

**Edition:**
1991

**Price:**
$6.95

**Pages/Run Time:**
152

**ISBN:**
0812045270

**Media:**
Book

**Principal Subject:**
Taking Care Of Your Child

**Secondary Subject:**
Choosing A Caregiver

**Age Group:**
Infants & Toddlers (0–3)

# KEYS TO CHOOSING CHILDCARE

### Description:

This author promises to "assist you in selecting the best possible childcare services with the least amount of time and effort." The effects of childcare on the child, the child's individual needs, and the mother's needs are all addressed in the first few chapters. The pros and cons of childcare, choices, and types of childcare are discussed in Chapters 7 through 13. Individual chapters discuss the different options, such as in-home caregivers, home childcare providers, centers, and other alternatives. Chapters 14 through 21 explain what to look for in general that would apply to any arrangement, such as budget and quality. Three sections offer information about specific types of caregivers—family childcare home, childcare center, and in-home childcare. The author provides tips on searching for and gathering facts on each type of care, as well as how to make that type of childcare work. Suggestions on how to prepare the child and the family for childcare, and what to expect during the adjustment period are also given. Included are detailed checklists giving specific points to look for in each of the childcare places parents visit. Questions to ask at different stages are also included.

### Evaluation:

The 43 chapters in this book total only 153 pages, including glossary and index. With each chapter being two to four pages long, the author's explanations are not swallowed up by lengthy discourse or relaying of one statistic after another. The author points out that the choice to go back to work is a very personal one and unique to each mother. Many different options are offered, including flexible scheduling and working from home. The author recognizes that while children are individually unique, they have certain growth patterns in common. The author describes how those growth patterns can fit into the schedule of outside childcare, which has benefits as well as liabilities. The nuts and bolts of the information is provided in the checklists, lists of interview questions, and rating system for comparing each facility/caregiver. Referral agencies, state licensing agencies, a list of references, and suggested equipment for preschool programs are included in some of the appendices. Explaining what to look for and how to look for it, this "just the facts, ma'am" approach can be a bit dry for some, but may prove to be time-efficient for many.

### Where To Find/Buy:

Bookstores, libraries, or order direct by contacting Barron's Educational Series, Inc. at 250 Wireless Boulevard, Hauppauge, NY 11788.

**Choosing A Caregiver**

# HOW TO HIRE A NANNY
## A Complete Step By Step Guide For Parents

★★★

## Description:

This step-by-step 96-page guidebook presents a progressive plan to hiring a nanny. The table of contents includes six sections. Section One discusses how to define the job or the nanny's role. This also includes fundamental issues (safety, health, discipline, etc.) as well as specific tasks (housekeeping, cleanup, etc.) and responsibilities (meals, bathing, etc.); worksheets are included. Section Two involves costs. Salary versus hourly wages, benefits, and filing state and federal employer tax forms are just some of the topics addressed. "Finding the Right Nanny," in Section Three, highlights the pros and cons of using an agency, how to interview, network, extend an offer, and more. Sections Four and Five focus on the management issue of having a nanny and the changes in family priorities, respectively. Self-explanatory examples are included throughout the book, such as examples of phone interviews, reference interviews, employment applications, and writing a classified advertisement. There is no index.

## Evaluation:

Logically ordered and concise, this reference offers an easy-to-follow plan for parents interested in hiring a nanny. Clearly written and appropriately detailed, this book guides you through the process of searching for, interviewing, hiring, and keeping a nanny. It also offers input on responsibilities your nanny will undoubtedly do, and how to understand current tax and employee regulations without feeling overwhelmed; a useful table is provided of "what to do" and "when to do it." Parents will find that this succinct resource provides a summary list of required activities so that finding the right nanny will be a relatively pain-free experience. For serious but busy parents, this book will be a big timesaver, arming them with all of the right tools to help in their decision. Although there is no index, the table of contents aptly serves as a competent compass to help parents find answers to their specific questions. This book is a handy resource and well worth the buy.

## Where To Find/Buy:

Bookstores and libraries.

**Overall Rating**
★★★
A true resource to guide busy parents; comprehensive and complete

**Design, Ease Of Use**
★★
Smooth, progressive flow; numerous worksheets to focus parents; no index provided

1–4 Stars

**Author:**
Elaine S. Pelletier

Elaine S. Pelletier is a business professional, wife, and mother of two children.

**Publisher:**
André & Lanier

**Edition:**
1994

**Price:**
$9.95

**Pages/Run Time:**
96

**ISBN:**
0963557572

**Media:**
Book

**Principal Subject:**
Taking Care Of Your Child

**Secondary Subject:**
Choosing A Caregiver

**Age Group:**
Infants & Toddlers (0–3)

## Overall Rating
★★
Good practical advice outlining the pros and cons of various childcare options

## Design, Ease Of Use
★★
Topics easy to find but not detailed in table of contents; some tables might need updating

1–4 Stars

## Author:
Sonja Flating

Sonja Flating, a childcare consultant, is a member of the Child Care Coalition in Sacramento, CA. This coalition is an organization that studies childcare and works with real estate developers in incorporating childcare into their master planning.

## Publisher:
Facts On File

## Edition:
1991

## Price:
$24.95

## Pages/Run Time:
173

## ISBN:
0816022321

## Media:
Book

## Principal Subject:
Taking Care Of Your Child

## Secondary Subject:
Choosing A Caregiver

## Age Group:
Infants & Toddlers (0–3)

**Choosing A Caregiver**

# CHILD CARE
## A Parent's Guide

## Description:
There are seven chapters in this 173-page book focusing on finding "the best child care." Chapter One offers the author's early childhood memories along with a "Self-Test" the results of which are to be used by parents as they narrow down their childcare choices. Chapters Two and Three offer suggestions on how to find the appropriate childcare for children based on their age and needs. Chapters Four and Five discuss in-home care and family daycare centers. Also provided are interview questions and ways to make the transition. Alternatives to childcare are addressed in Chapter Seven. Chapters Eight through Eleven offer an "action plan" for finding childcare (a step-by-step check-off list), an overview of employer-sponsored childcare options, ways to cope with guilt, and the long-term consequences of childcare. A resource listing, daycare center regulations by state, and an index complete the book. There are many sample charts, question and answer examples, and a bibliography for each chapter.

## Evaluation:
This guide offers practical advice on finding and evaluating a nanny, a daycare center, or an in-home care provider. Using a personal approach, the author provides basic suggestions and alternatives for parents looking for quality childcare. "Homework" assignments, given at the end of some chapters, help parents to discover needs specific to their own child's personalities. Good information is provided within this resource including things to look for in a care facility, questions to ask prospective caregivers, and a list of emergency instructions. This guide presents both the advantages and disadvantages of the various programs based on children's age and development needs. The book is weak, however, at helping children make the transition; one paragraph is devoted to this purpose whereas a chapter is devoted to the parents' transition. Well-written and easy to understand, this is a good first approach book for families considering daycare for their children. Other resources, however, will answer more in-depth questions.

## Where To Find/Buy:
Bookstores and libraries.

**Choosing A Caregiver**

# CHILD CARE CHOICES
Balancing The Needs Of Children, Families, And Society

★ ★

### Description:
Written by the architect of the Head Start program and a specialist in child and family policy issues, this 271-page book observes the childcare situation from a society's viewpoint. It explores the economic issues of childcare as well as the quality of care given and the obligations of a democratic society to provide families with "real choices" for raising responsible children. This text contains ten chapters. Chapters One and Two examine the childcare system with information on working mothers, a child's environment, and the various types of childcare available. Chapters Three through Seven focus on ways to meet a family's childcare needs and how to find quality care for infants, toddlers, school age children, and children with special needs. Chapter Eight addresses how companies are tackling the childcare issue. Chapter Nine outlines a unified system of childcare for the 21st century. Chapter Ten details a child allowance trust fund to create childcare options for families of infants and toddlers. There is an extensive reference section, followed by an author index and a subject index.

### Evaluation:
Although this book delves deeply into the challenges and solutions of our current childcare system, many new insights and ideas have come to pass since this book was copyrighted. This text is not about how to find and keep good childcare help. It is about understanding the system, so that society can offer parents good supportive childcare choices that best suits their family's needs and parenting goals. This book does a great job in gathering all of the information about the childcare system and what it will take to change the system to address the issues most worrisome to parents of today. The book offers well-presented proposals for revamping our present system to improve the quality and quantity of daycare services. These proposals are aimed at the educational system, the corporate environment, the family, and the child and health care systems (specifically social security). This resource is more of a treatise for policy changes than a "how-to" guide; parents will need to compare present-day policies of the childcare system, however, to determine the accurateness of this text.

### Where To Find/Buy:
Bookstores and libraries.

---

**Overall Rating**
★ ★
Treatise on the crisis in the childcare system with proposals for societal changes

**Design, Ease Of Use**
★ ★
Heavy textbook style; author and subject index, with an adequate table of contents

---

1–4 Stars

**Author:**
Edward F. Zigler and Mary E. Lang

Zigler, designer of the Head Start Program, Sterling Professor of Psychology and Director of the Bush Center in Child Development and Social Policy at Yale University, has earned many awards for his contributions. Lang specializes in child and family policy issues.

**Publisher:**
The Free Press (Macmillan)

**Edition:**
1991

**Price:**
$27.95

**Pages/Run Time:**
271

**ISBN:**
0029358213

**Media:**
Book

---

**Principal Subject:**
Taking Care Of Your Child

**Secondary Subject:**
Choosing A Caregiver

**Age Group:**
Infants & Toddlers (0–3)

**Choosing A Caregiver**

# CHILDCARE KIT
How To Recruit, Screen And Monitor Baby-Sitters And Caregivers

**Overall Rating**

★

Short, elementary, and concise information on how to find good childcare

**Design, Ease Of Use**

★

Resource contains no index; relies heavily on marginal table of contents

1–4 Stars

**Author:**

Faye D. Campeau

Faye D. Campeau has personal and professional experience, both as a parent, caregiver, and an owner/operator of a childcare referral service.

**Publisher:**

Childcare Publications

**Edition:**

1995

**Price:**

$9.95

**Pages/Run Time:**

63

**ISBN:**

1895292573

**Media:**

Book

**Principal Subject:**

Taking Care Of Your Child

**Secondary Subject:**

Choosing A Caregiver

**Age Group:**

Infants & Toddlers (0–3)

## Description:

This larger-sized 63-page book contains three major sections. The section following the Introduction contains information to help parents create their own personal childcare kit, definitions of some terms, and current childcare prices. The next section focuses on "outside-the-home childcare" and discusses safety inspections, how to check a caregiver's references, some suggested questions to ask potential prospects, and more. The rest of the guide deals with childcare in the home, including topics of how to find care whether for babysitting, full-time, or occasional care. Examples of interview questions, applications, reference check forms, checklists, agreements, and an orientation list for the home are given. Also provided are forms for daily schedules, safety expectations (outside play, infant and toddler equipment, etc.), medical release info, discipline statements, allergy/special diet information, and more. Black and white line drawings are repeated throughout this resource. There is no index.

## Evaluation:

This book, based on the author's personal experience as owner of a daycare operation and referral business, offers numerous generic forms that parents may find useful, but it provides little value in helping parents decide upon a caregiver. Overall, the guide seems hurried and incomplete. The redundancy and often misplaced clip-art style art is distracting at times—why is there a picture of a fire fighter in the section concerning observation of a daycare? These drawings could have been omitted. Many of the sample questions are droll and uninspiring—"What are your interests and/or hobbies?" "How will you entertain my children while I am absent?"—questions whose answers may perhaps result in an uninspiring caretaker. Other books offer similar forms with more homework done in their development. The content contained in this resource is very basic and hardly worth the price. Parents should look to other resources with better scope, more depth, and thorough content to help them make this important decision.

## Where To Find/Buy:

Bookstores and libraries, or order direct from Childcare Publications, 49 Evergreen Estates, Sudbury, Ontario, Canada P3G 1B3.

**Choosing A Caregiver**

# THE GOOD NANNY BOOK
How To Find, Hire, And Keep The Perfect Nanny For Your Child

## Description:

How to find, hire, and keep a nanny for your child is explained in this 276-page, eight chapter book. Chapter One focuses on whether or not a nanny is needed. Chapter Two—"Visualizing a Nanny from Heaven"—discusses realistic expectations. Chapters Three and Four offer suggestions on how to find a nanny and how to select a nanny, respectively. How to prescreen applicants, interview them, check their references, devise an application, and more are highlighted. Chapter Five presents an array of nannies from "heaven" and "hell"; various scenarios are illustrated along with questions to use to match a nanny's personalities with your family's needs. Chapters Six through Eight give information on setting up your home for a nanny, managing an employee, and living with a nanny. The Epilogue includes testimonials from parents and children on the good nannies in their lives, and from nannies who speak about their jobs. Three appendices offer a list of in-home childcare definitions, a sample work agreement, and childrearing tips. There is no index.

## Evaluation:

Most of this book is about the author's own experiences with nannies. At first glance, much of the book seems to offer sound advice and suggestions. But, the parent anecdotes, while interesting, are often a bit overdone and lengthy, perhaps used to fill in space to pad the book's real content. Although these real life situations lend an interesting point of view, the book still tends to be the author's biased singular opinion in many cases, often with far too much negativity. Her judgements about good and bad nannies are somewhat harsh and prejudicial ("Make sure if you hire a Queen Bee that she gets her own phone and is financially responsible for it."); these suppositions are not always based on performance, but rather assumed personality types. This resource would have fared better moving in a positive direction with the subject matter. Focusing on strategies to find a good nanny and letting the "down" side go would have been a better approach. There are other, better, resources.

## Where To Find/Buy:

Bookstores and libraries.

---

**Overall Rating**

★

Too much negative element to help you approach this process positively

**Design, Ease Of Use**

★

What? No index? You'll need help to find your way through this one

1–4 Stars

**Author:**
P. Michele Raffin

P. Michele Raffin is the coauthor of a previous book and has four children.

**Publisher:**
Berkley Books (Berkley Publishing Group)

**Edition:**
1996

**Price:**
$12.00

**Pages/Run Time:**
276

**ISBN:**
0425151336

**Media:**
Book

**Principal Subject:**
Taking Care Of Your Child

**Secondary Subject:**
Choosing A Caregiver

**Age Group:**
Infants & Toddlers (0–3)

**Crying & Soothing**

★★★★

**Overall Rating**
★★★★
Parent support and insight based on studies of thousands of infants

**Design, Ease Of Use**
★★★★
Checklists, quick reference charts to summarize points, parental anecdotes in margins

1–4 Stars

**Author:**
Sandy Jones

Sandy Jones, a recognized authority on crying babies, has written six books and has published numerous articles in major magazines.

**Publisher:**
Harvard Common Press

**Edition:**
2nd (1992)

**Price:**
$10.95

**Pages/Run Time:**
162

**ISBN:**
1558320458

**Media:**
Book

**Principal Subject:**
Taking Care Of Your Child

**Secondary Subject:**
Crying & Soothing

**Age Group:**
Infants (0–1)

# CRYING BABY, SLEEPLESS NIGHTS

**Recommended For:**
Taking Care Of Your Child

## Description:

Written by a "recognized authority on crying babies," this 162-page book details the meaning and importance of a baby's cries. The first of 11 chapters explains "Baby Crying Basics," including a quick reference chart listing different types of cries (16), descriptions, and what to do. Chapter Two follows with techniques for dealing with a baby's cries (motions, sounds, touch, etc.). Chapters Three and Five debunk the myths of babies sleeping through the night; included is evidence that contradicts those researchers who insist that babies should be trained to sleep using various behavior mod techniques. How to successfully feed your baby is the topic of Chapter Four with the focus on breastfeeding. Descriptions of possible causes of colic and ways to help a baby with colic are highlighted in Chapters Six and Seven. The effects of various diseases and drugs on a baby are presented in Chapter Eight along with advice on how to find a good match between you and a doctor for your baby. Chapter Nine deals with crying in older babies and toddlers. The book finishes with tips for parents on handling stress in Chapters Ten and Eleven.

## Evaluation:

Sleepless nights, a crying baby—these are things that either bring out the best or worst in a parent. In an era of parenting in which babies are being trained at an early age to "cry it out," Chapters Three and Five are especially enlightening. Sleep trainers who insist that the baby's cries should not interrupt the parents' sleep offer, as the author suggests, "seductive promises" that can easily convince them to buy into their methodology. The author cautions the reader about these sleep trainers' works, however, and their espoused "magic cures" which not only cause parents to override a baby's normal communication signals, but also shame parents into believing that they are being manipulated by their baby. On the contrary, this book offers insights as to why the baby *needs* to cry and why the parental role is to heed that cry. And it does so in a way filled with support and helpful techniques which can only be reassuring and comforting to any sleep-starved parent.

## Where To Find/Buy:

Bookstores and libraries.

**Crying & Soothing**

# THE FUSSY BABY
How To Bring Out The Best In Your High-Need Child

**Recommended For:**
Taking Care Of Your Child

## Description:

"A fussy baby can bring out the best and the worst in a parent. This book is designed to bring out the best," says Sears in his introduction. Various words are used to describe fussy babies throughout this 192-page book—colicky, fussy, high need. The underlying premise of this book, along with Sears' other books, is attachment parenting. The first two chapters of this 14 chapter guide highlight characteristics of high need babies along with explanations as to why they fuss. The next seven chapters focus on taking care of your baby. Topics focus on the early weeks of baby care, a detailed chapter on baby's cries, possible reasons for babies being colicky, and soothing, feeding, fathering, and taking care of your baby at night. Chapter Ten concentrates on avoiding mother burnout. Chapter 11 refutes the argument to let babies "cry it out" by describing the "shutdown syndrome"; patient anecdotes are used for illustration. Sears' attitudes toward disciplining high need children along with "the pay-off" or benefits of attachment parenting are the focus of Chapters 12 and 13. Chapter 14 is a case history of a family with a high need child.

## Evaluation:

If the reader is open to the concept of attachment parenting and is the parent of a "colicky" baby, this resource is a "must read." Although some of the book's content is duplicated in Sears' *The Baby Book*, this book includes more detail. The following sections are especially enlightening: Chapter 11, describing "shutdown syndrome" or the result of babies crying it out; Chapter 12, focusing on disciplining the high need child; and Chapter 13, for those who worry that attachment parenting will lead to a dependent child. Sears, as in his other books, supplies the reader with numerous anecdotes from other family situations; these examples can only comfort a parent who is struggling with a child that others describe as difficult. Sprinkled throughout this book, particularly in Chapters Five through Nine, are tips and tricks for soothing your baby. Sears states that "being fussy and demanding has survival benefits for these babies. If they didn't fuss, their needs might not be met." Parents of high need babies, then, will find this resource valuable, both for meeting the needs of the baby and their own.

## Where To Find/Buy:
Bookstores and libraries.

★★★★

**Overall Rating**
★★★★
Comforting explanations of why babies are colicky; tips for how to soothe them

**Design, Ease Of Use**
★★★
Well-organized table of contents with subheadings; small dense text due to book's size

1–4 Stars

**Author:**
William Sears, MD

Sears, "one of America's most renowned pediatricians," has been in practice for 20 years and authored 10 books. Currently, he's a clinical assistant professor of pediatrics at USC School of Medicine.

**Publisher:**
Penguin Books (Signet Books)

**Edition:**
1989

**Price:**
$5.99

**Pages/Run Time:**
192

**ISBN:**
0451163273

**Media:**
Book

**Principal Subject:**
Taking Care Of Your Child

**Secondary Subject:**
Crying & Soothing

**Age Group:**
Infants (0–1)

★★★

**Overall Rating**
★★★
Unique approach with emphasis on the nurturing qualities of a gentle touch for babies

**Design, Ease Of Use**
★★★
Table of contents vague, but index makes for easy navigation; beautifully illustrated

1–4 Stars

**Author:**
Peter Walker

Peter Walker is a physical therapist with over fifteen years of experience in working with children, parents, and parents-to-be. He offers baby massage workshops to midwives and other health-care professionals throughout the United Kingdom.

**Publisher:**
St. Martin's Griffin (St. Martin's Press)

**Edition:**
1995

**Price:**
$16.95

**Pages/Run Time:**
128

**ISBN:**
0312145454

**Media:**
Book

**Principal Subject:**
Taking Care Of Your Child

**Secondary Subject:**
Crying & Soothing

**Age Group:**
Infants (0–1)

**Crying & Soothing**

# BABY MASSAGE
## A Practical Guide To Massage And Movement For Babies And Infants

### Description:
This reference consists of four chapters detailing the benefits of baby massage. Chapter One talks about the importance of touch and explaining the healing potential of massage. Chapter Two includes general information about massage (supplies needed (oils), when not to do it, etc.) along with the specific benefits of baby massage; also included is a massage technique for newborn infants as well as a full body routine for infants two months and up. In Chapter Three parents will find how movement and flexibility exercises combined with massage can help children through the developmental stages of sitting, crawling and walking. The final section, Chapter Four, highlights how massage can help children with special needs, as well as how it can be used to assist with a few of the most common childhood illnesses, such as constipation, wind, colic, and congestion. There is an index and worldwide "Useful Addresses" for mother-to-mother support groups, childbirth education information, breastfeeding, and more.

### Evaluation:
For readers whose interest lies in this subject, this 128-page book will surely leave you satisfied. With more than 100 beautifully detailed full color photographs and line drawings, readers unfamiliar with massage techniques will come away from this book confident and charged to try the author's "soothing caresses." This is a well-written, easy-to-read guide extolling the virtues of touch between infant and parent. The information is based upon the author's ten years of experience as a physical therapist attending hundreds of mothers and babies. The book is meant to be read cover to cover. The author is careful to stress gentleness, patience, and consistency. The how-to instructions are clear and concise; a novice will have no trouble picking up the author's suggestions on how to calm an infant or encourage their flexibility and strength as they begin more movements. Parents eager to try new ways to work with a fussy baby or capitalize on the bonding period will no doubt find a treasure trove of tips here.

### Where To Find/Buy:
Bookstores and libraries.

**Equipment & Supplies**

★★★★

# BABY BARGAINS SECRETS

**Recommended For:**
Taking Care Of Your Child

## Description:

This 9" x 4-1/4" resource contains 333 pages of information on how to find bargains as parents prepare for a new baby. There are twelve chapters in this book's second edition. Chapter One discusses how a baby will monetarily change your life. Chapters Two through Four contain information on nursery necessities (furniture, bedding, layette). Chapter Five includes information on maternity/nursing clothes and equipment for feeding baby. Chapter Six addresses things around the house: baby monitors, toys, bath, food, high chairs, swings, and more. Chapter Seven discusses car seats, strollers, and carriers. Chapter Eight suggests ways for affordable baby proofing. Chapters Nine through Eleven offer the "best gifts for baby," "etcetera" (books, Internet websites, and choosing childcare), and lists of mail-order catalogs grouped by subject matter with contact information. In Chapter 12, the authors compare typical savings parents can attain if they use the book's suggestions. Child product sources and safety requirements of Canada are included in the appendix.

## Evaluation:

This revised second edition includes more brand name reviews, email suggestions from readers, an added section on playpens, baby bottles, formula, and money-saving advice. All of the information and prices have been updated. Overwhelmed at first glance through this book, parents will need to take some time because this resource covers a great many items. The reviews in the book are based upon the authors' experiences and those of parents interviewed. Reviews of selected manufacturers are rated on a star system from a Four Star rating ("Excellent-our top pick!") down to a One Star rating ("Poor—yuck! could stand some major improvement"). There is no advertising in the book, crediting the authors' intent to not accept money to "buy" favorable reviews, thus also helping to insure objectivity. Helpful "Smart Shopper Tips," "Wastes of Money," "Money Saving Secrets," and more are included throughout the book. Parents willing to do a bit of homework will find this resource offers the best bargains for anything their baby will need.

## Where To Find/Buy:

Bookstores and libraries, or order direct by calling (303) 442-8792 or (800) 888-0385.

**Overall Rating**
★★★★
Lots of helpful tips and useful information "guaranteed" to save parents at least $250

**Design, Ease Of Use**
★★★★
Intimidating at first but a 13-page index & a detailed table of contents make access easy

1–4 Stars

**Author:**
Denise Fields and Alan Fields
Denise and Alan Fields are consumer advocates who have been featured on *Oprah*, *The Today Show*, *Good Morning America*, and *Dateline NBC*. Their previous books include *Bridal Bargains*, *The Bridal Gown Guide* and *Your New House*.

**Publisher:**
Windsor Peak Press

**Edition:**
2nd (1998)

**Price:**
$13.95

**Pages/Run Time:**
333

**ISBN:**
1889392006

**Media:**
Book

**Principal Subject:**
Taking Care Of Your Child

**Secondary Subject:**
Equipment & Supplies

**Age Group:**
Infants (0–1)

## Overall Rating
★★★★

An expert assessment of the most (and least) necessary baby products

### Design, Ease Of Use
★★★★

Succinct, highly usable, with helpful page "tabs"; appendices offer contact info, etc.

1–4 Stars

### Author:
Ari Lipper and Joanna Lipper

Ari Lipper manages Albee's, a baby products store in New York City, where he and his wife, Joanna, also live.

### Publisher:
Dell Publishing (Bantam Doubleday Dell)

### Edition:
1997

### Price:
$9.95

### Pages/Run Time:
215

### ISBN:
0440507847

### Media:
Book

### Principal Subject:
Taking Care Of Your Child

### Secondary Subject:
Equipment & Supplies

### Age Group:
Infants (0–1)

---

Equipment & Supplies

# BABY STUFF
## A No-Nonsense Shopping Guide For Every Parent's Lifestyle

### Recommended For:
Taking Care Of Your Child

### Description:
"Reading this book should give you a good understanding of the products that are out there, how they work, which ones are necessities, and which ones are best for you to consider based on your lifestyle," is how the author introduces his 215-page guide to baby products. Drawing on his familiarity with baby-related items, Lipper gives a run-down of "must haves" (necessities), "might wants" (items to consider based on your budget), and "totally optional" products (frills). The products are divided into six main subject areas: the Nursery, the Layette, Carriages and Strollers, Getting Around, Food, and Safety, accessible by both a table of contents and page tabs. Each section describes the products, rates them, tells how long your baby may need them, what their "borrowability" is (and advice in case you do borrow an item), safety issues, and how to fit them into your budget (brand names, prices, where to buy). Also included are sections on where to shop to get the best value, borrowing tips, and nannies. Three appendices give timetables for products, brand names and prices, and a list of manufacturers' telephone numbers.

### Evaluation:
In the buying fever that often arrives even before baby does, parents hoping to purchase the best possible products for their baby find themselves unprepared for the expense and overwhelming array of baby items all of which tout themselves as "necessities." Ari and Joanna Lipper's book should prove to be a steady and expert guide to the world of baby products. Its no-nonsense evaluations of each baby item allow parents to purchase the necessities (the crib, diaper pail, clothing, thermometer, stroller, car seat, high chair, etc.), weigh and consider desirable items (bassinet, changing table, baby monitor, portable crib, etc.), and take a look at the "frills" (comforter, pram, jogging stroller, hip carrier/backpack, etc.). There is help here for every parent's budget: well-made, reasonably priced items are recommended while some pricier items are justly critiqued ("A crib is a crib. No matter if you pay $200 or $600 . . ."). In this age of consumerism, this book will save parents time, money, and frustration while showing them how to purchase the best products for their baby.

### Where To Find/Buy:
Bookstores and libraries.

**Equipment & Supplies**

# IBABY.COM
All Your Baby Needs

★★★

## Description:

This website is almost exclusively an online shopping source for baby items. The homepage offers several ways to shop, including going to the various departments (categories of similar items), gifts for babies (a list of gifts for a baby, with links to those products that they sell), best buys (lists of links to the best selling items), and a product search. In addition to the shopping opportunities, a baby registry is available to expectant parents who want to provide gift ideas for a baby shower. This registry can be edited/updated by the parent, or the site automatically updates the registry as purchases are made. To aid in planning for purchases for a new baby, the site also offers a new parent checklist that includes items and quantity of items needed to prepare for a newborn. To find a specific item, a visitor can access the product search function of the site. To use the site, a visitor first must register by submitting mailing information; an account number and password then is issued. Individual items are listed, with an illustration, product information, price, size, and color, if applicable.

## Evaluation:

One would expect an online shopping website to be overdone with sales pitches. However, we were amazed at the simple yet effective layout of this source. The departments are well-organized and offer a variety of ways to access products, depending on the customer's needs, without cluttering up the page. Similar to a traditional store, this site offers sale items and best buys. All products include colorful descriptions, in-stock status, price, and product number. Simply click the corresponding button to add the item to your "shopping cart." The online baby registry is a great time saver for anyone who cares to shop online. The new parent checklist is a helpful organizational tool, even if it is a bit dictatorial. For example, it recommends that 16 to 24 outlet plugs be purchased instead of suggesting the customer count his or her outlets. The product recall list is too confusing to be useful, unfortunately. Given the still prevalent concern about security, this site should add more information about its security measures. For ease of use, this site is topnotch. One caution: this site does not appear to make any evaluations or comparisons about the products offered; judgements must be made using other tools.

## Where To Find/Buy:

On the Internet at the URL: http://www3.ibaby.com/

---

**Overall Rating**
★★★
Useful tools to use when shopping for baby; good information on individual products

**Design, Ease Of Use**
★★★★
Excellent format, variety of ways to access the products

1–4 Stars

**Media:**
Internet

**Principal Subject:**
Taking Care Of Your Child

**Secondary Subject:**
Equipment & Supplies

**Age Group:**
Infants (0–1)

**Equipment & Supplies**

## Overall Rating
★★★
A useful planning tool for baby's arrival; includes small, easily-overlooked necessities

## Design, Ease Of Use
★★★
Helpful "checklist" format; monthly pregnancy calendars provided to track to-do list

1–4 Stars

## Author:
Susan Kagen Podell, MS, RD

Susan Kagen Podell, MS, RD is a Registered Dietitian and Certified Diabetes Educator, and the author of other books on nutrition.

## Publisher:
Main Street Books (Bantam Doubleday Dell)

## Edition:
1997

## Price:
$6.99

## Pages/Run Time:
212

## ISBN:
038547797X

## Media:
Book

## Principal Subject:
Taking Care Of Your Child

## Secondary Subject:
Equipment & Supplies

## Age Group:
Infants (0–1)

**Equipment & Supplies**

# CHECKLIST FOR YOUR FIRST BABY

## Description:

This book is designed to help new mothers-to-be organize and prepare for the arrival of a new baby. Focusing on pregnancy, birth, and the first six postpartum weeks, this book offers "checklists" for vital needs, helpful tips and information on a variety of topics. Section One discusses the first, second, and third trimesters, and changes you can expect through the months. Section Two contains information and checklists for health, nutrition, and exercise for the first trimester. Section Three looks at second trimester topics: how (and when) to announce the news, health insurance, equipping the nursery, purchasing maternity and baby clothes, childbirth classes, and bottle- vs. breast-feeding. Section Four includes a checklist of questions for one's pediatrician, choosing child care, and packing for the hospital during the third trimester. Section Five contains important tips for the weeks following the baby's birth: general care, the 6-week check-up, birth control choices, and traveling and playing with the baby. The last section is a "pregnancy calendar" to note appointments and stay organized until the birth.

## Evaluation:

The key to this little book's usefulness is in its design. It gives absolutely basic information for such things as nutrition and baby care (more comprehensively covered in other books) but contains reminders and checklists for little everyday necessities that bigger books may overlook. For example, how to choose maternity and baby wear while keeping costs down, nursery needs, what to pack for the hospital, and useful, practical baby care tips. Also helpful are the lists of suggested questions for one's health care provider before and after birth that may easily be forgotten in the thick of things (e.g. "What is your attitude about pain relief during labor?" "What type of breastfeeding tips can you provide me?" "When can I start exercising?"). Although the information offered here is very simple and basic, this book points the way towards getting the in-depth information one needs from the appropriate sources, while staying on top of the overall planning process for the baby's arrival.

## Where To Find/Buy:
Bookstores and libraries.

**Equipment & Supplies**

# GUIDE TO BABY PRODUCTS
Buy The Best For Your Baby

★ ★

## Description:

This 326-page guidebook is targeted to all consumers of baby products. Beginning with the statement that there is no guaranteed safety for a product made for children, the book then looks at the range of products currently sold in American markets and the availability of safety information on each product. Not all products are rated, but ratings are included when available. Topics covered include: backpacks/soft carriers, various infant beds, bathing accessories, bottlefeeding equipment, breastfeeding accessories, changing tables, child safety seats, clothing and footwear, baby foods, gates, hazard reduction/childproofing products, high chairs/booster seats, infant seats, monitors, nursery decor/accessories, playpens, strollers, swings, toilet-learning aids, toys, and walkers. Information is arranged alphabetically and with occasional photographs. Each section begins with information and advice on what to look for, rules on how to use some products, and a list of recalled products. Items selected for testing were based on information obtained from manufacturers. Manufacturers' contact information and an index are included.

## Evaluation:

Though the book is subtitled "Buy the Best for Your Baby," too little information was provided in most cases for a "best" evaluation. The introduction was somewhat disorganized and illogical. Is the assumption here that the consumer wants to buy the safest product for the least money? Or is safety the primary rating factor? Information on how products are rated and who is responsible for the rating should be presented more clearly—did the same parents who tested the products also rate them? The product listings contain maker and model, description, design info, and special features, but often there is no safety rating specific to that product, making evaluation difficult. It is unclear as to whether omission from these lists means the products were found unsafe or simply not supplied by the manufacturer. The text in these listings is small and hard to read. Photographs would be an added plus but there are too few to really be helpful. There is certainly a need for books like this one to facilitate consumers wading through the overwhelming mass of baby products, but this one falls short.

## Where To Find/Buy:

Bookstores and libraries.

**Overall Rating**

★★

Offers products that meet authors' or Consumers Union's safety standards

**Design, Ease Of Use**

★

Listing information is too small and lacks overall ratings; listing criteria unclear

1–4 Stars

**Author:**

Sandy Jones and Werner Freitag

Sandy Jones is a well-known expert on baby products and safety, and is the author of many books and articles for parents. Werner Freitag is a project leader at Consumers Union, where he has worked for over 30 years. He has helped draft baby product safety standards.

**Publisher:**
Consumer Reports Books

**Edition:**
5th (1996)

**Price:**
$14.95

**Pages/Run Time:**
326

**ISBN:**
0890438544

**Media:**
Book

**Principal Subject:**
Taking Care Of Your Child

**Secondary Subject:**
Equipment & Supplies

**Age Group:**
Infants (0–1)

## THE HEALTHY BABY MEAL PLANNER
Mom-Tested, Child-Approved Recipes For Your Baby And Toddler

★★★★

**Overall Rating**
★★★★
Innovative recipes for parents of infants and toddlers emphasizing taste and nutrition

**Design, Ease Of Use**
★★★★
Cross-referenced ingredients in index; mealplanner charts a+; delightful illustrations

1–4 Stars

**Author:**
Annabel Karmel

Having studied at the Cordon Bleu School of Cookery, this is Annabel Karmel's first book. She is also an accomplished musician and actress and has made numerous television appearances. She lives with her husband, Simon, and family in London.

**Publisher:**
Fireside (Simon & Schuster)

**Edition:**
1992

**Price:**
$15.00

**Pages/Run Time:**
192

**ISBN:**
0671750194

**Media:**
Book

**Principal Subject:**
Taking Care Of Your Child

**Secondary Subject:**
Feeding

**Age Group:**
Infants & Toddlers (0–3)

**Recommended For:**
Taking Care Of Your Child

**Description:**
This 192-page guide includes many recipes containing fresh ingredients, low animal fat, and little or no sugar or salt. There are five chapters, an index, and a listing of acknowledgments. Chapter One provides parents with information on milk (breastfeeding, bottlefeeding, cow's milk), why fresh foods are best to use in recipes, facts on the six essential nutrients for a child, and food allergies. Chapters Two, Three, Four, and Five contain age-specific recipes broken into the following age groups: four to six months, six to nine months, nine to twelve months, and toddlers. Each recipe contains a check box with a smiling face and a gloomy face to record a child's opinion of that recipe. An introduction precedes each chapter offering advice on various subjects such as meal planning, dealing with picky eaters, which quantities work best for specific age groups, and more. The index contains cross-references under each ingredient so that parents can access additional recipes that contain the same given ingredient.

**Evaluation:**
This is a upbeat recipe book offering many really good, nutritious, and fairly easy to make meals. The humorous illustrations add to the book's lightheartedness. The author has tried to serve the dietary needs of the whole family starting when the baby is about nine months old. This resource contains some very useful information. Tips on freezing storage times, the age at which some foods may be introduced, when to start weaning, and how to learn patience at mealtimes are just some highlights. The recipes are simple and well written. For busy parents, the author's inclusion of the smiling-gloomy faces at the end of each recipe will help serve as a reminder for which meals were successful and which were not. The age-specific meal planners are particularly helpful. Each planner is laid out day by day for one week, and includes breakfast, lunch, dinner, snacks, and bedtime food if appropriate.

**Where To Find/Buy:**
Bookstores and libraries.

**Feeding**

# SMALL HELPINGS
## A Complete Guide To Feeding Babies, Toddlers And Young Children

**Recommended For:**
Taking Care Of Your Child

## Description:

This 160-page hardcover book aims to provide nutritional recipes for parents of young children to establish a pattern of healthy eating that can be carried on through their lives. The author's premise is that a recipe has to be easy for busy parents; all use fresh, natural ingredients. The Table of Contents contains four sections, the first of which includes information on basic nutrition, food allergies, and sugar's effect on children's teeth. Section Two focuses on introducing solids to babies and presents food ideas for babies four months to 12 months of age. The third section offers ideas for feeding toddlers. It contains information about encouraging toddlers to eat good food, easing up on salt, eating out, and recipes including vegetables, pasta, fish, chicken, meat, and fruit. The final section discusses food for young children. Lunch box ideas, snacks, cookies, special treats, and "healthy fast food" are some of the topics discussed. Advice and "handy timesaving tips" are provided throughout for each stage of a child's development.

## Evaluation:

Whimsical drawings and bordered pages help make this recipe book a fun, easy to use manual. All of the basic food groups are covered and there is also information offered on meat alternatives and vegetarian diets. The recipes are elementary, but imaginative and each includes a portion count. The only objection we found in the book was the author's advice regarding "weaning." She did not reflect current info about when to start babies on cow's milk or solids. Interesting tips, notes, and advice are added for many of the recipes; for example, the author suggests mixing vanilla bean to simmering fruit as a way of adding sweetness without extra sugar, and using lemon juice on apples to help keep them from turning brown. Parents will get a sense from this well-written guide that regardless of which recipe they choose, it will be nutritious and most likely their child will like it! From "Mermaid Morsels" to "Tofu and Peanut Butter Stir-Fry," parents will find something in this guide to suit even the most discriminating of tastes.

## Where To Find/Buy:

Bookstores and libraries.

---

**Overall Rating**
★★★★
Nutritionally sound with quick and easy recipes using fresh, natural ingredients

**Design, Ease Of Use**
★★★
Simple, easy to reference; index good but not comprehensively cross-referenced

1–4 Stars

**Author:**
Annabel Karmel

Annabel Karmel, a best-selling author of previous cookbooks, has three young children.

**Publisher:**
Cole Publishing Group
(BBC Books/BBC Worldwide)

**Edition:**
1995

**Price:**
$14.95

**Pages/Run Time:**
160

**ISBN:**
1564260771

**Media:**
Book

**Principal Subject:**
Taking Care Of Your Child

**Secondary Subject:**
Feeding

**Age Group:**
Infants & Toddlers (0–3)

II. Caring For Your Child

Feeding

# BABY LET'S EAT

## Description:

Presented in five chapters, this 128-page recipe book offers recipes for baby and toddler foods. Chapter One discusses nutritional basics including information on proteins, carbohydrates, fats, vitamins, minerals, and more; a food chart for children ages one to three years old is provided with suggested serving sizes and recommended daily servings. Also discussed are various food preparation methods, foods to avoid (sugars, salts, fats, caffeine, dangerous), storing, etc. The next four chapters are divided by ages: 6 to 12 months, 12 to 18 months, 18 to 24 months, and 24 to 36 months. Within each chapter, the authors, one a chef and the other a nutritionist, detail hurdles and solutions specific to that age child along with a weekly menu chart for meal planning. The corresponding recipes (20–25) from the weekly menu chart then complete each chapter and are designed for use with the whole family. Recipes include breakfast foods, lunch items, dinner entrees, and snacks; they emphasize the use of non-sugar substitutes. The amount of preparation and cooking time are given along with how long the food can be stored in the refrigerator or freezer.

## Evaluation:

The strength of this recipe book that differentiates it from its counterparts is that it emphasizes family recipes along with the use of non-sugar substitutes, whole foods, and spices in lieu of salt. With its convenient spiral-bound design, colored recipe headings, and weekly meal planning charts for each age group, parents will find this guide easy to use. Whimsical illustrations accompany many recipes adding a light touch to a sometimes dull subject matter. The only difficulty some parents may find with this guide is that many recipes involve rather elaborate preparations, some uncommon ingredients, and lengthy preparation times of 30–45 minutes (not including cooking times). If parents consider the entrees to be family fare and not just menus to satisfy their toddlers' nutritional requirements, then this time may be well-spent. Otherwise, between busy schedules and finicky behaviors on the part of many toddlers, this time involved will become a source of frustration. However, if parents want to change their eating habits and prepare some healthful menus for their family, this is the book that can guide them.

## Where To Find/Buy:

Bookstores and libraries.

---

**Overall Rating**
★★★
Good application of nutrition basics to healthful recipes for each age group (6–36 mos.)

**Design, Ease Of Use**
★★★★
Spiral-bound layout helpful; weekly meal planning charts; recipe index would be nice

1–4 Stars

**Author:**
Rena Coyle with Patricia Messing
Coyle is a mother and chef and Messing is a nutritionist.

**Publisher:**
Welcome Enterprises
(Workman Publishing)

**Edition:**
1987

**Price:**
$9.95

**ISBN:**
089480300X

**Media:**
Book

**Principal Subject:**
Taking Care Of Your Child

**Secondary Subject:**
Feeding

**Age Group:**
Infants & Toddlers (0–3)

**Feeding**

# FEED ME! I'M YOURS

## Description:

Lansky has included in her book's third edition "new information, but it is still basically the same book." Recipes have been collected for "their nutrition, convenience, and fun." This 143+ page book is divided into 11 sections. The first couple of sections include information on preparing baby and finger foods. Following these sections are menus for toddler meals (breakfast, lunch, dinner, veggies, dessert, beverages) and snacks. Other chapters in this guide center on seasonal recipes, activities to do in the kitchen (crafts, various dough recipes, finger paints, paste, etc.), and birthday parties ideas for children ages one to five. The final section is a "potpourri" of ideas and information from other parents. Some included tips are methods for removing stains, first aid tips, traveling tips, and information on poisons. There is an index, which precedes an ingredient substitution list, and weights and measurements conversion list. Several pages of other selected print resources available from the publisher round out the book.

## Evaluation:

Divided into approximately eight main segments, this toddler baby food guide makes a wonderful addition to one's cookbook collection. This resource not only shows one how to blend and store fresh baby food, but also describes safe and nutritious finger foods, along with ways to add variety and balanced ingredients at mealtimes. There are recipes for teething biscuits, quick low sugar desserts, and recipes for specific seasons of the year. Some highlighted summer recipes include yogurt popsicles, water ices, and ideas for summer picnics; some of the recipes for winter include toasted pumpkin seeds and snow mousse. The birthday section offers insights on what activities are appropriate for specific ages, ideas for snack foods, cake ideas, and some fun preschool games. This is a delightful, helpful, and entertaining book that any parent concerned with their baby or child's nutrition and health will appreciate.

## Where To Find/Buy:

Bookstores and libraries, or order direct by calling (800) 338-2232.

---

★★★

**Overall Rating**
★★★
Fun and imaginative recipes for parents helping meet their child's nutritional needs

**Design, Ease Of Use**
★★★★
Straightforward with bold headings; spiral comb binding makes it easy to lay flat

1–4 Stars

**Author:**
Vicki Lansky

Vicki Lansky has authored over 25 books, and is well-known for her column in *Family Circle* magazine and *Sesame Street Parents' Guide Magazine*. She has also appeared on national TV shows like *Donahue*, *Oprah*, and *Today*.

**Publisher:**
Meadowbrook Press
(Simon & Schuster)

**Edition:**
3rd (1994)

**Price:**
$9.00

**ISBN:**
0671884433

**Media:**
Book

---

**Principal Subject:**
Taking Care Of Your Child

**Secondary Subject:**
Feeding

**Age Group:**
Infants & Toddlers (0–3)

## Overall Rating
★★★
An excellent overview of natural foods, nutritional requirements, and food substitutes

## Design, Ease Of Use
★★★★
Easily cross-referenced with large bold subheadings, numerous charts, bulleted tips

1–4 Stars

## Author:
Susan Tate Firkaly

Susan Tate Firkaly is a lecturer and an assistant professor in the School of Medicine at the University of Virginia. She is also the associate director for Health Promotion in the Department of Student Health.

## Publisher:
Betterway Books (F&W Publications)

## Edition:
2nd (1995)

## Price:
$9.99

## ISBN:
155870373X

## Media:
Book

## Principal Subject:
Taking Care Of Your Child

## Secondary Subject:
Feeding

## Age Group:
Infants & Toddlers (0–3)

**Feeding**

# INTO THE MOUTHS OF BABES
## A Natural Foods Nutrition And Feeding Guide For Infants And Toddlers

## Description:
With over 175 "economical, easy-to-make, vitamin-packed, preservative-free" recipes, this 160-page guide offers information on nutrition and natural foods for infants and children up to age three. There are fourteen chapters. Chapters One, Two and Three address the reasoning behind making your own baby food, what you'll need in your kitchen, and tips on shopping for whole foods (versus processed foods). The next two chapters discuss nutrition during pregnancy and for infants. Chapter Six contains information about breastfeeding, bottle-feeding, eating disorders, and introducing new foods. Information on food allergies can be found in Chapter Seven. The next four chapters include age-specific recipes for children ages six months to three years. Family recipes, recipes for children with allergies, and information on poisonous materials are contained in the final chapters. Many tables and charts are provided throughout. A bibliography, a list of further resources, a general index, and a recipe index are also given.

## Evaluation:
Much more than just a cookbook, this resource is a well-written guide on the preparation of natural foods and why they should be the cornerstone of nutrition for your family. This book's second edition offers excellent alternatives for parents wishing to steer their children away from a diet of sugar, salt, chemical additives, and high animal protein foods. This new version also includes updated nutritional information reflecting the currently recommended "food pyramid" as opposed to the four food groups. In this resource, parents will find a useful chart of food groups for those who chose not to eat meat, a timetable for introducing new foods, and a list of foods that can cause problems, such as choking and allergies. The recipes are easy, convenient, and tasty. Although these recipes contain no meat, this resource offers plenty of information for parents to decide which foods are best for their families. After reading this book, parents might feel compelled to take advantage of these great recipes and change their diet forever.

## Where To Find/Buy:
Bookstores and libraries, or order direct by calling (800) 289-0963.

**Feeding**

# SUGAR-FREE TODDLERS
Over 100 Recipes Plus Sugar Ratings For Store-Bought Foods

★★★

## Description:

Three main sections, supported by eight chapters, comprise this 170-page recipe book. The first section offers basic information on toddlers and nutrition, the plight of child obesity, and a toddler's nutritional requirements. The case for sugar-free foods is also presented. Chapter Two in this section contains information on common ingredients, nutritional quotients, a note about preparation times, and tips on freezing foods. Section Two (Chapters Three through Eight) includes over 100 of the authors' sugar-free recipes. These are grouped into categories that include: main dishes; biscuits, crackers, muffins and breads; drinks; snacks; sauces, syrups, and spreads; and cookies, cakes, and bars. Following Chapter Eight is a section entitled "Sugar Ratings For Store-bought Foods" which offers side-by-side product evaluations. This section includes which sweetener has been used, a "Toddler Rating," (toddler-tested evaluation), calorie count, and further comments on the store-bought product. An index completes the book.

## Evaluation:

The author emphasizes that although she worked full-time when her daughter was young, she wasn't "fanatical about health food," but she was concerned about finding nutritious alternatives to highly refined food. This is a situation many parents will appreciate. With over 100 recipes, this guide strives to suggest nutritional, good-tasting food with no refined sugars or refined flours. Each recipe lists the toddler rating, prep time, nutritional quotient (based on an approximation of a toddler's daily nutritional requirements), and servings count. Simple black line illustrations enhance the overall "toddler" theme. The recipes are clear and well-organized. There are useful hints for preparing day care lunches as well as brown bag lunches. The author has done a fine job of providing substitutions such as carob, nonfat dry milk powder, and hints on using vegetable cooking spray as an alternative. For parents concerned about their child's sugar intake, this book will be a welcome addition to their kitchen library.

## Where To Find/Buy:

Bookstores and libraries, or order direct by calling (800) 234-8791.

**Overall Rating**
★★★
User-friendly recipes with consistent ingredients; includes nutritional quotients

**Design, Ease Of Use**
★★★★
Easy to flip through; helpful index

1–4 Stars

**Author:**
Susan Watson

**Publisher:**
Williamson Publishing

**Edition:**
1991

**Price:**
$9.95

**Pages/Run Time:**
170

**ISBN:**
0913589578

**Media:**
Book

**Principal Subject:**
Taking Care Of Your Child

**Secondary Subject:**
Feeding

**Age Group:**
Toddlers (1–3)

★★★

## Overall Rating
★★★

Strong in providing information on the merits of nutrition coupled with 250+ recipes

### Design, Ease Of Use
★★★

Clear, well-organized; non-threatening textbook format

1–4 Stars

### Author:
Karin Knight, RN and Jeannie Lumley

Kari Knight is a registered pediatric nurse who has worked in the public health system in the Los Angeles area. Jeannie Lumley is employed by a major recording company in their public relations department.

### Publisher:
Quill (William Morrow & Company)

### Edition:
2nd (1992)

### Price:
$13.00

### ISBN:
0688103588

### Media:
Book

### Principal Subject:
Taking Care Of Your Child

### Secondary Subject:
Feeding

### Age Group:
Infants & Toddlers (0–3)

**Feeding**

# THE BABY COOKBOOK, REVISED EDITION
Tasty And Nutritious Meals For The Whole Family That Babies And Toddlers Will Also Love

## Description:
This 368-page guide provides information on the importance of healthy nutrition. This revised edition incorporates updated vitamin and mineral charts, info on fluoride, childhood obesity, microwave cooking, and crockpot cooking. Including 250+ recipes to be used for the whole family, this resource is divided into two parts. Part One contains basic information on nutrition (proteins, fats, cholesterol, fiber, etc.) and its importance to infants; dairy products, nursing bottle syndrome, allergies, introducing solids, and childhood obesity are also addressed. "Balanced menus" for baby and toddler breakfasts, lunches, dinners, and snacks are also included. Part Two provides recipes for the family and "special children's recipes" for: vegetables, legumes, tofu, cheese and eggs, fish, poultry, meats, grains and pasta, soups, breads, desserts, fruit and milk drinks, and stocks and sauces. The pros and cons of microwave cooking are given along with crockpot recipes. Growth and feeding charts, a general index, and a recipe index are also provided.

## Evaluation:
This well-written nutrition/feeding/recipe guide will serve as a valuable resource to start a child off on a smart and healthy way of eating. When to offer, what to feed, and how to prepare are all facets covered in this book. Recipes have been prepared with thought to nutrition, cost, and convenience in mind. The author includes a personal diary of her own baby's feeding progression so that parents can also keep their own child's feeding patterns in perspective. There are recipes for light meals, family meals, safe microwave meals, and slow crockpot cooking recipes; over 100 recipes are new to this edition. Vitamin tables, protein charts, and a twelve month summary of when to introduce solids are just some of the enhancements of this book. The recipes are practical, nutritious, and simple to execute. Grouped by categories, the recipes are low in sodium and contain almost no sugars. Addressing the needs of the baby as well as the family, this cookbook will most likely see much use when added to the family library.

## Where To Find/Buy:
Bookstores and libraries.

**Feeding**

# THE COMPLETE NEW GUIDE TO PREPARING BABY FOODS

★★★

### Description:

Beginning with "Nutrition" and ending with "Finger Foods," this 385-page book contains 14 chapters on how to prepare foods for your baby. Chapters One through Three speak to the importance of good nutrition, how to get the most for your money (including reading the labels), and information on feeding your baby (breastfeeding, introducing solids, balanced menu, digestive difficulties, etc.). Chapter Four offers advice on the best equipment for easy preparation. Chapters Five and Six address safe storage for food and a "Baby Food System," which offers suggestions on ways to plan and save time, how to use leftovers, and how to modify recipes. Chapters Seven through Twelve provide information on the four basic food groups (cereals, fruits, vegetables, proteins) along with desserts and beverages. The last two chapters offer recipes for "quick" baby foods and finger foods. There are three appendices, a bibliography, a section on how to prevent choking, and several child growth charts. A general index and a separate recipe index are also given.

### Evaluation:

Here is a very complete and well-written guidebook with a great deal of supporting information and additional resources. By providing practical easily made recipes, she strives to guide parents and caregivers towards a more balanced diet. The general principles of good nutrition are presented along with food selections that provide the essential calories, proteins, carbohydrates, fats, vitamins, and minerals that young children need. The book then goes further and explains the concept and process of introducing solids and/or new foods to your baby and how to avoid digestive and allergic reactions. There are over 100 nutritious and economical recipes for baby foods that parents can make at home. Even if parents only use a few recipes from this book, it will be money well-spent. It will start their baby off on developing the good feeding habits they probably wished they had learned as a child.

### Where To Find/Buy:

Bookstores and libraries, or order direct from Bantam Books, Dept. HN 12, 2451 S. Wolf Road., Des Plaines, IL 60018.

**Overall Rating**
★★★
For do-it-yourselfers interested in economics & health benefits of homemade baby food

**Design, Ease Of Use**
★★★
Small print; indexed separately by topic & recipe; numerous charts given (growth, etc.)

1–4 Stars

**Author:**
Sue Castle
Sue Castle, the author of several parenting books, currently writes and produces television programming on parenting, childcare, and nutrition issues. Castle has a B.A. in psychology form Smith College and an M.A. in Social Psychology from Columbia University.

**Publisher:**
Bantam Books (Bantam Doubleday Dell)

**Edition:**
3rd (1992)

**Price:**
$4.99

**Pages/Run Time:**
385

**ISBN:**
0553291831

**Media:**
Book

**Principal Subject:**
Taking Care Of Your Child

**Secondary Subject:**
Feeding

**Age Group:**
Infants (0–1)

II. Caring For Your Child

★★

## Overall Rating
★★
Encourages healthy creative cooking from scratch

## Design, Ease Of Use
★★
Font of subheadings sometimes difficult to read; "block-cut" illustrations are attractive

1–4 Stars

## Author:
O. Robin Sweet and Thomas Bloom

Sweet is an author, childbirth educator, and former pediatric nurse for 10 years. Bloom is an author, food educator, and former Professor of food science and food management at the University of Minnesota, The University of Wisconsin, and Florida State University.

## Publisher:
Macmillan (Prentice Hall Macmillan)

## Edition:
1994

## Price:
$12.00

## Pages/Run Time:
190

## ISBN:
0020453701

## Media:
Book

## Principal Subject:
Taking Care Of Your Child

## Secondary Subject:
Feeding

## Age Group:
Infants (0–1)

Feeding

# THE WELL-FED BABY
Easy Healthful Recipes For The First 12 Months

## Description:
This guide was the result of Sweet and Bloom's adoption of a six month old Russian baby who was malnourished and suffering from rickets. Supported by seven major sections with an introduction and concluding index, this 190-page resource strives to instill healthy cooking techniques and nutritional recipes for parents of infants. Chapter One discusses the changing feeding and diet requirements of babies and toddlers. Recommendations and advice are given in an age-specific format for children ages six months to 12 months of age. Chapter Two offers recipes for breakfasts. How to prepare your own grains is a highlight of this chapter. Chapters Three, Four, and Five include recipes for breads, lunches, and dinners, respectively. Chapters Six and Seven follow with the topics of soups, snacks, and desserts. At the conclusion of the book, there are two additional sections which contain advice for eating out with young children and a listing of contributing chefs.

## Evaluation:
Parents will certainly find this to be a good resource in providing information on healthy ways to prepare nutritious meals. Based upon the input from professional chefs and other food professionals, and tested within numerous families, a lot of good basic information is provided in this resource. Tips are given on food sanitation and safety; avoiding cross-contamination, such as the transfer of salmonella bacteria; food allergies; a feeding guide on food texture; and more. The recipes are simple and easy to execute, listing serving amounts for each along with age-specific recommendations. Each recipe is laid-out in a step-by-step format. One refreshing item about this book is its global approach in terms of its recipe content. Parents will appreciate such diverse recipes as tabbouleh salad, rice congee, and basmati rice and chicken as inspired by some of the most accomplished chefs.

## Where To Find/Buy:
Bookstores and libraries.

**Feeding**

# 365 FOOD KIDS LOVE TO EAT

### Description:

Offering their "practical, comprehensive, easy-to-follow" cookbook, the authors of this 365+ page book list 365 one page recipes "designed with kid's palates and appetites in mind." The book begins with sections offering tips on "table management for families" (manners), some suggestions for healthful eating ("trim fats from meats," etc.), and food substitutions and equivalences; a list of measuring conversions is provided at the back of the book. The table of contents lists all recipes which are grouped by category (23) including: baby foods, beverages, breads and muffins, breakfast, fruits, do-it-yourself, peanut butter, lunch boxes, salads, sandwiches, soups, snacks, cookies, designer foods, pasta, vegetables, meats, poultry, fish, desserts, parties, holidays, and foreign foods. Each category includes a facing page that lists the recipes included within that section. Some recipes include a one sentence "note" (offering the authors' personal anecdote or advice) or a suggested activity to do while preparing the food. There is no index.

### Evaluation:

There is a plethora of available cookbooks to help parents prepare recipes that not only provide children with healthy eating habits, but can also be prepared quickly and easily. Not so with this one. Recipes in this guide contain many ingredients that children will certainly like—corn syrup, sugar, and chocolate to name a few—but not generally accepted as healthy. Additionally, many of the recipes involve quite elaborate steps. Since children's eating desires fluctuate dramatically from one day to the next, commonsense dictates that spending considerable time preparing a child's food is time ill-spent. The food prepared using these recipes is good, but it would be better presented to the entire family with possible success for the toddler or preschooler child. Some ingredients for the baby food recipes are ill-advised. Some recipes call for milk, suggesting breast or formula milk until the baby is six months old (and then what?), others include egg or honey with no warning about allergies. Look to other better researched guides to feeding your child.

### Where To Find/Buy:

Bookstores and libraries.

---

**Overall Rating**
★
Tasty recipes that often involve elaborate preparation or unhealthy ingredients

**Design, Ease Of Use**
★★
Grouped by category (23) in the table of contents with no back-up index

1–4 Stars

**Author:**
Sheila Ellison and Dr. Judith Gray

Ellison, with a BA degree in psychology from USC, has volunteered on behalf of children, and founded community youth groups and mentoring programs. Gray is internationally known as an author, teacher, and speaker on future trends in education.

**Publisher:**
Sourcebooks

**Edition:**
1995

**Price:**
$12.95

**Pages/Run Time:**
365

**ISBN:**
1570710309

**Media:**
Book

**Principal Subject:**
Taking Care Of Your Child

**Secondary Subject:**
Feeding

**Age Group:**
Infants & Toddlers (0–3)

**★★★★**

**Overall Rating**
★★★★
Advice is adaptable for any parenting style; practical and thorough information

**Design, Ease Of Use**
★★★★
Many charts and worksheets serve as tools for the reader; family success stories

1–4 Stars

**Author:**
Rebecca Huntley

Rebecca Huntley is a child and family therapist, parent educator for a community college, social worker, and counselor with 18 years of experience. She also is the parent of three boys.

**Publisher:**
Parenting Press

**Edition:**
1991

**Price:**
$14.95

**Pages/Run Time:**
102

**ISBN:**
0943990343

**Media:**
Book

**Principal Subject:**
Taking Care Of Your Child

**Secondary Subject:**
Sleep

**Age Group:**
Infants & Toddlers (0–3)

**Sleep**

# THE SLEEP BOOK FOR TIRED PARENTS
## Help For Solving Children's Sleep Problems

**Recommended For:**
Taking Care Of Your Child

## Description:

This book provides "solutions that will help you get your family's sleep patterns back on track." Chapter titles include "Sleepless Nights," "Building the Basics," "The Trouble Spots," "Four Basic Approaches," "Plan for Success," "Put Theory into Practice," and "The Parent's Side." Four major techniques to dealing with sleeping problems are offered: The Family Bed, Cry-It-Out, Teaching in Small Steps, and Living With It. Chapter One describes what sleep problems are, offers help in diagnosing a sleep problem, and gives guidelines for determining the right time to deal with the problem. Chapter Two goes into the basics of sleeping—biological rhythms, sleep patterns, reasons for difficult sleep, and tips to avoid sleep problems. Chapter Three touches on most sleep problems that can occur. The four approaches to dealing with sleep problems are described in Chapter Four. The process of working through a problem, from identification to congratulations, is explained in Chapter Five. Chapter Six discusses putting the four theories into practice. Lastly, Chapter Seven discusses parental guilt, taking care of the parents' needs, and what to do when nothing works.

## Evaluation:

Every parent knows that too often sleep doesn't always come easily or peacefully to their son or daughter. Sometimes it doesn't seem to come at all. The author offers options to solve a child's sleeping problems that would apply to a variety of parenting styles. She believes that sleep problems are unique to every person, and therefore, the solution should be customized to fit the problem and people involved. The author begins by giving the reader basic background information about what sleep disorders are and why they occur. From this, the reader gains a good general understanding of the typical problems that may apply to his or her family. The reader can then identify which approach would work best for their family and develop a plan for a solution. Included throughout are suggestions, stories, charts, worksheets, and tables about how other families have dealt with similar problems. The author makes no attempt to judge or preach about the "right way" to deal with these problems. By including a variety of parenting styles and by adapting the methods to each style, the author not only accepts the variety, but reinforces the reality that there are as many parenting styles as there are parents, each with its pros and cons.

## Where To Find/Buy:

Bookstores, libraries, or order direct by calling (800) 992-6657.

**Sleep**

# THE FAMILY BED
## An Age Old Concept In Child Rearing

★★★

## Description:

The author, the mother of two children and a former La Leche League counselor, wrote this book from her experience with her daughter who would not sleep alone, and after discovering that many parents solved this problem by "...tak(ing) the child to bed...." This book explores the benefits of allowing babies and older children to sleep with their parents, and the modern "taboo" against the practice. The first five chapters discuss current beliefs and attitudes towards shared sleeping, why and how parents began allowing their children to sleep with them, concerns and fears about it, and the psychological importance to the child. The next two chapters include a history of shared family sleep from medieval times onwards, and observations of sleep arrangements in various cultures throughout the world. Chapters Eight through Ten discuss the needs of the infant and older child, how siblings fit into the picture, and marital relations. The last three chapters discuss special circumstances (hospitalization, adopted children), nighttime parenting (discipline) as a continuum of daytime parenting, and the benefits of the family bed.

## Evaluation:

Of the many ways in which modern society alienates its members, putting a baby to sleep in a separate room, some argue, may be one of the most subtle. As we learn from this book, the concept of shared sleep is hardly new—families have been sharing beds since the beginning of time. Many of the "scientific" reasons of why shared sleeping is so bad are discredited here, and experts and parents alike have been looking twice at the practice. Sharing sleep, the author argues, is practical (no more getting up in the middle of the night to breastfeed) and psychologically beneficial (babies and young children may feel more secure); it also ends the difficulty of putting a child to bed—when they are secure enough to sleep by themselves, they will. Especially interesting is the "brief history" of family sleeping, and the gradual rise of "sterile child rearing" that reached its zenith in the 1940s. Parents interested in or curious about the idea of the shared family bed will find this a persuasive and informative read.

## Where To Find/Buy:

Bookstores and libraries.

**Overall Rating**
★★★
Persuasively presents the practical and psychological benefits of shared family sleep

**Design, Ease Of Use**
★★★★
Extremely well written and researched

1–4 Stars

**Author:**
Tine Thevenin

The author began this book as a research report before it grew into a book manuscript. She was born in the Netherlands, and is the mother of two children. She has also been a counselor for La Leche League.

**Publisher:**
Avery Publishing Group

**Edition:**
1987

**Price:**
$9.95

**Pages/Run Time:**
159

**ISBN:**
0895293579

**Media:**
Book

**Principal Subject:**
Taking Care Of Your Child

**Secondary Subject:**
Sleep

**Age Group:**
Infants & Toddlers (0–3)

★★★

## Overall Rating
★★★
Rationale and tips for finding a "sensitive solution to your baby's sleepless nights"

## Design, Ease Of Use
All subtopics listed under chapter headings in table of contents; useful photographs

1–4 Stars

## Author:
William Sears, MD

Sears, "one of America's most renowned pediatricians," has been in practice for 20 years and authored 10 books. Currently, he's a clinical assistant professor of pediatrics at USC School of Medicine.

## Publisher:
Penguin Books USA (Plume)

## Edition:
1987

## Price:
$11.95

## Pages/Run Time:
203

## ISBN:
0452264073

## Media:
Book

## Principal Subject:
Taking Care Of Your Child

## Secondary Subject:
Sleep

## Age Group:
Infants & Toddlers (0–3)

Sleep

# NIGHTTIME PARENTING
How To Get Your Baby And Child To Sleep

## Description:
Sears has written this guide to answer the question, "Should I let my child cry it out at night, or console my crying child?" His goal, in this 203-page, 17 chapter book, is "to help parents and children achieve sleep harmony" . . . "lessening your child's night-waking and increasing your ability to cope." Sears draws on both his experience as a father of eight and from returns of a questionnaire sent to patients. The foundation of the book, as with all of Sears' books, lays in the tenets of attachment parenting (where babies and caregivers best form a secure relationship by being very connected to each other's cues); Chapter One explains this in detail. Other chapter topics deal with the difference between baby and adult sleep, where baby should sleep, dealing with night-waking, food that helps sleep, nighttime fathering, demands of the high need child, SIDS, sleep disorders, nap times, single nighttime parenting, and more. Sears asserts throughout his book the importance of babies and young children "sharing sleep" with their parents; in other words, sleeping in the parents' bed.

## Evaluation:
Does Sears answer the question, "Should I let my child cry it out at night?" You bet. His points are well-made, using both research findings and anecdotes from parents. Everyone agrees that a baby's cries are a baby's language. However, as Sears asserts, "if the baby's cries fall on deaf ears, he is less motivated to cry" . . . "the baby loses trust that the caregiver will respond." One can always find arguments to defend any parenting style; parents and advisors to parents should read all the viewpoints and choose one that resonates with them. Sears' book represents a point of view that some parents will strongly embrace and others will just as strongly reject, research or no research. A weakness of this book, however, is that some areas need updating. For example, since 1987 (its copyright date), new research has come to light regarding SIDS, including the pros and cons of sleeping with your baby. Also, special situations, such as working mothers, need some extended suggestions and support, especially since this is the norm for many households.

## Where To Find/Buy:
Bookstores and libraries.

# SLEEP
## How To Teach Your Child To Sleep Like A Baby

### Description:

This six chapter, 214-page book aims to answer the question "How can I get my child to sleep through the night?" Based on "in-depth interviews with more than two dozen of today's leading experts in sleep research, pediatric medicine, and child psychology," the author has also conducted a "thorough" review of the research that has been done; the "experts" are listed in the Acknowledgments and literature reviewed is cited in the Resources section. Chapter One reviews children's sleep patterns and problems. Then Chapter Two describes ways to deal with "bedtime battles" while Chapter Three offers techniques for managing "middle-of-the-night awakenings." Chapter Four focuses on what to do to help children who have nighttime fears. "Where should your child sleep?" is the topic of Chapter Five outlining pros and cons of various sleep locations (family bed, bassinet, crib, big bed, etc.). "Special Situations" are addressed in Chapter Six and include circumstances that interfere with a child's sleep (siblings, twins, babysitter, travel, divorce, preemies, sleep disorders, etc.). No index is given.

### Evaluation:

This book's intention is admirable given the amount of discussion today focusing on sleep issues and how many experts can't agree on how to handle sleep problems. Supplying parents with information on all the different methods that are available allows parents to compare methods and make their decision based on their family's needs. To this goal, organization elements in this book would have made this search more rewarding. Yet, there are no details in the table of contents and there is no index. Instead, parents will need to read the entire text, write down names and page numbers of methods, and jot down notes because there are no other ways to relocate the information. The author does highlight various sections within the chapters with titles such as "The Beat-Him-To-The-Punch Approach" or "The Reassuring Approach," but this offers little real help. A comparison chart that contrasts such things as amount of parental involvement or absence, the length of time needed to resolve sleep problems, etc. would be more helpful along with cross-references to page numbers. Parents should use this as a start but keep their paper and pen handy.

### Where To Find/Buy:

Bookstores, libraries, or order direct by contacting Mail Order Department, Simon & Schuster, 200 Old Tappan Road, Old Tappan, NJ 07675.

---

**★★★**

**Overall Rating**
★★★
Useful for cross-examining the various methods available for teaching children to sleep

**Design, Ease Of Use**
★
No index, minimal table of contents makes searching for specific methods impossible

1–4 Stars

**Author:**
Tamara Eberlein

Eberlein has written over 200 articles on parenting, health, and psychology. Her work has appeared in magazines such as *Redbook*, *Good Housekeeping*, *Family Circle*, and more. She is a graduate of the Georgetown University School of Languages and Linguistics.

**Publisher:**
Pocket Books
(Simon & Schuster)

**Edition:**
1996

**Price:**
$5.99

**Pages/Run Time:**
214

**ISBN:**
0671880381

**Media:**
Book

---

**Principal Subject:**
Taking Care Of Your Child

**Secondary Subject:**
Sleep

**Age Group:**
Infants & Toddlers (0–3)

II. Caring For Your Child

★★

**Overall Rating**
★★
Good overview of sleep issues, pros and cons of various methods, and practical tips

**Design, Ease Of Use**
★★★★
Easily read with bulleted tips, inset blocks of advice and parental quotes; succinct

1–4 Stars

**Author:**
Vicki Lansky

Lansky is a mother and author. She can also be read regularly in *Sesame Street's Parent Guide* section and in *Family Circle* where she writes the "HELP!" column.

**Publisher:**
The Book Peddlers

**Edition:**
2nd (1991)

**Price:**
$6.95

**Pages/Run Time:**
131

**ISBN:**
0916773191

**Media:**
Book

**Principal Subject:**
Taking Care Of Your Child

**Secondary Subject:**
Sleep

**Age Group:**
Infants & Toddlers (0–3)

Sleep

# GETTING YOUR CHILD TO SLEEP . . . AND BACK TO SLEEP
## Tips For Parents Of Infants, Toddlers, And Preschoolers

**Description:**

The ten chapters of this 131-page guide highlight many of the facets of children's sleep. Chapter One discusses a baby's sleep patterns during the first six months, while Chapter Two offers tips on developing bedtime routines for a baby. Chapters Three and Four focus on how to deal with baby's cries and colic. Chapter Five offers tips for getting a "night waker" back to sleep. Whether or not to allow a baby or child to share the parents' bed is the topic of Chapter Six. Helping parents cope with loss of sleep is Lansky's focus in Chapter Seven. "Naptime" how-tos and suggestions for older children are discussed in Chapter Eight, while Chapter Nine discusses "reasonable bedtime routines" for older children. The last chapter offers strategies for helping children handle their nighttime fears, bad dreams, and night terrors. A one page index concludes the book as well as a list of other suggested resources. Each chapter contains bulleted tips, blocked insets of highlighted advice and parental quotes, and sometimes organizational contacts or products.

**Evaluation:**

Lansky has provided an overview here of all prevailing theories on how to deal with sleep issues from having baby "cry it out" to sleep arrangements in "the family bed." Although she presents the pros and cons of these sleep issues, most often Lansky's opinion is center stage following her line of reasoning that she had "made peace with the fact that sleep as [she] had known it was no longer to be part of [her] life" and "it was somehow okay." While this may not bide well with those who seek sleep training methods to teach their baby to sleep, Lansky, does, however, offer strategies and support to overcome the tiredness plaguing many parents in the early months and years. She balances her opinions with quotes from parents who have tried the reverse of Lansky's suggestions and also had success. While not a definitive guide, Lansky's guide gives parents a plan for dealing with sleep issues. Parents will get practical tips ("play a radio, with an automatic shut-off timing feature") and support ("learn to make jokes about your lack of sleep"). They can then look to other resources if necessary for additional support or how-tos.

**Where To Find/Buy:**

Bookstores, libraries, or order direct by calling (612) 475-3527 or (800) 255-3379.

**Sleep**

# SLEEPING THROUGH THE NIGHT
How Infants, Toddlers, And Their Parents Can Get A Good Night's Sleep

★ ★

## Description:

This professional in pediatric sleep disorders addresses the issue of children sleep behaviors by explaining typical sleep basics and problems. The introductory chapters explain sleep and behaviors, and give a general review of basic parenting skills and behavior management strategies. Part Two explains how to establish good sleep habits by addressing common problems and recommending coping strategies for those problems, while Part Three discusses common sleep problems and disorders. Adult sleep problems are touched on in Part Four. Suggested bedtime books for children and resources for parents are included in the appendices. Each chapter begins with a story of a parent-child situation which is used to illustrate the topic of discussion. "This book provides practical techniques and tips on how to get infants and toddlers to sleep through the night . . . Included are steps on how to get babies to fall asleep and sleep through the night, as well as answers to commonly asked questions," the author writes. Issues addressed throughout the book include waking during the night, sleeping in the parents room/bed, parents with different styles, and more.

## Evaluation:

"This book, designed for parents who need a user-friendly method to get their child to sleep through the night, addresses the practicalities of life" says the author. She makes good on her claim in this self-help book written by a professional who avoids technical, medical terms that can overwhelm an already tired parent. Even the explanations of adult sleep disorders are understandable. Mindell provides an overview of sleep patterns and behaviors without regurgitating statistics and studies. Clear, simple, sound advice is offered for most sleep concerns. Descriptions of a parent's problem are usually provided as well as answers to their specific questions. Parents who are not first-time parents may find that the information provided is a little too basic not offering any new or creative solutions. Others may have difficult with the author's suggestion to schedule baby's sleep and time parental response. This book is perhaps most useful to parents wishing to establish sleep habits from the beginning. Some parents may find this book more useful than other similar resources focused on this topic. Upon acceptance, they will gladly welcome this guide's lack of clinical jargon, its concise nature, and its easily digestible style.

## Where To Find/Buy:

Bookstores and libraries.

**Overall Rating**
★★
Advice from a professional that is easy to understand and practical to use

**Design, Ease Of Use**
★★★
Chapters are divided into relevant sections that are short, yet descriptive

1–4 Stars

**Author:**
Jodi A. Mindell, PhD

Mindell is Pediatric Clinical Director of the Sleep Disorders Center at Allegheny University of the Health Sciences in Philadelphia, holds degrees in clinical psychology, is a professor of psychology, and author of numerous publications on pediatric sleep disorders.

**Publisher:**
HarperPerennial (HarperCollins)

**Edition:**
1997

**Price:**
$13.00

**Pages/Run Time:**
291

**ISBN:**
0062734091

**Media:**
Book

**Principal Subject:**
Taking Care Of Your Child

**Secondary Subject:**
Sleep

**Age Group:**
Infants & Toddlers (0–3)

II. Caring For Your Child

Sleep

# HELPING YOUR CHILD SLEEP THROUGH THE NIGHT
A Guide For Parents Of Children From Infancy To Age Five

**Overall Rating**

★

Considers child's developmental issues, but backed up only by personal research

**Design, Ease Of Use**

★★★★

Well-organized, concrete steps presented for each age; each chapter stands on its own

1–4 Stars

**Author:**

Joanne Cuthbertson and Susie Schevill

Cuthbertson and Schevill are both mothers and married to pediatricians.

**Publisher:**

Main Street Books (Doubleday/Bantam Doubleday Dell)

**Edition:**

1985

**Price:**

$11.95

**Pages/Run Time:**

246

**ISBN:**

0385192509

**Media:**

Book

**Principal Subject:**

Taking Care Of Your Child

**Secondary Subject:**

Sleep

**Age Group:**

Infants & Toddlers (0–3)

## Description:

Written by two mothers, this 246-page resource is "devoted to showing you how to establish and maintain good sleeping habits for your children." An introduction outlines various elements of sleep including the "science of sleep" (bio rhythms, physiology), security objects. possible locations of sleep, bedtime rituals, and more. The remaining five chapters highlight the authors' sleep training methods, advice, and discussions of sleep disruptions (in light of habits, development, and specific situations) for various age groups: from birth to four months, five to nine months, ten to 18 months, 18 months to three years, and three years to five years. Each chapter is designed to stand on its own. It is suggested, however, that parents, read the introduction prior to turning to the chapter that corresponds to their child's age. A Q & A segment is included at the end of each chapter. A bibliography, suggested bedtime books for children, and an index conclude the resource.

## Evaluation:

Of the various sleep training methods that exist, this resource considers reasons for sleep interruptions along with the child's developmental stage. The main problem we found, however, with this method is that it has not been tested by large controlled studies. It is based on the authors' reading and experience with their own children and friends' children. One concern in particular we had involves training a three day old newborn. It is suggested that after the newborn receives their "focal feeding" (at about 11 pm), upon waking later they should be comforted to sleep, and if need be, offered a bottle of water (or glucose water), and then placed in bed. This "stretching" the time between feedings is the heart of the authors' method. Many pediatricians and family physicians, though, advise newborns be fed on demand. Nursing mothers are also advised not to use a bottle for several weeks due to nipple confusion on the part of the infant. And what if the baby, who, research states, is naturally inclined to be drawn to sweet tastes, decides the glucose water is a fine substitution for milk? Look to other more sound resources for help in getting your child to sleep.

## Where To Find/Buy:

Bookstores and libraries.

**Sleep**

# SOLVE YOUR CHILD'S SLEEP PROBLEMS

## Description:

This 250-page book addresses the issues of sleeplessness and how it affects the parents as well as the child. Ferber states that "when your child's sleep patterns cause a definite problem for you or for him, then he has a sleep problem." Throughout the book, he describes the tired, frustrated, and angry responses of parents with a young child who will not settle into the normal routines of the family. Ferber then offers reassurance to parents that these problems have nothing to do with poor parenting, nor is it a "stage" that must be waited out. Instead, he describes problematic "sleep associations" (nursing or bottle, rocking, holding, cuddling, music) that a parent must "begin to correct" from infancy onward. He advocates scheduled daytime feedings (both nursing and bottles) and naptimes, no nighttime feedings, his "progressive waiting" program (not heeding child's waking cries for specific time intervals), and "door-closing" techniques (holding door closed from the outside until child returns to and stays in bed). Ferber states that sleeping alone is necessary to teach an infant or child to see himself as an independent individual.

## Evaluation:

Charts, graphs, recording worksheets, programmed steps, and tables are integral parts of Ferber's solution to "sleep problems." These strategies help distract the reader from the inherent problems present in Ferber's argument for sleep training. On one hand, he states that pediatricians "recommend that you try to follow your infant's cues." Then Ferber suggests that a baby should learn to "self-comfort" himself without rocking, touching, bottles, nursing, or pacifiers; that this fundamental assumption is best for infants is disputed by many. He also describes the importance of our natural circadian rhythms— "if your child's circadian rhythms are disrupted, her sleep-wake patterns deteriorate." Then he devotes the rest of his book to explain how to ignore an infant's nighttime "wants," and how to change these circadian rhythms by scheduling a baby's sleeping pattern so it more clearly mirrors an adult's. Doing so, he believes will help adults and babies sleep through the night. The detail throughout the book is dense. This book dictates steps, and offers warnings and threats ("Take the steps necessary to correct [sleep problems]. If you do not, it may persist for months, even years."). Look for resources more soundly based on infant development.

## Where To Find/Buy:

Bookstores and libraries.

---

**Overall Rating**

★

Dry description of how to regulate children's sleep habits, full of contradictions

**Design, Ease Of Use**

★★

Dense text, reliance on charts, graphs, tables; must be read cover-to-cover

1–4 Stars

**Author:**

Richard Ferber, MD

Ferber, an authority in the field of children's sleep problems, directs the Sleep Lab and the Center for Pediatric Sleep Disorders at Children's Hospital in Boston. He also teaches at Harvard Medical School and is a pediatrician.

**Publisher:**

Fireside (Simon & Schuster)

**Edition:**

1985

**Price:**

$12.00

**Pages/Run Time:**

250

**ISBN:**

0671620991

**Media:**

Book

---

**Principal Subject:**

Taking Care Of Your Child

**Secondary Subject:**

Sleep

**Age Group:**

Infants & Toddlers (0–3)

**Sleep**

# ON BECOMING BABYWISE, BOOK ONE
Learn How Over 500,000 Babies Were Trained To Sleep Through The Night The Natural Way

**Overall Rating**
★
Detached technique not well-grounded in recommended child care advice

**Design, Ease Of Use**
★
Difficult to find direct tips or strategies; few graphics

1–4 Stars

**Author:**
Gary Ezzo and Robert Bucknam, MD

**Publisher:**
Multnomah Publishers

**Edition:**
2nd (1998)

**Price:**
$9.99

**Pages/Run Time:**
223

**ISBN:**
1576734597

**Media:**
Book

**Principal Subject:**
Taking Care Of Your Child

**Secondary Subject:**
Sleep

**Age Group:**
Infants (0–1)

## Description:

The author states in his preface that his book is "more than an infant-management concept; it is a mind-set for responsible parenthood." Chapter One describes the importance of establishing and maintaining a family, as opposed to being "child-centered or mother-centered." A historic overview of "feeding philosophies" is presented in Chapter Two, along with the "The Babywise Alternative" or "parent-directed feeding" (PDF) which is described as a "24 hour infant-management strategy designed to help moms connect with their babies and their babies connect with them." Throughout the remainder of the book, Ezzo compares and contrasts PDF with "hyperscheduling on one extreme and attachment parenting at the other" in his discussions of babies' sleep, feedings, waketime, naptime, parental response to babies' cries, and more. He presents statistical findings from a number of studies, "including the ones we commissioned in our pursuit of establishing *Babywise* norms for sleep, weight gain, and average length of time our mothers breast-fed their babies." A new chapter to this revised edition discusses PDF as it relates to multiple births; Ezzo also offers pointers for "starting late."

## Evaluation:

This book offers another strategy for "teaching good sleep habits" starting from day one of a newborn's life. Ezzo suggests parents observe and tune in to their newborn's inherent feeding and sleeping schedule. He then offers his "flexible schedule" which then dictates when they should eat, when they should sleep, when they can play; nursing mothers are admonished to "stabilize [their] lactation." Readers should note, however, that the author has no medical background or apparent credentials to speak on this subject. Numerous physicians and lactation consultants have written to decry Ezzo's methods, his own original church has distanced themselves from his stance, and his work is almost in direct contradiction to the American Academy of Pediatrics' statement on breastfeeding. In addition, a number of "failure to thrive" cases in babies have been linked to this method. Throughout, Ezzo speaks in a compassionless detached tone. At one point, he likens a mother's emotional response to a baby's cries as "set[ting] the stage for child abuse." He offers much misinformation and advice dangerous to a baby's health. Parents should check other resources that better address their needs while ensuring their baby's well-being.

## Where To Find/Buy:

Bookstores and libraries.

# CHAPTER TWO—UNDERSTANDING YOUR CHILD'S GROWTH & LEARNING

"They grow up so fast!" One minute a baby is crying indiscriminately, the next they need consoling about their "owie." A baby awkwardly grabs at the mobile in their crib; before you know it, they are steering their tricycle in circles round the park. Childhood is but a fleeting period compared to a lifetime, but the experiences and interactions during these formative years will have effects lasting the rest of a child's life.

Child development experts place great importance on the first three years of a child's life. This period offers opportunities to substantially impact a young child's future abilities, skills, attitudes, personality, social interactions with others, their way of looking at the world, and their self-esteem. The latest research shows that the quality of care and variety of experiences given to a child during the first three years contributes substantially to their brain development. Neglecting a child's needs and their inherent quest for answers to make sense of their world may have irreversible effects. How do parents begin to fulfill this overwhelming responsibility? Their first step is to gain an understanding of their child's development process.

The paragraphs that follow will introduce general and specific issues parents will encounter as they observe their baby or toddler, and begin to understand how their child grows and makes sense of their world. Following this introduction are our recommendations for resources that can help parents deal with each of these concerns.

## General Overviews

Most parents understand well-known developmental milestones such as "they'll be walking at one, talking at two." Although children's rates of development vary from one child to the next, each child does follow a certain progression physically, that is, they progress from lying down to rolling over, sitting up, pulling up to stand, standing, walking, running, climbing, and so on. Their fine motor skills (eye-hand coordination) progress from seeing a confusing field of objects, to seeing one desired object and intentionally trying to grasp it with their whole hand. From there, babies progress to finger control as they develop their "pincer grasp" and begin to manipulate smaller objects. Eventually, young children will be able to coordinate all of these efforts as they learn to cut with scissors, write their own name, and pick up bugs.

However, some parents, preoccupied with their child's physical development, fail to realize that their child develops in other ways at the same time. For example, children's language development follows another sequence. It starts with a baby's first cry that communicates his or her needs, and progresses to smaller units of sound (babbling). Then one-word utterances begin to take shape, and so on, until children are speaking sentences that adults can fully comprehend.

In addition, children's emotional patterns of responding to situations and other people are being developed and refined from birth—"Should I be fearful of this new situation or should I be confident? Is it okay to be mad, sad, or frustrated? If I do something naughty, do my mommy and daddy still love me? What kind of things do I do that make people like me?"

During this crucial period of time, children's cognitive abilities are also developing by leaps and bounds. Children are quickly forming, adapting, and refining concepts in their brain to make sense of their environment. They work toward distinguishing the differences between similar things—"is this a cat or a dog?" They work toward understanding the relationship between things and how these things are organized in their world—"a cat and a dog are both animals." And children actively work toward understanding cause-and-effect relationships and figuring out how things work . . . much to our chagrin when we find something other than a videotape in the VCR.

Children also develop socially, going from a "me-centered" universe to an "us-centered" universe. Their first interactions concentrate on how to get their needs met with their parent or caregiver. Then, as they play with others, they continue to develop their social interaction skills. Initially, children may play in the same vicinity as other children but not actually participate with them (parallel play). Eventually, children actively engage in fantasy play and games with their peers—"you be the mommy, I'll be the baby." As they experience more social interactions, children better understand appropriate ways of responding to friends, adults, and strangers.

Development, however, does not happen in a vacuum, as both research and common sense would dictate. The impact parents and caregivers have on a child's development has been demonstrated over and over again through positive and negative examples. A child's growth and learning in the first five years, when properly guided by parents and caregivers, will afford any child the best possible start in life. For example, by knowing what is developmentally appropriate and inappropriate at any given stage or age, adults will have a better grasp on how to address specific situations such as discipline, sibling relationships, and toilet training to name a few. Also, once a child's general development is understood, parents can more successfully choose activities that can capitalize on their child's skills and interests rather than frustrating or boring their child.

In the pages that follow, we have recommended resources that offer parents a general overview of child development. Some of these resources focus on a specific age group's development, while others focus on the entire period from birth through the toddler years (and, in some cases, beyond). These resources may not necessarily go into the specifics and how-tos of subjects like discipline or toilet training. But they will offer parents a wonderful overview of how an infant develops into a young child, and how parents can make that a positive experience for all. As your parenting skills and style develop alongside your child, an all-inclusive guide can not only help answer your general questions, but help you realize the magnitude of this adventure.

All-inclusive guides, by their very nature, are useful at presenting the big picture, but usually don't offer in-depth information in any one area. Whenever you find you need help in a specific area, check other recommendations we have made for specific issues we have identified, such as the following:

- Behavior & Discipline
- Choosing Activities & Games
- Toilet Training

## Behavior & Discipline

"How can I get my child to behave?" As a child struggles with their growing drive for independence and autonomy, they invariably test the limits, as well as parents' patience and resolve. But discipline is not about control, at least not parent-control. As one educator pointed out, "Where did we ever get the crazy idea that in order to make children do better, first we have to make them feel worse?" Children will naturally make mistakes, sometimes by accident, sometimes intentionally. The long-term goal of discipline is not to make children pay for their mistakes. It is not an opportunity to show who is the boss and in charge. The long-range goals of discipline should be independence (to make one's own informed decisions), responsibility (for one's actions), and self-control (to learn by one's efforts). Most child development experts believe that discipline should be another arena for parents to teach children how to make good decisions, live with consequences, and problem-solve.

In our research, we have found that the resources we reviewed typically fall somewhere along the continuum of three different parenting styles (authoritarian, permissive, democratic), each of which approach discipline differently. Some offer a style that places the parent in complete command—the child is told to behave "because I said so." Others place the child in complete control—the parents say "do what you want because we love you." The resources we have found that embody long-range goals of discipline, however, treat children's mistakes not as punitive opportunities but as a shared learning process. Children learn that there are natural and logical consequences to their choices; they learn that if they make a mistake, they must then figure out a way to solve their problem. In this approach, parents are not placed in an adversarial role but are considered "facilitators" of this process. The child's behavior doesn't place the parents and child at odds with each other, but simply extends the learning relationship to other contexts.

The excellent resources we have recommended in this section differentiate between developmental issues and intentional actions: for example, a toddler's natural curiosity to play with an "off-limits" object versus a preschooler's act of intentionally grabbing something to gain attention. To ease parents' frustrations, these resources offer strategies, tips, and constructive advice about handling such discipline problems as hitting playmates, not picking up toys, not getting ready for bedtime, and more.

## Choosing Activities & Games

Nothing is more fun than finding an activity to do with a child . . . unless that activity frustrates them, bores them to tears, or involves too much preparation. Knowing the progression of a child's development will better serve parents as they work toward finding age-appropriate activities to do with their child. Since children are working at different skills at different ages, activities that would be done with an infant will naturally be different than activities that will be done with a toddler. Some will overlap. Much of it involves trial and error.

Infants respond well to activities that promote touching, bonding, soothing, and security. Toddlers, on the other hand, want to impact and control their environment. Activities might include things that can be manipulated, taken apart, and put together. Some toddlers (and especially preschoolers) crave imaginative play. They engage in role-play and imaginative play with their peers, taking turns being the important people in their daily lives or characters from books or movies.

If activities are introduced at a time when children are not developmentally ready, either the child will get frustrated and give up, or the parent will wonder why they bothered to begin with. It is important to understand child development in light of the various activity resources that exist. We have recommended some excellent resources that will not only stimulate your child but also motivate you to try other activities. Many of these recommended resources include various subjects, involve simple or inexpensive materials, concentrate on a given skill or concept (eye-hand coordination), and include ways to extend the activity if it was a success. Most important, these activities are open-ended, focusing on the process and not the product; there are no right or wrong ways for the child to participate. This leads to success and the wonderful feeling of mastery.

## Toilet Training

This is a parenting issue that continues to be controversial. Some experts claim that toilet training should begin before a child turns one, while others claim that training should definitely be finished before children enter the challenges of the "terrible twos," when they begin to demand that parents relinquish control. Most child development experts, however, believe that toilet training, or what is now considered by some to be "toilet learning," should begin when children have reached certain readiness milestones, such as being aware of the elimination process and expressing it in words ("potty," "wet," etc.). Other readiness signs include disliking wet or soiled diapers, staying dry for several hours, waking up dry after a nap, being anxious to please parents, being able to pull their clothes off quickly, and of course, asking to use the toilet!

While some toilet teaching/learning methods insist that children can learn to use the toilet early, this is considered by critics to be a battle that parents will not win, and which may negatively impact a child's self-esteem and need for independence. Unfortunately, many parents feel pressured to get their child toilet-trained before their child is ready. This is partly due to past practices and partly due to the inability or unwillingness of some preschools or childcare centers to accept a diapered child into the facility's program.

Once again, if parents are properly equipped with the developmental information they need to understand their child's growth and learning, they will be best able to make informed decisions about this important rite of passage in their child's life. The resources we have included here discuss readiness signs, the equipment needed, how to ease your child into the process, how and when to reward your child, how to deal with accidents, how to toilet train your child at night, how to deal with bedwetting, and more.

As in the previous section, we have divided our resource recommendations into several categories to help focus your search for answers. Be sure to read the full-page review of any recommended resource to be sure it will be the best resource to address your family's specific needs and questions.

Additional resources that highlight some of these topics are also described in Chapter Three—"Strengthening Your Family," especially those resources designed for new fathers. We also refer parents to Chapter Four—"All-Inclusive Overviews About Parenting" which contains more general discussions of these parenting issues.

Remember that parenting is an adventure! Although the scenery continues to change along the way, the trip should be one that brings forth mutual learning, understanding, comfort, enjoyment, and memories to cherish and share.

*"Little things affect little minds."*

—Benjamin Disraeli

**General Overviews**

★★★★

**Overall Rating**
★★★★
An informative look at how important quality care is on a child's brain development

**Design, Ease Of Use**
★★★★
Well-laid out site; downloadable QuickTime movie clips require lots of hard disk space

1–4 Stars

**Publisher:**
Yahoo!.com

**Media:**
Internet

**Principal Subject:**
Understanding Your Child's Growth & Learning

**Secondary Subject:**
General Overview

**Age Group:**
Infants & Toddlers (0–3)

# I AM YOUR CHILD

**Recommended For:**
Understanding Your Child's Growth & Learning

**Special Resource For:**
Correlating the latest in brain research with suggested advice for raising young children

**Description:**
Founded by Rob Reiner, Michele Singer Reiner and others, this national "public awareness and engagement campaign to make early childhood development a top priority for our nation "offers eight options at the website homepage. "Key Issues" and "Brain Facts" highlight how undeveloped a child's brain is at birth. As the brain develops, the child's experiences and attachments within the first three years directly impact his emotional development, learning abilities, and how he functions later. Parents' "most pressing questions" and responses from "experts" are listed under "Parent Questions." "Ages & Stages" detail child development from prenatal to age three, and "top experts" (Brazelton, Bowman, Koop, Perry) offer their child development advice and insight via downloadable QuickTime movie clips. A list of summarized resources also is available. For those interested in working on behalf of children, two options offer information on this site's campaign, along with ways for communities to promote the cause.

**Evaluation:**
With recent attention focused on the plight of our nation's children and the lack of quality childcare, this campaign is timely. If you're a working parent with a child in daycare, you won't be guilt-tripped here. This site offers "ten guidelines that can help parents and other caregivers raise healthy, happy children and confident, competent learners." The guidelines aren't novel ("talk, read and sing to your child," "use discipline as an opportunity to teach," etc.). But, coupling them with the latest in brain research gives parents rationale for giving and demanding quality care for their child, especially during those first three years. Opportunities exist every day to contribute to the healthy development of a child's brain through experiences, affection and other ways, and this site reinforces this message. You won't find chats here, you won't find humor or a light-handed look at parenting. This site takes its position seriously. Those seriously interested in the welfare of children should visit and become informed, too.

**Where To Find/Buy:**
On the Internet at the URL: http://www.iamyourchild.org/. Also available is a CD-ROM (1997) and a videotape (1997, 30 minutes). Both of these resources are free (there is a $5.00 shipping and handling fee), and can be received by contacting the I Am Your Child Campaign at (202) 338-4385, by FAX at (202) 338-2334, or through the mail at 1010 Wisconsin Ave., NW, Suite 800, Washington, D.C. 20007.

**General Overviews**

# I'M TWO YEARS OLD!
Everything Your Two-Year-Old Wants You To Know About Parenting

★ **Recommended For:**
Understanding Your Child's Growth & Learning

## Description:
The advice the author offers in this book is specifically for the parents of a two-year-old child, and is written from the perspective of a two-year-old. In it, the child tries to tell the parent why she behaves the way she does and what she needs from the parent. It is organized alphabetically into 71 separate issues, including bedtime battles, dressing, lying, nightmares, transitions, and many others. Each issue is introduced by a brief (a third of a page) scenario that illustrates the situation. The two-year-old then suggests different ways a parent could help her deal with the situation. Each one-sentence suggestion is followed by a description of why that suggestion would work. The author says the book is "about looking through the world through the eyes of a two-year-old." And "while the book is written in a child's voice, it certainly goes beyond the words and thought processes of a two-year-old." Each issue is addressed in two to five pages.

## Evaluation:
Written for a very specific audience—the parents of a two-year-old—the author successfully educates the reader about the needs of that age child. Using the voice of the two-year-old to convey the book's point is more purposeful than just cute. It challenges parents to look at the world from a child's point of view, something most parents wouldn't take the time to do. There are valid reasons for the temper tantrums, fears, and power struggles, the author and her two-year-old voice suggest, with very specific suggestions about how to deal with them. For example, regarding tantrums, "Sometimes I just lose it," the child says, suggesting that a day's accumulation of frustration sets her off. Sound familiar? The suggestions for dealing with each problem (in this case: "stay near me," "help me move on," and "avoid my trigger points" are followed by an expanded explanation. Issues are listed alphabetically in the table of contents. One has only to go to the appropriate section and, two to four brief pages later, receive solid, excellent advice on how to deal with the problem. The advice given is gentle, loving, and full of common sense. At the very least, readers will finish this book and if they're lucky, they will have rediscovered an ability to see the world through a child's eyes.

## Where To Find/Buy:
Bookstores and libraries.

★★★★

**Overall Rating**
★★★★
Excellent advice in a cute format that offers a new perspective for parents

**Design, Ease Of Use**
★★★★
Topics organized alphabetically in table of contents; offers "to-the-point" advice

1–4 Stars

**Author:**
Jerri Wolfe, PhD

Wolfe holds a PhD in family resource management, an MS in education, and is a certified family life educator. She also teaches seminars and courses on family management and parenting issues, and is the author of numerous articles on parenting and family issues. She is married, with an eight-year-old daughter.

**Publisher:**
Becker & Mayer! Books/Pocket Books (Simon & Schuster)

**Edition:**
1998

**Price:**
$10.00

**Pages/Run Time:**
196

**ISBN:**
0671003380

**Media:**
Book

**Principal Subject:**
Understanding Your Child's Growth & Learning

**Secondary Subject:**
General Overview

**Age Group:**
Toddlers (1–3)

II. Understanding Your Child's Growth & Learning

**Overall Rating**
★★★★
The concept of "touchpoints" helps explain the dynamics involved as a child develops

**Design, Ease Of Use**
★★★★
Easy to read, well-illustrated, lots of open space, and well-indexed

1–4 Stars

**Author:**
T. Berry Brazelton, MD

T. Berry Brazelton, MD is Associate Professor of Pediatrics at Harvard Medical School and Chief of the Child Development Unit at the Boston Children's Hospital Medical Center. Dr. Brazelton is considered a leading authority on child development.

**Publisher:**
Addison Wesley Publishing (Merloyd Lawrence)

**Edition:**
1992

**Price:**
$16.00

**Pages/Run Time:**
480

**ISBN:**
020162690x

**Media:**
Book

**Principal Subject:**
Understanding Your Child's Growth & Learning

**Secondary Subject:**
General Overview

**Age Group:**
Infants & Toddlers (0–3)

## General Overviews

# TOUCHPOINTS
## Your Child's Emotional And Behavioral Development

**Recommended For:**
Understanding Your Child's Growth & Learning

**Description:**

Dr. Brazelton introduces his book as a "map of infancy and of early child development." The purpose of this map is to help parents navigate the predictable ups and downs, and spurts and stalls that happen along the way in raising a child. This book maps out not only the physical growth of a child, but psychological development as well, helping parents achieve an understanding of what happens as a child struggles to reorganize and incorporate each new achievement. As such, this book illustrates in three parts the "touchpoints" of development (from the newborn to the three-year-old child), challenges to development (discipline, fears, sleep problems, and more), and the child's allies in development (grandparents, friends, etc.). "Touchpoints" is a concept that Dr. Brazelton has developed to label the predictable times that occur just before a surge of rapid growth. At this time, a child's behavior falls apart and he becomes difficult to understand. "Touchpoints," in his words, become a window for viewing the "great energy that fuels a child for learning," that pushes him toward greater autonomy.

**Evaluation:**

*Touchpoints*, Dr. Brazelton's latest book on child development, includes much of the information found in his other books (such as *Mothers and Infants* and *The Earliest Relationship*). While those books targeted professionals who would be offering support or services to parents, this book is specifically for parents. As such it is less technical and easier to read. The same amount of comprehensive detail is provided, but it is arranged in a much more digestible manner. Breaking the book into three sections also makes it easier to reference when one is trying to solve problems and particular parental challenges, from headaches and stomach aches to television. The final section on "Allies in Development" is light, only 40 pages out of this 480-page book. This could be a whole additional book, since it addresses the value of interactions in a child's life—the past and how it is passed on (parents, grandparents), and the child's evolving relationships with peers and others. Many valuable insights and new research findings are interpreted in this book; it is a good book to have as new parents.

**Where To Find/Buy:**
Bookstores and libraries.

**General Overviews**

# TOUCHPOINTS, VOLUME 2
## The First Month Through The First Year

★★★★

**Recommended For:**
Understanding Your Child's Growth & Learning

**Special Resource For:**
Understanding a baby's development (using a videotape)

## Description:

This is the second videotape in a series of three hosted by T. Berry Brazelton, "America's preeminent baby doctor." Here he illustrates ways that families can understand their new baby from one month to 15 months of age. Five families are the focus of this 45 minute videotape, all of which were presented in the first videotape: a family with a "trying" child and older sibling, a single mom, a couple with a very busy dad and toddler, a couple who had a premature baby, and older first-time parents. Throughout the videotape, Brazelton expands upon the various "touchpoints" these families encounter. Touchpoints are "periods of time that precede a rapid growth in learning for both child and parent." As Brazelton explains, "Touchpoints are predictable and can help parents make decisions on how to handle their children." The camera and Brazelton detail certain age ranges—one to four months, five to six months, seven to eight months, nine to 12 months, 12–15 months—and the 15+ touchpoints included within these age groupings. Touchpoints include sleeping, feeding, motor skills, cognitive development, negativism, teasing, and more.

## Evaluation:

Brazelton's charismatic manner once again holds the segments of the tape together as he introduces each new "touchpoint." Again, the honesty and humanness of the families involved contribute to the personal and warm tone of this film. The viewer is bound to find his/her baby in this film, whether that baby be fussy, calm, sleepy, or alert. The viewer can't help but benefit from watching the struggles and joys these families experience which are common to all parents, especially new parents. With his familiar tone and sunny attitude, Brazelton walks you through the babies' various milestones—object permanence, stranger anxiety, pincer grasp, sitting up, standing, walking, etc.—And does a fine job of explaining their importance in light of the babies' cognitive, emotional and physical growth. In fact, this video very neatly sums up the contents of his TV show and gives you the highlights in a tidy brief clip.

## Where To Find/Buy:

Bookstores, libraries, videotape dealers, or order direct by calling (800) 756-8792.

**Overall Rating**
★★★★
Details major milestones babies encounter from one month of age to 15 months

**Design, Ease Of Use**
★★★★
Split screen with parents & baby; narration closely coincides with babies' actions

1–4 Stars

**Publisher:**
Pipher Films

**Edition:**
1991

**Price:**
$29.99

**ISBN:**
1878983105

**Media:**
Videotape

**Principal Subject:**
Understanding Your Child's Growth & Learning

**Secondary Subject:**
General Overview

**Age Group:**
Infants (0–1)

II. Understanding Your Child's Growth & Learning

## Overall Rating
★★★★

Combines research & concrete examples of toddlers' thoughts, feelings and responses

## Design, Ease Of Use
★★★

Textbook-like at times, but offers bulleted highlights, clear headings, bold case studies

1–4 Stars

## Author:
Alicia F. Lieberman

Lieberman is professor of psychiatry at the University of California, San Francisco, and senior psychologist of its Infant-Parent Program. She is world-renowned for her work on mother-child attachment.

## Publisher:
The Free Press
(Simon & Schuster)

## Edition:
1995

## Price:
$12.00

## Pages/Run Time:
244

## ISBN:
0028740173

## Media:
Book

## Principal Subject:
Understanding Your Child's Growth & Learning

## Secondary Subject:
General Overview

## Age Group:
Toddlers (1–3)

---

### General Overviews

# THE EMOTIONAL LIFE OF THE TODDLER

### Recommended For:
Understanding Your Child's Growth & Learning

### Description:

Lieberman, a senior psychologist who has studied mother-child attachments, presents her research and observations of how a toddler "thinks, feels, and responds to the challenges of growing up, and how parents can help them meet these challenges with greater self-confidence and joy." This 244-page book is divided into ten chapters with an index and a chapter-by-chapter reference section. Chapters One through Three explore the toddler and his need to reconcile his new-found yearning for independence with his need for his parents' secure base. Chapters Four through Six explain the varieties in toddler temperaments (easy, slow to warm up, active, difficult) along with how parents' temperaments can interplay; separate chapters illustrate the developments of the active and shy toddler. The next two chapters focus on toddlers' anxieties and how specific age-related anxieties (toilet training, siblings, nighttime fears, separation, etc.) can be addressed. The impact of divorce on the toddler is the topic of Chapter Nine while Chapter Ten focuses on the effects of placing a toddler in childcare.

### Evaluation:

Don't be taken aback by the textbook-like manner in which this book is presented. Lieberman does an excellent job of stating the scientific background and research for her generalizations while at the same time illustrating her points through specific toddler "case study" examples. She presents an interesting proposition in stating that the extreme fluctuations in toddler moods often mirror feelings parents had in their own childhood that may or may not have been successfully dealt with and that now result in anxious parental reactions. Lieberman does an excellent job of bringing the toddler's behavior back into the here-and-now, however, by offering concrete tips in bulleted highlights where appropriate and necessary. This is not a book on discipline although parents will naturally strive to better handle their toddler's actions with reactions that are based on an in-depth understanding of the toddler's drives and needs. Parents will certainly get that understanding within this book.

### Where To Find/Buy:
Bookstores and libraries.

**General Overviews**

# KNOW YOUR CHILD
## An Authoritative Guide For Today's Parents

**Recommended For:**
Understanding Your Child's Growth & Learning

**Description:**
Based on the underlying theme of temperament, this resource is divided into three major parts. Part One focuses on the differences in children and parents. Human development, the significance of temperament, parenting styles (secure, insecure, intimidated, over-interpretive, etc.), and the "goodness of fit" between parenting styles (attitudes and expectations) and children's temperament are some of the topics addressed in this first section. Part Two discusses the developing child from infant to adolescent. Some of the topics covered include social, cognitive development, and emotional development along with gender identity, and the child's self-esteem. The final section, Part Three, focuses on family issues. Content in this section addresses children with special needs, the debate over IQ scores, roles of parents and siblings, and the effect of working mothers. An extensive reference section and index conclude this 397-page resource.

**Evaluation:**
Based on the authors' 30 year longitudinal study, their 20 years of experience editing the annual volume of Progress in *Child Psychiatry and Child Development*, and their 40+ years of teaching and consulting practice, this book is exceptionally strong on research with advice for direct application. With its intent to cover the wide span of research that has been done on this subject, this guide does have a tendency sometimes to get weighted down with much theory and explanation. Parents may want more content on specific subjects upon reading this volume. There are several important themes running through this book. One, that babies are different from the start and one difference is their temperament. Also, infants are equipped with the necessary biological makeup that allows them to socially interact with the world around them. Finally, there are many good ways to be a good parent and what is important is the "goodness of fit." A very strong advocate of the parent, this resource offers useful information for those parents who "know their children, and are not bewildered by the contradictory advice they read and hear."

**Where To Find/Buy:**
Bookstores and libraries.

---

**Overall Rating**
★★★★
Strong advocate of "fit" between parents and child; good mix of research & application

**Design, Ease Of Use**
★★★
Although textbook like at first glance, reads well and is concise; easily referenced index

1–4 Stars

**Author:**
Stella Chess and Alexander Thomas

Stella Chess and Alexander Thomas, both professors of psychiatry at New York University Medical Center, founded the modern study of temperament in 1956. They received an award from the Society for Research in Child Development for contributions to child development

**Publisher:**
Jason Aronson

**Edition:**
2nd (1996)

**Price:**
$40.00

**Pages/Run Time:**
397

**ISBN:**
1568218346

**Media:**
Book

**Principal Subject:**
Understanding Your Child's Growth & Learning

**Secondary Subject:**
General Overview

**Age Group:**
Infants & Toddlers (0–3)

**★★★★**

**Overall Rating**
★★★★
Especially valuable for parents of twins; emphasizes family harmony and peer insight

**Design, Ease Of Use**
★★★
Excellent text, light on illustrations

1–4 Stars

**Author:**
Connie L. Agnew, MD, Alan H. Klein, MD, Jill Alison Ganon

All authors are parents and reside in Los Angeles, California. Agnew, a perinatologist, specializes in the care of high-risk mothers and infants. Klein, a pediatrician, specializes in high-risk infant care. Ganon is a professional writer and editor.

**Publisher:**
HarperPerennial
(HarperCollins Publishers)

**Edition:**
1997

**Price:**
$16.00

**Pages/Run Time:**
304

**ISBN:**
0062734601

**Media:**
Book

**Principal Subject:**
Understanding Your Child's Growth & Learning

**Secondary Subject:**
General Overview

**Age Group:**
Infants (0–1)

## General Overviews

# TWINS!

Expert Advice From Two Practicing Physicians On Pregnancy, Birth, And The First Year Of Life With Twins

**Recommended For:**
Understanding Your Child's Growth & Learning

**Description:**

The authors begin by acknowledging that twins are "miraculous . . . You're starting out on a truly epic journey." Throughout the book, readers hear both from health care professionals and other parents of twins. Introductory chapters discuss how twins are conceived, how to find the "right practitioner," and why the reader needs to take responsibility for a healthy start in their pregnancy. Fetal development is considered from several perspectives: "Your Developing Twins," "Your Pregnant Body," "Symptoms That May Be Ongoing," "The Checkup," "Transitions" (a forum for special issues and conditions), and "Roundtable Talk" in which parents and physician participants respond to an array of topics concerning the twins in their lives. Also provided are chapters on labor and delivery followed by an expanded discussion of postpartum issues which focus on the whole family. The first year of life with twins is described in a format similar to that used for fetal development—"Your Growing Twins," "Parental Questions and Concerns," "Roundtable Talk," and more. An emphasis is placed on developmental milestones, family harmony, and safety measures to consider.

**Evaluation:**

This book speaks both to readers who are pregnant and, more specifically, to those who are pregnant with twins. As expectations and conditions of the pregnancy are described, comparisons are often noted in relation to the "singleton mom." Similar to other books on pregnancy, the reader is told what to expect during her prenatal visits to the physician. In addition, helpful considerations for choosing a prenatal caregiver are offered. Unusual to this book are chapters that not only detail the progression of both the developing fetus and the first year of life, but also thoughtfully introduce the reader to other peers in "Roundtable Talk." Here prospective parents will find comfort in knowing their concerns are shared by others, as well as attaining advice from specialists. Throughout the book, consideration and guidance is offered to support family harmony. Thanks to its organization, bold highlights, and index, it is also easily referenced. Relevant charts and a ten-page resource guide are included to help support parents. Overall, this book can be comfortably read from cover-to-cover.

**Where To Find/Buy:**
Bookstores and libraries.

**General Overviews**

# THE HURRIED CHILD
Growing Up Too Fast, Too Soon

### Recommended For:
Understanding Your Child's Growth & Learning

## Description:

This 217-page guide is divided into two main parts. Part One—"Our Hurried Children"—contains four chapters. These chapters describe the concept of childhood, attributes of the "hurried child," the influence of parents, education, and the media on children and adolescents' development, and the myth of the "Superkid." Part Two—"Hurried Children: Stressed Children"—has five chapters. These chapters identify children's responses to responsibilities that contradict numerous developmental recommendations. The achievements and limitations of the major stages of child development are highlighted, as well as how "hurrying" a child has negative effects on their "normal" course of development intellectually, emotionally, and socially. Suggestions and advice are also given on how families might socialize children and how to help children in distress. Bold sub-headings, sample contract sheets (to track adult expectations), and bulleted facts and information are given. A notes section (by chapter) and index conclude the text.

## Evaluation:

Although its copyright is dated, this classic continues to warrant attention. Elkind states that certain societal changes have caused parents to believe in the "Superkid," one who is more competent (than development shows) and can take on new responsibilities emotionally, socially, and intellectually. In effect, he says, we hurry their growth in our own best interests, then rationalize our decisions, and ignore the gross effects our decisions have on our children. He cites examples such as early childcare, latchkey kids, greater home responsibilities, early schooling, etc. At first glance, he appears to make sweeping generalizations ("The truth is that children . . . are less well off today that they were a couple of decades ago.") or project his strong opinions ("those who would teach young children about AIDS, nuclear war, and child abuse are really dealing with their own anxieties and fears . . ."). But upon closer examination, he backs up his statements with research studies, statistical evidence, and news headlines. This is an insightful, if not alarming, view that parents should include in their research about childcare and early schooling.

## Where To Find/Buy:
Bookstores and libraries.

---

**Overall Rating**
★★★★
Often opinionated with generalizations, but backed by solid research & statistics

**Design, Ease Of Use**
★★
Larger type; but must be read cover to cover to find its "needle-in-a-haystack" points

1–4 Stars

**Author:**
David Elkind, PhD

David Elkind, a worldwide advocate for the protection of childhood, is a professor of child study and senior resident scholar at the Lincoln Filene Center of Tufts University.

**Publisher:**
Addison-Wesley Publishing

**Edition:**
2nd (1988)

**Price:**
$14.00

**Pages/Run Time:**
217

**ISBN:**
0201073978

**Media:**
Book

**Principal Subject:**
Understanding Your Child's Growth & Learning

**Secondary Subject:**
General Overview

**Age Group:**
Infants & Toddlers (0–3)

**Overall Rating**
★★★★
Rich, thought-provoking site full of quality information

**Design, Ease Of Use**
★
Despite attractiveness, clarity and ease of use, little can be successfully printed

1–4 Stars

**Media:**
Internet

**Principal Subject:**
Understanding Your Child's Growth & Learning

**Secondary Subject:**
General Overview

**Age Group:**
Infants & Toddlers (0–3)

## General Overviews

# ZERO TO THREE
Young Explorers

**Recommended For:**
Understanding Your Child's Growth & Learning

### Description:

Zero To Three, a nonprofit national organization founded in 1977 and "dedicated solely to advancing the healthy development of babies and young children," offers an extensive website that covers hundreds of topics of interest to parents of children from birth to three years of age. The site's homepage options include access to its "Parent Information" sections (information on dozens of topics and an extensive resource list), "Choosing Quality Child Care," "Developmental Milestones," "Tip of the Week," information about the organization's campaign to increase public awareness of the developmental importance of a child's first three years, classes and curriculum offered by the national Training Institute, and an online bookstore. Also offered are a selection of parenting—and grandparenting—experiences written by parents and caregivers. Reference sections include topics such as adoptive parents, beginnings of literacy, infants and toddlers in groups, dynamic play therapy, peer group entry skills, infant massage, grandparents and young children, selecting childcare, and much more. The Developmental Milestones section offers information on young infants (birth to eight months), "explorers" (eight to 18 months) and Toddlers and Two-Year Olds (18 months to 3 years). Its board of directors includes national experts from top universities and medical centers.

### Evaluation:

"By age 1, [a child's] brain is 80 percent developed," this website's authors say. "And during the first years of life, a child has already developed a sense of empathy and curiosity, a feeling of connection to others, and the ability to relate and communicate with others." There may be no better description of this website than that. The site provides clear and complete information about basic topics of interest to parents and caregivers of toddlers. It is in its richer layers, however, that it truly distinguishes itself. Parents and grandparents offer heartfelt and poignant accounts of what their involvement with their children and grandchildren mean in their lives. National experts discuss thought-provoking topics not found elsewhere. Witness intriguing essays on such subjects as "gourmet babies" (babies who want for nothing), "Grandparents Give in Many Ways," and "How Men and Children Affect Each Other's Development." One unfortunate web design disappointment: because of the text and background colors chosen, attempts to print pages will turn out blank. On the whole though, this is a site that inspires, that draws forth empathy, and that informs and encourages connections between parent and child, among parents, and throughout a virtual community.

### Where To Find/Buy:

On the Internet at the URL: http://www.zerotothree.org/

**General Overviews**

# GROWING TOGETHER
## A Parent's Guide To Baby's First Year

### Description:

This 260-page, 11 chapter book discusses the development of baby from birth through 12 months of age. Each of baby's first six months is discussed in its own chapter. Chapter Ten covers six to nine months, and Chapter Eleven covers nine to twelve months. Over 230 black-and-white and color photographs are included in this book showing baby's developmental stages from just minutes after birth up to the first birthday. In the month-by-month chapters, developmental stages discussed include large and fine motor skills, language/social development, cognitive skills, and more. In addition to tracking baby's development, there are chapters on parenting style and feeding your baby (breastfeeding, bottlefeeding, and solids). Sears advocates an "attachment" style of parenting, which basically starts with a close attachment between mother and baby after birth; responding to baby's needs, language, and cries; breastfeeding with infant-led weaning; wearing baby in a baby carrier (or arms); sharing sleep with baby; and father involvement.

### Evaluation:

Sears writes that his three goals in writing this book are "to help you know your baby, to help you and your baby feel right, and to help all of you to enjoy one another." With all the information presented and the proud way in which he has shared his personal photos, it certainly appears that he has met these goals. The many photographs in the book, which were taken by Sears and his wife of their sixth child, illustrate a well baby's milestones as well as the little steps. The simple format and organization of the book make the book very easy to read. Information is relatively easy to find, with large and well-placed subject headings. In some chapters, there are also some helpful ideas and activities for things to do with your baby at the different growth stages. Sears presents a strong argument for the attachment style of parenting, which he believes cannot help but make parents and baby enjoy each other more. *Growing Together* is a fine nuts-and-bolts book for what to expect in baby's first year.

### Where To Find/Buy:

Bookstores, libraries, or order direct by calling (708) 451-1891 or by contacting La Leche League International at P.O. Box 1209, Franklin Park, IL 60131-8209.

---

**Overall Rating**
★★★
A clearly written, easy to read book on baby's development

**Design, Ease Of Use**
★★★★
Simple chronology of baby's development; large headings make info easy to find

1–4 Stars

**Author:**
William Sears, MD

William Sears, MD, is a pediatrician in private practice, Assistant Professor of Pediatrics at the University of Southern California, and a lecturer on parenting and child care. Dr. Sears and his wife, Martha, an accredited La Leche League Leader, have eight children.

**Publisher:**
La Leche League International

**Edition:**
1987

**Price:**
$14.50

**Pages/Run Time:**
260

**ISBN:**
0912500360

**Media:**
Book

**Principal Subject:**
Understanding Your Child's Growth & Learning

**Secondary Subject:**
General Overview

**Age Group:**
Infants (0–1)

General Overviews

# INFANTS AND MOTHERS
Differences In Development

## Description:

Dr. Brazelton has recorded in this book a narrative on the first year of life for three different baby types. Through this book's 300 pages, Brazelton traces the month-by-month reactions of three different types of babies—average, quiet, and active. The first chapter (of fourteen) explains the importance of noticing, understanding, and accepting each infant's individuality and unique differences. Through each succeeding chapter, Dr. Brazelton tries to illustrate the learning process that both parent and infant undertake as they take in new information, digest it, and organize it for later use. By understanding how each child is essentially "wired" at birth to respond to stimulation, parents are better equipped to adapt their parenting styles and the environment they provide their babies. Through each chapter, he illustrates how parents and infants learn from each other. He also reveals how over-stimulation can be "tuned-out" by the baby, and how under-stimulation can actually slow the baby's development. This revised edition reflects the changing status of the family, including single parents and working mothers and fathers.

## Evaluation:

Brazelton's running commentary of his observations and evaluations as he interacts with infants makes this book unique. A mother who feels overwhelmed and unsure if she is adequate will appreciate the insights offered on a new baby's internal conflicts. As a new parent, you won't find advice, specific support, or techniques for the challenges of parenthood. Nor does this book seek to intellectualize the process of becoming a parent. It is, rather, an illustration of how three families (with different types of babies) adapted to and cared for their babies while the babies adapted to their new world; what the families did and how they felt are highlighted. This book, then, this quite interesting, but it is very detailed and most new parents will not have the time or attention span to get through it. It is better read in retrospect or to have read while waiting for the birth of a new infant. Professionals working with parents of infants will also find it to be a useful tool.

## Where To Find/Buy:

Bookstores and libraries.

---

**Overall Rating**
★★★
A valuable book illustrating the individual needs of different "types" of infants

**Design, Ease Of Use**
★★★★
Well done, easily followed and easily referenced; loaded with photographs of babies

1–4 Stars

**Author:**
T. Berry Brazelton, MD

T. Berry Brazelton, MD is Associate Professor of Pediatrics at Harvard Medical School and Chief of the Child Development Unit at the Boston Children's Hospital Medical Center. Dr. Brazelton is considered a leading authority on child development.

**Publisher:**
Bantam Doubleday Dell (Merloyd Lawrence)

**Edition:**
2nd (1983)

**Price:**
$16.95

**Pages/Run Time:**
300

**ISBN:**
0440506859

**Media:**
Book

**Principal Subject:**
Understanding Your Child's Growth & Learning

**Secondary Subject:**
General Overview

**Age Group:**
Infants (0–1)

II. Understanding Your Child's Growth & Learning

**General Overviews**

# YOUR TWO-YEAR-OLD
12 To 24 Months

★★★

## Description:

Written by co-founders of the Gesell Institute, this 148-page resource highlights the development of a two year old; much of the book is directed toward the "disequilibrium" age of two-and-a-half years, or "the terrible twos." Divided into nine chapters, the first two chapters describe the transition into toddlerhood along with general characteristics of toddlers in terms of motor, language, social, and emotional changes. Chapter Three focuses on toddlers' social interactions with others, while "techniques" for dealing with toddlers' behavior on "difficult days" are offered in Chapter Four. Chapter Five describes major "accomplishments and abilities" (language, motor, visual, language, adaptive play, etc.) of the two year old and the two-and-a-half year old. Chapter Six outlines typical daily routines (eating, bath and dressing, bedtime, and elimination), while Chapter Seven focuses on the "mental life" of toddlers, or how they view the world. Chapter Eight describes differences in children's development. Chapter Nine offers "Stories from Real Life." Lists of toys, equipment, and books for children are included in the four appendixes, as well as books for parents of two year olds.

## Evaluation:

As the second in a series of ten books, this one outlines the toddler's development and behavior better than the first of the series. Here, parents will find not only a sensitive portrayal of the tender, yet tumultuous two year old, but also some positive concrete tips for dealing with toddler behavior, especially in Chapter Four. Suggestions, such as how to take advantage of the toddler's ritualistic tendency, accepting security measures (teddy bears, blankets, etc.), giving face-saving commands, avoiding certain things (terms like "later"), using distractions, etc., are clearly described. Chapter Six offers help for handling daily routines with the Q & A segment in Chapter Nine underscoring this chapter's advice. Although Chapters Two, Three, Four, and Six highlight what to expect from toddlers, no discussion is afforded the role of discipline. Parents will need other resources to supplement this topic. Also, the discussion in Chapter Eight is minimal; the role of temperament in explaining the range of toddler behaviors is ignored. Good for a general discussion, this resource offers parents an overall scan of their toddler's development and behaviors.

## Where To Find/Buy:

Bookstores, libraries, or order direct by contacting Dell Readers Service, Box DR, 1540 Broadway, New York, NY 10036.

**Overall Rating**
★★★
Thorough discussion of the "terrific and terrible" twos; minimal info of temperament

**Design, Ease Of Use**
★★★★
Easily read; chapters broken up by subtopics or ages; many black and white photos

1–4 Stars

**Author:**
Louise Bates Ames, PhD and Frances L. Ilg, MD

Ames is a lecturer at the Yale Child Study Center and assistant professor emeritus at Yale University. Both Ilg and Ames are co-founders of the Gesell Institute of Child Development at Yale.

**Publisher:**
Dell Trade (Dell Publishing/ Bantam Doubleday Dell)

**Edition:**
1976

**Price:**
$10.95

**ISBN:**
0440506387

**Media:**
Book

**Principal Subject:**
Understanding Your Child's Growth & Learning

**Secondary Subject:**
General Overview

**Age Group:**
Toddlers (1–3)

## General Overviews

★★★

**Overall Rating**
★★★
Offers developmental tidbits on baby's first year milestones

**Design, Ease Of Use**
★★★
Succinct with segment headings; great examples of baby's development; canned presentation

1–4 Stars

**Publisher:**
Congress Entertainment, Ltd.

**Edition:**
1985

**Price:**
$19.98

**ISBN:**
1560940883

**Media:**
Videotape

**Principal Subject:**
Understanding Your Child's Growth & Learning

**Secondary Subject:**
General Overview

**Age Group:**
Infants (0–1)

# A JOURNEY THROUGH THE FIRST YEAR OF LIFE

## Description:
Narrated by Dr. Burton L. White, an educational psychologist, and Judith Nolte, editor of *American Baby* magazine, this 45 minute videotape affords parents a sequential glimpse into their child's development during the first year of life. Divided into six segments from "Hello World" (the first month) to "Walking Tall" (the 11th and 12th months), this video illustrates baby's milestones concerning motor skills (gross and fine), sensory development (hearing, sight, sound, touch), language development, problem-solving skills (cause-effect, etc.), and social and emotional development. Each segment includes a brief introduction by the two narrators followed by footage of babies illustrating each concept. Brief parent interviews are interjected throughout. A preview heading signals the onset of the next stage along with a written synopsis of what is achieved, for example, "Sitting On Top of the World"—sitting up during the seventh and eighth months. A recap is given after each discussion before the next stage is introduced.

## Evaluation:
White, known for his extensive research (38+ years) in the arena of child development, along with Nolte, whose magazine is well-known by most new parents, offer this good, but canned, description of a baby's first year. Parents will find direct examples to help understand their baby's development along with indirect advice on ways to enhance their baby's discovery of their world. Although not focusing on how to take care of a baby, this video would be a helpful tool in a parenting education class on understanding the developmental needs of newborns and babies. The examples are very well-done, the information is succinct, and the parent narratives, although lacking spontaneity, are appropriate venues for the narrators' discussions. The only negative element of this tape is its canned, prepackaged nature of presentation. However, it offers valuable informative, it's not too expensive compared to other videos available, and it would be a good shower present for first-time parents.

## Where To Find/Buy:
Bookstores, libraries, videotape dealers, or order direct by calling (800) VHS-TAPE. It can also be ordered through Library Video Company at (800) 843-3620, through FAX at (610) 645-4040, or online at http://www.libraryvideo.com.

**General Overviews**

# YOUR AMAZING NEWBORN

★★★

## Description:

Authors Marshall and Phyllis Klaus combine their years of experience in the field of newborn development with 120 photographs of babies less than two weeks old to present information on how babies and those who love them bond in the first days of life. This 113-page book is presented in ten chapters, including: "Before Birth: Dawning Awareness"; "The First Minutes"; "Waking to the World"; "Newborn Sight"; "Newborn Hearing"; "Touch, Taste and Smell"; "Motions and Rhythms"; "Expressions and Emotions"; "The Newly Adopted Baby"; and "The Newborn Family." The black and white photographs range from fetal images to newborns up to two weeks of age. The photos are used to illustrate ways babies and their families instinctively move toward and within "an intimate and reciprocal choreography." Also included is an authors' preface, a notes section, and an index.

## Evaluation:

Make no mistake here: the eyes have it. Or, in the case of these tiny newborns, their entire cherubic faces. *Your Amazing Newborn* uses more than 100 black and white photos of babies less than two weeks old to illustrate how newborns and their families find one another and naturally bond, when allowed the instinctual closeness they crave. The Klaus' expertise in the field allows them to present the most up-to-date findings on how newborns develop. While the photos will draw your attention first, you'll come back for the information contained within the text itself. Readers will view images of a newborn less than one hour old crawling unassisted to the mother's breast, recognizing the parents' voices, and shutting out unwanted sights and sounds. Experience here the first gaze, the first reach, the first spark of recognition "that ignites a lifetime bond." This is a priceless book for all who love innocence and breathtaking inner wisdom of a newborn. It would also make a delightful gift for prospective parents.

## Where To Find/Buy:

Bookstores and libraries.

**Overall Rating**
★★★
Beautiful book that inspires awe at the miracle of a newborn

**Design, Ease Of Use**
★★★
Effective combination of text and black and white photographs

1–4 Stars

**Author:**
Marshall H. Klaus, MD, and Phyllis H. Klaus, CSW, MFCC

Klaus, neonatologist and researcher, teaches pediatrics at the University of California, San Francisco, School of Medicine, and is author of several works in that field. Klaus teaches and practices psychotherapy at the Erikson Institute in Santa Rosa.

**Publisher:**
Perseus Books

**Edition:**
1998

**Price:**
$20.00

**Pages/Run Time:**
113

**ISBN:**
0738200131

**Media:**
Book

**Principal Subject:**
Understanding Your Child's Growth & Learning

**Secondary Subject:**
General Overview

**Age Group:**
Infants (0–1)

## General Overviews

# BABYHOOD
## Stage By Stage, From Birth To Age Two:
## How Your Baby Develops Physically, Emotionally, Mentally

**Overall Rating**
★★★
An interesting and in-depth look at child development

**Design, Ease Of Use**
★★
Rather heavy text but it is easily cross-referenced; graphics would help the monotony

1–4 Stars

**Author:**
Penelope Leach, PhD

Penelope Leach was educated at Cambridge University and the London School of Economics, where she received her PhD in Psychology and lectured on psychology and child development. For four years she ran a study on the effects of babies on their parents.

**Publisher:**
Alfred A. Knopf

**Edition:**
2nd (1983)

**Price:**
$17.00

**Pages/Run Time:**
400

**ISBN:**
0394714369

**Media:**
Book

**Principal Subject:**
Understanding Your Child's Growth & Learning

**Secondary Subject:**
General Overview

**Age Group:**
Infants & Toddlers (0–3)

### Description:

Babyhood is a book of 400+ pages and 31 information-loaded chapters. Written from the point-of-view of the developing child, it aims to create an ideal model of care, contact and communication between child and parents. The information is arranged to cover five age periods (first six weeks, to three months, to six months, to 12 months, to toddler). Similar topics are reviewed in each section, noting what has changed and how the child has developed. Each age period is introduced with a discussion of the child's normal patterns, or in the case of newborns, the lack of pattern, and how to help ease a child's distress as she settles into them. Within each period particular patterns are explained. For example, the physical patterns of feeding, sleeping, elimination, and crying may be discussed followed by the development of motor control, sensory input and meaning-making, hearing and making sounds, (the beginning of language development), and so on. Each of the age periods is summarized and a table included in each chapter to help you review normal behaviors, stages, and comments for the child's development to this point.

### Evaluation:

Outdated in some respects, this book does not go into the details of how to hold or feed or clean a baby. Instead it addresses the larger view of where a baby is at each stage of her development, i.e. physically, emotionally, and mentally. Its goal is to teach a new parent how to assess their child, offering baselines for a "good" physical state, as well as emotional and mental states. While the first 70 pages or so review what parents need to know on diet, sleep needs, normal crying, and elimination, the more interesting material begins with Chapter Five on the "difficulties of getting settled." Using her descriptions of "miserable babies, jumpy babies, sleepy babies and wakeful babies," Leach illustrates how a parent can benefit from understanding and assessing their baby's development. As patterns begin to make sense, the reader is tempted to flip forward to the next section to see what comes next about a given topic, like language, sleeping, etc. We believe you'll find that Leach has managed to create a fascinating book on child development and an intimate look at the parent-child interaction that goes into that development.

### Where To Find/Buy:

Bookstores and libraries.

**General Overviews**

# FIRST FEELINGS
Milestones In The Emotional Development Of Your Baby And Child

★★★

## Description:

This 247-page, six chapter book focuses on the emotional development of children from birth to 48 months of age. The authors, a psychiatrist and child development researcher, offer advice on how parents can take an active role in understanding the emotional stages in their child's life. Subheadings within each chapter include: "Observing Your Baby," "Creating a Supportive Environment," and "Reviewing Your Support." Six emotional milestones and various "Dimensions of Human Emotion" are given in the introduction. Chapter One (birth to three months) discusses baby's personality and parental personality styles. The second chapter (two to seven months) deals with forming relationships and attachment periods. Chapter Three (three to ten months) contains info on communication, while Chapter Four (nine to 18 months) delves into the emergence of a child's sense of self. Chapter Five (18–36 months) and Chapter Six (30–48 months) include topics such as emotional thinking and expression, how a child's personality functions, emotional memory, repression, and more.

## Evaluation:

This resource aims to orient parents "to the broader issues that must be addressed before a solution to the particular drama or problem is found." Using years of research and clinical experience, the authors present an abundance of information from studies that support the theories contained in this guide. Although the book reads like a textbook or doctoral thesis at times, it helps bridge the gap found in resources that simply address a child's physical and cognitive growth. By considering this guide's "milestones" that mark the emotional development of a child, parents will be able to more clearly identify some of the more common difficulties encountered along a specific stage in their child's development and find ways to help them deal with events more effectively. Parents will also be better able to appreciate their child's special abilities by taking a look at and understanding their child's first feelings in life. This is a well-written, well-researched book worthy of every parent's attention.

## Where To Find/Buy:

Bookstores and libraries, or order direct from Penguin Books by Mail, Dept. BA Box 999, Bergenfield, NJ 07621-0999.

**Overall Rating**
★★★
Based on research, this book fills a need not often addressed by other resources

**Design, Ease Of Use**
★★
Heavy, reads like a textbook at times; small type on newsprint makes reading difficult

1–4 Stars

**Author:**
Stanley I. Greenspan, MD, and Nancy Thorndike Greenspan

Stanley Greenspan, MD, is a practicing psychiatrist and chief of the Clinical Infant and Child Development Research Center of the Division of Maternal and Child Health and the National Institute of Mental Health. Nancy Thorndike Greenspan is a health economist.

**Publisher:**
Penguin Books

**Edition:**
1985

**Price:**
$12.95

**Pages/Run Time:**
247

**ISBN:**
0140119884

**Media:**
Book

**Principal Subject:**
Understanding Your Child's Growth & Learning

**Secondary Subject:**
General Overview

**Age Group:**
Infants & Toddlers (0–3)

General Overviews

## YOUR ONE-YEAR-OLD
### The Fun-Loving, Fussy 12 To 24-Month-Old

**Overall Rating**

★★

Good overall discussion of toddlers' development and this "often difficult year of life"

**Design, Ease Of Use**

★★★★

Easily read; chapters broken up by subtopics or ages; many black and white photos

1–4 Stars

**Author:**

Louise Bates Ames, PhD, Frances L. Ilg, MD, & Carol Chase Haber, MA

Ames is a lecturer at the Yale Child Study Center and assistant professor emeritus at Yale University. Both Ilg and Ames are co-founders of the Gesell Institute of Child Development at Yale. Haber, a school psychologist, is a trained and qualified Gesell Examiner.

**Publisher:**

Dell Trade (Dell Publishing/ Bantam Doubleday Dell)

**Edition:**

1982

**Price:**

$10.95

**ISBN:**

0440506727

**Media:**

Book

**Principal Subject:**

Understanding Your Child's Growth & Learning

**Secondary Subject:**

General Overview

**Age Group:**

Toddlers (1–3)

### Description:

Written by co-founders of the Gesell Institute, this 178-page resource highlights the development of a toddler; much of the book is directed toward the median age of 18 months. Divided into 11 chapters, the first two chapters describe the transitions from babyhood into toddlerhood. Chapter Three offers general characteristics of toddlers including motor, language, social, and emotional changes; the "disequilibrium" apparent between 15 and 21 months is also discussed. Chapter Four describes major "accomplishments and abilities" (language, fine motor, large motor, etc.) and is divided into three month age segments from 12 to 24 months. Chapter Five focuses on toddlers' social interactions with others, while Chapter Six outlines typical daily routines (sleeping, feeding, elimination, bath and dressing). "Techniques" to deal with emerging behavior for this "often difficult year of life" are offered in Chapter Seven. Chapter Eight focuses on the "mental life" of toddlers. Chapter Nine describes differences in children's development. Chapters 10 and 11 offer "real stories" and a quiz for parents. Lists of toys and books for children and adults are included in the three appendixes.

### Evaluation:

Although some information in this book reflects the book's copyright date, parents will glean a good overall picture of the young toddler's emerging abilities, personality, and behavior. Written in a straightforward manner, this guide reflects the historical practices of Dr. Arnold Gesell who was instrumental in child observational studies from the 1930s onwards. While most areas are still pertinent in terms of a toddler's development, some areas should be taken lightly, such as the advice to introduce toddlers to reading at 15 to 18 months; most experts nowadays suggest a much earlier age of three to six months. Additionally, we found the discussion in Chapter Nine rather bizarre as it described variances in children's development. Theories presented suggest that these individual differences occur due to a child's anatomical structure (endomorph, ectomorph, mesomorph), basic level of health, mother-child match, or other reasons; current discussions focus on children's temperament, and the roles of parenting style, environment, and biology. Good as a general guide, we suggest parents use this with other resources to learn about their young toddler.

### Where To Find/Buy:

Bookstores, libraries, or order direct by contacting Dell Readers Service, Box DR, 1540 Broadway, New York, NY 10036.

**General Overviews**

# THE FIRST TWELVE MONTHS OF LIFE
## Your Baby's Growth Month By Month

★★

## Description:

Using a month-by-month format, this 302-page reference provides information on an infant's development from birth to twelve months. There are fourteen "Chapters." The first two offer general information for parents on Caesarean birth and the newborn (basic senses, feeding and sleeping patterns, breastfeeding/bottlefeeding, and more). The next three chapters address the infant's first three months including postpartum blues, depression, colic, baby's schedule, early learning, sensory-motor abilities, vocal and visual stimulation, immunizations, and more. Chapter Six highlights infants' fourth month and their visual powers, exercising baby, introducing solid foods, etc. The remaining eight chapters address specific milestones that appear monthly in an infant's development. Some of these include separation anxiety, language, motion, obedience, independence, and walking to name a few. A book list for parents is included as well as a ten-page index.

## Evaluation:

This reference is a good choice for following an infant's developmental progression on a month-to-month basis during their first year of growth. Although this guide reads much like a textbook for a child development course, its consistent format and style help make it more easily read and less forbidding. The author provides monthly growth charts, numerous black and white photographs, and uses a two-column format throughout. She also supplies an overview at the introduction of each chapter that succinctly captures the main elements of that stage in an infant's growth. Infant development is fully addressed, albeit in a rather dense fashion with few subheadings to break up the text. Many areas of baby care, however, need updating, namely the advice concerning breastfeeding and sleeping positions. Much of the material is supported by such notables as Dr. T. Berry Brazelton and Dr. Mary D. Ainsworth. However, with the 1993 copyright date, this guide might best be used as a supplemental companion to a more current in-depth resource that discusses baby care and child development.

## Where To Find/Buy:

Bookstores and libraries.

**Overall Rating**
★★
Good overall discussion of child development, needs more depth and updating on care

**Design, Ease Of Use**
★★★
Although it reads much like a textbook, parents will gain easy access to subject matter

1–4 Stars

**Author:**
Theresa Caplan

Theresa Caplan is carrying on the vision of Frank Caplan, Founder of the Princeton Center for Infancy and Early Childhood who authored the first edition of this book. She is currently Director of the Center.

**Publisher:**
Perigee Books
(Berkeley Publishing)

**Edition:**
2nd (1993)

**Price:**
$15.95

**Pages/Run Time:**
302

**ISBN:**
0399518045

**Media:**
Book

**Principal Subject:**
Understanding Your Child's Growth & Learning

**Secondary Subject:**
General Overview

**Age Group:**
Infants (0–1)

II. Understanding Your Child's Growth & Learning

## General Overviews

# RIGHT FROM BIRTH
Building Your Child's Foundation For Life—Birth To 18 Months

**Overall Rating**
★★
Scientific facts without translation into any practical or innovative parenting advice

**Design, Ease Of Use**
★★★
Chapters are well-defined, well-organized; scientific info is easily understandable

1–4 Stars

**Author:**
Craig T. Ramey, PhD and Sharon L. Ramey, PhD

Craig and Sharon Ramey are researchers interested in how to permanently enhance the development of children. Over the past 30 years, they have studied children from all walks of life and at every level of development, from "at risk" to gifted.

**Publisher:**
Goddard Press

**Edition:**
1999

**Price:**
$19.95

**Pages/Run Time:**
261

**ISBN:**
0966639715

**Media:**
Book

**Principal Subject:**
Understanding Your Child's Growth & Learning

**Secondary Subject:**
General Overview

**Age Group:**
Infants & Toddlers (0–3)

### Description:

Section One—"What We Have Learned"—consists of ten chapters and addresses child development from a scientific perspective. Here the authors discuss a baby's neurobiology and the effects of emotional and social stimulation on brain development. In addition, the authors present a list of the "Seven Essentials" a baby needs daily from a parent: encouragement, mentoring, celebration, rehearsal, protection, guidance, and communication. Section Two—"Your Baby's Development"—is comprised of six chapters: "Getting Oriented and Building Trust" (the first month), "Discovering the World" (two to three months), "Becoming a Social Being" (four to six months), "Thinking and Experimenting" (seven to ten months), "Independence" (11 to 14 months), and "Self-Competence" (15 to 18 months). At the end of each chapter in Section Two, the authors provide a list of activities a parent can do to address each of the seven essentials outlined in Section One.

### Evaluation:

The authors promise to address three issues concerning parenting. First, they will describe what the newest research really says. Second, they will focus on the child's total development, including growth, learning, social interactions, emotional development, and communication. Third, they will teach the reader how to put that knowledge to good use. The authors achieve two of those promises. What stands out about this book is the recitation of scientific fact after scientific fact. That can be a plus, in that the reader is aware of the sources for the authors' parenting philosophy, a trait often lacking in other parenting how-to books. However, the authors' conclusions are disappointing in their lack of new insight. For example, they state that, "there are noticeable differences in children's rates and levels of development" and that, "babies flourish when their needs get well-timed, trustworthy, positive responses." This is not new. In addition, they often don't answer their own questions, such as "When Should Parents Start to Set Limits?" in their discussion on "Discipline with Forethought and Kindness." The scientific information is worthwhile for those with time to ingest it and draw from it their own practical applications. Those wishing more practical direct advice will want to look elsewhere.

### Where To Find/Buy:

Bookstores and libraries.

**General Overviews**

# YOUR CHILD AT PLAY: ONE TO TWO YEARS
Exploring, Daily Living, Learning, And Making Friends

## Description:

One in a series of four, this 219-page resource details the development of toddlers from the age of one to two. Divided into three parts and 12 chapters, this book was written by two developmental psychologists "as a practical guide for parents who are faced with the everyday challenges of living with a toddler." The book is organized according to topics rather than ages to allow for differences in toddlers' rates of growth. Each part delivers advice to parents as they try to handle the "competing objectives" their toddler faces, such as independence versus independence, learning versus playing, and so on. Part One— "Exploration"—focuses on the various ways toddlers explore their environment along with issues that arise as parents want to encourage exploration but keep it in bounds. Part Two—"Everyday Living"—focuses on the toddler's strife for independence through daily routines such as sleeping, eating, etc. Part Three—"Play and Learning"—explores what the toddler learns through different kinds of play such as physical games, toys, reading books, and interactions with adults, children, and pets.

## Evaluation:

Parents looking for a basic overview of their toddler's growth and development will find it here. This resource, although dated, offers an assortment of short tips from "hundreds of families." It contains advice ranging from how to reasonably accommodate a toddler's desire to play with water to how to maintain one's sanity while going out in public. Not an end-all for subjects such as discipline, beginning toilet training (featured in the next book of the series), or sibling relationships, nonetheless, this book does a good job of reassuring parents that the behaviors their toddler is displaying are most likely "normal." User-friendly in tone, each chapter begins with a typical dialog scene between parents and a toddler highlighting the characteristics discussed in that chapter. Numerous black and white photographs are also included. Providing a general perspective on what to expect or reassurance for behaviors already encountered, this book is good as a starter for other resources that provide more details.

## Where To Find/Buy:

Bookstores and libraries.

---

**Overall Rating**
★★
Good for general overview of a toddler's growth and development

**Design, Ease Of Use**
★★★
Meager index but detailed table of contents suffices; user-friendly language and tone

1–4 Stars

**Author:**
Marilyn Segal, PhD and Don Adcock, PhD

Both authors are development psychologists. Segal is the director of the Family Center at Nova University in Florida and also a professor of human development. Adcock, a professor of early childhood development, is the associate director at the Family Center.

**Publisher:**
Newmarket Press

**Edition:**
1985

**Price:**
$14.95

**Pages/Run Time:**
219

**ISBN:**
0937858536

**Media:**
Book

**Principal Subject:**
Understanding Your Child's Growth & Learning

**Secondary Subject:**
General Overview

**Age Group:**
Toddlers (1–3)

**General Overviews**

# DIARY OF A BABY
What Your Child Sees, Feels, And Experiences

**★★**

**Overall Rating**
★★
Voice of the child seems more poetic than realistic

**Design, Ease Of Use**
★★
Adequate combination of the poetic and factual; age specific sections

1–4 Stars

**Author:**
Daniel N. Stern, MD

Daniel N. Stern, MD is a professor of psychology at the University of Geneva and an adjunct professor of psychiatry at Cornell Medical Center. He is the author of four other parenting books, and is a father of five.

**Publisher:**
BasicBooks
(Perseus Books Group)

**Edition:**
2nd (1998)

**Price:**
$13.00

**Pages/Run Time:**
165

**ISBN:**
0465016405

**Media:**
Book

**Principal Subject:**
Understanding Your Child's Growth & Learning

**Secondary Subject:**
General Overview

**Age Group:**
Infants (0–1)

## Description:

This story is a personal diary of a baby during five different parts of its life: six weeks, four-and-a-half months, 12 months, 20 months, and four years. The background for the author's theory of how a baby views its world is based on three things: a variety of facts based on research, the author's speculations on those facts, and the author's imagination. For each age group, the author believes the baby has a different level of conceptual understanding of its world. At six weeks, the level of understanding is called the "World of Feelings." At four-and-a-half months, it is the "Immediate Social World." At 12 months, it is the "World of Mindscapes." Twenty months is described as the "World of Words," and four years is the "World of Stories." At the beginning of each age group discussion, the author introduces the child's new abilities and capacities. Each age group includes either two or four different experiences, or diary entries, written from the perspective of the baby. Before each diary entry, the author provides the context of the experience. Following each, the author comments on the diary entry and describes what the child has experienced.

## Evaluation:

Stern says that one reason for this book is to fulfill parents' desire to know "what is going on inside [their] baby's head at many key moments." He continues by stating that "it is your interpretations that help her to define herself and structure of her world." However, the voice of Joey, the "baby" who writes the diary entries, is not how one would imagine a baby's thoughts and expressions to be formed. For example, at six weeks the author uses the descriptive "thin and taut" in rather a sophisticated manner. Joey's language at four-and-a-half months also makes comparisons between Mother's face and the sky, clouds, and water. The entries seem less like sincere attempts to delve into the actual mind of a baby and more like an opportunity to showcase the author's talents for poetry and prose. In contrast, the language Joey uses at age four is very realistic of how a four year old expresses himself. Also, in the four-year-old section, the author adds Joey's Story, a verbal interchange that describes the event, in addition to the diary entry. The contrast between the two are clever. The explanations of each age's conceptual levels are moderately interesting, but the interpretations are not enough to make this book worthwhile for a thorough understanding of a baby's developmental process.

## Where To Find/Buy:

Bookstores and libraries.

# MY TODDLER
## The Beginning Of Independence

### Description:

This 217-page guide is from the "Stepping-Stones" series for Christian parents by Dr. Paul Warren of the Minirth Meier New Life Clinics. There are seven chapters primarily focusing on a toddler's development from age one to three. Physical Development is the focus of Chapter One including the topics of what to expect, how to deal with eating habits, potty training, safety, and more; brief highlights of the changes engulfing the "terrible twos" are also given. Chapter Two deals with the toddler's need for independence and dependence; a toddler's negativism, ways to promote their independence, and the caregiver's role are discussed. Social development, language development, and reducing stress in a parent's life are addressed in Three through Five. Chapter Six offers discipline strategies—how to control a one-year-old, historical roots of discipline, the Biblical roots of discipline, positive discipline, and more. Chapter Seven offers the author's closing comments. There is no index. An anecdote format is used throughout.

### Evaluation:

While many other resources detail a toddler's growth and development in more a textbook-like fashion, many readers will appreciate this book's narrative short story format. Dr. Warren's humor and friendly writing tone immediately sets the reader at ease. The book's larger print makes it more easily read than other resources. The table of contents neatly lists major subtopics within the book and the bold subheadings help delineate issues. However, an index would have proved a supportive backup as would bulleted tips, highlights, or chapter summaries. This guide is based on the new King James Version of the Bible and reflects those teachings in a subtle fashion aiming for a balanced approach to childrearing. Warren's underlying message is that parents can build trust and independence within young children by understanding toddlers' physical, mental, social, and emotional needs and development. Parents will find many good tips and strategies here but they'll need other resources for back-up.

### Where To Find/Buy:

Bookstores and libraries, or order direct by calling (800) NEW-LIFE.

**Overall Rating**

★★

Good basic info on understanding and encouraging toddlers with a Christian theme

**Design, Ease Of Use**

★★

Easy to read; table of contents highlights major subtopics but an index would be helpful

1–4 Stars

**Author:**

Dr. Paul Warren

Paul Warren, MD is a behavioral pediatrician, adolescent medicine specialist, medical director of the Minirth Meier New Life Clinic in Richardson, Texas, and maintains an active outpatient practice. He is a popular speaker on child and adolescent issues.

**Publisher:**

Thomas Nelson Publishers

**Edition:**

1994

**Price:**

$10.99

**ISBN:**

0785283471

**Media:**

Book

**Principal Subject:**

Understanding Your Child's Growth & Learning

**Secondary Subject:**

General Overview

**Age Group:**

Toddlers (1–3)

**Overall Rating**
★★
Tone makes reader feel removed; needs clearer tips and suggestions

**Design, Ease Of Use**
★★
Chapter topics are often misleading; author sometimes digresses from book's intent

1–4 Stars

**Author:**
Marilyn Segal, PhD

Marilyn Segal, PhD, is the founder and Dean Emeritus of the Family and School Center in Florida. She has five children and 13 grandchildren. She has written 19 books. She also produces the TV show, "To Reach a Child."

**Publisher:**
Newmarket Press

**Edition:**
2nd (1998)

**Price:**
$16.95

**Pages/Run Time:**
226

**ISBN:**
1557043329

**Media:**
Book

**Principal Subject:**
Understanding Your Child's Growth & Learning

**Secondary Subject:**
General Overview

**Age Group:**
Infants & Toddlers (0–3)

General Overviews

# YOUR CHILD AT PLAY: 2 TO 3 YEARS
Growing Up, Language, And The Imagination

**Description:**

The author of this book uses many tools and more than 100 photographs to describe her concepts and explain her information. One of the volumes in the *Children At Play* series, the author's message is that the child's family members should get down and play with the child on a regular basis, which will enhance the child's growth and learning. She divides the way children play into four categories. The first is about exploring and discovering new things, including finding out how things work, new territories, and new concepts. Everyday living is another way children play. This includes making everyday routines, such as preparing for mealtimes and bedtimes, a learning game. Children of this age also love to help out. Developing relationships and making connections with other people is discussed in a third section. It includes development of a child's sense of self and interactions with others. Language development, including the ability to listen and express, is addressed in the fourth section. Pretending, active and constructive play, and conversations are all reviewed.

**Evaluation:**

The author states that the anecdotal information provided in this book "exemplify playful strategies for inviting compliance and encouraging children to explore, to master new skills, and to engage in imaginative play." At the beginning of each section, Segal describes how that particular type of play encourages a specific area of development. She then generally explains what toddlers like and don't like during this phase, how this phase compares to earlier phases, and the different behaviors that can result due to these developmental phases. Most explanations begin with an anecdote, followed by a description of how that anecdote typifies a two-year-old in that situation. The author explains all of this in a textbook fashion, and her topics sometimes digress from the subject of two-year-olds' play. It would be more helpful to have included a more concise list of activities for child and parent to play, without burying them in anecdotes. Other subjects, such as sibling rivalry, should have been addressed in another context. Perhaps most oddly, when reading this book, one gets the feeling that children are being studied from behind a one-way mirror, instead of down on the floor, as part of the child's world.

**Where To Find/Buy:**

Bookstores, libraries, or order direct by contacting Newmarket Press at 18 East 48th Street, New York, NY 10017.

**General Overviews**

# GETTING TO KNOW YOUR ONE-YEAR-OLD

★★

### Description:

This book is the first in the "Magical Years" series of three. Within this book there are ten chapters and a "Conclusion." There is no index. The first chapter highlights what a parent might expect developmentally from their one-year-old. Chapters Two and Three address physical growth and intellectual development. Language and social development follow in Chapters Four and Five, and emotional development is the focus of Chapter Six. Discipline, the importance of daily routines, and nutrition are the subjects of Chapters Seven through Nine. Chapter 10 provides information on baby proofing and keeping a one-year-old out of harm's way. The conclusion is a reflection of the first year as well as a look ahead. At the beginning of each chapter there is a situational narrative setting the stage for the topic discussed. A question and answer section concludes each chapter. "Time Capsules" recap the developmental milestones within each chapter providing general guidelines for different stages of growth in a progressive manner.

### Evaluation:

This 216-page resource offers good general information on a one-year-old's development up to the second year of their life. Questions about walking expectations, discipline, daily routines, nighttime wakings, and nutrition and weight are just some of the topics addressed in this guide. Unfortunately, much of the information is presented in short, concise blocks leaving the reader begging for more complete details. Parents may find themselves having to plow through some situational content before they reach their desired subject. Some of the chapters, however, do offer additional reading materials that help to complement the chapter's related topic. The "How to Help" sections also help make up for the rather brief explanations. We suggest parents use the authors' bulleted tips and advice within each chapter for quick reference. While not a well-organized text, parents might find this book helpful as a companion to a more comprehensive text.

### Where To Find/Buy:

Bookstores and libraries, or order direct from Publishers Book and Audio Mailing Service, P. O. Box 120159, Staten Island, NY 10312-0004.

---

**Overall Rating**
★★
Snippets of information touching on the major development stages from 13 to 24 months

**Design, Ease Of Use**
★
An index would help to find specific information more easily

1–4 Stars

**Author:**
Janet Poland and Judi Craig, PhD, consulting editor

Poland, writer and former newspaper editor, graduated from Grinnell College, and has a graduate degree in political science from the University of Wisconsin. Craig is a clinical psychologist with more than 27 years experience counseling parents and children.

**Publisher:**
Skylight Press
(St. Martin's Press)

**Edition:**
1995

**Price:**
$4.99

**Pages/Run Time:**
216

**ISBN:**
0312954182

**Media:**
Book

**Principal Subject:**
Understanding Your Child's Growth & Learning

**Secondary Subject:**
General Overview

**Age Group:**
Toddlers (1–3)

II. Understanding Your Child's Growth & Learning

# HOW TO READ YOUR CHILD LIKE A BOOK

**Overall Rating**
★★
Good content, although too concise for most subjects

**Design, Ease Of Use**
★
Vague titles in table of contents; book follows sequentially and smoothly along; no index

1–4 Stars

**Author:**
Lynn Weiss, PhD

Lynn Weiss, PhD, is a child and adult psychotherapist, as well as a marriage, family, and mental health counselor. She also hosts a radio talk show in Dallas/Fort Worth and is a frequent commentator for CNN.

**Publisher:**
Meadowbrook Press
(Simon & Schuster)

**Edition:**
1997

**Price:**
$8.00

**Pages/Run Time:**
213

**ISBN:**
0671521241

**Media:**
Book

**Principal Subject:**
Understanding Your Child's Growth & Learning

**Secondary Subject:**
General Overview

**Age Group:**
Infants & Toddlers (0–3)

## Description:

There are five "developmental stages" to this resource guide. Stage One addresses "Trust" and includes information on children ages birth to eighteen months. It focuses on topics such as crying, fear, irritability, and more. Each topic is further divided into five subtopics: "Your Child's Behavior," "What Your Child May Be Thinking or Feeling," "What It Means," "What To Do," and "What Not To Do." Stage Two addresses "Identity" issues for children eighteen months to three years old. Some of the topics covered are feelings, aggressive behavior, separation anxiety, and more. Stage Three focuses on the "Competence" of three to four year olds and Stage Four explores "Power"—how four and five year olds test and push limits. Stage Five discusses issues of "Self-Control" for children five to six years of age. Following these sections is a section on "Parting Remarks" which talks about responsible parenting. The book concludes with an "Assessment Checklist for Preschoolers" and a resource list. There is no index.

## Evaluation:

This 213-page book does a good job of trying to help the reader comprehend each of the five developmental stages, presenting information in a logical, understandable sequence. However, some of the advice is rather concise and parents may find themselves asking for more information on a specific issue. The table of contents is vague with subtopic titles such as, "Expanding Interests," "Making Things Happen," etc.; a supporting index would have greatly helped this guide. Variances in children's personalities and developmental levels have not been keenly addressed in this guide. The reader will need to look beyond the author's concise suggestions keeping in mind that there is more than one way to address these developmental issues depending upon the personality of their child. Parents will most likely find this resource guide a better companion to a more comprehensive reference, instead of being used as a stand alone cure-all.

## Where To Find/Buy:

Bookstores and libraries, or order direct by calling (800) 338-2232.

**General Overviews**

# RAISING A HAPPY, UNSPOILED CHILD

★★

## Description:
Based upon White's 38 years of observation, this 253-page book focuses on a child's social development and "how to raise an absolutely wonderful 22 month old child." White found that two-year-olds who were socially capable retained those qualities at the age of 6 compared with those children who were "overindulged and spoiled." His study then focused on parent-child interactions in the early months to see how to avoid dealing with the "terrible twos." The introduction explains his methodology. The book is divided into seven chapters. Chapters 1–5 are divided by age range (birth to five-and-a-half months, five-and-a-half to seven-and-a-half months, seven-and-a-half to 12 months, 12 months to 14 months, 14–22–30 months, and 22–30–36 months) and offer development information and suggestions. Subtopics within each chapter include discussions of normal social development, the development of a social style, how to guide your child through this stage, and more. Chapter Six presents "Special Topics" such as "hazards" (late parenting, prematurity, etc.), effects of caregivers and grandparents, and more. Chapter Seven offers White's concluding remarks.

## Evaluation:
White's research is one of the few studies based on natural observations of children in their homes. His research methodology is well-outlined, extensive, and somewhat scientifically founded; White admits that neither he nor anyone else has developed a reliable measure for the many facets of a baby's social development. This leaves the reader questioning the study's objectivity especially when reading what seems to be White's personal opinion at times. Will White's suggestions actually work—can parents avoid the "terrible twos" by following his advice as they "discipline" their baby at the critical stage from five-and-a-half months to seven-and-a-half months? It's up to parents to read his work and adopt or reject his philosophy according to their own parenting beliefs. His writing style tends to be heavy textually, not making for light reading. But all that aside, White offers an in-depth glimpse at the inner workings and interactions of the young child. If parents can distinguish between White's personal opinion and child development facts, they will enjoy reading about the changes their child goes through.

## Where To Find/Buy:
Bookstores and libraries.

**Overall Rating**
★★
Interesting glimpse at a child's social development but based on a questionable study

**Design, Ease Of Use**
★
Textbook-like; vague table of contents; good summaries at end of chapters; index given

1–4 Stars

**Author:**
Burton L. White

White is the director of the Center for Parent Education in Newton, Massachusetts, and the designer of the Missouri New Parents as Teachers Project. He is the father of four (now grown) children and lives in Waban, Massachusetts.

**Publisher:**
Fireside (Simon & Schuster)

**Edition:**
1995

**Price:**
$11.00

**ISBN:**
0684801345

**Media:**
Book

**Principal Subject:**
Understanding Your Child's Growth & Learning

**Secondary Subject:**
General Overview

**Age Group:**
Infants & Toddlers (0–3)

★★

**Overall Rating**
★★
Brief, basic information given; best used as a refresher by busy already informed parents

**Design, Ease Of Use**
★
Navigation frustrating at times; no index, broad table of contents' titles

1–4 Stars

**Author:**
Janet Poland and Judi Craig, PhD, consulting editor

Poland, writer and former newspaper editor, graduated from Grinnell College, and has a graduate degree in political science from the University of Wisconsin. Craig is a clinical psychologist with more than 27 years experience counseling parents and children.

**Publisher:**
Skylight Press (St. Martin's Press)

**Edition:**
1995

**Price:**
$4.99

**Pages/Run Time:**
212

**ISBN:**
0312955820

**Media:**
Book

**Principal Subject:**
Understanding Your Child's Growth & Learning

**Secondary Subject:**
General Overview

**Age Group:**
Toddlers (1–3)

# SURVIVING YOUR TWO-YEAR OLD

## Description:

There are ten chapters in this resource focusing on what to expect developmentally from a child when they reach 30 to 36 months of age. Chapters discussed within the book include information on physical growth along with intellectual, language, emotional, and social development. Also provided are suggestions on how to set limits, the importance of daily routines, food and nutrition, and tips and advice on safety (in the house, around water, outdoors, and toys). At the beginning of each chapter there is a situational narrative setting the stage for the topic discussed. A general preview is also given that highlights the major points of the topic to be addressed. Within each chapter there are "How to Help" sections, as well as a concluding "Time Capsule" section which provides an overview of the material presented. Additionally, each chapter has a concluding question and answer section which provides situational problems and options for a variety of solutions. There is no index.

## Evaluation:

One of three in the "Magical Years" series, this 212-page book attempts to address issues such as how to encourage creativity, when to correct your child's language use, how to cope with disobedience, and when to teach reading and writing. This resource provides good elementary information with some hands-on techniques. While the topics addressed are all important, unfortunately the author fails to do justice to the issues by not providing enough detail. The bulleted "How to Help" sections and the "Time Capsules" sections are both highlights of the book and best used by busy parents who need a quick refresher on any given subject matter. A cross-referenced index should have been included since the table of contents provides rather broad and vague titles. For general bare bones basics about a two-year-old's development, this book will do; but parents seeking a more comprehensive text will want to use this guide only as an informational companion.

## Where To Find/Buy:

Bookstores and libraries, or order direct from Publishers Book and Audio Mailing Service, P. O. Box 120159, Staten Island, NY 10312-0004.

**General Overviews**

# CHILD DEVELOPMENT: THE FIRST TWO YEARS
A Comprehensive Guide To Enhancing Your Child's Physical And Mental Development

## Description:

Divided into five age segments, this 47 minute videotape describes developmental changes for babies and toddlers. The first segment (birth to three months) offers general information about physical development, feeding (breastfeeding and bottlefeeding), the importance of touching and bonding, and ways to stimulate your baby. Segment Two (three to six months) discusses the how-tos of introducing solids along with advice on using playpens and interacting with your baby. The next segment illustrates the developmental changes that occur between the ages of six and 12 months as many babies gain head and lower body control, added mobility, and motor skills such as crawling, pulling to stand, and walking. Tips on childproofing, introducing finger foods, and language acquisition are provided. The final two age segments are combined (12 to 18 months; 18 to 24 months) and feature developmental information about toddlers. Suggested milestones for physical development, language skills, and emotional development are given.

## Evaluation:

As parents watch this video, they will no doubt be captivated by the engaging footage of babies going about the process of growing up. However, the accompanying information is bleak and does not do justice to such an important topic. For example, considerable footage is used to show a baby exploring his food bowl, yet little time is given to how language develops (other than constant reminders to talk to your baby). Extensive time is afforded to how to read a commercial baby food jar, while insignificant time is allowed for discussing children's cognitive development; no mention is made of cause-effect relationships, object permanence, and other facets important for baby's mental growth and social development. The video is divided into neat little age packages, but the narration jumps around. One minute the narrator discusses a baby's early growth, but the next minute, she discusses a toddlers' physical development. A continuum of how a baby changes into a toddler is useful but in this videotape it gets confusing. Other videotapes offer more in-depth information on this important subject. Check out those resources over this one.

## Where To Find/Buy:

Bookstores, libraries, videotape dealers, or order direct by calling (212) 674-5550. It can also be ordered through Library Video Company at (800) 843-3620, through FAX at (610) 645-4040, or online at http://www.libraryvideo.com.

---

**Overall Rating**
★
Minimal information on many facets of child development

**Design, Ease Of Use**
★★
Engaging videotape footage; narration confusing (jumps around age group to age group)

1–4 Stars

**Publisher:**
V.I.E.W.

**Edition:**
1993

**Price:**
$24.98

**ISBN:**
0803015232

**Media:**
Videotape

**Principal Subject:**
Understanding Your Child's Growth & Learning

**Secondary Subject:**
General Overview

**Age Group:**
Infants & Toddlers (0–3)

## General Overviews

# MADELEINE'S WORLD
## A Child's Journey From Birth To Age Three

**Overall Rating**

★

Author uses the medium of a novel to record his daughter's growth from infancy to age 3

**Design, Ease Of Use**

★

No way to reference this novel; chapters related to child's age would have been helpful

1–4 Stars

**Author:**

Brian Hall

Hall has written two novels, two nonfiction books, and articles for various magazines. He lives in upstate New York with his wife and two daughters.

**Publisher:**

Houghton Mifflin

**Edition:**

1997

**Price:**

$20.00

**ISBN:**

0395870593

**Media:**

Book

**Principal Subject:**

Understanding Your Child's Growth & Learning

**Secondary Subject:**

General Overview

**Age Group:**

Infants & Toddlers (0–3)

### Description:

The author, a father of two daughters, has written this biography to record the growth of his daughter, Madeleine, as she progress from being an infant to a three year old. Divided into three parts with numerous chapters within each, he uses humor, observation, and developmental information to chart his daughter's developmental milestones. This 262-page novel also includes a bibliography list of "Madeleine's Books." No table of contents or index are included.

### Evaluation:

Novel approach, yes, but easily read, not necessarily. This novel is written in three parts and one might assume each part pertains to one year of Madeleine's development, but this isn't so. It would have been perhaps mundane, but more useful, to have chapters that pertained to each month of a child's life. Even though children develop at different rates, this would have improved the reader's ability to hunt for a particular phase. Certainly entertaining at times, Hall's style is overly doting and precious as he writes about his daughter's motives. His writing aptly expresses the wonderment he senses from his daughter as she learns about the world around her. He also sprinkles developmental information within the confines of this journalistic work. This is a cute way to introduce parents to how children develop, but unfortunately a bit too cute at times, giving the reader the sense that the author is too close to his subject to be impartial. This one is not great for a quick or seasoned view of infant and child development, but good for parents who are looking for a model on how to record their own child's development.

### Where To Find/Buy:

Bookstores and libraries.

**General Overviews**

# THE MAGIC YEARS
Understanding And Handling The Problems Of Early Childhood

## Description:

Written by a past professor of child psychoanalysis, this 305-page resource discusses childhood fears, anxieties, and neurosis in its aim to promote mental health within children. Divided into five parts, with nine chapters, this guide relies heavily on the writings of Anna Freud (ego psychology, early childhood development), Rene Spitz (psychology of infancy), Heinz Hartmann and Ernst Kris (psychoanalytic ego psychology), and Jean Piaget (child's construct of reality). The author states that the information provided comes from case studies in which the child's history has allowed emotional disturbances to develop, but that it is difficult to definitively describe how to avoid these disturbances. Part One focuses on anxiety, the ego, mental health, and more. Parts Two, Three, and Four respectively discuss characteristics and conflicts facing the child during the first eighteen months, from 18 months to three years, and from three years to six years of age. A conclusion is provided in Part Six along with a three-page index.

## Evaluation:

Not a book for the faint of heart who haven't the time to concentrate and discern the author's intent, this book is packed with psychoanalytical jargon and heavy rhetoric. For those parents who prefer theory mixed with suggested practice, we recommend they select other resources offering a more balanced approach in discussing children's cognitive, emotional, and social development. The bottom line premise of this book is good. It concludes that "parents need not be paragons; they may be inexperienced, they may be permitted to err . . . to employ sometimes a wrong method or an unendorsed technique," but that as long as the bonds between parent and child are strong, they have a good chance of rearing a mentally healthy child. Unfortunately, this message often gets lost in the shuffle between the author's espousing of her psychoanalytic background and the case studies she presents. Suited more for the educator who can deliver this message more concretely to parents, save this one for when you have ample time on your hands, the ability to concentrate, or nothing better to read.

## Where To Find/Buy:

Bookstores and libraries.

---

**Overall Rating**

★

Strictly based on psychoanalytic studies, this resource emphasizes parent-child bond

**Design, Ease Of Use**

★

Heavy rhetorical text with substantial psychoanalytic discussions; minimal index

---

1–4 Stars

**Author:**

Selma H. Fraiberg

Fraiberg was professor of child psychoanalysis and director of the Infant-Parent Program of San Francisco General Hospital, University of California School of Medicine. Her articles were published widely in professional and popular magazines.

**Publisher:**

Fireside (Simon & Schuster)

**Edition:**

1996

**Price:**

$12.00

**Pages/Run Time:**

305

**ISBN:**

0684825503

**Media:**

Book

---

**Principal Subject:**

Understanding Your Child's Growth & Learning

**Secondary Subject:**

General Overview

**Age Group:**

Infants & Toddlers (0–3)

**Overall Rating**
★★★★
Great comprehensive resource for all parents and caregivers—a "must have"

**Design, Ease Of Use**
★★★★
Age-appropriate contents; detailed chronological index useful for referencing

1–4 Stars

**Author:**
Elaine Martin

**Publisher:**
Running Press Book Publishers

**Edition:**
1988

**Price:**
$12.95

**Pages/Run Time:**
183

**ISBN:**
0894716174

**Media:**
Book

**Principal Subject:**
Understanding Your Child's Growth & Learning

**Secondary Subject:**
Activities & Games

**Age Group:**
Infants & Toddlers (0–3)

# BABY GAMES
The Joyful Guide To Child's Play From Birth To Three Years

**Recommended For:**
Understanding Your Child's Growth & Learning

## Description:

This revised and updated 183-page book is organized into twelve chapters and culls a wide variety of activities. The author suggests that the book be used as a play resource to find the child's and parent's own favorite games and rhythms of play. The first six chapters relate to activities in infancy and are broken down into three month time frames; subsequent chapters represent six month time frames because of the developmental pattern changes that occur at about eighteen months. The author, however, advises not limiting oneself to the book's timetables and categories, but rather to use the entire book depending upon the needs of the child and parent. Chapter One, then, begins with activities for ages birth to three months, progressing through Chapter Nine with activities for children 30 to 36 months of age. Movement, water play, music, kitchen and art activities, indoor and outdoor games—all are presented. Chapter Ten lists recordings, television, video/computer programs, books, and public entertainment resources. Information about toys and birthday/holiday activities are also given.

## Evaluation:

This book's strength lies in its organizational elements. The index, divided into ten sections, lists all activities for quick and easy use. The music section includes traditional folk songs and rhymes and the specific locality or country of origin has been indicated (when possible). Some unusual art activities include colored pasta, string painting, or Jell-O painting. Other sections include word play, changing/dressing games, and quiet activities. The "Calendar of Holidays" (within Chapter 12's "Birthdays, Unbirthdays, Holiday, and Other Excuses for a Party") gives a thoughtful and informative review of traditional holidays celebrated in various countries. Groundhog's Day, New Year's, Shrovetide, Afrikomen, Mardi Gras, and Sham-al-Nessin are but a sampling. Books, poems, songs, games, activities, and more are included for most holidays. This guidebook is well written with a wealth of information for parents, teachers, and caregivers. It is a helpful, entertaining resource to be kept close at hand.

## Where To Find/Buy:

Bookstores and libraries, or order direct from Running Press Book Publishers at 125 South Twenty-second Street, Philadelphia, Pennsylvania 19103.

**Activities & Games**

# GAMES TO PLAY WITH TWO YEAR OLDS

**Recommended For:**
Understanding Your Child's Growth & Learning

## Description:

The author organizes the activities and games into the following categories: language, running and jumping, animal, car, art, counting, teddy bear, imagination, nursery rhyme games, singing games, cooking games, nature games, and quiet games. Within each category, the games are further divided into the age groups of young twos, middle twos, and older twos. The table of contents lists each game in its appropriate category, then identifies which skills that particular game helps to develop, such as language, creativity, imagination, self-expression, thinking, listening, imitation, observation, fun, coordination, body awareness, and many others. The index lists the games, either by name or major component (such as crayons). Prior to the descriptions of these games, the author describes the guidelines for growth of skills in the following categories: motor, auditory and visual skills; language and cognitive skills; and self-concept skills.

## Evaluation:

This book is a simple listing of games and activities that are age appropriate for two-year-old children. Each game is described on one-page and requires only a few simple steps. All the games assume the involvement of another person, including the activities in the section about car games. Many of the games involve, of course, pretending and singing. A minimum amount of pre-play preparation, such as cutting out pictures from a magazine, is required for some of the games. The beauty of this book is that the games do not require a lot of expensive toys or other props. For example, puppets in the puppet game are made out of popsicle sticks and stickers. Because so few and only basic props are required, these activities would be the saving grace of keeping a two-year-old entertained in circumstances where a child could easily become restless, such as on an airplane, in a waiting room, or any formal function. Every parent should keep a copy of this book on hand.

## Where To Find/Buy:

Bookstores, libraries, or order direct by contacting Gryphon House, Inc. at 10726 Tucker Street, Beltsville, MD 20705.

---

**Overall Rating**
★★★★
Excellent games that don't require a lot of props, rather creativity and imagination

**Design, Ease Of Use**
★★★★
A few simple instructions on one page; all games listed by skill and age

1–4 Stars

**Author:**
Jackie Silberg

Jackie Silberg has spent years working with young children. Through her radio and television appearances, parenting workshops, and seminars, she has shown thousands of parents and teachers how to make learning exciting for young children.

**Publisher:**
Gryphon House

**Edition:**
1993

**Price:**
$14.95

**Pages/Run Time:**
279

**ISBN:**
0876591691

**Media:**
Book

---

**Principal Subject:**
Understanding Your Child's Growth & Learning

**Secondary Subject:**
Activities & Games

**Age Group:**
Toddlers (1–3)

II. Understanding Your Child's Growth & Learning

★★★★

## Overall Rating
★★★★
Outstanding array of activity categories, open-ended and based on discovery approach

## Design, Ease Of Use
★★★★
Detailed table of contents makes up for lack of index; attractive with explicit drawings

1–4 Stars

## Author:
Amy Nolan

Nolan has a BFA in art and an MS in elementary education. She has been affiliated with The Children's Museum in Boston for the past seven years, first as the manager of Playspace and later as a freelance writer.

## Publisher:
Pocket Books
(Simon & Schuster)

## Edition:
1997

## Price:
$12.00

## Pages/Run Time:
245

## ISBN:
0671528572

## Media:
Book

## Principal Subject:
Understanding Your Child's Growth & Learning

## Secondary Subject:
Activities & Games

## Age Group:
Toddlers (1–3)

Activities & Games

# GREAT EXPLORATIONS
100 Creative Play Ideas For Parents And Preschoolers From Playspace At The Children's Museum Boston

## Recommended For:
Understanding Your Child's Growth & Learning

## Description:
Developed by the manager of Playspace (part of the Children's Museum in Boston), this 245-page resource offers the center's favorite art, science, music, cooking, and dramatic play experiences. The age-appropriate activities focus on the "whole" child, emphasize a discovery-based approach to learning, are open-ended, and involve simple, inexpensive materials. The author's intent is for activities and materials to be "as accessible as possible to as many people as possible." Activities are grouped according to categories—arts and crafts, science, outside, seasonal, quiet, music and movement, pretend play, and cooking. Each activity usually is explained in two pages with a list of materials, recommended ages, length of time needed, directions, "what your child is learning," and ways to extend the activity. Additional sections offer information about Playspace's philosophy, the role of play in a child's development, the rationale behind the activities that were chosen, how to get started, what basic supplies should be kept on hand, how to set up the activities, where to buy supplies, how to display a child's work, and more.

## Evaluation:
Parents won't find any other book of activities that beats this one. It's chockfull of a wide range of activities, not just placing emphasis on art, language, or other areas that are generally the focus of other resources. For example, many other resources neglect some categories and skills such as science, pretend play, self-expression, mathematics, cooking, and problem-solving. This guide includes all these arenas and more. All activities are developmentally sound with the process highlighted and not the product. The author offers parents the opportunity to extend the activities inviting a continuation of the learning experience. Although designed specifically for children between the ages of 18 months and five years, the author also provides a section that explains how activities can be adapted for younger and older children. Some of the activities may take a little more parent time in getting set up than others, but this book offers parents and their child excellent ideas for engaging in play together.

## Where To Find/Buy:
Bookstores, libraries, or order direct by contacting Mail Order Department, Simon & Schuster, Inc., 200 Old Tappan Rd., Old Tappan, NJ 07675.

**Activities & Games**

# I LOVE YOU RITUALS
Activities To Build Bonds And Strengthen Relationships With Children

★★★★

**Recommended For:**
Understanding Your Child's Growth & Learning

## Description:

*I Love You Rituals* is a collection of activities and games to play with children. Most of the activities involve touch, with the goal of bringing adult and child closer together in a warm, healthy relationship. The author writes, "I love you rituals put life in focus, shifting from getting ahead to getting together and from valuing material wealth to valuing one another." This 208-page book has 11 chapters. Chapters One through Three give some information and background about the emotional, psychological, and physical needs of children. Also discussed in these chapters are reasons why children and adults need these rituals and interactions. Chapters Four through Eleven present the activities and games. They are divided by chapters according to types of games. For example, there are "Positive Nursery Rhymes," "Interactive Finger Plays," "Silly Interactions," "Relaxing Games," "Cuddling and Snuggling Games," and more. The author also addresses the subject of abused children in parts of the book. Additionally, Bailey gives specific advice for activities that may cause negative reactions in abused children.

## Evaluation:

This is a delightful book that most adults need. It also serves as a terrific reminder that children and the time spent with them are ultimately more important than our busy schedules and to-do lists. The easy-to-read format of this book, with its large print and animated illustrations, makes this book inviting and fun rather than a chore to read. Activities and games are so easy to pick out, that parents can open the book to virtually any page (after Chapter Three) and find something fun to do with their child. Bailey's underlying goal behind these activities, besides the mere fun of doing them, is the investment in children to help them grow, develop, and bond in a healthy way. Chapters One, Two, and Three, which discuss topics such as why children need touch and rituals and how adults can become better parents and caregivers, are general but very informative. Bailey's sensitivity toward and concern for abused children are reflected in her discussions on abused children and ways to help these children. This resource will find itself well-loved and well-used in any parenting library.

## Where To Find/Buy:

Bookstores, libraries, or order direct by calling (800) 842-2846 or (407) 366-0233. It can also be ordered by Fax at (407) 366-4293 or through Loving Guidance at P.O. Box 622407, Ovieda, FL 32762.

**Overall Rating**
★★★★
Activities and games are fun and help build bonds between child and adult

**Design, Ease Of Use**
★★★★
Extremely easy to use and read, with many delightful illustrations

1–4 Stars

**Author:**
Dr. Becky Bailey

Dr. Becky Bailey is an associate professor at the University of Central Florida and the president of Loving Guidance, Inc. She is a highly acclaimed, dynamic speaker known nationally for her books, lectures, and workshops.

**Publisher:**
Loving Guidance

**Edition:**
2nd (1997)

**Price:**
$19.95

**Pages/Run Time:**
208

**ISBN:**
1889609056

**Media:**
Book

**Principal Subject:**
Understanding Your Child's Growth & Learning

**Secondary Subject:**
Activities & Games

**Age Group:**
Infants & Toddlers (0–3)

**Activities & Games**

★★★★

**Overall Rating**
★★★★
Inspiring story will inspire parents to view the more immediate world of their child

**Design, Ease Of Use**
★★★★
Simple narrative story format coupled with beautiful photographs works well

1–4 Stars

**Author:**
Rachel Carson

Rachel Carson, the late "the patron saint of the environmental movement," authored the text of *The Sense of Wonder*. Photographer Nick Kelsh, coauthor of *Naked Babies* with Anna Quindlen, lives in Philadelphia with his family.

**Publisher:**
HarperCollins

**Edition:**
2nd (1998)

**Price:**
$20.00

**Pages/Run Time:**
107

**ISBN:**
006757520X

**Media:**
Book

**Principal Subject:**
Understanding Your Child's Growth & Learning

**Secondary Subject:**
Activities & Games

**Age Group:**
Infants & Toddlers (0–3)

# THE SENSE OF WONDER

**Recommended For:**
Understanding Your Child's Growth & Learning

**Description:**
Author Rachel Carson originally wrote this story in 1956 as an essay entitled "Help Your Child to Wonder." In 1964, she expanded the essay into this story. It was published posthumously in 1965. When photographer Kelsh read Carson's story, he was inspired to create a set of photographs to augment the story for a new edition. Kelsh received the help of Carson's biographer, who wrote the introduction and explained the background of this story. It was written about Carson's experiences with her young nephew and their adventures in the Maine wilderness. The story is written to reflect the importance of developing and maintaining a child's sense of wonder and also is about retrieving one's own sense of wonder to share with the child. Kelsh's photography supplements the story with photographs of the natural world: artful close ups of insects on tree bark, autumn leaves, stones on a beach, as well as pounding surf and forest scenes.

**Evaluation:**
All of the self-help and how-to books on the market struggle to be the most complete and up-to-date authority on how to raise a happy, healthy child. This story, written in 1964, takes a small aspect of parenting—developing a sense of wonder in a child—and through it instills in the reader the desire to be the best parent there is. "If a child is to keep alive his inborn sense of wonder without any such gift from the fairies, he needs the companionship of at least one adult who can share it, rediscovering with him the joy, excitement, and mystery of the world we live in," Carson writes. The photographer, so inspired by reading the original story, developed a series of photographs to illustrate what he believed the author was trying to express. Throughout the book are stunning photographs of the natural world. This book seems more like a coffee table book than a manuscript to teach one how to parent, and that is why this book works. It allows the reader, parent or not, to step back and take a look at the world around him and appreciate all that is good. The resulting inspiration is sure to enhance one's parenting instincts.

**Where To Find/Buy:**
Bookstores and libraries.

**Activities & Games**

# TREASURED TIME WITH YOUR TODDLER
## A Monthly Guide To Activities

**Recommended For:**
Understanding Your Child's Growth & Learning

## Description:

The activities listed are divided into sections, each pertaining to a month of the year. There are four or five activities listed for each month, depending on the number of weeks in that month, and generally activities are related to that month's theme. The themes, or treasures as the author calls them, for the months are: January, winter; February, love; March, music and movement; April, spring; May, the outdoors; June, summer; July, freedom; August, beating the heat; September, color and shapes; October, counting and ABCs; November, thankfulness; and December, holiday. Each weekly chapter includes book suggestions, recipes, verses or songs, and activities. Weekly themes are borrowed from a nursery rhyme or Mother Goose rhyme. In the beginning of the book, the author supplies a list of materials to have on hand. At the beginning of each month, the author describes the theme of the month, how it can be related to the toddler's development, related weekly themes, and other thoughts.

## Evaluation:

"Children's literature is a wonderful foundation on which to base a child's entire education," and Mother Goose stories and rhymes are still powerful ways to introduce children to literature, author Brennan believes. That is why each weekly theme is related to a Mother Goose or other nursery rhyme. As good a place as any to start. This book has the look and feel of a great big coloring book, which can itself be a joy for a reader, because it gives him or her the excuse of playing with baby to partake in a little joyful down-at-eye-level playing. There is a wonderful mix of suggested books to read (descriptions included), songs based on familiar melodies, recipes for food and homemade concoctions, and activities such as games, exercise, and plays. The weekly themes purposefully attempt to teach the child something about his life or environment. For example, being sick is one of the weekly themes in January (appropriate for many children at this time of year). One weekly theme in March, "Wee Willie Winkie," teaches a child about sleep and going-to-bed routines. Books, recitations, recipes, and all activities are then centered around this theme. This book, combined with a box full of the recommended supplies, would make an excellent gift for parent or toddler.

## Where To Find/Buy:

Bookstores, libraries, or order direct by calling (800) 284-8784 or (501) 372-5450.

★★★★

**Overall Rating**
★★★★
Activities are organized by themes important to toddler; they teach and entertain

**Design, Ease Of Use**
★★★★
Organized chronologically by month; themes are clever, interesting, and relevant

1–4 Stars

**Author:**
Jan Brennan

Jan Brennan holds a BA in child development and an MS in reading. She homeschools her three sons in Connecticut.

**Publisher:**
August House

**Edition:**
1991

**Price:**
$14.95

**Pages/Run Time:**
189

**ISBN:**
187483127X

**Media:**
Book

**Principal Subject:**
Understanding Your Child's Growth & Learning

**Secondary Subject:**
Activities & Games

**Age Group:**
Toddlers (1–3)

II. Understanding Your Child's Growth & Learning

★★★★

## Overall Rating
★★★★
300 commonplace and unusual games, many of them accompanied by songs or rhymes

## Design, Ease Of Use
★★★
Activities listed alphabetically or by category; list of skills practiced would be useful

1–4 Stars

## Author:
Jackie Silberg

Silberg presents concerts, workshops and keynote addresses at early childhood conferences all over the U.S. She holds a MS degree in early childhood education from Emporia State University in Kansas where she is a Distinguished Alumna.

## Publisher:
Gryphon House

## Edition:
1997

## Price:
$12.95

## Pages/Run Time:
191

## ISBN:
0876591829

## Media:
Book

## Principal Subject:
Understanding Your Child's Growth & Learning

## Secondary Subject:
Activities & Games

## Age Group:
Toddlers (1–3)

## Activities & Games

# 300 THREE MINUTE GAMES
## Quick And Easy Activities For 2–5 Year Olds

### Recommended For:
Understanding Your Child's Growth & Learning

### Description:
Designed to be used as a companion to one of Silberg's many other books (500 Five Minute Games), this 191-page book offers 300 "stimulating games that challenge the imagination" and are age-appropriate for toddlers and preschoolers. Silberg is an "acclaimed speaker, teacher, and trainer on early childhood development and music." Activities within her book are grouped within 14 categories including animal games, bath games, book games, exercise games, imagination games, music games, outside games, quiet games, storytelling games, stuck inside games, stuffed animal games, thinking games, transition games, and waiting games. Poems, rhymes, or songs accompany most activities. Step-by-step directions are given along with occasional black line drawings. A skill or concept that is practiced by doing the activity is also provided. These skills range from "develops imagination" to "practices language skills" to "teaches about propulsion." An index lists activities alphabetically by name.

### Evaluation:
This is definitely one of Silberg's better books. She does an excellent job here of compiling the more commonplace activities ("Playing in the Tub"—bring all sorts of unbreakable things into the tub) with the more unusual, often humorous activities ("Here's Some Soup"—pretend to make soup in the tub and add all sorts of vegetables while you stir it . . . but, with the admonition "Do not drink the bath water"). Not just for fun, these games are also developmentally sound. Heavy emphasis is placed on language skills and young children will delight in the rhythms of the poems, songs, and rhymes included with many of the activities. Silberg's other books list activities by recommended age of the child. This one does not, leaving the assessment of the activity's success up to the parent and child where it rightfully belongs since no two children's developments are alike. Many activities seem more geared toward the two and three year old range, but parents can, of course, adapt and expand these activities for the older preschooler. This would make a great gift for parents of toddlers or preschoolers at their child's birthday.

### Where To Find/Buy:
Bookstores and libraries.

**Activities & Games**

# 365 OUTDOOR ACTIVITIES YOU CAN DO WITH YOUR CHILD

**Recommended For:**

Understanding Your Child's Growth & Learning

## Description:

This 430-page book offers parents "activities that foster a love of learning and a sense of family, neighborhood, and community." The 365 activities fall into 25 categories. They are grouped alphabetically in the table of contents and the body of the book and by category in the index. Categories include: backyard fun, beach activities, environmental activities, gardening, imagination games, natural science, old-fashioned games, seasonal activities, recycled/reused household materials, sports, toys and gadgets, and more. Each activity is fully contained on one-page and includes a list of materials in the margin along with safety reminders and optional materials when applicable. Also included is a small illustration for each activity along with a narrative description of how to do the activity. The authors' safety tips are included in the introduction along with suggested tips for outdoor play ("tailor the competition to your child," "foster team spirit," etc.). Advice is also given on how to use this book to reduce indoor TV watching.

## Evaluation:

Not involving a lot of preparation, the ideas in this compact (4" x 6") little book will be of great help for parents intent on either reliving games and adventures from their youth and/or or intent on eliminating (or limiting) their family's TV watching and/or coming up with fun, spontaneous ways of interacting with their children outdoors. Although many of the activities are designed more for elementary school-aged children, creative parents of toddlers and preschoolers will be able to adapt many of these activities for their child. The suggested activities are open-ended, prepared easily and spontaneously, and complete with understandable directions. Many activity resources focus on arts and crafts. This resource, then, is a great idea book about what one can do with one's child outside the house and fills the gap left by other resources.

## Where To Find/Buy:

Bookstores and libraries.

**★★★★**

**Overall Rating**
★★★★
Fun, easily prepared games and adventures generally using very little materials

**Design, Ease Of Use**
★★★
Arranged alphabetically and by category; age group categories would be helpful too

1–4 Stars

**Author:**
Steve Bennett and Ruth Bennett

Steve Bennett has written more than 35 books in the fields of parenting, family computing, and business management. Ruth Bennett is a landscape architect who has designed parks, playgrounds, and public places in many U.S. cities. They have 2 children and live TV-free.

**Publisher:**
Adams Media

**Edition:**
1993

**Price:**
$6.95

**Pages/Run Time:**
430

**ISBN:**
1558502602

**Media:**
Book

**Principal Subject:**
Understanding Your Child's Growth & Learning

**Secondary Subject:**
Activities & Games

**Age Group:**
Infants & Toddlers (0–3)

II. Understanding Your Child's Growth & Learning

Activities & Games

**★★★★**

**Overall Rating**
★★★★
Comprehensive guide primarily beneficial for caregivers and educators of infants

**Design, Ease Of Use**
★★★
Icons show ages for activities; good table of contents & section indexes, no main index

1–4 Stars

**Author:**
Debby Cryer, Thelma Harms, and Beth Bourland

Ms. Cryer, Harms, and Bourland are with the Frank Porter Graham Child Development Center, University of North Carolina, Chapel Hill, North Carolina

**Publisher:**
Addison-Wesley Longman (Addison-Wesley Publishing)

**Edition:**
1987

**Price:**
$23.25

**Pages/Run Time:**
193

**ISBN:**
0201213346

**Media:**
Book

**Principal Subject:**
Understanding Your Child's Growth & Learning

**Secondary Subject:**
Activities & Games

**Age Group:**
Infants (0–1)

# ACTIVE LEARNING FOR INFANTS

**Recommended For:**
Understanding Your Child's Growth & Learning

**Description:**

This 193-page activity guidebook is one of five in a series. This comprehensive book is made up of four activity sections and a planning guide for those working with infants, newborn to 12 months of age. Section One—"Planning for Infants"—includes ideas for developing a schedule, making interest centers, and an environment that is positive; a sequential developmental list of what "Baby Can" do are also offered. Section Two—"Activities for Listening and Talking"—contains activities (books, pictures, conversation, etc.) that promote talking and listening. "Activities for Physical Development" offers ideas to develop babies' large and small muscles. Section Four—"Creative Activities"—uses art, blocks, dramatic play, and music to develop babies' senses, imagination, and art enjoyment. The final section, "Activities for Learning from the World Around Them" focuses on nature, numbers, the five senses, size, shape, and color. Separate indexes are included for each section. Each activity contains an icon corresponding to the age range (0 to five months, five to nine months, nine to 12 months) appropriate for the activity.

**Evaluation:**

One of Addison-Wesley's "Active Learning Series," this reference specifically focuses on the newborn to one year old infant. It provides numerous developmental activities covering the areas of creativity, community, listening and talking, physical development, and learning about the environment. The book does not have an overall index but it does have a detailed table of contents and section indexes. Each activity includes: skills the baby will need, where the activity can be done (indoors, outdoors), how long it could take, and how many babies can do the activity; the icons give a quick visual cue for caregivers trying to find an age-appropriate activity. Although designed primarily for educators of young infants, this guidebook will also be a useful reference for parents seeking ideas and suggestions on things to do with their baby. The checklists and materials lists are invaluable sources for organizing one's self and guiding an infant's education. Parents will benefit from buying the series; these will be a much used resource.

**Where To Find/Buy:**
Bookstores and libraries.

**Activities & Games**

# MORE THINGS TO DO WITH TODDLERS AND TWOS

**Recommended For:**
Understanding Your Child's Growth & Learning

## Description:

This 212-page book containing 17 chapters was written for parents as well as teachers and caregivers of toddlers. The chapters generally are organized by types of activities. Some of the chapter subjects/ activities include cognitive development activities, learning to communicate, communicating with music, getting in touch with senses, art, pretending (dramatic play), gross motor development, and social development. Things to make, experiments, songs to sing, playground activities, and more are provided in these chapters. Chapters at the end of the book focus more on the adults (teacher or parent)—developing a curriculum, discussions about children's behaviors, developing routines, handling problem behavior, and the parent-teacher relationship. A list of resources related to the chapter subjects/activities is given at the end of most chapters. In the last chapter of the book, the author speaks personally to those in the early childhood profession about "staying alive and growing" in that profession. The book does not include an index.

## Evaluation:

Karen Miller provides numerous fun, creative activities and ideas in her book. This book, which is a sequel to her *Things To Do With Toddlers And Twos*, is a welcome supplement to the first book. Parents who do not already have the first book, however, may want to get a copy, as *More Things To Do With Toddlers And Twos* periodically references activities from the first book. Not only does *More Things To Do With Toddlers and Twos* provide activities and ideas for parents and caregivers who need help in the creative department, it also contains helpful information about the developmental stages of toddlers, advice on structuring activities and guiding toddlers, and, for teachers and caregivers, working with parents. Miller's presentation and tone show that this is not just a book filled with fun, time-consuming activities, but one in which the mental, physical, and emotional development of children are a priority. Whether you are a teacher or parent, your personal library will benefit from having this one on the shelf. An index would have been helpful.

## Where To Find/Buy:

Bookstores and libraries.

★★★★

**Overall Rating**
★★★★
Great activities; emphasis placed on understanding and working with the toddler

**Design, Ease Of Use**
★★★
Generally easy to read; lack of an index makes it difficult to find specific info

1–4 Stars

**Author:**
Karen Miller

Miller is also the author of *Ages and Stages*, and *The Outside Play and Learning Book*. In her 20+ years in the childcare field, she has been a teacher for Head Start, director of four different childcare centers, and has been involved with two major childcare organizations.

**Publisher:**
Telshare Publishing

**Edition:**
1990

**Price:**
$14.95

**Pages/Run Time:**
212

**ISBN:**
0910287082

**Media:**
Book

**Principal Subject:**
Understanding Your Child's Growth & Learning

**Secondary Subject:**
Activities & Games

**Age Group:**
Toddlers (1–3)

II. Understanding Your Child's Growth & Learning

★★★★

**Overall Rating**
★★★★
Excellent combination of theory, practice, and concrete examples to encourage reading

**Design, Ease Of Use**
★★★
Laborious reading in first half, the Treasury and various indexes are well-organized

1–4 Stars

**Author:**
Jim Trelease

Trelease, a graduate of the University of Massachusetts, was an award-winning artist and writer for *The Springfield Daily News* for 20 years. He works full-time addressing parents, teachers, and professional groups on the subjects of children, literature, and TV.

**Publisher:**
Penguin Group
(Penguin Books USA)

**Edition:**
4th (1995)

**Price:**
$13.95

**Pages/Run Time:**
387

**ISBN:**
0140469710

**Media:**
Book

**Principal Subject:**
Understanding Your Child's Growth & Learning

**Secondary Subject:**
Activities & Games

**Age Group:**
Infants & Toddlers (0–3)

# THE READ-ALOUD HANDBOOK

**Recommended For:**
Understanding Your Child's Growth & Learning

## Description:

Trelease's 387-page, ten chapter handbook is two books in one. The first half presents evidence that supports reading aloud to children while the second half contains his "Treasury of Read-Alouds." Chapters One and Two focus on why and when parents should read to their child. Chapter Three presents the progressive stages for reading aloud based upon the child's development; also listed are the types of books that are recommended for a child's given age (wordless books, picture books, etc.). The "Dos and Don'ts of Read-Aloud" is the subject of Chapter Four, while Chapter Five highlights various programs that have implemented read-alouds and had positive results. Chapter Six deals with setting up home, school, and public libraries. The drawbacks of TV are covered in Chapter Seven while the benefits of Sustained Silent Reading (SSR) are explained in Chapter Eight. Chapter Nine explains how to use Chapter Ten—the Treasury (200+ pages). Books are separated by type (wordless, predictable, picture, etc.). Each book includes a one paragraph synopsis, suggested age range, other books by that author, other books that are related to the subject, and more.

## Evaluation:

Now in its fourth edition, this book has remained a timeless classic. Recently revised with updated statistics, new research and anecdotes, and current children's literature additions, this book continues to appeal to parents and teachers. Although quite a bit of the book's first half is dedicated to children of school age, we recommend parents of babies and young children wade through it. Some of the reading is tedious and laborious, bordering on the feel of a textbook. However, Trelease does a great job interjecting numerous family and classroom examples to break up the serious tone of his message— "a nation that doesn't read much doesn't know much." His treatise is that children should be read to from the time they are a few months old if for nothing else than to hear the sounds of language. The Treasury is well-organized allowing parents to either seek out other books by the same author or books along the same theme. Well-researched and with tons of great ideas for young readers, this one would be a great shower present for a new mother or father.

## Where To Find/Buy:

Bookstores and libraries.

**Activities & Games**

# GAMES BABIES PLAY
## From Birth To Twelve Months

### Description:

This 97-page activity book is divided into four age groups: birth to three months, three to six months, six to nine months, and nine to 12 months. At the beginning of each age group, the author describes, on one-page, the developmental milestones of each age in areas such as sensory, social, emotional, and cognitive development. Then following these descriptions, the author outlines a series of games and activities for baby that are appropriate to that age group. Descriptions of each activity range from half a page to two pages in length.

### Evaluation:

Finally! A book that memorializes in print the ages-old child-tickler Eentsy Weentsy Spider. If you don't remember all the words, or have a bet that your partner is doing it wrong, this is the book for you. At 97 pages, the focus of this book is simple in scope: games to play with your baby. Most of the activities involve singing and many involve some sort of touch and/or movement. Very few of the activities require any kind of prop. The few props that are required do not consist of fancy, specialized toys. Interaction between baby and parent is all that is required. Games are very simple and some are familiar standbys. In addition to Eentsy Weentsy Spider, some of the more familiar games are included such as Pat-A-Cake and Airplane Baby. The descriptions of the games and activities are simple and clear to understand. This would be a useful guide for any parent, grandparent, or childcare provider.

### Where To Find/Buy:

Bookstores, libraries, or order direct by calling (800) 255-3379, or by contacting Practical Parenting Books-By-Mail at 15245 Minnetonka Blvd., Minnetonka, MC 55345.

---

**Overall Rating**
★★★
Activities are easy to play anywhere and uncomplicated to learn

**Design, Ease Of Use**
★★★★
Activities are arranged alphabetically and by age-appropriateness

1–4 Stars

**Author:**
Vicki Lansky

Lansky is the author of many books for parents, including *Feed Me I'm Yours*, *Practical Parenting Tips*, and *Welcoming Your Second Baby*. Lansky's ideas can be found in her column for *Sesame Street* magazine *Parents' Guide* and *Family Circle* magazine.

**Publisher:**
Book Peddlers

**Edition:**
1993

**Price:**
$8.95

**Pages/Run Time:**
97

**ISBN:**
0916773337

**Media:**
Book

**Principal Subject:**
Understanding Your Child's Growth & Learning

**Secondary Subject:**
Activities & Games

**Age Group:**
Infants (0–1)

## Overall Rating
★★★
Simple everyday games based on child's developmental level using household items

## Design, Ease Of Use
★★★★
Table of contents arranged by baby's age, index arranged by subject

1–4 Stars

## Author:
Shari Steelsmith

Shari Steelsmith and her husband are the parents of two sons. This is Ms. Steelsmith's first activities book for children. She is also the author of *How to Open and Operate a Home-Based Day-Care Business.*

## Publisher:
Parenting Press

## Edition:
1995

## Price:
$9.95

## ISBN:
0943990815

## Media:
Book

## Principal Subject:
Understanding Your Child's Growth & Learning

## Secondary Subject:
Activities & Games

## Age Group:
Infants & Toddlers (0–3)

**Activities & Games**

# PEEKABOO AND OTHER GAMES TO PLAY WITH YOUR BABY
Tools For Everyday Parenting Series

## Description:
This 120-page book is a collection of over 100 activities and baby games that parents and caregivers can use for interacting with their infant or toddler. Separated into 15 age-specific sections (by month from newborn to 12 months old, then by 12 to 15 months and 15 to 18 months), it also includes a section on choosing or making age-appropriate toys and a section on reading with babies and toddlers. A half page of information introduces each section with highlights of that stage of development. Also included are simple songs, rhymes, and numerous illustrations. A materials list is provided for each activity and usually includes everyday household items (magazines, cardboard, glue, etc.). Book resource lists for parents, babies, and toddlers are provided at the end of the book. The "Subject Index" concludes the book and separates the games and activities described in the book into seven sections (language games, learning games, movement games, sensory games, sound games, things to make, and visual games).

## Evaluation:
This is a whimsical book with ideas for activities and games that children and adults will find fun to do together. The author has carefully tried to put together simple games that involve the five senses of sight, sound, touch, taste, and smell. Differences in children's personalities and safety concerns have also been considered. The book sports a generalized table of contents divided by baby's age month-by month and the "Subject Index" does a great job of backup. Parents will find many unique activities in this concise guide from making collages by taping contact paper with the sticky side out on the refrigerator to "painting" with shaving cream, and more. Each activity capitalizes on the developmental milestones at a particular age. Descriptions include a list of materials along with additional information to ensure success. The book is in a non-standard 8.5 x 5.5 size, with an easy-to-read typeface and bold subheadings. This entertaining collection should provide many good times between parents and children.

## Where To Find/Buy:
Bookstores and libraries, or order direct by calling (800) 992-6657.

**Activities & Games**

# PLAY, LEARN, & GROW
## An Annotated Guide To The Best Books And Materials For Very Young Children

### Description:
Stating that it is a "highly selective, evaluative collection development resource guide," this 439-page guide highlights books and other media (not games or toys) for use with children under the age of five. Over 5,000 print and non-print titles were evaluated by librarians and early childhood educators in compiling this list. The importance of the parent/adult's role in engaging a child to read begins the book. The next sections discuss the importance of choosing quality materials, a "developmental portrait" for infants through five year olds (characteristics, what they enjoy, sample book titles), criteria used for selecting the book's content, and more. The remainder of the book contains the annotated list of books and media arranged alphabetically by title, with bibliographic information, an assigned general category (wordless, concept, etc.), age range, and more. Three appendices are included (professional resources, publisher contacts, organizations) along with five indexes to access entries (by name, subject, age/ category, age/purchase priority, and format).

### Evaluation:
Reading aloud is certainly an activity that young children and infants enjoy with their parents. At first glance though, it seems that this bulky text, with all its resources arranged alphabetically, will provide endless agony. Do parents have to wade through all the annotations to find appropriate books for their child? Fortunately not. This inherent problem can be circumvented if parents make good use of the indexes as they search for materials pertinent to their needs, such as a search for "all books for a preschooler that have to do with dinosaurs." Parents will find the information contained within this resource complete, easily accessible in a variety of ways, and well-summarized. It should prove helpful to parents struggling with what to buy in the bookstore or what to search for in the local library. However, its primary target audience is early childhood educators and those involved with library media. It is pricey for parents and other resources are available that offer similar (even more current) listings for less money. We recommend parents use these editions over this text.

### Where To Find/Buy:
Bookstores and libraries.

---

★★★

**Overall Rating**
★★★
Complete listings of annotated children's resources based on defined criteria

**Design, Ease Of Use**
★★★★
Arranged alphabetically by title with 5 indexes listing resources by subject, age, etc.

1–4 Stars

**Author:**
James L. Thomas

**Publisher:**
R.R. Bowker
(Reed Reference Publishing)

**Edition:**
1992

**Price:**
$30.00

**ISBN:**
0835230198

**Media:**
Book

**Principal Subject:**
Understanding Your Child's Growth & Learning

**Secondary Subject:**
Activities & Games

**Age Group:**
Infants & Toddlers (0–3)

II. Understanding Your Child's Growth & Learning

**Activities & Games**

★★★

**Overall Rating**
★★★
Comprehensive guide primarily beneficial for caregivers & educators of one-year-olds

**Design, Ease Of Use**
★★★
No main index, but detailed table of contents and section indexes ease navigation

1–4 Stars

**Author:**
Debby Cryer, Thelma Harms, and Beth Bourland

Ms. Cryer, Harms, and Bourland are with the Frank Porter Graham Child Development Center, University of North Carolina, Chapel Hill, North Carolina

**Publisher:**
Addison-Wesley Longman (Addison-Wesley Publishing)

**Edition:**
1987

**Price:**
$18.60

**Pages/Run Time:**
218

**ISBN:**
0201213354

**Media:**
Book

**Principal Subject:**
Understanding Your Child's Growth & Learning

**Secondary Subject:**
Activities & Games

**Age Group:**
Toddlers (1–3)

# ACTIVE LEARNING FOR ONES

## Description:

This 218-page activity guidebook is one of four in Addison-Wesley's "Active Learning Series." This comprehensive book is made up of four activity sections and a planning guide for those working with children between 12 and 24 months of age. Section One—"Planning for Ones"—includes ideas for developing a schedule, making interest centers, and an environment that is positive; how to write an activity plan for each child is also included. Section Two—"Activities for Listening and Talking"—assists you with activities (books, pictures, conversation, etc.) that promote talking and listening. "Activities for Physical Development" offers ideas to develop children's large and small muscles. Section Four—"Creative Activities"—uses art, blocks, dramatic play, and music to develop children's senses, imagination, and art enjoyment. The final section—"Activities for Learning from the World Around Them"—focuses on nature, the senses, size, shape, color, and numbers. Separate indexes are included for each section.

## Evaluation:

This reference is one of the Addison-Wesley "Active Learning Series" specifically focused on the one-year-old toddler. It provides a wonderful source of developmental activities covering the areas of creativity, community, listening and talking, physical development, and learning about the environment. The book does not have an overall index but it does have a detailed table of contents and section indexes. Each activity has an approximate time completion, with a suggested optimal number of children participating. Also noted is whether the activity is more appropriately experienced indoors or outdoors. Although designed primarily for educators of young children, this guidebook can also serve as a quality reference for parents seeking ideas and suggestions on things to do with their one-year-old. The checklists and materials lists are invaluable sources for organizing one's self and guiding a one-year-old's education.

## Where To Find/Buy:

Bookstores and libraries.

**Activities & Games**

# ACTIVE LEARNING FOR TWOS

★★★

## Description:

Boasting 330 pages, this guidebook contains five sections of activities for two-year-olds. "Planning for Twos" suggests ideas for setting up an environment conducive for "good care and avoid(ing) problems"; this section also shows how to plan activities so that things will run smoothly. The second section includes activities to help those working with two-year-olds make the best use of listening and talking skills. Large and small muscle activities comprise Section Three. There are exercises and activities for using your legs, arms, and back through walking, running, climbing, and balancing, as well as developing the muscles in your hands and fingers. Section Four deals with art, blocks, dramatic play, and music. The final section focuses on activities involving nature, the senses, size, shape, color and numbers. Materials lists (and suggested "notes") and "Activity Checklists" accompany each section. Each Section has its own index preceding the section along with a rationale on why the activities are important.

## Evaluation:

This reference is one of the Addison-Wesley "Active Learning Series" specifically focused on the two-year-old toddler. It provides a wonderful source of developmental activities covering the areas of creativity, community, listening and talking, physical development, and learning about the environment. The book does not have an overall index but it does have a detailed table of contents and section indexes. Each activity has an approximate time completion, with a suggested optimal number of children participating. Also noted is whether the activity is more appropriately experienced indoors or outdoors. Although designed primarily for educators of young children, this guidebook can also serve as a quality reference for parents seeking ideas and suggestions on things to do with their two-year-old. The checklists and materials lists are invaluable sources for organizing one's self and guiding a two-year-old's education. Buy the series; these will be a much used resource.

## Where To Find/Buy:

Bookstores and libraries.

**Overall Rating**
★★★
Offers a wealth of activities and organizational tools, along with supporting rationale

**Design, Ease Of Use**
★★★
Comprehensive table of contents makes up for a lack of index; section indexes provided

1–4 Stars

**Author:**
Debby Cryer, Thelma Harms, Beth Bourland

Debby Cryer, Thelma Harms, and Beth Bourland collaborated with the Frank Porter Graham Child Development Center (University of North Carolina) in Chapel Hill, North Carolina in the development of this guidebook.

**Publisher:**
Addison-Wesley Longman (Addison-Wesley Publishing)

**Edition:**
1988

**Price:**
$23.25

**Pages/Run Time:**
330

**ISBN:**
0201213362

**Media:**
Book

**Principal Subject:**
Understanding Your Child's Growth & Learning

**Secondary Subject:**
Activities & Games

**Age Group:**
Toddlers (1–3)

## Activities & Games

### Overall Rating
★★★
Most activities are unusual and capitalize positively on what toddlers like to do

### Design, Ease Of Use
★★★
Comprehensive index and bold headings make it easily read; graphics would help

1–4 Stars

### Author:
Karen Miller

Karen Miller has spent over 20 years in the child care field. She has been a teacher for Head Start, a director of child care centers, and has held numerous other child care positions, one involving curriculum development for two major child care organizations.

### Publisher:
Telshare Publishing Company

### Edition:
1984

### Price:
$14.95

### Pages/Run Time:
167

### ISBN:
091028704X

### Media:
Book

### Principal Subject:
Understanding Your Child's Growth & Learning

### Secondary Subject:
Activities & Games

### Age Group:
Toddlers (1–3)

# THINGS TO DO WITH TODDLERS AND TWOS

## Description:
This 167-page guide contains ten chapters, organized according to different types of toddler behaviors (sticking fingers in holes, climbing, etc). It is a compilation of ideas and activities and designed to set up a foundation for interactive fun between caregiver and child. Chapters One through Four explore games and activities involving cause and effect, playing with water, noise makers (toys that shake, rattle, bang, twang, etc.), and art activities. Chapter Five highlights activities that use the senses (textures, taste, etc). Pretending and dramatic play are covered in Chapter Six, while Chapter Seven focuses on language development (singing, fingerplays, things to do with pictures, etc.). Chapter Eight and Nine offer activities that show how things work together (stacking and puzzles) and various types of movement (climbing, throwing, pushing, crawling, etc.). Chapter Ten discusses "special problems" of toddlers in groups. These include clinging, sharing, frustration, and attention to name a few. An appendix, bibliography, and index conclude the resource.

## Evaluation:
The author's intent is to describe activities that will provide a stimulating environment for toddlers. She resists applying age-specific guidelines to those activities, however, leaving that up to the parent; she is also adamant that the book is not a discussion of child development. However, she suggests that various activities she has described can enhance a toddler's newly acquired capabilities or offer a positive redirection of unacceptable behaviors. Many activities are unusual (marbles/bubble in a tube, pulleys, record player art, etc.) and sure to capture the interest and fascination of any toddler. Many capitalize on themes of science, math, reading, and other subject areas without appearing too intrusive or instructional. All activities involve open-ended exploration and are derived from the author's observation of what toddlers like to do. This is an unusual basis not often found in other activity resources which focus more on the teachable objective rather than the discovery element. Sure to offer fun experiences whether used in a home or in an educational context, this resource has much to offer.

## Where To Find/Buy:
Bookstores, libraries, or order direct by calling (800) 343-9707.

**Activities & Games**

# WELCOME TO COOKING WITH YOUNG CHILDREN

### Description:

This site's goal is to encourage early childhood teachers and parents of young children to increase their use of cooking as an activity with young children. "Cooking provides children with a sense of personal achievement by giving them a peek into the adult world they so often imitate in their play," Dambra says. "Most teachers would agree that cooking is a valuable experience, yet very little takes place in classrooms today." Categories on the homepage include: Cool Cooking, Cooking with Heat, Summer Fun, Recipes for Creating, Lunch Ideas, and Early Childhood Links; all categories contain subsections appropriate for toddlers. The site has an impressive collection of early childhood education links and simple recipes developed especially for kids.

### Evaluation:

Now here's a small site that delivers what it promises. Dambra has assembled a tidy but downright delightful collection of information important to early childhood educators and parents of small children. Where else can parents find, in one convenient location, recipes for goop, flubber, smelly playdough, puffy paint, finger paint and soap crayons? All that can be found and more in just one section: Stuff To Create With. Dambra's sense of fun, sincerity, and dedication to early childhood education make this a site to visit. It's not flashy, but it accomplishes just what it sets out to do—encourage adults to become more involved in activities with the children around them.

### Where To Find/Buy:

On the Internet using the URL: http://members.aol.com/Sgrmagnlia/cooking.html

---

**Overall Rating**
★★★
Recipes your toddlers won't want to miss

**Design, Ease Of Use**
★★★
Straightforward layout

1–4 Stars

**Author:**
Marianne E. Dambra
Dambra is an early childhood educator.

**Media:**
Internet

**Principal Subject:**
Understanding Your Child's Growth & Learning

**Secondary Subject:**
Activities & Games

**Age Group:**
Toddlers (1–3)

★★★

**Overall Rating**
★★★
Useful book lists (based on author's favorites) and valuable support for reading aloud

**Design, Ease Of Use**
★★
Book lists need highlights; no ISBNs provided for suggested books

1–4 Stars

**Author:**
Dorothy Butler

A native of New Zealand, Dorothy Butler is a teacher, bookseller, and author, as well as a worldwide recognized children's literature advocate.

**Publisher:**
Heinemann (Reed Elsevier)

**Edition:**
2nd (1998)

**Price:**
$15.95

**Pages/Run Time:**
261

**ISBN:**
0435081446

**Media:**
Book

**Principal Subject:**
Understanding Your Child's Growth & Learning

**Secondary Subject:**
Activities & Games

**Age Group:**
Infants & Toddlers (0–3)

**Activities & Games**

# BABIES NEED BOOKS
Sharing The Joy Of Books With Children From Birth To Six

**Description:**
This book focuses on the why, what, when, and hows of introducing children to reading and books. It contains 261 pages, seven chapters with age-specific book lists, a conclusion, supplemental book lists, and an index. Chapter One offers supportive testimony of why children should be involved with books, with Chapter Two plunging into the mechanics of reading with babies. The chapters following (Three through Seven), offer information in a progressive format for children up to age five. Different aspects of children's books are highlighted, such as the value of various illustration methods, the types of books to choose from (board books, alphabet, collections, etc.), the benefits of "theme" and "story" books for children, and more. Some of the book lists for each age category offer a short synopsis of the books, as well as the author and publisher. The concluding "Supplementary Book lists" section has been prepared by children's literature specialists and is intended to be used as a complementary supplement to the main book. There is an extensive index.

**Evaluation:**
This is a handy and valuable resource that focuses solely on the early childhood years. The author's intent is admirable—to list books that will involve children deeply, spark their imagination and curiosity, and establish a lifelong habit and appreciation of reading. There are old and new books, best-sellers, classics, and hard-to-find books, and all are worthy and respected. The shortcomings of this resource can only be found in its abruptness in stopping at six years of age, but its compact package makes it handy to carry around. We also wish the author had supplied ISBNs for recommended books to make searches a bit easier for parents, librarians, and bookstores. It is very well-presented, well-written with supportive information, and easily navigable. Although the author is most adamant about reading and this dominates the book (sometimes intrusively), the lists and evaluation of the books are great resources. Parents will find their time floundering at the bookstore cut drastically.

**Where To Find/Buy:**
Bookstores and libraries.

**Activities & Games**

# 365 DAYS OF BABY LOVE
Playing, Growing And Exploring With Babies From Birth To Age 2

### Description:
The authors, two experienced mothers who also happen to be sisters, state in their introduction, "We believe that the magic of childhood lives in the everyday moments." This book aims at offering a wide variety of games, toys, crafts, interactions, and exercises to help you fill those everyday moments with meaningful activities. Filled throughout with children's drawings, this book is organized in an easy-to-use style with one activity per page, often with enclosed "Wit & Wisdom" captions with tips from other parents across the country. The book contains 26 individual sections, with many ideas included in each section for such areas as "Caregiving," "Language and Sound," "Everyday Toys," "Nature," "Art," "Dad's Time," and "Food and Nutrition." Each of the 26 sections starts with activities appropriate for infants and progresses up through activities for two year olds; no age specifications are listed for each activity to account for individuals' variations. When necessary to the activity, a list of materials precedes the activity's description.

### Evaluation:
Readers will find in this book a plethora of interesting games, activities, and interactions to engage in with their baby. This book emphasizes a baby's need to make choices and exercise his/her will, with activities that promote a baby's interactive abilities and development. The toys, crafts, and music sections are particularly valuable, including such cheap, easy-to-make items as a "permanent photo," created by keeping a series of school photos in one frame, or "finger tapping" devices created by sewing buttons on a child's old pair of gloves. Some of the other activities, however, feel too directed for both babies and mothers. The magic of motherhood lies in the spontaneity and freedom of being able to structure time with one's child in unique ways. But, if a mother is looking for ideas which can be tailored to her interactions with her child and/or she does not have an extended family to rely on, this resource can be a lifesaver now and then.

### Where To Find/Buy:
Bookstores and libraries.

---

**Overall Rating**
★★★
Many ideas for playing with your baby

**Design, Ease Of Use**
★
"Flip-through" style with no index; recommended ages not included on activities

1–4 Stars

**Author:**
Sheila Ellison and Susan Ferdinandi

Sheila Ellison is the author of the "365" series of parenting books, including *365 Days of Creative Play*. Susan Ferdinandi is the Assistant Director and teacher at the Little School in Benicia, CA. Both are experienced mothers, and are also sisters.

**Publisher:**
Sourcebooks

**Edition:**
1996

**Price:**
$12.95

**Pages/Run Time:**
416

**ISBN:**
1570711100

**Media:**
Book

---

**Principal Subject:**
Understanding Your Child's Growth & Learning

**Secondary Subject:**
Activities & Games

**Age Group:**
Infants & Toddlers (0–3)

II. Understanding Your Child's Growth & Learning

**Activities & Games**

# BABY SIGNS
How To Talk With Your Baby Before Your Baby Can Talk

★★★

**Overall Rating**
★★★
Comprehensive argument, backed up by case studies, for teaching early communication

**Design, Ease Of Use**
★
Lack of index makes it difficult to find specifics; large subheadings somewhat useful

1–4 Stars

**Author:**
Linda Acredolo, PhD and Susan Goodwyn, PhD

Acredolo is a Professor of Psychology at the University of California at Davis. Goodwyn is an Associate Professor of Psychology at California State University, Stanislaus. Both have been teaching Baby Signs to parent, teachers, and pediatricians for the past 10 years.

**Publisher:**
Contemporary Books (NTC/Contemporary Publishing)

**Edition:**
1996

**Price:**
$12.95

**ISBN:**
0809234300

**Media:**
Book

**Principal Subject:**
Understanding Your Child's Growth & Learning

**Secondary Subject:**
Activities & Games

**Age Group:**
Infants (0–1)

## Description:

This 163-page ten chapter reference focuses on how to take advantage of your baby's non-verbal communication, their signs and gestures, and teach them to "talk" before they can. Chapters One and Two give a brief overview of the meaning of "baby signs," and how babies use it to communicate before they are old enough to speak. Chapters Three through Five contain information on how to begin teaching baby signs ("hat," "bird," "flower," "fish," "more") and how to progress toward more advanced baby signs; emphasis is on selecting a non-verbal cue that is mutually understood between parent and child. Stories about babies who sign are highlighted in Chapter Six, while Chapter Seven discusses the transition from signing to speech. The final three chapters include answers to parents' questions, an illustrated section of suggested baby signs, and interactive poems using baby signs. There is list of suggested books at the close of the book for parents interested in learning more about infant sign language research. This resource contains no index.

## Evaluation:

Enhanced by black and white photographs and whimsical illustrations, this guide offers parents ways to enrich their interactions with their child through early signing. Based on ten years of research with families, the authors believe that a baby's ability to create and respond to gestures ("bye-bye," "no," "yes," etc.) can lead to better communication. By teaching children "baby signs," parents can hasten the process of learning to talk, jump start their child's intellectual development, enhance their self-esteem, and form a stronger bond between parent and child. This book provides a comprehensive argument for and interesting case studies of early communication which, when employed and practiced regularly, can certainly help parents meet their babies' needs early on. Hopefully later editions will include an index making this guide quite a bit easier to explore. Emphasizing that there are no "correct" signs except those established between parent and child, this book, however, is worth struggling through.

## Where To Find/Buy:
Bookstores and libraries.

**Activities & Games**

# GAMES TO PLAY WITH TODDLERS

★★

## Description:

This 285-page book includes ten sections of activities for children ages 1 to 2 years. Sections include: growing & learning games, teddy bear games, the kitchen, the outdoors, laughing & having fun, art & singing, car games, special bonding, bath & dressing, and finger & toe games. Silberg uses her experience as a teacher and trainer in early childhood development to detail games for toddlers ages 12 to 15 months, 15 to 18 months, 18 to 21 months, and 21 to 24 months. Originating from a variety of cultures and ethnic backgrounds, the games selected for each age group focus on coordination, language, observation, listening skills, imitation, nature appreciation, creativity, and other areas. The games progress in a step-by-step format with their intended objective—"What your toddler will learn"—noted at the bottom of each page. Also included are "Guidelines for Growth" a list of specific actions that illustrate toddler growth in motor, auditory & visual skills, language & cognitive skills, and self-concept skills.

## Evaluation:

Readers will be pleased at the opportunity to "pick and choose" games based upon skill set/objective and interest. Additionally, grouping activities by age makes it relatively easy for parents/ caregivers to determine where their child falls in terms of their developmental growth. For example, a 14 month old child might succeed at a game that is "appropriate" for an 18 month old. Or if a caregiver wishes to help a child in a certain area, like language skills, progressive games are given to serve that purpose. But remember these are, as always, "average" developmental guidelines. The games encompass both indoor and outdoor activities. Care is made to utilize common objects which are used in everyday situations. Alternative methods of play are offered for most games encouraging further creativity and exploration. Many of the games, however, are fairly commonly known: playing catch, throwing beanbags, Thumbkin, etc. Other books offer unique alternatives; this resource can be used to back up some of these.

## Where To Find/Buy:

Bookstores and libraries.

**Overall Rating**
★★
Over 100 toddler games described, many of which are commonplace—"playing ball"

**Design, Ease Of Use**
★★★★
Well-organized with easy-to-use cross-referencing; listing the game's objective is useful

1–4 Stars

**Author:**
Jackie Silberg

Silberg, an acclaimed speaker, teacher, trainer of early childhood development and music, is also a regular columnist for *Instructor* magazine. She is an adjunct lecturer in preschool education at Emporia (Kansas) State University, and has hosted a children's TV program.

**Publisher:**
Gryphon House

**Edition:**
1993

**Price:**
$14.95

**ISBN:**
0876591632

**Media:**
Book

**Principal Subject:**
Understanding Your Child's Growth & Learning

**Secondary Subject:**
Activities & Games

**Age Group:**
Toddlers (1–3)

**★★**

**Overall Rating**
★★
Refreshing global approach; a bit heavy on rhetoric

**Design, Ease Of Use**
★★★★
Detailed table of contents, thorough reference and index sections, bold subheadings

1–4 Stars

**Author:**
Peggy Jenkins, PhD

Peggy Jenkins is the founder and director of a nonprofit educational service organization called "Joyful Child Inc." Dr. Jenkins is also a seminar leader in parent/teacher education, and a consultant in the area of behavior/learning styles.

**Publisher:**
Aslan Publishing

**Edition:**
1996

**Price:**
$16.95

**Pages/Run Time:**
257

**ISBN:**
0944031668

**Media:**
Book

**Principal Subject:**
Understanding Your Child's Growth & Learning

**Secondary Subject:**
Activities & Games

**Age Group:**
Infants & Toddlers (0–3)

## Activities & Games

# THE JOYFUL CHILD
A Sourcebook Of Activities And Ideas For Releasing Children's Natural Joy

**Description:**

This book centers on releasing the inner joy within ourselves and our children. Incorporating quotes throughout from philosophers, authors, and the Bible, this 257-page guide is divided into three parts. Part One discusses various philosophies and ideas for releasing "Natural Joy." Subtopics include defining joy and exploring the foundations of joy; self-esteem, values, and universal principles; teaching relationships (parents, child, teachers) along guidelines for the transmission of consciousness and attitudes; and looking at four different types of children—DISC (Dominate, Influencing, Supportive, and Conscientious). Part Two suggests activities in art, music, games, and more. Part Three shows parents how to bring it all together by focusing on creating a lesson plan, discussing the value of prayer, and the joy of serving. An Appendix portrays Dr. Robert Muller's "World Core Curriculum." A ten-page reference and resources section is included as well as an eight-page index.

**Evaluation:**

Jenkins' book details her argument for helping children and parents release their inner joy to become more caring and compassionate individuals. "Joy, as an expression of love, is a healing energy much needed by humanity and the planet at this time," and this is the author's stated purpose. Gleaning information from various philosophies on the topics of joy and inner peace, this guidebook expounds upon the virtues of "The Golden Rule" and how parents can modify their behavior as well as their children's towards this end. Despite the book's heavy spiritual flavor and sometimes preachiness, many families will find valuable information to interweave into their daily lives. The author's global approach helps extend the joyful child's awareness beyond national boundaries to understand their interconnection with everyone and everything. The author has taken great care to give a variety of resources for each chapter.

**Where To Find/Buy:**

Bookstores and libraries, or order direct by calling the publisher at (707) 542-5400, or Joyful Child, Inc. at (602) 494-3383.

**Activities & Games**

# JOYFUL PLAY WITH TODDLERS
Recipes For Fun With Odds And Ends

★★

### Description:

This resource contains 126 pages of things to make and do with toddlers utilizing everyday "odds and ends." It begins with ideas for improving parenting skills by explaining how young children learn and explore. There is a brief (one-page) checklist on how to babyproof your home, as well as a list of those items not suitable for making toys. The second chapter talks about setting limits, behavior, acknowledging feelings, power struggles, and regaining calm. The book progresses onto toys and games with suggestions of safe household items to use and how toddlers and parents might turn them into playthings. These include games using boxes, milk cartons, old clothes, kitchen utensils, and more. The "Activities" segment includes water and outdoor play, make-believe adventures, music and art, and cooking. An index is included. The book's main intent is to offer suggestions for on-the-spot games and activities for toddlers.

### Evaluation:

Parents, teachers, and caregivers will find this quick idea guide a useful resource. It offers simple activities, such as bird watching, listening to sounds, and ladder stepping, as well as more advanced activities, such as cooking and threading pasta necklaces. There is also advice on how to find free or inexpensive art materials. The book is unique in its dedication of describing a set of fun and creative games utilizing household items. Each activity is easily accessible via the Table of Contents and Index. Safety tips concerning water activities and how to babyproof your home are invaluable saves. This guidebook is full of practical, fun ideas and would make a worthwhile addition to your family library.

### Where To Find/Buy:

Bookstores and libraries, or order direct by calling (800) 992-6657.

**Overall Rating**
★★
Useful activities to stimulate toddlers without digging into their parents' pocketbooks

**Design, Ease Of Use**
★★★★
Small size makes it easy to use; loaded with illustrations and written concisely

1–4 Stars

**Author:**
Sandi Dexter

Sandi Dexter is a parent and teacher who has been involved with preschoolers for 12 years. She is a collector of odds and ends from around her home and community, putting them to good use for toddler play and learning.

**Publisher:**
Parenting Press

**Edition:**
1995

**Price:**
$9.95

**ISBN:**
1884734006

**Media:**
Book

**Principal Subject:**
Understanding Your Child's Growth & Learning

**Secondary Subject:**
Activities & Games

**Age Group:**
Toddlers (1–3)

**Activities & Games**

★★

**Overall Rating**
★★
250+ baby games described, many of which are commonplace (peekaboo, shake, etc.)

**Design, Ease Of Use**
★★★
Clear format; simple instructions & illustrations; games listed alphabetically in index

1–4 Stars

**Author:**
Jackie Silberg

Silberg has authored numerous books on child development and is a regular columnist for the teacher magazine *Instructor*. She is also an adjunct lecturer in preschool education at Emporia (KS) State University, and has hosted her own children's television program.

**Publisher:**
Gryphon House

**Edition:**
6th (1993)

**Price:**
$14.95

**Pages/Run Time:**
286

**ISBN:**
0876591624

**Media:**
Book

**Principal Subject:**
Understanding Your Child's Growth & Learning

**Secondary Subject:**
Activities & Games

**Age Group:**
Infants (0–1)

# GAMES TO PLAY WITH BABIES

## Description:

Silberg uses her experience as a teacher and trainer in early childhood development to detail games for infants ages 0 to three months, three to six months, six to nine months, and nine to 12 months. This 286-page book includes eight sections of activities for babies, parents, and caregivers. Sections include: growing & learning games, special bonding games, kitchen games, laughing & having fun, art & singing, bath & dressing, finger & toe games, and going to sleep games. Originating from a variety of cultures and ethnic backgrounds, the games selected for each age group focus on hand-eye coordination, language, observation, listening skills, bonding, exploration, body awareness, and other areas. The games progress in a step-by-step format with their intended objective—"What your baby will learn"—noted at the bottom of each page. Also included are "Guidelines for Growth" a list of specific actions that illustrate babies' growth in motor, auditory & visual skills, language & cognitive skills, and self-concept skills.

## Evaluation:

Being able to "pick and choose" activities based upon daily routines (sleep, having fun, bonding, etc.) and interest (fingers, toes, singing, etc.) will delight many parents. By listing the appropriate age for each activity along with the activity's intent, parents will find this resource a help in their child's development. Each game contains very easy instructions with minimal preparation time and planning. Most of the activities are fairly commonplace as those described in some of her other books—"Where Did It Go?" (covering a toy with a cloth), "Shake, Shake, Shake" (filling containers with objects), etc. Although some rhymes, songs, and poems are offered, other resources place more emphasis on language experiences. The black and white illustrations are adequate but incomplete. The page layouts make for quick navigation but are uninspiring. The alphabetical index is comprehensive. For parents searching for an impromptu game, this source will help. Other resources, however, offer a wider selection of unusual activities, along with the more commonplace, to keep a little one (and parents) focused and interested.

## Where To Find/Buy:

Bookstores and libraries.

**Activities & Games**

# MORE GAMES TO PLAY WITH TODDLERS

★★

### Description:

This 271-page guide contains 200+ games and activities for toddlers and is divided into twelve sections. Each game is explained on one-page and includes a recommended age. Step-by-step instructions are given with occasional illustrations. Each game notes what a child will learn from the activity. A "Guidelines for Growth" chart lists developmental skills in terms of motor, auditory, and visual skills; language and cognitive skills; and self-concept skills. The first four sections include block games, bouncing games, games involving color and shape, and language games. Quiet and outside games, rhyming games, games involving running and jumping, and seasonal games follow. The final sections include singing games, toy games, and social games which use cooperation, coordination and imitation skills. The Table of Contents lists all the games, which age the activity is appropriate for, and what skill is reinforced ("coordination," "listening," etc.). An annotated list of books for toddlers and an index are given.

### Evaluation:

Caregivers, as well as parents, will certainly find this a useful book. Each game contains very easy instructions with minimal preparation time and planning. These games involve few materials, although most of the activities are just as commonplace as those described in her first book—walking around the house pointing out a given color, stacking blocks, etc. The novelty with this edition, however, is the emphasis on language with more rhymes, songs, and poems offered. By listing the appropriate age for each activity along with the activity's intent, parents will find this resource a help in their child's development. The black and white illustrations are adequate but incomplete. The page layouts make for quick navigation but are uninspiring. The index is comprehensive and cross-referenced. For parents searching for an impromptu game, this source will help. Other resources, however, will offer a wider selection of unusual activities, along with the more commonplace, to keep a busy toddler focused and interested.

### Where To Find/Buy:

Bookstores and libraries.

**Overall Rating**
★★
A fun overview of some of the more common games for children ages 12 to 24 months

**Design, Ease Of Use**
★★★
Simply organized with clear instructions; some illustrations

1–4 Stars

**Author:**
Jackie Silberg
Jackie Silberg has a degree in education from the University of Missouri, Kansas City, and a master's degree in early childhood education from Emporia State University in Kansas. She is also a teacher, a keynote speaker, and an accomplished musician.

**Publisher:**
Gryphon House

**Edition:**
1996

**Price:**
$14.95

**ISBN:**
0876591780

**Media:**
Book

**Principal Subject:**
Understanding Your Child's Growth & Learning

**Secondary Subject:**
Activities & Games

**Age Group:**
Toddlers (1–3)

II. Understanding Your Child's Growth & Learning

**Activities & Games**

## DAYCARE PROVIDERS HOME PAGE

**Overall Rating**

★★

Connects daycare providers through email contact and hosts numerous activities

**Design, Ease Of Use**

★★

Straightforward navigation

1–4 Stars

**Media:**

Internet

**Principal Subject:**

Understanding Your Child's Growth & Learning

**Secondary Subject:**

Activities & Games

**Age Group:**

Toddlers (1–3)

### Description:

This site was developed by a professional home daycare provider for daycare providers. It offers access to a daycare providers' discussion l ist, craft and activity ideas, and an extensive set of links for childcare providers, parents, and educators. Link groupings include lists of websites specifically for daycare providers, preschool development sites, preschool activity sites, special needs and medical information sites, daycare businesses and organizations on the Web, daycare software and other products and services for daycare providers, as well as childcare referral agencies, information for parents, and kids' sites. The site is hosted by iComm, a Canadian nonprofit organization devoted to offering other organizations access to the Internet. Developed by a home daycare provider for the "sharing of information and ideas concerning the providing of professional services by daycare/childcare providers," this site offers two options at their homepage along with numerous links to child-related sites. The first option is connection to "The Daycare Provider's Mailing List." This email access offers daycare providers, parents, and others an opportunity to enter into discussions and share ideas. Instructions are given on how to subscribe and how to leave the list; a warning is offered that subscription often brings over 100 messages each day. The second option—"Cindy's Cardfile—Circle, Craft and Activity Ideas"—presents 12 sections of activities ranging from "drama, fairy tales, families, and flowers" to "shapes, space, stories, transportation, and weather." Activities within these sections can be printed and include activity title, materials needed, and the procedure. Roughly 3 activities are given per page.

### Evaluation:

While the Daycare Providers Home Page definitely is targeted to daycare providers, it offers much that will be of interest to parents. The list of links alone is worth the visit. It offers, probably unwillingly, a wealth of information to parents on how the business end of a daycare is run, down to suggested software packages and accounting systems. More importantly, here are childcare referral agencies and parenting resources across the World Wide Web. The "cardfile" of crafts and activities offers many ideas. Topic headings demonstrate the breadth of offerings: paint and color; safety, science and sea; shapes, space, stories, transportation and weather; drama, fairy tales, families, and flowers; and more. It is the "seasons" series of activities that catches the eye, with its yearlong calendar of fun. This is a somewhat simple, straightforward site offered with a good heart by a daycare provider obviously committed to enhancing her entire profession.

### Where To Find/Buy:

On the Internet at the URL: http://www.icomm.ca/daycare/index.html

**Activities & Games**

# THE INFANT & TODDLER HANDBOOK
Invitations For Optimum Early Development

## Description:

This 105-page book is organized in seven chapters, each with its own introduction. Chapter One includes information on infant/toddler social, motor, language, and cognitive development skills. Chapter Two continues with information on designing an interesting and responsive environment encouraging exploration. Chapters Three through Seven present age-specific learning "invitations"—to look & listen, touch, communicate, move, and discover & solve problems. The author defines "invitations" as a means of providing infants and toddlers with "appropriate learning opportunities, activities, and materials which help them grow in all areas of development." Each "invitation" includes the child's "emerging ability," the "caregiver role," and lists of activities related to that "invitation" divided by age groups (three and six month breakdowns). Two appendices are also included. Appendix A includes a list of books, records, and other resources. Appendix B is a table for matching caregiving activities to a child's individual temperament.

## Evaluation:

The layout of this book is methodical, and although there is no index, the table of contents serves as a clear path to tap the book's information. The author's suggestion—to convert the activities to cards, organize them in a file box, and use them according to a child's age and development—is a good one. The result of this would be a convenient curriculum guide for either caregivers or parents. Particularly well done are the "Role of the Caregiver" sections in Chapters Three, Five, and Seven. Some research data is given to justify and validate the suggested activities. For example, information is provided on how language-related activities (talking, singing, reading) encourage the development of the left side of the brain; visual-spatial materials (mobiles, music, stacking toys) encourage the development of the right side of the brain. The author then offers activities to satisfy both kinds of experiences. Used with other more comprehensive activity guidebooks, caregivers in particular will find this book useful for creating a caring and interactive environment.

## Where To Find/Buy:

Bookstores and libraries.

---

★★

**Overall Rating**
★★
Offers multi-level activities for infants & toddlers, but not useful as a sole resource

**Design, Ease Of Use**
★★
Good bold headings; no illustrations; activity index by "invitation" would be helpful

1–4 Stars

**Author:**
Kathryn Castle, EdD

**Publisher:**
Humanics Limited

**Edition:**
1994

**Price:**
$16.95

**Pages/Run Time:**
105

**ISBN:**
0893340383

**Media:**
Book

**Principal Subject:**
Understanding Your Child's Growth & Learning

**Secondary Subject:**
Activities & Games

**Age Group:**
Infants & Toddlers (0–3)

**Activities & Games**

# CHOOSING YOUR CHILDREN'S BOOKS
## 2 To 5 Years Old

**Overall Rating**

★

Limited choices for encouraging young readers, based on loose selection criteria

**Design, Ease Of Use**

★★★★

Large print, easily portable; organized first by category, alphabetically in the index

1–4 Stars

**Author:**

Valerie White, BA, Cert.Ed.

White is an experienced teacher of English and school media specialist. She holds a degree in English, with a Postgraduate Certificate in Education.

**Publisher:**

Bayley & Musgrave

**Edition:**

1994

**Price:**

$5.95

**Pages/Run Time:**

78

**ISBN:**

1882726103

**Media:**

Book

**Principal Subject:**

Understanding Your Child's Growth & Learning

**Secondary Subject:**

Activities & Games

**Age Group:**

Toddlers (1–3)

**Description:**

Twelve "chapters" comprise this 78-page guide to children's literature developed by the author, an English teacher and school media specialist. Her introduction briefly highlights young children's literacy development along with suggestions for encouraging young readers. She also gives an overview of the types of books this age group enjoys. The children's books White recommends are arranged alphabetically within the following 12 categories: alphabet books, counting books, concepts, nature, rhymes, wordless, simple stories, folk tales, bedtime books, families, and starting school. Bibliographic information is included for each along with a one paragraph annotation; illustrations from these annotated books are included at times. The guide is the author's personal selection and criteria used for selecting the materials was "by doing a lot of reading!" The book includes choices from the classics, award winners, multicultural, and modern stories. It is the first in a series of three.

**Evaluation:**

The author's husband states in his foreword that this book was created as a more simple version of the heavy reference books that are available about children's literature. Then he continues by saying that they envisioned a slim guide with large print that "could be easily brought to the bookshop or library to make a selection." Their vision is a reality here. This guide is slim, does have large print, and certainly can be easily packed for an outing. However, it won't take long for parents and children to read through all of the resources listed within this guide book. Each category roughly contains about 12–20 choices, certainly not an overabundance considering the hungry reading appetites of this age group. We do like the author's intent of having something a bit more portable. But we also know that parents and their children will be better served investing in one of the more extensive resources that are available. These won't cost much more but offer more choices and variety than contained within this volume.

**Where To Find/Buy:**

Bookstores and libraries.

**Activities & Games**

# EARLYCHILDHOOD.COM

## Description:

Sponsored by a school supply store specializing in arts and crafts materials, this site offers information for both parents and early childhood education professionals. Options at the site include "arts-n-crafts," articles and resources, forums to share one's ideas, post concerns and questions to others, and an avenue for individuals or organizations to publish articles and comments. A list of education-type links also is provided. Articles offer advice and information from "early childhood experts" such as Bev Bos, Evelyn Petersen, and others. Articles written specifically for parents focus on listening skills, reading to children, and teaching thinking skills at home. Also given is narrative advice from Bev Bos along the topics of children's book literacy, music, "parenting basics," and separation anxiety. Other articles concentrate on issues that typically concern professionals—creating thematic curriculums, multi-age classrooms, assessment and evaluation, technology in the classroom, and more.

## Evaluation:

While this site's supply of craft ideas makes it worth a visit, its depth is limited and the commercial nature of its presentation makes one question the sources and experts used. For example, an article on how puzzles can influence a child's development turns out to be written by the marketing director for a puzzle company in a not-even-thinly disguised pitch to link her company's puzzles—by name—with successful childhood development. Although the author and her commercial affiliation are clearly stated, the site would be better enhanced by clearly separating its information sections from its commercial "pitches." One pleasant surprise is a list of interesting links. And while its discussion boards are confusing to navigate, in the end it is this site's arts and craft projects that offer parents the most reason to visit. Unfortunately, few of those projects are appropriate for—or interesting to—toddlers. Parents of toddlers may want to hang on to this site address for the future, when their child is ready for butterfly collages, magnet art, and grocery sack backpacks. Other sites offer parents of young children much more.

## Where To Find/Buy:

On the Internet at the URL: http://www.earlychildhood.com

---

**Overall Rating**
★
Little information, heavy commercialism and craft projects too old for toddlers

**Design, Ease Of Use**
★★★
Clear path, simple and colorful design

1–4 Stars

**Publisher:**
Discount School Supply

**Media:**
Internet

**Principal Subject:**
Understanding Your Child's Growth & Learning

**Secondary Subject:**
Activities & Games

**Age Group:**
Toddlers (1–3)

II. Understanding Your
Child's Growth & Learning

## Activities & Games

# SELF-ESTEEM ACTIVITIES
## Giving Children From Birth To Six The Freedom To Grow

### Description:

This 169-page book focuses on age-specific self-esteem activities for children age birth to six years. These games and activities are arranged to parallel the authors' suggested five steps of a child's emotional development. These five stages include trust, self-awareness, competence, power, and self control. The table of contents separates the activities for each of these five stages and orders them by age: birth to 18 months, 18 months to three years, three to four years, four to five years, and five to six years. There is no index. One activity or game is described on each page. Each activity includes the following information: its purpose, the materials needed, how to do the activity, what was learned, and ways to extend the activity (other projects or activities). The authors, Angie Rose, Ph.D., and Lynn Weiss, Ph.D. are professionals whose collective educational backgrounds include child development, effective parenting strategies, anthropology, and mental health.

### Evaluation:

This guidebook provides parents a very simple approach for interacting with their children in an educational way. The introduction neatly explains the five developmental steps children experience as they become emotionally healthy, self-controlled individuals. The age-specific breakouts, separated by the five emotional development stages, allow parents to quickly find an appropriate game. It would have also been helpful to have an index to look for an activity based on the learned outcome from each game. The "What Next?" section at the end of each activity points towards a future goal, or next step, and serves as another way to measure your child's development and growth. All activities focus on building a child's self-esteem. They are easy to follow and well-planned, albeit often mundane and commonplace—blowing kisses, playing with playdough, etc. This resource, although well-intentioned for parents looking to develop a strong sense of self-esteem in their child, will only serve as a start.

### Where To Find/Buy:

Bookstores and libraries.

---

**Overall Rating**

★

Book's intent is admirable but activities are rather droll and uninteresting

**Design, Ease Of Use**

★★

Easy to read but wide margins and a lot of white space provide little text

1–4 Stars

**Author:**

Angie Rose, PhD, and Lynn Weiss, PhD

Angie Rose has a PhD in early childhood development and education. She is also the specialist in Education for Responsible for Parenthood (EFRP) for the Dallas Independent School District. Weiss is a psychotherapist and hosts a daily radio call-in program.

**Publisher:**

Humanics Limited

**Edition:**

1994

**Price:**

$17.95

**Pages/Run Time:**

169

**ISBN:**

0893340464

**Media:**

Book

**Principal Subject:**

Understanding Your Child's Growth & Learning

**Secondary Subject:**

Activities & Games

**Age Group:**

Infants & Toddlers (0–3)

**Activities & Games**

# 365 DAYS OF CREATIVE PLAY
For Children 2 Years & Up

## Description:

With a brief introduction describing the benefits of a child's experiences with play, this 377+ page book describes 365 activities that can be done with children aged two years and older. Activities are grouped into 13 categories "all of which tap into the child's creative potential." The activities do not need to be done in order but a balance between all categories is included when the activities are done sequentially. Included categories are: Art, Construction, Craft, Dance, Education, Environment, Family, Foods and Cooking, Games, Horticulture, Make-Believe, Music, and Nature. There is no table of contents, but an index lists the activities and activity number by these categories. Suggested safety tips is provided along with a list of materials, supplies, and equipment. Each activity is fully explained on one-page with a list of materials, directions, and a child's illustration of the activity also given. The authors also note that all the activities and their materials comply with safe environmental standards.

## Evaluation:

Although the activities are designed "for children 2 years and up," that's convenient for selling the book but not a fair description of its contents. Most of the activities are designed for the older child or parent. Involving considerable adult preparation at times, these activities will creatively challenge the parent but do little for their child's self-confidence or self-esteem. The other problem with this book is in its organization. Additional information needs to be included for each activity such as: the activity's category, the suggested age range, and the objective/skill that is being enhanced. Listing the activities by category in the index, without a table of contents or general alphabetical listing, makes subsequent searches for an activity difficult. The "365 Days" format, of course, fits in neatly with doing one activity a day with your child. But the book is bulky (a spiral-bound format would be more useful) and some activities are fairly common (make popsicles with your child). Check out other resources that build on children's developmental abilities, not adults'.

## Where To Find/Buy:

Bookstores and libraries.

---

**Overall Rating**

★

Great for enhancing the parent's creative potential, less so for the child's

**Design, Ease Of Use**

★

No table of contents, index lists activities by category only; needs a spiral format

1–4 Stars

**Author:**

Sheila Ellison and Dr. Judith Gray

Ellison, with a BA degree in psychology from USC, has volunteered on behalf of children, and founded community youth groups and mentoring programs. Gray is internationally known as an author, teacher, and speaker on future trends in education.

**Publisher:**
Sourcebooks

**Edition:**
3rd (1995)

**Price:**
$12.95

**Pages/Run Time:**
377

**ISBN:**
1570710295

**Media:**
Book

**Principal Subject:**
Understanding Your Child's Growth & Learning

**Secondary Subject:**
Activities & Games

**Age Group:**
Toddlers (1–3)

## Overall Rating
★★★★
Good information offered in a step-by-step format for a specific parenting dilemma

## Design, Ease Of Use
★★★★
Highlighted advice with numerous charts and tables

1–4 Stars

## Author:
Rex Forehand, PhD and Nicholas Long, PhD

Forehand is a research professor of clinical child psychology and director of the Institute for Behavioral Research at the University of Georgia. Long is an associate professor of pediatrics and director of pediatric psychology at the University of Arkansas.

## Publisher:
Contemporary Books (NTC/Contemporary Publishing)

## Edition:
1996

## Price:
$14.95

## Pages/Run Time:
256

## ISBN:
0809232650

## Media:
Book

## Principal Subject:
Understanding Your Child's Growth & Learning

## Secondary Subject:
Behavior & Discipline

## Age Group:
Toddlers (1–3)

---

**Behavior & Discipline**

# PARENTING THE STRONG-WILLED CHILD
The Clinically Proven Five-Week Program For Parents Of Two- To Six-Year-Olds

## Recommended For:
Understanding Your Child's Growth & Learning

## Special Resource For:
Parenting a strong-willed child

## Description:
This book is divided into four sections. Each of the first three parts describes a different dimension of the guide's five-week program strategy. Part One explains the factors that cause or contribute to strong-willed behavior. Considered factors include such topics as temperament, parenting styles, parental conflict, divorce, alcohol abuse, and television. Techniques of the five-week program are the focus of Part Two broken down week by week, and day by day in some segments. Part Three centers on ways to develop a more positive environment in the family and home. The purpose of this part is to show ways to enhance and maintain the positive behavior changes that occurred via the five-week program. The final section, Part Four, combines what parents have learned in the first three parts. It offers parents suggestions, advice, and strategies for managing specific behavior problems commonly occurring in young, strong-willed children (temper tantrums, aggression, bedtime and mealtime problems, etc).

## Evaluation:
This 256-page book focuses on the specific challenge of parenting a strong-willed child. Offering a five-week easily followed guide, this program is based on a clinical treatment program that is backed by over 30 years of collective research. Unusual to this study is that the authors have also done follow-up work 15 years later with families who have used their technique finding continued success. This approach uses a positive, step-by-step, clearly outlined strategy that discusses ways for parents to seek manageable solutions to their children's difficult behavior. This book will dictate your full attention and should not be used simply as a reference aid, although the comprehensive index makes for easy navigation in finding information on any specific topic. The tables, charts, and worksheets work hard to illustrate concepts, and are very useful for the success of the program. Parents who are anxious and frustrated about the behavior of their strong-willed child need to take a look at this useful resource.

## Where To Find/Buy:
Bookstores and libraries.

## Behavior & Discipline

# POSITIVE DISCIPLINE: THE FIRST THREE YEARS
From Infant To Toddler—Laying The Foundation For Raising A Capable, Confident Child

**Recommended For:**
Understanding Your Child's Growth & Learning

## Description:

Part One—"Welcoming Baby: Learning to Live in Your New Family"—has three chapters regarding ways to prepare for the new child in the family and getting to know the child. Part Two—"How Children Grow: Learning and the Stages of Development" offers four chapters highlighting how children learn trust and autonomy. Part Three—"Getting to Know Your Unique Child: Temperament and Age Appropriateness"—addresses the child's temperament, what makes a child unique, and development. Part Four—"Sleeping, Eating, and Toileting: You Can't Make 'Em Do It"—addresses three of the biggest concerns about caring for an infant and toddler. Part Five—"Getting Along in the Great Big World: Discipline and Life Skills"—addresses a range of topics, including social skills, discipline, building self-esteem, bonding, feelings, and language development. The last section, Part Six—"Keeping Your Family Strong: Care and Support for Parents and Children"—discusses, in separate chapters, how to choose childcare and how to build a support network.

## Evaluation:

The authors state that one of the primary goals of the book is to encourage parents to "love our children enough to teach them, to set wise boundaries, to say no when we must, and to help them to live peacefully and respectfully in a world filled with other people." The authors gently give the reader first an understanding about life from the child's perspective. They also empathize with the reader about all the ways a family changes with the birth of a child. In this book, the authors don't ask the reader to adopt a new parenting style or work through a series of exercises. Instead, they offer a reasonable, reassuring philosophy of balance. Balance baby's needs with mother's needs and the family's needs. Hold, but not constantly. Love, but don't smother. Discipline, but don't punish. This book is less about discipline, and more about what a child is experiencing and thinking, along with the reasons behind their actions. The author believes that through that understanding, parents will learn to have patience and experience positive interactions with their child. The authors manage to explain their parenting style without the ever present "do this, or else" attitude so evident in many other resources, making this one of the more balanced, supportive, and reassuring books available.

## Where To Find/Buy:

Bookstores, libraries, or order direct by calling Empowering People at (800) 456-7770, through mail at P.O. Box 1926, Orem, UT 84059, or through FAX at (801) 762-0022.

★★★★

**Overall Rating**
★★★★
Well balanced, reasonable, practical information

**Design, Ease Of Use**
★★★★
Information well organized, easy to read, and presented in a helpful manner

1–4 Stars

**Author:**
Jane Nelsen, EdD, Cheryl Erwin, MA, and Roslyn Duffy

Nelsen is coauthor of the Positive Discipline series, and is a speaker and education specialist. Erwin is a private family therapist, consultant, speaker, and author. Duffy is a childcare director, counselor, parent, education specialist, and speaker

**Publisher:**
Prima Publishing

**Edition:**
1998

**Price:**
$16.00

**Pages/Run Time:**
281

**ISBN:**
0761515054

**Media:**
Book

**Principal Subject:**
Understanding Your Child's Growth & Learning

**Secondary Subject:**
Behavior & Discipline

**Age Group:**
Infants & Toddlers (0–3)

II. Understanding Your Child's Growth & Learning

**★★★★**

**Overall Rating**
★★★★
Excellent for beginning a discussion on discipline in a parenting education class or forum

**Design, Ease Of Use**
★★★★
To the point with major necessary tips highlighted; includes a wrap-up & quick tips

1–4 Stars

**Publisher:**
TMW Media Group

**Price:**
$29.98

**Media:**
Videotape

**Principal Subject:**
Understanding Your Child's Growth & Learning

**Secondary Subject:**
Behavior & Discipline

**Age Group:**
Toddlers (1–3)

---

**Behavior & Discipline**

# STOP STRUGGLING WITH YOUR CHILD

**Recommended For:**
Understanding Your Child's Growth & Learning

## Description:

Reiterating the points of their book by the same title, these "parenting experts" detail their four-step process for minimizing family conflicts and maximizing a child's self-esteem. The ultimate goals of this method are to help parents move from major power struggles to minor ones and, by doing so, increase a child's self-concept. The four steps are: "Don't Use Your Mouth, Use Your Routine"; "Treat 'Em As A Team"; "Make A Correction With A Connection"; and "See The Small Successes Along The Way." They suggest that if parents change their own behavior, children will change theirs. They also suggest that following these steps gives children opportunities to become cooperative, to practice problem-solving, and to take responsibility for themselves. Parents are encouraged to separate themselves from the problem, to not get hooked into fights, and to think with reason, not anger. At the end of this 30 minute tape, the authors offer "Quick Tips" for solving conflicts such as not picking up belongings, fights in the car, not doing chores, clothing choices, and more.

## Evaluation:

This would be a marvelous tape to use in a parent education class. It clearly outlines the major points involved in most current positive discipline resources in a succinct, concise manner. By combining footage from the authors' workshop and from real-life family scenarios, the authors do a good job at identifying major conflicts parents face. The connection they make between parent-child power plays and self-esteem is well made and is one not often addressed in other resources. By realizing that power struggles often earmark a child's need for attention, but also noting that reducing conflicts helps to bolster a child's self-esteem, many parents will have a reason to want to change their own behavior. Parents can increase their own self-esteem by taking themselves out of the fight and stepping back to watch their child become more responsible. Although this video is a bit pricey for at-home viewing, busy parents will appreciate its conciseness and application.

## Where To Find/Buy:

Bookstores, libraries, videotape dealers, or order directly by calling TMW Media Group at (310) 577-8581 or Total Marketing Services, Inc. at (800) 262-3822. Orders can also be taken online by Total Marketing Services at http://www.videoalliance.com/.

**Behavior & Discipline**

# AVOIDING POWER STRUGGLES WITH KIDS

★★★★

**Recommended For:**
Understanding Your Child's Growth & Learning

## Description:

The authors of *Parenting with Love and Logic* highlight their parenting technique—that "love" allows children to grow through their mistakes while "logic" allows children to live with the consequences of their choices. This 65-minute audiotape focuses on the "Science of Control." The authors believe that if parents take all the control away from kids, kids will fight to get control in negative ways (power struggles); conversely, the more control parents give away, the more control they will have. The authors give four steps to dealing with potential power struggles. First, parents need to diffuse a problem by saying something like "no problem." Then, they need to use "thinking words" (what the parent will do) as opposed to "fighting words" (what the child has to do). Next, children should be given choices that the parent can live with, and finally, the authors state that "parents should hope and pray" the child makes the wrong decision so they will receive some real world learning experience when "it's affordable." Tips for dealing with specific situations are given (bedtime, eating, chores, watching TV, schoolwork, and more).

## Evaluation:

Parents who don't have the time to read the authors' book will glean the important points through this audiotape. It generally tends to be succinct, although the authors do ramble at times leaving the listener wondering where they are going. Most parents will appreciate how this technique doesn't focus on them solving problems but instead focuses on their child. The authors state that this will still keep the parent in control but avoid the "brain drains" and conflicts. Parents are taken out of the hotbed of anger, lectures, and threats which tend to make children resentful of them. Instead, the parent becomes available to offer empathy for the child's mistakes (but no "I-told-you-sos"). The authors make a good point about encouraging children to make choices (without danger involved) and live with the consequences at an early age—when "it's affordable" and not devastating to their lives. Of particular use for many parents will be the numerous verbal examples given for what to say in given situations. Parents will find this tape a good reflection of the authors' key points and worth their time and money.

## Where To Find/Buy:

Bookstores and libraries, or order direct by calling (800) 338-4065.

---

**Overall Rating**
★★★★
Offers parents verbal cues for staying in control of potential conflicts with their child

**Design, Ease Of Use**
★★★
Rambles at times, but fairly succinct in identifying main points; concrete examples given

1–4 Stars

**Author:**
Jim Fay and Foster W. Cline, MD

Foster W. Cline, MD, is a child and adult psychiatrist. He specializes in working with difficult children. Jim Fay has 31 years of experience as an educator and principal. He is an educational consultant and won many awards in the education field.

**Publisher:**
The Love and Logic Press

**Edition:**
1996

**Price:**
$11.95

**Pages/Run Time:**
65

**ISBN:**
0944634311

**Media:**
Audiotape

**Principal Subject:**
Understanding Your Child's Growth & Learning

**Secondary Subject:**
Behavior & Discipline

**Age Group:**
Toddlers (1–3)

★★★★

### Overall Rating
★★★★
Relaxed approach includes tips for specific problems based on logical consequences

### Design, Ease Of Use
★★★
Lots of story copy to get beyond; good cross-referencing in index

1–4 Stars

### Author:
Foster Cline, MD and Jim Fay

Foster W. Cline, MD is a child and adult psychiatrist. He specializes in working with difficult children. Jim Fay has 31 years of experience as an educator and principal. He is an educational consultant and won many awards in the education field.

### Publisher:
Pinon Press

### Edition:
1990

### Price:
$18.00

### Pages/Run Time:
225

### ISBN:
0891093117

### Media:
Book

### Principal Subject:
Understanding Your Child's Growth & Learning

### Secondary Subject:
Behavior & Discipline

### Age Group:
Toddlers (1–3)

---

**Behavior & Discipline**

# PARENTING WITH LOVE AND LOGIC
## Teaching Children Responsibility

### Recommended For:
Understanding Your Child's Growth & Learning

### Description:
Divided into two parts, this 225-page book centers on using love and logic while parenting. The authors define love as not permissive or tolerant of disrespect, but that which allows children to make mistakes and live with the logical consequences; logic is centered in the consequences themselves. Parenting then becomes an issue of offering your child choices along with empathy if your child makes mistakes in the process. The first part of the book discusses general parenting issues: self-concept, setting limits, offering choices, consequences, etc. Each chapter in part one recites a proverb, specific to the topic. The second part focuses on 41 love and logic "Pearls" (tips) for dealing with problems parents encounter during the first twelve years of their children's lives. Included here is advice about dealing with peer pressure, temper tantrums, fears and monsters, negative body language, and more. The second part is intended to be used in conjunction with part one. An index is included along with information about "Love and Logic" seminars.

### Evaluation:
This book's approach focuses on providing children the "opportunity for a joyful, productive, and responsible adult life." The book's relaxed writing style sets a comfortable, down-to-earth mood and it is easily read. The author has thoughtfully anticipated and incorporated important parental issues in the index which are not clearly noted in the detailed table of contents. For instance, drug use, runaways, diseases, and suicide are all generally included in Pearl 8—"Crisis Situations"—but are also listed separately in the index. The two part format allows the "Love and Logic Parenting Pearls" to validate the first section. The book offers many interesting issues with sound advice not often included in other books with the same subject material. Some of these issues include pet care, back seat car battles, table manners, bossiness, teeth brushing, and telephone interruptions. Other resources offer positive approaches to dealing with children's behavior; this book's unique approach makes it a helpful resource to be used in conjunction with them.

### Where To Find/Buy:
Bookstores and libraries. An audiotape version (3 1/2 hours long; 1997; ISBN No. 0944634389) of this book is also available for $24.95 by contacting The Love and Logic Press at (800) 338-4065.

**Behavior & Discipline**

# POSITIVE DISCIPLINE
Revised Edition

## Recommended For:
Understanding Your Child's Growth & Learning

## Description:
Drawn from the beliefs of Alfred Adler and Rudolf Dreikurs, "positive discipline" is defined as firmness with dignity, kindness, and respect. The goals are twofold: to teach children self-discipline, responsibility, cooperation, and problem-solving skills; and to always be positive with no humiliation for the child or the adult. Key concepts to this discipline practice include: treat mistakes as opportunities to learn, seek solutions to problems together as a family (rather than blame), believe that children do better when they feel better, the "significant seven" of successful people ("I am capable," etc.), children listen to parents when they feel listened to, and more. Nelsen's newly revised edition contains more examples of how to use encouragement to motivate children along with her emphasis on understanding and applying the importance of "social interest" (concern for others, the community, and the environment). The chapter on natural and logical consequences has also been revised.

## Evaluation:
This 258-page, ten chapter resource offers a combined approach of understanding family dynamics (parenting styles, birth order/siblings, etc.) and child temperament, so that a better understanding of the child's goal/behavior is reached and communication patterns improved. Parents will not only learn ways to interpret their child's mistakes differently but also ways to enhance their family interactions. By offering parents constructive ways to approach a child's mistake, through developing problem-solving strategies as a family and by making decisions together, Nelsen offers strong alternatives to techniques that no longer work for parents, such as punitive discipline. If parents are looking for solutions to specific problems, they might well read one of her other books, Positive Discipline A–Z. The questions at the end of each chapter help to refocus parents (or parent groups) into the essential ingredients of Nelsen's method. The book must be read cover-to-cover to understand the philosophy and gain its benefits, but these benefits will outweigh the time needed to digest the material and practice its suggestions.

## Where To Find/Buy:
Bookstores, libraries, or order direct by calling (800) 456-7770. An audiotape version (90 minutes; no publishing date given) of this book is also available for $10.00 (ISBN No. 0679460411), as well as a videotape version (two-part, two-hours long; 1988) for $49.95. Both can also be ordered by calling (800) 456-7770.

---

★★★★

**Overall Rating**
★★★★
Emphasizes communication, respect, and dignity between parents and children

**Design, Ease Of Use**
★★★
Numbered highlights, bulleted tips, summaries useful; must be read cover-to-cover

1–4 Stars

**Author:**
Jane Nelsen, EdD
Nelsen is a licensed marriage, family, and child therapist, and was an elementary school counselor and a college instructor in child development for ten years. She is the mother of seven children and has thirteen grandchildren.

**Publisher:**
Ballantine Books
(Random House)

**Edition:**
3rd (1996)

**Price:**
$11.00

**Pages/Run Time:**
258

**ISBN:**
0345402510

**Media:**
Book

**Principal Subject:**
Understanding Your Child's Growth & Learning

**Secondary Subject:**
Behavior & Discipline

**Age Group:**
Toddlers (1–3)

**★★★**

### Overall Rating
★★★
An interesting and in-depth examination at a child's first two years of development

### Design, Ease Of Use
★★★★
Very well-organized with chart and narrative summaries; boxed hints throughout

1–4 Stars

### Author:
Claire B. Kopp, PhD with Donna L. Bean

Dr. Claire B. Kopp is a noted developmental psychologist and a professor at the University of California at Los Angeles. This book is the result of her nearly three decades of work with children and parents, as well as her own experiences as a mother and grandmother.

### Publisher:
W. H. Freeman

### Edition:
1994

### Price:
$14.95

### ISBN:
0716724995

### Media:
Book

### Principal Subject:
Understanding Your Child's Growth & Learning

### Secondary Subject:
Behavior & Discipline

### Age Group:
Infants & Toddlers (0–3)

---

**Behavior & Discipline**

# BABY STEPS
The "Whys" Of Your Child's Behavior In the First Two Years

### Description:
This 279-page resource focuses on understanding the behavior of infants and young children as related to their development. Four main sections, or "Previews," divide the book into monthly segments from birth to three months, four to seven months of age, and eight to twelve months of age; babies' development at fifteen to twenty-four months is divided into three month intervals. Each section contains a developmental overview for the entire preview period (roughly a three to four month period) followed by a "snapshot" summarizing the major milestones of this age. Additional subsections describe motor skills, visual perception, language, cognitive skills, social skills, emerging self-concepts, and emotions. Boxed "Hints" are provided throughout in the margins. A "Developmental Close-Up" at the end of each age group offers detailed discussions on age-relevant topics (grasping, toilet-training, etc.). Charts of developmental milestones for the first two years (divided into each skill type) completes the book along with additional reading and reference lists, and an index.

### Evaluation:
This very comprehensive, well-organized resource may seem at first glance to be yet another textbook, but parents will find it to be extremely user-friendly. Many resources focus on children's behavior and how to deal with it; they often gloss over the impact a child's development has on his or her behavior. This resource takes a different stance, albeit at times in a roundabout way, that certain behaviors are normal if better understood. Parents need to make judicious use of the developmental milestone charts at the end of each Preview. These charts also list behaviors that may not be appropriate, thereby suggesting possibly delayed development. Parents are advised to contact their pediatrician; every child is unique and the guidelines given are merely guidelines. With this understanding, this book is definitely a resource well worth a parent's time.

### Where To Find/Buy:
Bookstores and libraries.

**Behavior & Discipline**

# CHANGE YOUR CHILD'S BEHAVIOR BY CHANGING YOURS
13 New Tricks To Get Kids To Cooperate

## Description:

This 198-page guide is divided into three parts. The book is based on two premises of "proactive parenting" which are listed in Part One: changing adult behavior will change a child's behavior, and children's inappropriate behavior is mostly age-appropriate. Part Two offers tips on how to handle thirteen of challenging behaviors for children from birth to age six (bedtime, siblings, eating, going places, etc.). Part Three discusses the relationship between parents, childcare providers, and teachers. Each chapter follows the same format: a scenario of a child-parent conflict, a description of the developmental trait that provides impetus for the behavior, a section explaining typical parental reactions, a section which relates the child's behavior to a similar adult behavior, and a section suggesting alternative reactions to a child's behavior. Each chapter includes a "Bibliotherapy" section which lists reading resources to be used between parent and child to teach about that particular behavior.

## Evaluation:

The authors suggest that if parents look at their own adult behavior, they will be able to understand more clearly the behaviors of their children; "adults throw tantrums, pout, take revenge, and refuse to cooperate. It's just that our actions are cloaked in adult rhetoric. . . ." This resource's unique approach is positive, upbeat, and refreshing; it offers parents encouragement and motivational techniques to change their adult behavior. Although all behaviors aren't addressed, this guidebook offers great concise advice and suggestions for "on-the-go" parents. Of special interest are the sections within each chapter titled "Stop! Rewind Your Own Tape." These snippets relating adult behaviors to the child's will not only help parents relate to what is going on with their child, but may also in effect offer parents alternatives for communicating with their child. This guide's use of icons and consistent formatting makes it very user-friendly and a quick read. For busy parents on the fly, this book will prove to be a big help.

## Where To Find/Buy:

Bookstores and libraries.

---

★★★

**Overall Rating**
★★★
An upbeat and concise guide on how to deal with and overcome challenging behaviors

**Design, Ease Of Use**
★★★★
Clear format for each chapter using icons, catchy titles, compact; light-hearted tone

1–4 Stars

**Author:**
Barbara Chernofsky, MS and Diane Gage

Barbara Chernofsky, MS, is a child-care specialist for the NBC affiliate KNSD-TV, in San Diego. Diane Gage has written eight books and is the Director of Corporate Relations for Sharp HealthCare in San Diego.

**Publisher:**
Three Rivers Press (Crown Publishers/Random House)

**Edition:**
1996

**Price:**
$14.00

**Pages/Run Time:**
198

**ISBN:**
0517884631

**Media:**
Book

**Principal Subject:**
Understanding Your Child's Growth & Learning

**Secondary Subject:**
Behavior & Discipline

**Age Group:**
Toddlers (1–3)

II. Understanding Your Child's Growth & Learning

**★★★**

## Overall Rating
★★★
This sound practical and philosophical guide will complement any home library

## Design, Ease Of Use
★★★★
Detailed table of contents; anecdotes throughout; highlighted blocks of info

1–4 Stars

## Author:
William Sears, MD, and Martha Sears, RN

William Sears, MD, is a Clinical Assistant Professor of Pediatrics at the University of Southern California School of Medicine. Martha Sears, RN, is a registered nurse and certified childbirth educator.

## Publisher:
Little Brown and Company

## Edition:
1995

## Price:
$13.95

## Pages/Run Time:
316

## ISBN:
0316779032

## Media:
Book

## Principal Subject:
Understanding Your Child's Growth & Learning

## Secondary Subject:
Behavior & Discipline

## Age Group:
Toddlers (1–3)

### Behavior & Discipline

# THE DISCIPLINE BOOK
Everything You Need To Know To Have A Better-Behaved Child—From Birth To Age Ten

## Description:
This 316-page book includes 19 chapters on discipline strategies for young children. The book centers on ten principles. These include a healthy relationship between parent and child ("attachment parenting"), knowing your child, (understanding age appropriate behavior), being respectful of authority, setting limits, obedience expectations, modeling discipline, nurturing self-confidence, shaping your child's behavior, raising compassionate children, and communicating effectively. To expound on these principles, the book is divided into three parts. Part One focuses on promoting desirable behavior; 11 chapters deal with child development, temper tantrums, anger, sleep, and more. Part Two, with five chapters, highlights pros and cons of methods for correcting undesirable behavior (spanking, timeout, etc.) along with specific situations (hitting, whining, bad language, etc.). Part Three discusses lifelong discipline, including morals and manners, sexuality, and disciplining special children. A sample discipline plan is also offered.

## Evaluation:
This is most certainly one of the better books on discipline. William Sears, M.D. and Martha Sears, R.N. have combined their professional and personal experiences (parents of eight children) to develop a philosophy of discipline whose purpose is to equip children with the tools they will need to succeed in life. The philosophy is backed up with practical advice. It is well-researched, well-written, and easily comprehended. The book is both advocate and champion of parents looking for answers to questions about behavior, beginning with the "connection" of breastfeeding, then carrying through to a lifelong discipline plan. And because discipline has many facets, it provides general guidelines for parents to analyze behavior problems within their families as well as providing a definitive and positive approach to raising well-adjusted, well-behaved children; solutions to some specific behavior problems will need to be found elsewhere. This book has much to offer parents so they can feel confident as they raise their child.

## Where To Find/Buy:
Bookstores and libraries.

**Behavior & Discipline**

# POSITIVE DISCIPLINE A–Z
1001 Solutions To Everyday Parenting Problems

★★★

### Description:

This 354-page reference book is divided into three parts. Part One offers "basic positive discipline parenting tools." Some of the 27 topics discussed within this part include: family meetings, choices, consequences, follow-through, humor, special time together, and more. Part Two offers "positive discipline solutions." Some of the issues addressed include adoption, bedtime hassles, disrespect, divorce, materialism, defiance, whining, and more. Part Three offers "short tips" (one paragraph each) for avoiding common problems encountered by parents of young children and teenagers. Each issue is discussed and a plan detailed using the bold subheadings: "Understanding Your Child, Yourself, and the Situation"; "Suggestions"; "Planning Ahead to Prevent Future Problems"; "Life Skills Children Can Learn"; "Parenting Pointers"; and "Booster Thoughts." A "How to Use This Book" section offers six guidelines to help your child gain courage, confidence, and life skills. A comprehensive index is also included.

### Evaluation:

Although certainly not addressing ALL of a preschoolers' discipline problems, this book directs parents to advice and suggestions on some of the most common. This well-written, easily understandable resource offers 1000+ solutions to issues such as birth order, cruelty to animals, masturbation, tattling, and more. Its value lies in that it offers not only advice, but also encourages parents by presenting "pointers" and reinforcing "Booster Thoughts" for each discipline solution. The authors' purpose is twofold: to enable parents to increase their self-confidence while solving problems with their children; consequently their children will be presented with positive models so they can become successful at problem-solving on their own. The authors stress that parents need to focus on enjoying their child by using understanding, compassion, and wisdom, instead of seeking perfection as a goal. Offering logical and practical advice, parents should look to this resource as one of the better guides for teaching discipline to their child.

### Where To Find/Buy:

Bookstores and libraries, or order direct by calling (916) 632-4400 or (800) 456-7770. FAX orders can be placed by calling (800) 377-2811.

---

**Overall Rating**
★★★
Short, simple "what to do" solutions that not only support the parent but also the child

**Design, Ease Of Use**
★★★★
Alphabetical listing of "problems"; consistent, bold headings separate sections

1–4 Stars

**Author:**
Jane Nelsen, EdD, Lynn Lott, MA, MFCC, and H. Stephen Glenn

Jane Nelsen, EdD is a lecturer and has authored previous books. Lynn Lott, MA, MFCC is a speaker and therapist. H. Stephen Glenn pioneered the Developing Capable People course which teaches skills for living and building strong relationships.

**Publisher:**
Prima Publishing

**Edition:**
1993

**Price:**
$14.95

**Pages/Run Time:**
354

**ISBN:**
1559583126

**Media:**
Book

**Principal Subject:**
Understanding Your Child's Growth & Learning

**Secondary Subject:**
Behavior & Discipline

**Age Group:**
Toddlers (1–3)

II. Understanding Your Child's Growth & Learning

★★★

**Overall Rating**
★★★
Offers parents verbal cues for staying in control of potential conflicts with their child

**Design, Ease Of Use**
★★★
Rambles at times, but fairly succinct in identifying main points; concrete examples given

1–4 Stars

**Author:**
Jim Fay with Foster W. Cline, MD

Jim Fay, with over 30 years experience in education, is one of America's most sought-after consultants and presenters. He is the author of over 90 books, tapes, and articles on parenting and positive discipline.

**Publisher:**
The Love and Logic Press

**Edition:**
1996

**Price:**
$11.95

**ISBN:**
0944634354

**Media:**
Audiotape

**Principal Subject:**
Understanding Your Child's Growth & Learning

**Secondary Subject:**
Behavior & Discipline

**Age Group:**
Toddlers (1–3)

**Behavior & Discipline**

# LOVE ME ENOUGH TO SET SOME LIMITS
Building Your Child's Self-Esteem With Thoughtful Limit Setting

**Description:**

Using an interview format, the writers of *Parenting with Love and Logic* highlight their parenting technique. They believe that "love" allows children to grow through their mistakes while "logic" allows children to live with the consequences of their choices. This 65 minute audiotape explains how to set limits and offer children choices. Tips for dealing with specific situations are also given (homework, bedtime, clothes, music, friends, chores, using the car, curfews, sibling fights). The authors believe that setting firm limits builds children's self-concept and self-esteem and that children "desperately need limits." They differentiate between "fighting words" (telling them what not to do) and "thinking words" (giving them choices while implying the consequences will always be there). Fay states that if parents use thinking words, dignity, and respect, then their children will treat their parents the same way. A "direct correlation" between good school performance and setting limits on early behaviors is also suggested.

**Evaluation:**

Parents who don't have the time to read the authors' book will glean the important points through this audiotape. It generally tends to be succinct, although the authors do ramble at times leaving the listener wondering where they are going. Several concrete examples of how to deal with certain situations are given, a quality lacking in one of their other tapes. Although mostly directed at parents of teenagers, parents of younger children will be able to pick out main ideas; in fact, Fay states that limits are established when parents begin responding to children's cries. Of particular use for many parents will be the numerous verbal examples given for what to say in given situations. Emphasis was on parents doing mental preparation by rehearsing what they will do and say to their child before a repeated behavior occurs. They state that this will put the parent in control and avoid "brain drains" and arguments. Parents will find this tape a good reflection of the authors' key points and worth their time and money.

**Where To Find/Buy:**

Bookstores and libraries, or order direct by calling (800) 338-4065.

**Behavior & Discipline**

# THE NEW FIRST THREE YEARS OF LIFE
The Completely Revised And Updated Edition Of The Parenting Classic

★★★

## Description:

Based on White's 38 years of observation and research, this 384-page book consists of two sections. The first section details "The Seven Phases of the First Three Years of Life." This includes an initial section offering guidelines for a child's first eight months and a concluding overview of educational developments that occur within the first three years. The seven phases are broken down into age groups: birth to six weeks, six to 14 weeks, three-and-a-half to five-and-a-half months, five-and-a-half to eight months, eight to 14 months, 14 to 24 months, and 24 months to 36 months. Each phase begins with an introduction, then describes a child's general behavior, apparent interests, educational/learning developments, recommended and not recommended child-rearing practices, recommended materials, and behaviors triggering the onset of the next phase. Section Two spotlights child rearing topics such as spoiling, sibling rivalry, discipline, substitute childcare, older first-time mothers, toilet training, and more. An index is included as well as a list of recommended readings.

## Evaluation:

White's book is one of the few books based on natural observations of children in their homes. His methodology is well-outlined and somewhat scientifically founded. However, as White states in his concluding remarks, a project designed to carry out his ideals was incorrectly set up due to government misinterpretation. Final test results then, comparing children in this project with others in terms of their achievement in language, intelligence, and social behavior, were incorrect. This leaves parents questioning whether or not his suggestions actually work—can parents avoid the "terrible twos" by following his philosophy as he promises? All that aside, White offers a valid in-depth glimpse at the inner workings of the young child. If parents can distinguish between his personal opinion and child development facts, they will relish reading about the changes their child goes through. His writing style is down-to-earth, although sometimes textbook-like. Offering a balance between strict authoritarian styles of parenting and laissez-faire, this book has stood the test of time in its popularity with parents.

## Where To Find/Buy:

Bookstores and libraries.

**Overall Rating**
★★★
Presents a balance between strict and permissive parenting based on 38 years of research

**Design, Ease Of Use**
★★★
Excellent index, ample table of contents; differentiation between subheadings awkward

1–4 Stars

**Author:**
Burton L. White

Burton L. White is the director of the Center for Parent Education in Newton, Massachusetts, and the designer of the Missouri New Parents as Teachers Project. He is the father of four (now grown) children and he lives in Waban, Massachusetts.

**Publisher:**
Fireside (Simon & Schuster)

**Edition:**
4th (1995)

**Price:**
$14.00

**ISBN:**
0684804190

**Media:**
Book

**Principal Subject:**
Understanding Your Child's Growth & Learning

**Secondary Subject:**
Behavior & Discipline

**Age Group:**
Infants & Toddlers (0–3)

II. Understanding Your Child's Growth & Learning

II. Understanding Your Child's Growth & Learning

**Behavior & Discipline**

★★★

**Overall Rating**
★★★
Bailey shows a great deal of insight into children and how to work with them

**Design, Ease Of Use**
★★★
Logical structure; rather heavy on text, not easily perused at a glance; worksheets

1–4 Stars

**Author:**
Dr. Becky Bailey

Dr. Bailey is an associate professor of Early Childhood Education and Development at the University of Florida. She is a speaker and the author of numerous research articles, audiotapes, and five books.

**Publisher:**
Loving Guidance

**Edition:**
3rd (1997)

**Price:**
$21.95

**Pages/Run Time:**
325

**ISBN:**
188960903X

**Media:**
Book

**Principal Subject:**
Understanding Your Child's Growth & Learning

**Secondary Subject:**
Behavior & Discipline

**Age Group:**
Toddlers (1–3)

# THERE'S GOTTA BE A BETTER WAY: DISCIPLINE THAT WORKS

## Description:

The author presents and defines what she believes are the two typical yet flawed methods of raising children: the punitive guidance system (power over the child) and the permissive guidance system (power under the child). She also explains that the child can likewise exercise power over (aggressiveness) the adult as well as power under (passiveness) the adult in order to get needs met. The author then suggests the "responsibility guidance system" in which the child learns to have personal power, which will "develop fully functioning, caring, creative, and responsible people." The remainder of the book shows how to achieve and use this system to develop personal power in the child. Exercises are included in most of the chapters; these exercises generally serve as tools for the reader to gain a better understanding of not only children, but the reader as well. The appendix contains "Letters To Parents" (an English and a Spanish version) for teachers to send to students' parents requesting information about their customs and culture, a list of "Children's Literature That Supports Limits And Rules," and "References." There is no index.

## Evaluation:

This book is full of insights into the behaviors of children—and adults as well. Bailey does not merely offer the reader methods to use to direct and guide children, but she first delves into the reader's past to allow the reader to do some self-examination. Through this unique and perhaps even sometimes painful approach, the reader can see the guidance system(s) by which she was raised and how these methods and beliefs may have carried over into her way of raising or teaching her children or students. By better understanding her own background, the reader can have a greater appreciation of the guidance system and methods that Bailey presents. And Bailey does give many illustrations and examples to support her teachings. The many exercises in this book are probably more helpful to the teacher or caregiver than the parent who is reading the book. If the exercises are completed, they will make the reader stop and think. The appendix material contain some valuable references. The lack of an index is unfortunate, as there is much information in the book and no quick way to look up specific topics.

## Where To Find/Buy:

Bookstores, libraries, or order direct by calling (800) 842-2846 or (407) 366-0233. It can also be ordered by Fax at (407) 366-4293 or through Loving Guidance at P.O. Box 622407, Ovieda, FL 32762.

# TIME-IN
## When Time-Out Doesn't Work

★★★

## Description:

Time-In offers an alternative method for dealing with bad behavior. Its focus is on discipline as a means to teach rather than punish. The author describes the four "puzzle pieces" available to use during discipline: Act, Ask, Attend, and Amend. Each of these puzzle pieces is described in a chapter. There are four steps a parent goes through to use the "Time-In" discipline, according to the author. The first is to stop the unwanted behavior, the second is to ask what lesson the child should learn about the issue, the third is to use the puzzle pieces in any order or combination, and the fourth is to notice the pieces that the child responds to. The author also compares Time-In with Time-Out and other methods of discipline, suggests ways to put the puzzle pieces together, and addresses parental anger. Throughout the book, there are very brief examples of negative behavior and how each can be dealt with using the Time-In method. Also included are suggestions for using the Time-In method for positive reinforcement outside of the discipline process.

## Evaluation:

The "Time-In" method is a mature way to handle difficult behavior situations. It teaches the child to think for himself, reason out his behavior, empathize with the person toward whom the behavior was directed, and take responsibility for his actions. When a child misbehaves, the parent becomes a role model by using the Time-In method instead of reacting on impulse with useless or destructive punishments. The author suggests that the parent give serious consideration to what lesson is to be learned from each experience. Examples offer useful illustrations of the intent of the four tools, although the actual descriptions of the tools need clarity. "Ask" is used to help a child discover for herself what she needs to learn. "Act" refers to parental intervention. "Attend" means paying attention to what is immediately needed using each opportunity to teach values and responsibility. "Amend" is atonement for loss, injury, or insult. The author begins each of these four discussions by describing what that tool means, and then suggests how and when to use each tool. Not all four tools need to be used in all situations, and the author stresses tailoring the method to each child and each circumstance. At only 74 pages, the book is a quick read and a viable system for changing negative behaviors.

## Where To Find/Buy:

Bookstores and libraries.

**Overall Rating**
★★★
Interesting concept offering parents four tools to use while dealing with problems

**Design, Ease Of Use**
★★★
Easy-to-read layout; information is concise

1–4 Stars

**Author:**
Jean Illsley Clarke

Jean Illsley Clarke is a parent educator and consultant. She has authored several books, including books on self-esteem and leadership. She lives with her family in Minnesota.

**Publisher:**
Parenting Press

**Edition:**
1999

**Price:**
$9.95

**Pages/Run Time:**
74

**ISBN:**
1884734286

**Media:**
Internet

**Principal Subject:**
Understanding Your Child's Growth & Learning

**Secondary Subject:**
Behavior & Discipline

**Age Group:**
Toddlers (1–3)

**Behavior & Discipline**

# WITHOUT SPANKING OR SPOILING
## A Practical Approach To Toddler And Preschool Guidance

**Overall Rating**
★★★
Lots of information for dealing with early childhood problems in a workbook format

**Design, Ease Of Use**
★★★
Table of Contents is comprehensive but best read cover to cover; numerous worksheets

1–4 Stars

**Author:**
Elizabeth Crary

Elizabeth Crary is a parent educator who has over 20 years of experience in teaching parenting classes. She currently teaches at North Seattle Community College in Seattle, Washington.

**Publisher:**
Parenting Press

**Edition:**
2nd (1993)

**Price:**
$14.95

**Pages/Run Time:**
126

**ISBN:**
0943990742

**Media:**
Book

**Principal Subject:**
Understanding Your Child's Growth & Learning

**Secondary Subject:**
Behavior & Discipline

**Age Group:**
Toddlers (1–3)

## Description:

Based on parent effectiveness training, behavior modification, transactional analysis, and the Adlerian-Dreikurs approach, the methods in this guidebook are designed for use with toddlers and preschoolers. This 126-page guide is separated into seven chapters. Chapter One focuses on three "support skills" for guiding children: parental values, developing reasonable parental expectations, and encouraging self-esteem. Chapter Two offers a problem-solving approach for dealing with challenging behaviors. Chapters Three through Six detail strategies for avoiding conflicts, encouraging appropriate behavior, instilling new behaviors, and modifying inappropriate behavior. Chapter Seven integrates these strategies by showing how two parenting situations were resolved using the author's techniques. Appendix One offers "150 ideas for common problems" with ten examples of how to use the techniques in the book to solve problems. Appendix Two includes summary sheets for the book's featured "Ten Tools." An index is also given.

## Evaluation:

By offering 32 alternatives to spanking, and over 150 ways to resolve many of the conflicts parents experience today, this is truly a working resource. The numerous worksheets, exercises, and charts included in this resource will be of great help to many parents, caregivers, and teachers. By helping to isolate and break down problem behaviors, parents will be more apt to take a proactive stance rather than reacting negatively to issues. Parents are encouraged to determine what their goals are for their children, then choose the best course of discipline, and develop their own "effective, loving style of parenting." Although not necessarily an easily-read book, it is a resource well worth parents' time if they are finding themselves in a quandary about which type of discipline is best. Based upon the personalities of the parent and child, this book may offer parents some welcome relief and additional ideas for how to deal with conflicts that arise.

## Where To Find/Buy:

Bookstores and libraries, or order direct by calling (800) 992-6657.

**Behavior & Discipline**

# KIDS ARE WORTH IT!
Giving Your Child The Gift Of Inner Discipline

★★★

### Description:

This book is based upon the author's parenting theory of teaching children to believe, think, and respect themselves, thus, becoming responsible, resourceful, resilient, and loving individuals who have the gift of inner discipline. She shows how to do this in 14 chapters. Chapter Two speaks to three kinds of families: "Brickwall," "Jellyfish," and "Backbone" and the characteristics of each; how they respond to various situations is explained throughout the rest of the book. Chapter topics include: keeping your cool, dealing with serious problems (getting your child out of jail, etc.), money, toilet training, sexuality, and more. The author demonstrates that her "answer [to these situations] is more an approach to parenting than a collection of techniques." The author further states that having an attitude in which parents believe kids are worth it, treating them in a way parents would want to be treated, and behaving in a way that leaves dignities intact will provide an environment to help children develop self-discipline.

### Evaluation:

The underlying theme in this book is "The Golden Rule." Drawing from her experience as a nun, and now as a parent of teenagers, the author outlines an approach that allows the child to be responsible for themselves instead of being reliant on external rewards, incentives, and punishments. It is a refreshing point-of-view, and clearly outlined and illustrated. The book's 253 pages offers insights on why discipline is not learned through threats and bribes, offering instead the impetus to teach children HOW to think. The book also provides good news about the strong-willed child, and how to buffer your child from the dangers of sexual promiscuity, drug abuse, and other self-destructive behavior. Although heavy with text at times, this book and its inspirational quotes, will help parents find alternative ways to deal with "problems." Although superficially more relevant for parents of teenagers, parents of young children will glean a well-thought out foundation for "disciplining" their toddler or preschooler.

### Where To Find/Buy:

Bookstores and libraries.

---

**Overall Rating**
★★★
Unique approach clearly presented and well-illustrated; expect long-term use

**Design, Ease Of Use**
★★
Adequate table of contents & index; heavy text style, caps in chapter subheadings help

1–4 Stars

**Author:**
Barbara Coloroso

Barbara Coloroso, a former schoolteacher, is an internationally known speaker in the areas of parenting, teaching, positive school climate, and nonviolent resolution.

**Publisher:**
Avon Books
(Hearst Corporation)

**Edition:**
1994

**Price:**
$12.00

**Pages/Run Time:**
253

**ISBN:**
0380719541

**Media:**
Book

---

**Principal Subject:**
Understanding Your Child's Growth & Learning

**Secondary Subject:**
Behavior & Discipline

**Age Group:**
Toddlers (1–3)

# HOW TO TALK SO KIDS WILL LISTEN & LISTEN SO KIDS WILL TALK

**Overall Rating**
★★★
Practical down-to-earth tips to guide communications between parent and child

**Design, Ease Of Use**
★
Lots of information presented in a cluttered, rather distracting format

1–4 Stars

**Author:**
Adele Faber and Elaine Mazlish

Adele Faber and Elaine Mazlish are both graduates of New York University, and have taught at the New School for Social Research in New York and the Family Life Institute of Long Island University.

**Publisher:**
Avon Books
(Hearst Corporation)

**Edition:**
1980

**Price:**
$12.00

**Pages/Run Time:**
242

**ISBN:**
0380570009

**Media:**
Book

**Principal Subject:**
Understanding Your Child's Growth & Learning

**Secondary Subject:**
Behavior & Discipline

**Age Group:**
Toddlers (1–3)

## Description:

This guidebook presents communication methods that "affirm the dignity and humanity of both parents and children." This 242-page, seven chapter book is based on the authors' six years of experience with parents in their workshops. Numerous exercises, sample dialogues, and cartoon "dos" and "don'ts" are given for each chapter. The authors suggest that parents first flip through the book, but then progress through the chapters slowly in order doing the exercises as they go; they advise parents not to skip over any of the activities. The first chapter is about helping children deal with their feelings. Chapter Two focuses on cooperation. Chapters Three and Four include alternatives to punishment and encouraging autonomy, respectively. Chapter Five highlights ways to praise children. Chapter Six discusses how to free children from "playing roles," i.e., self-fulfilling statements. Chapter Seven shows parents how to put to use the suggestions from the book. A summary, some additional resources, and an index conclude the book.

## Evaluation:

This resource offers valid parenting points and great problem-solving strategies, but it tends to be a laborious read. Sample conversations interspersed throughout, response "fill-ins" for the reader, and amateurish cartoons make deciphering information a difficult and fatiguing operation. Despite inclusion of an index, readers may need to re-review the material in order to ferret out tips for specific topics. For some issues, the authors have written "scenes" to help the reader understand the proposed principles. Instead, these dialogues are confusing. The authors try to recoup in each chapter by including "A Quick Reminder" that sums up major points, but these lead to overkill and the weary search for information plods on amongst the poor style format. If parents are intent on reviewing this book, they need to thoroughly peruse the "How to Read and Use" section at the beginning.

## Where To Find/Buy:

Bookstores and libraries. An audiotape version (1995) of this book is also available for $12.00 (ISBN No. 0671520717).

**Behavior & Discipline**

# TODDLERS AND PARENTS
## A Declaration Of Independence

★★★

### Description:

Brazelton, a pediatrician and parenting advocate, offers advice to parents and caregivers working with toddlers. Within the 249 pages of his book, he intermixes narrative paragraphs, set in a story-type format, with explanations of a toddler's actions and interactions. The book is divided into 11 chapters. The first chapter deals with the one-year-old's "Declaration of Independence" while the next three chapters focus on 15 month old toddlers in family daycare, in sibling relationships, and living with a single parent (single mother, single father, working single mother). Subsequent chapters deal with the toddler at 18 months old, at two years old, and at 30 months old. Three of these chapters outline family scenarios and characteristics of the "Withdrawn Child," the "Demanding Child," and the "Unusually Active Child." A chapter is devoted to the 30 month old toddler's experience at daycare, followed by chapters describing a toddler's sense of self and inner control; the importance of setting limits, the value of fantasy and imaginative play, language acquisition, role playing, and more are also described.

### Evaluation:

While other resources have a tendency to be read much like a textbook, this one reads more like a novel. As a result, the toddler's behavior comes alive via the story vignettes used throughout to introduce Brazelton's responses to discipline situations, developmental issues, and more. However, this method of delivery results in a book that can't be read lightly; parents will need to read it from cover to cover to get the information and advice they need to help them through this possibly tumultuous time, and they will be unable to just jump in anywhere to get concise, succinct answers to their questions. Although an index is available, cross-references won't be of any assistance, if parents haven't read the chapter from the start to understand the dynamics of the sample family and the issues Brazelton addresses. On the other hand, if parents have the time to absorb Brazelton's engaging story telling style, they will glean some good advice and answers to their concerns. Otherwise, they need to look to other better organized resources that offer information in parent-sized bites.

### Where To Find/Buy:

Bookstores and libraries.

**Overall Rating**
★★★
Interesting interplay between fictional stories, professional advice, and description

**Design, Ease Of Use**
★
Rambling, must be read cover to cover to get exact information; table of contents vague

1–4 Stars

**Author:**
Brazelton is clinical professor of pediatrics at Harvard Medical School and Chief of the Child Development Unit at the Boston Children's Hospital Medical Center. He is a leading authority on child development and a parent/family advocate.

**Publisher:**
Dell Trade (Dell Publishing/ Bantam Doubleday Dell)

**Edition:**
2nd (1989)

**Price:**
$17.95

**Pages/Run Time:**
249

**ISBN:**
0440506433

**Media:**
Book

**Principal Subject:**
Understanding Your Child's Growth & Learning

**Secondary Subject:**
Behavior & Discipline

**Age Group:**
Toddlers (1–3)

# DISCIPLINE WITHOUT SHOUTING OR SPANKING
Practical Solutions To The Most Common Preschool Behavior Problems

## Overall Rating
★★

Concise dos and don'ts of 30 common behavior problems presented in a "first-aid" style

## Design, Ease Of Use
★★★★

Table of contents lists all behaviors; easily read (bold headings, consistent format)

1–4 Stars

## Author:
Jerry Wyckoff, PhD and Barbara C. Unell

Jerry Wyckoff is a family therapist and adjunct professor in the Human Development and Family Life Department of the University of Kansas. Barbara Unell has written numerous articles, three books, and is an editor for *Twins* magazine.

## Publisher:
Meadowbrook Press
(Simon & Schuster)

## Edition:
1984

## Price:
$6.00

## Pages/Run Time:
135

## ISBN:
0671544640

## Media:
Book

## Principal Subject:
Understanding Your Child's Growth & Learning

## Secondary Subject:
Behavior & Discipline

## Age Group:
Toddlers (1–3)

## Description:
Containing 30 of the most common behavior problems, this 135-page guidebook offers nonviolent suggestions for disciplining preschoolers. A glossary of discipline terms begins the book followed by an outline of developmental milestones for children one to five. The authors suggest that parents read this first to understand their child's developmental stage so they can determine whether a certain kind of behavior is appropriate or not. The remainder of the book contains "chapters" of typically three pages each focusing on a given behavioral problem (aggression, messiness, dawdling, sibling rivalry, etc.). Each chapter offers a description of the problem, ways to prevent the behavior from occurring in the first place, ways to solve the problem (dos and don'ts), and a closing narrative that details a real-life situation in which parents successfully handled the problem. The two appendices include a checklist for childproofing your home and a feeding guide for young children. There is also a follow-up index.

## Evaluation:
This handy book is for parents seeking brief, immediate, and direct practical answers to parenting questions concerning behavior and discipline. Based on over twenty years of behavioral research and the principal of "separating the child from the behavior," this book stresses nonviolent solutions while instilling self-esteem. It is well-laid out, in a quick, easy-to-read format. In their introduction, the authors thoughtfully guide you through the text describing how best to use this resource. Seven "ABCs" of disciplined parenting are offered to help focus parents: determine the specific behavior to be changed, describe to the child exactly how you would like them to change their behavior, praise, avoid power struggles, supervise children's play, and don't dwell on bad behavior. Although parents won't find in-depth answers here for solving more extreme behavioral problems (lying, stealing, etc.), parents will find it a helpful and handy reference used in conjunction with other behavioral guides.

## Where To Find/Buy:
Bookstores and libraries, or order direct by calling (800) 338-2232 or (612) 930-1100.

**Behavior & Discipline**

# 365 WACKY, WONDERFUL WAYS TO GET YOUR CHILDREN TO DO WHAT YOU WANT
Tools For Everyday Parenting Series

## Description:

This is a 102-page "idea book," offering 365+ suggestions for encouraging positive behavior in young children. The table of contents supports nine sections. Each section is further divided into three to five subtopics. The first section is a review of "Magic Tools" and the ideas in the book are based on five points. These points include acknowledging good behavior, avoiding problems, setting limits, accepting feelings, and reducing power struggles. Other sections of the book involve developmental issues (saying "no," throwing food, etc.), safety conflicts (sharp knives, etc.), trouble with other kids (hitting, not sharing, etc.), everyday problems (whining, won't go to bed, etc.), and parenting in public (won't leave the park, tantrum in stores, etc.). Each subtopic includes a statement and definition of the problem, ideas of how to solve the problem, and a list of other resources. A "Just For Parents" section discusses ideas for alleviating frustration. The final section offers a list of additional resources for parents, followed by an index.

## Evaluation:

Here is a light-hearted, comical look at how parents can solve inappropriate behavior in their young child and still keep their sense of humor. This book gives parents idea after idea on how to keep their sanity and still maintain a relationship with their children. Easy-to-read and in an unconventional format (5.5" x 8.5" soft cover), this "wacky" book delivers short, numerous, "pick-and-choose" suggestions for a wide variety of common, everyday problems. This resource also includes several development charts, reflective notes, and a brief index. The suggestions and ideas are always set to the positive side, while the reinforcing cartoons add a humorous approach that simply reiterates the text. It would have been more useful to use the cartoon format to illustrate other ways to deal with the problem other than simply repeating the text's message. Although not a comprehensive "text," this book would make for good conversation or a springboard for other tried-and-true methods within a parent forum.

## Where To Find/Buy:

Bookstores and libraries, or order direct by calling (800) 992-6657.

---

**Overall Rating**
★★
Light-hearted & entertaining book offering practical suggestions for everyday problems

**Design, Ease Of Use**
★★★
A quick read; both the contents and index are helpful; cartoons fun but rather repetitive

1–4 Stars

**Author:**
Elizabeth Crary

Elizabeth Crary has been a parent educator for 20 years and the author of 27 other books for parents and children.

**Publisher:**
Parenting Press

**Edition:**
1995

**Price:**
$9.95

**Pages/Run Time:**
102

**ISBN:**
0943990793

**Media:**
Book

---

**Principal Subject:**
Understanding Your Child's Growth & Learning

**Secondary Subject:**
Behavior & Discipline

**Age Group:**
Toddlers (1–3)

**Behavior & Discipline**

# GENTLE DISCIPLINE
50 Effective Techniques For Teaching Your Children Good Behavior

**★★**

### Overall Rating
★★
Short, concise solutions probably won't satisfy most parents' needs for in-depth advice

### Design, Ease Of Use
★★
Strong chapter subheadings & bulleted highlights useful; index would be helpful

1–4 Stars

### Author:
Dawn Lighter, MA

Dawn Lighter, MA, is a family therapist. She has an MA in Family Counseling from the University of San Diego.

### Publisher:
Meadowbrook Press
(Simon & Schuster)

### Edition:
1995

### Price:
$6.00

### Pages/Run Time:
107

### ISBN:
0671527010

### Media:
Book

### Principal Subject:
Understanding Your Child's Growth & Learning

### Secondary Subject:
Behavior & Discipline

### Age Group:
Toddlers (1–3)

### Description:
This 107-page book is based on three steps toward growth: awareness, learning new skills, and getting support. It focuses on a nonviolent, gentle approach to discipline. The book has five parts. Part One offers parents ten ways of avoiding conflicts with their child (ignoring, walking away, choices, humor, etc). Parts Two and Three center, respectively, on improving communication (clear commands, family meetings, etc.) and shaping your child's environment (simplify, enrich, limit, and organize). General guidelines for children, with positive and negative consequences, are given in Part Four, and Part Five closes with ten ways parents can meet their own needs. There is a listing of further suggested readings and resources as well as a two-page bibliography. Each of the 50 techniques typically is covered in one-page and the age groups for which this technique works best are given at the end of the explanation. Most of the techniques are suitable for the 2 to 19 year old age range. No index is provided.

### Evaluation:
Offering 50 simple, effective techniques for disciplining your child, this book focuses on teaching children good behavior, rather than simply punishing bad behavior. Many valuable solutions are given for parents on correcting misbehavior using a nonviolent authoritative approach. These solutions, however, are quite concise; parents wishing more in-depth examples will need to look elsewhere. Not only addressing the child's behavior, this guide is unique by taking into account parental bad habits as well; topics such as avoiding alcohol, not undermining your partner's authority, and recognizing when to seek psychological help are addressed in Part Five. The author also recommends various ways parents can stay in shape, physically and psychologically, so they can function better as a parent. The book is logical and sequential. It speaks to all families, regardless of lifestyles or environment, and would be useful in everyone's family library combined with other resources on behavior and discipline.

### Where To Find/Buy:
Bookstores and libraries, or order direct by calling (800) 338-2232.

**Behavior & Discipline**

# NO MORE TANTRUMS
## A Parent's Guide To Taming Your Toddler And Keeping Your Cool

★★

### Description:

Offering a "helpful compilation of parent-tested, child-tested solutions to . . . troublesome areas in child rearing," this 168-page, 18 chapter book strives to help parents deal with toddlers' behaviors. Chapter One offers parents tips on how they can keep calm during a child's outburst. Chapters Two through Five discuss sibling issues. These include how to manage a sibling's behaviors towards a new baby (sulking, pouting, etc.), along with how parents can include the older child in the care of the new baby. Most other chapters address situations where tantrums may erupt. These situations include sharing with other children, talking back, nagging and whining, tattling, name-calling, as well as lying and stealing, to name a few. Some of the suggestions are in the form of dialogue, while "starred" paragraphs offer the authors' insight, alternatives, and advice. Also included are tips on getting a child to bed at the appropriate time and establishing accepted behaviors in public places. The book supports a full index.

### Evaluation:

Although the book's concise advice sometimes lacks depth, this upbeat guidebook does a good job of addressing toddler misbehavior. The book offers multiple solutions towards resolving sibling disputes, disciplining effectively, establishing rules, and encouraging positive habits in a sensitive, compassionate manner. The authors have wisely used humor in dealing with this subject matter, leaving the reader in a comfortable, no-stress environment. This approach shows parents the effectiveness of stepping back and thinking about their child's behavior first, before reacting to the heat-of-the-moment tantrum. Handling one's own temper first helps to eliminate the frequency of temper tantrums, suggest the authors. The book is easy to use with a larger print format. The index is a good back-up for a rather obscure table of contents with titles such as "The Taming of Some Shrews" and "War and . . . War." This resource will be best used to complement other books dealing with both the "whys" and "hows" of toddler behavior.

### Where To Find/Buy:

Bookstores and libraries.

---

**Overall Rating**
★★
Lighthearted tips for dealing with toddler behavior but solutions could use more depth

**Design, Ease Of Use**
★★
Spread out larger print is great; vague chapter titles aided by comprehensive index

1–4 Stars

**Author:**
Diane Mason, Gayle Jensen, and Carolyn Ryzewicz

Diane Mason, Gayle Jensen, and Carolyn Ryzewicz are parents with a history of credits in journalistic, entrepreneurial, and educational endeavors.

**Publisher:**
Contemporary Books (NTC/ Contemporary Publishing)

**Edition:**
1997

**Price:**
$12.95

**Pages/Run Time:**
168

**ISBN:**
0809230704

**Media:**
Book

**Principal Subject:**
Understanding Your Child's Growth & Learning

**Secondary Subject:**
Behavior & Discipline

**Age Group:**
Toddlers (1–3)

II. Understanding Your Child's Growth & Learning

**Overall Rating**

★★

Surface explanations for understanding a child's behavior; emphasis is on "the system"

**Design, Ease Of Use**

★

No index; somewhat obscure table of contents

1–4 Stars

**Author:**

Thomas W. Phelan, PhD

Dr. Thomas W. Phelan is a lecturer on child discipline and Attention Deficit Disorder. He is a registered PhD Clinical Psychologist who founded the Illinois Association for Hyperactivity and Attention Deficit Disorder. He also appears on both radio and TV.

**Publisher:**

Child Management

**Edition:**

2nd (1995)

**Price:**

$12.95

**Pages/Run Time:**

180

**ISBN:**

0963386190

**Media:**

Book

**Principal Subject:**

Understanding Your Child's Growth & Learning

**Secondary Subject:**

Behavior & Discipline

**Age Group:**

Toddlers (1–3)

## Behavior & Discipline

# 1-2-3 MAGIC
## Effective Discipline For Children 2–12

### Description:

This 180-page, nine-chapter guidebook highlights "one of the most popular child rearing programs in the country" developed by the author, a clinical psychologist, in 1984. The book's intent is to arm parents with a discipline method for children ages two to twelve that involves no shouting, arguing, or spanking. Some of the issues presented include controlling obnoxious actions, testing/manipulations children use, encouraging good behavior, tantrums, and more. The "1-2-3 Magic" system relies on, as the author states, the belief that children "are born unreasonable and selfish, and it is our job to help them become the opposite." He further details the method's use for behaviors that parents want stopped (hitting, etc.) or started (chores, etc.), the six types of testing and manipulation children use, and more. This newer edition also includes four new chapters for teachers of preschool to junior high, a chapter on dealing with behaviors in public, active listening, building self-esteem, and other topics. There is no index.

### Evaluation:

The intent of the 1-2-3 system is a step process of disciplining children in a positive, caring environment. For example, when parents encounter unreasonable behavior, they say, "That's 1"; this is the first warning. If no change occurs in the child's behavior, parents then hold up another finger and say, "That's 2." If there still is no change, then "3" sends the child off to his room for the "time out." The book further explains how to get him to his room and other facets of the process. After the timeout, nothing further is said about the behavior. The guide is easy to understand, sometimes using a dialogue style format for clarity. So much emphasis is placed on the "system" that the book falls short on giving depth to the real issues of discipline. Very short, basic explanations are given for a variety of topics. An index would have helped for a rather obscure table of contents. This is just another attempted "cure-all" for inappropriate behavior in children. Check out more than this resource for a more balanced view.

### Where To Find/Buy:

Bookstores and libraries, or order direct by calling (800) 442-4453. A videotape version (120 minutes, 1990) of this book is also available for $44.98 (ISBN No. 0963386131) by calling (800) 442-4453.

**Behavior & Discipline**

# MAKING THE "TERRIBLE" TWOS TERRIFIC!

★★

## Description:

This 184-page book is based on Rosemond's "benevolent dictatorship" disciplinary style. As he states, successful parenting includes "Management, as opposed to punishment; Proactivity, as opposed to reactivity; Assertiveness, as opposed to anger; Consistency, as opposed to unpredictability; and Communication, as opposed to confusion." He aims to provide parents with a resource that is "low on theory and high on service" as their child moves through the "terrible twos." This guide supports seven chapters. Chapters One through Three discuss ways to understand a two-year-old, how to encourage their healthy development, and methods of managing discipline. Chapter Four talks about toilet training, and the final chapters, Five through Seven, contain information on bedtime routines, aggressive behaviors, and daycare versus parent care. Most chapters focus on the author's point of view primarily based on books by Dr. Burton White. Chapters contain parent anecdotes about the given topic and finish in a question and answer format.

## Evaluation:

Rosemond interjects humor, his professional experience in psychology, and his consistent principles to help parents understand and cope with their two-year-old's development. His point is that a household must be parent-centered, not child-centered. Successful parenting in his terms means three things need to happen: that children need to "pay more attention to the adult than the adult does to the child," children need to do as told, and parents must have the last word ("because I told you so"). He also offers tips on how to discipline (spanking is acceptable and defined). This guide must be read cover to cover since the titles in the table of contents and chapter subheadings are rather vague. Rosemond also has a tendency to ramble while dismissing others' points of views and espousing his own. The Q & A format at the end of each chapter is helpful for focused input on any given subject. Parents looking to strike a balance between an authoritarian parenting style and an attachment style may find their answers in this guidebook.

## Where To Find/Buy:

Bookstores and libraries.

---

**Overall Rating**
★★
Useful tips & support for parents trying to balance authoritarian and attachment styles

**Design, Ease Of Use**
★
Table of contents vague, subheadings absent in some chapters; Q & A format for each topic

1–4 Stars

**Author:**
John Rosemond

John Rosemond is a family psychologist and director of the Center for Affirmative Parenting (CAP) in Gastonia, North Carolina. CAP is a national organization whose purpose is to provide families with advice and guidance in the raising of their children.

**Publisher:**
Andrews and McMeel (Universal Press Syndicate)

**Edition:**
1993

**Price:**
$8.95

**ISBN:**
0836228111

**Media:**
Book

**Principal Subject:**
Understanding Your Child's Growth & Learning

**Secondary Subject:**
Behavior & Discipline

**Age Group:**
Toddlers (1–3)

**Behavior & Discipline**

# DR. JAMES DOBSON ON PARENTING
The Strong-Willed Child And Parenting Isn't For Cowards

## Description:
This book contains two complete books written by Dobson. Reference notes follow each book. The first book, The Strong Willed Child (copyright 1978), has nine chapters. These include discussions about "Shaping the Will," "Protecting the Spirit," common parenting errors, sibling rivalry, hyperactivity, an evaluation of effecting parenting, and more. The second book, Parenting Isn't For Cowards (copyright 1987), has 12 chapters. This book discusses the challenge of parenthood, offers feedback from 35,000 parents about their children and themselves, gives suggestions for parents of young children, ways to handle "power games," and more. It also provides suggestions and advice to parents of adolescents, a question and answer chapter, and finishes with Dobson's inspired "Final Thought." There is an appendix following the second book consisting of a questionnaire/survey. There are numerous tables and explanatory charts interspersed throughout the book.

## Evaluation:
This book rests primarily on Dobson's stated purpose to "verbalize the Judeo-Christian tradition regarding discipline of children and to apply those concepts to today's families." We would then hope that numerous scripture verses would be quoted to support his position, perhaps coupled with results from more recent child development studies regarding behavior and discipline. Instead, Dobson takes on a decidedly defensive posture lambasting many respected child development theorists. Dobson's first book begins with a story of how he taught his willful dog to obey commands by striking him. Dobson continues this analogy stating that "corporal punishment [a small switch or belt] . . . is a teaching tool by which harmful behavior is inhibited. . . ." He further states that he makes no attempt to validate or prove his suggestions and perspectives. If one wants a historical perspective on behavior and discipline, this resource can be helpful. Otherwise, other books offer a more well-rounded Christian base from which to parent.

## Where To Find/Buy:
Bookstores and libraries.

---

**Overall Rating**
★
Offers a historical basis, sprinkled with some scripture, for using corporal punishment

**Design, Ease Of Use**
★
Chapter titles in table of contents are rather obscure; does not contain an index

1–4 Stars

**Author:**
James Dobson, PhD

James C. Dobson, PhD, is founder and president of Focus on the Family. He has served as a consultant to the White House on family matters, has a national radio program, and was Associate Clinical Professor of Pediatrics at the USC School of Medicine for 14 years.

**Publisher:**
Inspirational Press
(BBS Publishing)

**Edition:**
1997

**Price:**
$12.99

**Pages/Run Time:**
501

**ISBN:**
0884861775

**Media:**
Book

**Principal Subject:**
Understanding Your Child's Growth & Learning

**Secondary Subject:**
Behavior & Discipline

**Age Group:**
Infants & Toddlers (0–3)

**Behavior & Discipline**

# THE NEW DARE TO DISCIPLINE

### Description:

These eleven chapters convey the author's approach towards disciplining children, which is based on his "understanding of the Judeo-Christian concept of parenting that has guided millions of mothers and fathers for centuries." Chapter One gives the author's premise by stating that, in order to be successful, parents must have courage, consistency, conviction, diligence, and enthusiasm. Chapters Two and Three discuss philosophies and methods as well as examining five concepts the author refers to as "commonsense" child rearing. Chapter Four is set in a question/answer format, and Chapters Five and Six discuss reinforcement principles. Chapters Seven, through Nine focus on the discipline needed in learning situations and the barriers involved. Chapter Ten discusses morality, and Chapter Eleven offers suggestions on how mothers can cope with the rigors of parenting. Also included are a "Notes" section and an appendix listing narcotic drugs, their costs, indications of use, and slang vocabulary.

### Evaluation:

This revised 277-page edition centers on the author's strong feelings about discipline and how parents should employ his techniques based upon the Scripture. He rarely backs up his premises, however, with quotes from the Bible. Focusing heavily on the author's ego and less so on parents' and children's needs, many parents will come away annoyed. Many of the concepts in this resource border on the ridiculous. For example, although the author suggests that corporal punishment should be an "infrequent occurrence," he belabors the hows, whens, whys, and whats (paddle or switch) of spanking throughout his book in an obviously defensive posture. He even has an opinion on how long a child should be allowed to cry after discipline (with the caveat that maybe the child needs another spanking). No back-up rationale for discipline is tendered other than Dobson's opinion. Other experts in the field treat misbehavior in a more well-founded manner.

### Where To Find/Buy:

Bookstores and libraries. An audiotape version (1993) of this book is also available for $14.99 (ISBN No. 0842374299).

**Overall Rating**
★
Strong on the author's philosophy without offering alternatives for discipline

**Design, Ease Of Use**
★
Contains no index; difficult to find specific information through all of the fluff

1–4 Stars

**Author:**
James Dobson

James Dobson, a licensed psychologist, is president of Focus on the Family. He has earned several honorary doctorates and holds a PhD in child development. He resides in Colorado with his wife. They have two grown children.

**Publisher:**
Tyndale House Publishers

**Edition:**
2nd (1992)

**Price:**
$12.99

**Pages/Run Time:**
277

**ISBN:**
0842305068

**Media:**
Book

**Principal Subject:**
Understanding Your Child's Growth & Learning

**Secondary Subject:**
Behavior & Discipline

**Age Group:**
Toddlers (1–3)

## Overall Rating
★

Most advice is obvious and too simplistic; heavy reliance on acronyms for some messages

## Design, Ease Of Use
★

Consistent chapter format nice, but has a vague table of contents with no index to help

1–4 Stars

## Author:
Thomas J. Dishion, PhD and Scot G. Patterson

Dishion is a child psychologist, family therapist, and research scientist at the Oregon Social Learning Center. He is also an associate professor of counseling at the University of Oregon. Patterson has a BS in psychology and has been a coauthor of other books.

## Publisher:
Castalia Publishing

## Edition:
1996

## Price:
$10.95

## Pages/Run Time:
126

## ISBN:
0916154130

## Media:
Book

## Principal Subject:
Understanding Your Child's Growth & Learning

## Secondary Subject:
Behavior & Discipline

## Age Group:
Toddlers (1–3)

### Behavior & Discipline

# PREVENTIVE PARENTING WITH LOVE, ENCOURAGEMENT, AND LIMITS
## The Preschool Years

## Description:
The authors define preventive parenting as an approach that requires parents to pay attention to their children's needs, interests, and behavior, and take into account what their children are learning from the way parents respond to situations. Within this 126-page book, parents will find eight chapters dealing with behavior and discipline. The authors recommend parents read the book cover to cover sequentially. The chapters have been designed to be read in about ten minutes. A story vignette introduces each chapter with a concluding summary and home practice activities which are divided into two sections—a basic skill and an advanced skill. Chapter topics focus on: observing parent-child interactions ("key events"), teaching cooperation, focusing on positive behavior, using incentives, setting limits, using consequences and time out, "coaching children's friendships," and establishing family cohesiveness. No index is provided. A one-page list of resources is given.

## Evaluation:
Saving harried parents time is an admirable goal, since their time is at a premium. But, there's inherently a danger in not giving parenting topics the time they rightly deserve and, in effect, simplifying things too much, as it has been done in this resource. Certainly parents can handle more than a ten minute slice of advice for understanding the roots of their child's behavior and how best to approach discipline. Yet, the authors dedicate little time here and too much time explaining the hows, whys, and why-nots of using incentives to change behavior. The authors place great importance on "key events," but rarely deal with them in-depth opting instead for the most obvious explanation or a convenient acronym to guide parents—"the PIE recipe for incentives." Parents reading this guide will get the impression that most behaviors can be modified by using a sticker, a star chart, or a cute keyword. They will most likely be left with more problems than they started with, like how to get rid of those stickers and star charts.

## Where To Find/Buy:
Bookstores, libraries, or order direct by calling (541) 343-4433 or contacting Castalia Publishing, P. O. Box 1587, Eugene, OR 97440.

**Behavior & Discipline**

# TODDLERS
Love And Logic Parenting For Early Childhood

### Description:

The authors, "internationally recognized parenting experts," offer their technique referred to as "love and logic parenting." "Love" allows children to grow through their mistakes while "logic" allows children to live with the consequences of their choices. This 114-minute audiotape (in two parts) is conducted in an interview-type format with numerous anecdotal stories. The authors believe that parents lay the foundation for their child's ability to internalize appropriate behavior and that this can be developed from the time a child is 6 months old; the critical period is when they are 8–12 months old. Descriptions of what parents do wrong and how they can better deal with issues (tantrums, testing limits, public displays, etc.) are given. Key practices involve: creating a parent-centered environment (where parents "say what they mean and mean what they say"); dealing with situations without anger, frustration, or threats; not rescuing children from consequences; treating situations with consistency; and more.

### Evaluation:

The authors suggest that raising a toddler is not unlike training an animal. In fact, they state that one of the two things parents should do is to take a good dog discipline course. Although, this philosophy may help put some frustrated parents back in control who feel powerless, other parents may feel even more frustration. Numerous stories are given about what parents do wrong with warnings that the teenage years will then be troubled and riddled with drugs, disrespect, and other problems. Few positive examples are offered, and few practical strategies are given for dealing with situations; for example, for problems while shopping, it's suggested that someone else come along separately so they can drive the child back home if need be. The format flows like a Siskel & Ebert episode with the authors playing off one another. This rambling tape fails to give parents constructive input and it's chockfull of warnings. Parents will be better served reading their book instead of wasting time and money on this medium.

### Where To Find/Buy:

Bookstores and libraries, or order direct by calling (800) 338-4065.

---

**Overall Rating**
★
Rather negative with emphasis on warning parents who don't follow this philosophy

**Design, Ease Of Use**
★
Authors/interviewees tend to ramble with numerous anecdotal stories

1–4 Stars

**Author:**
Jim Fay and Foster W. Cline, MD

Foster W. Cline, MD is a child and adult psychiatrist. He specializes in working with difficult children. Jim Fay has 31 years of experience as an educator and principal. He is an educational consultant and won many awards in the education field.

**Publisher:**
The Love and Logic Press

**Edition:**
1997

**Price:**
$17.95

**ISBN:**
0944634443

**Media:**
Audiotape

---

**Principal Subject:**
Understanding Your Child's Growth & Learning

**Secondary Subject:**
Behavior & Discipline

**Age Group:**
Toddlers (1–3)

★★★★

**Overall Rating**
★★★★
Presents both toilet training philosophy & practice using a "parent-as-coach" attitude

**Design, Ease Of Use**
★★★★
Helpful index, excellent checklists, parent anecdotes, bulleted tips

1–4 Stars

**Author:**
Jan Faull, MEd

Jan Faull, MEd, is a parent educator with 20 years of experience teaching toilet training practices to parents. Author of a Q & A parenting column for the Online magazine *Family Planet*, she is also a regular parenting expert on a local television station in Seattle, WA.

**Publisher:**
Raefield-Roberts & Parenting Press

**Edition:**
1996

**Price:**
$13.95

**Pages/Run Time:**
132

**ISBN:**
0965047709

**Media:**
Book

**Principal Subject:**
Understanding Your Child's Growth & Learning

**Secondary Subject:**
Toilet Training

**Age Group:**
Toddlers (1–3)

# MOMMY I HAVE TO GO POTTY!
## A Parent's Guide To Toilet Training

**Recommended For:**
Understanding Your Child's Growth & Learning

**Description:**

Based on four main points—respect, positive attitude, environment, and moderation, this 132-page book shows parents how to toilet train their child. There are nine chapters. Chapter One highlights "readiness" signs for toilet training; a checklist is given. Chapters Two and Three include toilet training in "Grandma's Day" and where to begin today. Chapters Four through Six discuss what do to if a parent's plan for training doesn't work, what kinds of reward systems do work, and how to deal with power struggles. Night Training and bedwetting are discussed in Chapter Seven, and Chapter Eight focuses on problems such as constipation, bowel retention and encopresis. The final chapter summarizes all of the information by also discussing parenting styles and "final tips." Checklists, "Stories from the Bathroom" (parent narratives), and tables are interspersed throughout the book. Appendix A illustrates a graph showing "average children's toilet training progress." A suggested reading section and an index round out the book.

**Evaluation:**

With checklists, bulleted ideas and tips, and personal experience stories from parents, this resource is one of the better ones available to help parents toilet train their child. Faull states her advice is for today's broad-based group of parents. These are parents, she explains, who realize that there are differences in approaches from one generation to the next and that each child learns to use the toilet in their own unique way. Guidelines are given so parents can recognize developmental signs in their child. These will ensure that toilet training will be successful with "as little emotional upheaval as possible, in a time frame attuned to the child." Many parent narratives are given to introduce and support the author's message. This lends a personal, down-to-earth, easy-going style to the book. Although not all aspects of toilet training are addressed (twins/ multiples, children with special needs), readers will glean a goodly amount of information to send them on their way towards success without diapers.

**Where To Find/Buy:**

Bookstores and libraries, or order direct by calling (800) 992-6657.

**Toilet Training**

# KEYS TO TOILET TRAINING

**Recommended For:**
Understanding Your Child's Growth & Learning

## Description:

This is one book in Barron's Educational Series entitled *Keys to Parenting*. There are more than 30 other books in this series, each addressing a particular parenting issue. Here, the author addresses all the issues regarding potty-training in six parts and 30 chapters. At only 130 pages, the chapters are fairly brief. Part One—"How Children Are Different"—explains toddler development and temperament. Part Two—"The Basics"—explains a child's readiness, getting ready, purchasing a potty, and rewards. Part Three—"Common Toilet Training Problems"—discusses resistance, regression, and other problems. "More Challenging Problems" (Part Four) addresses constipation, withholding bowel movements and wetting. "Working with Others" (Part Five) explains training in situations such as with working parents, grandparents, and other caregivers. Part Six—"Family Life"—talks about related issues, such as reacting to a new baby, reasoning with the preschooler, variances between homes of separated or divorced parents, and bathroom language. Commonly asked questions and their answers are listed following the chapters.

## Evaluation:

Common sense is the key, author Zweiback reassures. ". . . every solution to a problem has to be grounded in common sense," she says. Therefore, generally caring parents don't have to worry that some event during the training process will emotionally damage the child, and this generally sets the tone of this book. It doesn't try to convince parents that they should or should not adopt a particular philosophy. The information is provided in a brief, practical, easy to read manner that simply provides the basics without filling parents up with a lot of background, statistics, quotations from studies, or other perceived extraneous information. The basics outlined in Part Two are based on the work and theories of T. Berry Brazelton. Included in this book is a chapter not found in many discussions about toilet training—diet and its effect on training. In short, this book lives up to its "how-to" status by being just that. It provides straightforward information on how to potty train without making judgments about situations, threatening that certain behaviors will damage a child forever, delving into the history of potty training, or spouting endless facts and studies that serve no useful purpose to busy parents.

## Where To Find/Buy:

Bookstores, libraries, or order direct by calling (800) 645-3476 or contacting Barron's Educational Series at 250 Wireless Boulevard, Hauppauge, NY 11788.

---

★★★★

**Overall Rating**
★★★★
Excellent how-to information without being preachy or too wordy

**Design, Ease Of Use**
★★★
Information is straightforward, well-organized, easily understood; graphics absent

1–4 Stars

**Author:**
Meg Zweiback, RN, CPNP, MPH

Meg Zweiback is a nurse practitioner and family consultant. She has authored other *Parenting Keys* volumes, including *Keys to Parenting Your One-Year Old*, *Keys to Parenting Your Two-Year Old*, and *Keys to Preparing and Caring for Your Second Child*.

**Publisher:**
Barron's Educational Series

**Edition:**
1998

**Price:**
$6.95

**Pages/Run Time:**
130

**ISBN:**
0764103431

**Media:**
Book

---

**Principal Subject:**
Understanding Your Child's Growth & Learning

**Secondary Subject:**
Toilet Training

**Age Group:**
Infants & Toddlers (0–3)

★★★

**Overall Rating**
★★★
A good amount of useful information sprinkled with humor in a concise book

**Design, Ease Of Use**
★★★★
Complete index; bulleted tips; lists of contacts for supplies and children's stories for aid

1–4 Stars

**Author:**
Vicki Lansky
Vicki Lansky has authored over 25 books, and is well-known for her column in *Family Circle* magazine and *Sesame Street Parents' Guide Magazine*. She has also appeared on national TV shows like *Donahue*, *Oprah*, and *Today*.

**Publisher:**
Bantam Books
(Bantam Doubleday Dell)

**Edition:**
2nd (1993)

**Price:**
$6.99

**Pages/Run Time:**
107

**ISBN:**
0553371401

**Media:**
Book

**Principal Subject:**
Understanding Your Child's Growth & Learning

**Secondary Subject:**
Toilet Training

**Age Group:**
Toddlers (1–3)

Toilet Training

# TOILET TRAINING
## A Practical Guide To Daytime And Nighttime Training

### Description:
Consisting of 107 pages and eight chapters, this guide presents information on toilet training your preschooler. Chapter One advises parents on how to tell if their child is ready. Chapter Two details the choices available for toilet training (potty chairs, adult toilet adapter seats, footstools, and the family toilet). Chapters Three and Four discuss how to begin training along with opinions from noted child development experts (Brazelton, Leach, Ames, Azrin/Foxx). Chapter Five includes advice on working with an uncooperative child. Chapters Six through Eight focus on toilet training under special circumstances, handling accidents, and dealing with bed-wetting. Interspersed throughout the book are bulleted tips, explanatory illustrations, and additional resources for parents along with lists of books, videos, games, and "surrogate" dolls that wet and use the toilet for children. Contact information for mail-order companies that carry potty seats and diapers is included. A single-page index completes the book.

### Evaluation:
This is a basic, no nonsense guide offering clear advice for parents looking to toilet train their children. The author has done a fine job of defining toilet training, preparing parents for what to expect, and delivering a variety of solutions from which parents can choose, based upon their child's age and personality. This book thoughtfully includes the addresses and telephone numbers of valuable toilet training resources making it not only useful but unique. Of special interest to parents will be the six-page section that highlights further reading material for children; the publisher and telephone number are included for each book. This guide does well interweaving tips from parents, humorous illustrations, and bulleted advice. Parents of boys will appreciate the "For Boys Only" section which shows how much fun it can be turning the "blue" toilet bowl water green. With her usual humorous flair and concise advice, Lansky fans won't be disappointed. This guide is succinct and addresses all toileting issues.

### Where To Find/Buy:
Bookstores and libraries, or order direct by calling (800) 255-3379.

**Toilet Training**

# PARENTS™ BOOK OF TOILET TEACHING

### Description:

The author of this 128-page guidebook on toilet teaching toddlers states that "the philosophy presented here is one of common sense and a balance between parents' rights and children's needs." The book has ten chapters. Chapter One speaks to parents about when to start training their child—"Don't Start Too Early." The author then suggests reading Chapters Two through Six in order. These chapters include a discussion of readiness, preparing your toddler for toilet learning, a step-by-step plan, dealing with "the learning period" and accidents, and staying dry during the night. Chapters Seven through Nine center on common difficulties, how the feelings and attitudes of parents can affect toilet teaching, and how to keep everything in perspective. The final chapter is a review of the book in the form of frequently asked questions from parents. There is a conclusive index, including references to other resources which are used throughout the guide.

### Evaluation:

Well-organized and sensible, this resource nudges parents towards successfully teaching their young child how to use the toilet in an unhurried, natural progression. Parents are taught how to instill reassuring daily routines, how to ease into the transition from diapers to underpants, and how to talk to their child to reinforce success. Once parents have determined that their child is ready, Chapter Four offers a step-by-step plan that guides the transfer towards no diapers. Despite its copyright date, this guide book is very good at not advancing the process before the toddler is ready. It continues this reminder throughout with warnings not to proceed before following a previous step. For parents that are having difficulties with toilet teaching, such as bedwetting or late toilet learning, the book offers an address and home telephone number of a physician in this field. Even though the book's copyright date is 1983, we called this number and it works! This is a sensitive book worthy of your time.

### Where To Find/Buy:

Bookstores and libraries.

---

**Overall Rating**
★★★
Succinct positive advice on toilet learning/teaching with good clarity of ideas

**Design, Ease Of Use**
★★
Small print; bold headings would help highlight info

1–4 Stars

**Author:**
Joanna Cole

Joanna Cole is a former elementary school teacher and graduate of City College of New York with a BA in psychology. She is a writer specializing in books and articles for and about children.

**Publisher:**
Ballantine Books
(Random House)

**Edition:**
1983

**Price:**
$5.99

**Pages/Run Time:**
128

**ISBN:**
0345343328

**Media:**
Book

**Principal Subject:**
Understanding Your Child's Growth & Learning

**Secondary Subject:**
Toilet Training

**Age Group:**
Toddlers (1–3)

II. Understanding Your Child's Growth & Learning

## ★★

**Overall Rating**
★★
Sorts out research info on "effective methods" in a simple easy-to-understand manner

**Design, Ease Of Use**
★★
Alot of information in a compact book, small print; table of contents & index are helpful

1–4 Stars

**Author:**
Charles E. Schaefer, PhD and Theresa Foy DiGeronimo

Dr. Charles Schaefer is a renowned child-care expert and the author and co-author of several books. Theresa DiGeronimo is an experienced medical writer and has a master's degree in education.

**Publisher:**
Signet (Penguin Group/ Penguin Putnam)

**Edition:**
2nd (1997)

**Price:**
$5.99

**Pages/Run Time:**
235

**ISBN:**
0451192125

**Media:**
Book

**Principal Subject:**
Understanding Your Child's Growth & Learning

**Secondary Subject:**
Toilet Training

**Age Group:**
Toddlers (1–3)

# TOILET TRAINING WITHOUT TEARS

## Description:

Separated into four sections, this 235-page resource offers parents several different toilet teaching methods in a "positive, nurturing" way. Part One carries information on basic toilet training. Besides teaching several approaches to toilet training, it also includes tips on establishing early hygiene habits. Approaches discussed include "The Readiness Approach," "The Early Approach," and "The Rapid Approach." Part Two highlights special situations such as delayed toileting, toilet training the resistant child of three-and-a-half to five, helping children with delayed bowel and bladder control, and bedwetting. Part Three offers tips for training caregivers and ways to toilet train children while traveling. Part Four addresses techniques in training the mentally and physically challenged child. There are two appendices. Appendix A lists toilet training products and Appendix B provides additional reading and video resources. The "Notes" section lists chapter by chapter references; with a concluding index.

## Evaluation:

This resource encourages parents to take on the role of a teacher and encourage their child, avoiding the extremes of being either too strict or too lax. The author advises parents to maintain a warm and loving attitude, offering more positive than negative feedback. This is a well written, well-meaning book which gives the author's ten general guidelines while addressing "the most effective methods of toilet training." This allows parents to choose the one that fits their needs and their child's developmental readiness. This resource gives all methods fair treatment by offering both the advantages and disadvantages of the methods discussed. There are numerous charts, illustrations, and tables to help parents decide which method may work best for them. It is a practical guide without prejudice, offering parents suggestions and essential tips on how to effectively toilet train their child. For parents entering into this phase of their child's development, this resource may contain the information they're looking for.

## Where To Find/Buy:

Bookstores and libraries, or order direct by calling (800) 253-6476.

**Toilet Training**

# GOOD-BYE DIAPERS

★★

## Description:

This 192-page resource contains 13 chapters. Each chapter contains bold subheadings for specific topics covered. The first section focuses on attitude, the process of elimination is described next, followed by advice on choosing a potty. Chapter Four discusses several approaches to toilet training, with Chapters Five through Seven focusing on the "first steps," saying "good-bye" to diapers, and the one-day intensive approach (the Azrin-Foxx method). Information for toilet training the older child is offered in Chapter Eight with "General Tips" discussed in Chapter Nine. Chapters 10 through 13 include ways to prevent bedwetting, encopresis (fecal soiling), toilet training the special needs child, and stories of parental experiences in toilet training their children. The stories are fictional but are inspired by real situations. They are presented to give parents examples of the various approaches outlined in the book. The author focuses on parental attitude throughout stating it makes toilet training either an "ordeal . . . or . . . a joyful challenge."

## Evaluation:

This guide's main focus is on attitude first before introducing parents to toilet training techniques. The author does a good job of outlining various techniques, all approached with a positive attitude. Parents can then decide which are most appropriate for their child's needs and design a toilet training program specific to their child. The "Special Situations" section is sensitive to blind, deaf, and autistic children, as well as children with ostomies, spina bifida, cerebral palsy, mental retardation, attention deficit hyperactivity disorder, and more; also addressed are tips for toilet training twins and multiples. Good general information is provided in this resource to offer parents choices best suited for their situations. The type in this book is small, no illustrations are given for the various methods or the potty training equipment that are available, and no index is provided. Sympathetic towards families searching for answers to toilet training concerns, this guide may help parents get started, but they'll need other sources too.

## Where To Find/Buy:

Bookstores and libraries, or order direct by calling (800) 788-6262, x1.

**Overall Rating**
★★
Approach emphasizes parental attitude; multiple techniques need elaboration

**Design, Ease Of Use**
★
No index, small print, and no graphics make the hunt for specific information difficult

1–4 Stars

**Author:**
Batya Swift Yasgur

**Publisher:**
Berkley Books
(Berkley Publishing Group)

**Edition:**
1994

**Price:**
$4.99

**Pages/Run Time:**
192

**ISBN:**
0425141853

**Media:**
Book

**Principal Subject:**
Understanding Your Child's Growth & Learning

**Secondary Subject:**
Toilet Training

**Age Group:**
Toddlers (1–3)

**Toilet Training**

# POTTY TRAINING YOUR BABY
## A Practical Guide For Easier Toilet Training

### Overall Rating
★

Stress-free approach, but many parents may find it stressful as THEY become trained

### Design, Ease Of Use
★★

Adequate but vague titles in table of contents; bold subheadings throughout chapters

1–4 Stars

### Author:
Katie Van Pelt

Mother of three children, Katie Van Pelt draws from the potty training method handed down to her through three generations of her family, based on a commonsense approach and a loving environment.

### Publisher:
Avery Publishing Group

### Edition:
1996

### Price:
$5.95

### Pages/Run Time:
119

### ISBN:
0895296926

### Media:
Book

### Principal Subject:
Understanding Your Child's Growth & Learning

### Secondary Subject:
Toilet Training

### Age Group:
Toddlers (1–3)

### Description:
The author of this 119-page book believes that "potty training is more of a philosophy than a specific, step-by-step technique." General guidelines are given to toilet train children with "minimal stress." There are five chapters. Chapter One is dedicated to the "Early-Start Alternative." This approach is based on identifying the physical sensations of toileting to a child, practicing muscle control, and learning purposeful control. The author states that this technique can begin before the age of one and is generally completed by two years of age. Chapter Two discusses the "elements" needed for toilet training—a relaxed attitude, a healthy baby, a baby that can sit up, and the right potty. Chapters Three and Four specifically deal with training a one-year-old and a two-year-old child. Chapter Five focuses on bowel movements, and Chapter Six offers the author's final thoughts (avoiding negatives and teasing, using the "big potty," and dealing with accidents). An index is included.

### Evaluation:
Here is yet another opinion on toilet training based on a method that was handed down through three generations of the author's family. The author's intent was to gather and evaluate current information to show parents the success of her own method. The "Early-Start Alternative" bills toilet training as a time of bonding, learning, and enjoyment. It stresses patience, respect, and insight into your child's needs during this time in his development. There are, however, many contradictions in the author's statements. After stating that "potty training is more of a philosophy . . ." she then proceeds to give parents the step-by-step instructions for toilet training. She also emphasizes "taking an easy-going attitude toward training" and yet, one stage of her technique includes marching your child off to the toilet every 20 minutes over a several hour period. Overall, this book outlines ways to toilet train the parent more than it offers ways to train the child. Parents looking for the opposite will need to look to other resources.

### Where To Find/Buy:
Bookstores and libraries.

**Toilet Training**

# TOILET TRAINING IN LESS THAN A DAY

## Description:

This guide is about the Azrin-Foxx method of toilet training children where spanking and anger are excluded. This book contains seven chapters. Chapter One outlines concerns parents have about toilet training; many letters from mothers are included. Chapter Two details the method's background and success rate (children 20 months or older, who were "responsive to instructions, and whose parents desired the training, were trained . . ."). Chapters Three through Five discuss the general teaching plan, how to train your child, and what to expect and do after training. Chapter Six is a mother's account describing her thoughts and actions while training her son using the new method. The final chapter includes a reminder list of 99 questions and answers, a list of training materials and supplies, and reminder sheets for prompting/inspection (during training) and after training inspections. One appendix focuses on toilet training children with mental retardation. A short reference section for further reading and an index complete the book.

## Evaluation:

The authors claim "the average child required less than four hours to be trained . . . without assistance." Outdated, but still a bestseller, this book emphasizes a behavioral approach with a system of stimuli (the potty chair), rewards (candy, snacks), and punishment (verbal disapproval, but "spanking or other physical punishment is probably never necessary . . ."). The authors' method, first developed and successful for the profoundly retarded, was extended to address toilet training for all children. Their research states that children using this method learn fast because of the many factors the authors believe make learning pleasant, simple, and exciting. The training is intense and, in many ways, more a training for the parent than for the child. Areas not addressed that many newer resources include are nighttime training, bowel elimination, travel, medical problems that interfere with training, etc. Also not included are tips on weaning your child from the treats that reward toileting. Even though two million copies of this resource have been sold, there are currently better resources than this one available.

## Where To Find/Buy:

Bookstores and libraries.

---

**Overall Rating**
★
Focus is on quickness of learning with rewards and punishment; some areas not addressed

**Design, Ease Of Use**
★★
Must read chapter by chapter to understand the entire method; small text; good pictures

---

1–4 Stars

**Author:**
Nathan H. Azrin, PhD, and Richard M. Foxx, PhD

Azrin heads the Behavior Research Laboratory at Anna State Hospital, Anna, Illinois and is Professor of Rehabilitation at Southern Illinois University. Foxx is a research psychologist for the state of Illinois Department of Mental Health.

**Publisher:**
Pocket Books

**Edition:**
1974

**Price:**
$5.99

**Pages/Run Time:**
189

**ISBN:**
0671693808

**Media:**
Book

---

**Principal Subject:**
Understanding Your Child's Growth & Learning

**Secondary Subject:**
Toilet Training

**Age Group:**
Toddlers (1–3)

Toilet Training

# TOILET LEARNING
## The Picture Book Technique For Children And Parents

**Overall Rating**

★

Simple and basic but dumbing down the reader is irritating

**Design, Ease Of Use**

★

Outdated pictures & text; most tips for parents are hidden in the child's guide for part 2

1–4 Stars

**Author:**

Alison Mack

Alison Mack is a parent and has written previous child development books.

**Publisher:**

Little, Brown and Company

**Edition:**

1978

**Price:**

$11.95

**Pages/Run Time:**

109

**ISBN:**

0316542377

**Media:**

Book

**Principal Subject:**

Understanding Your Child's Growth & Learning

**Secondary Subject:**

Toilet Training

**Age Group:**

Toddlers (1–3)

## Description:

Organized in two parts, this 109-page book centers on toilet "learning," rather than toilet training, for young children reaching that development stage. The author suggests that "toilet learning presents a remarkable opportunity to evaluate your entire approach to child rearing as your personality and your child's become revealed to you." Part One includes nine topics. Some topics include a history of previous toilet training practices, the benefits of using the toilet, how to prepare yourself and your child for toilet learning, and more. There is also a sub-chapter entitled, "The Freud Complex," explaining the author's opinion of the psychiatrist Sigmund Freud and his theories on child care. This guidebook's second half— "Child's Guide to Toilet Learning"—uses a picture book technique to assist parents in helping their child get ready to use the toilet. It is an illustrated section explaining bodily functions to the child and how to use the toilet. A guide on how to use Part Two precludes this section. No index is given.

## Evaluation:

The only benefit of this book is the advice to not rush your child into toilet "learning." The author does a fine job of "beating up" Sigmund Freud and other toilet training practices trying to validate her technique (she even references a 1914 infant care book). The book, copyrighted in 1978, is dated in many respects. Part Two, the child's guide, should include illustrations and text that capture a child's attention, especially since this is the crux of the author's message to young children. Instead this is where most of the parent information is housed. Marginally artistic, these illustrations show children, horses, and various wildlife relieving themselves outdoors, as well as portraying firemen, policemen, babysitters, and grandpa on the toilet. Using terms like "wee-wee" and "doo-doo" nearly insults the intelligence of parents in its attempt to "train" them how to "train" their young children about bodily functions. There are better, more informative resources available on this subject.

## Where To Find/Buy:

Bookstores and libraries.

# Chapter Three—Strengthening Your Family

Proud parents feel like exclaiming to the world, "Look, everyone . . . here's our new baby!" Then as sleep deprivation begins to take its toll, new moms and dads fully realize the responsibility of learning to take care of their new baby. From the moment babies are born, they begin to search for ways to make a difference, to make an impact on those around them. Adults, too, often enter into parenthood with their own agenda, their own aspirations, dreams, and plans. They may wish to parent much like their parents did, or they may decide to seek a different approach. When a couple has a baby, they begin to entertain philosophical thoughts—"What is best for my baby? How do we nurture our child so she has the best start in life? What kind of family traditions do we want to start or continue or change? What values do we want to impart on our child? How can we make a difference in our child's life?"

As a couple settles in to life with their new baby, adjustments become apparent. Sometimes new parents may feel as if they are living in a vacuum, out of touch with "the real world." Attention is lavished on their new infant, but proud new parents may feel somewhat lost in the shuffle. They are no longer perceived as a couple, but are now considered a family unit. Whereas before they considered their own needs, now it seems as if they are integrally wrapped up in the needs of someone they barely know. Now couples often find it difficult to engage in activities that they routinely did before. Many times one parent becomes a primary caregiver for their baby, other times both parents share equally in the responsibility. However, these shifts in roles may place additional stresses on a couple's relationship, which can, of course, greatly impact the future of their family.

Parenting today is radically different than it was just a generation ago. Statistics show that more than 70 percent of parents return to work after the birth of their child, nearly 50 percent of marriages end in divorce, and 40 percent of children come from those divorces. Nowadays, new parents face issues that their parents did not usually have to deal with. Parenting concerns today focus on such things as how to continue working while raising a child, how to find quality childcare and ensure a child's safety to another individual, and how to find quality time as a family, much less time for one's self. The time constraints and pressures can become enormous, and male and female roles often become blurred. And through all this confusion, parents still want the best for their child.

Couples often seek guidance about how to strengthen their family through this possibly tumultuous time.

## General Overviews

In the past, parents' access to advice was limited. As they raised their children, parents generally chose either to listen to the experts of that time or recall how they themselves were raised. Resources that were available to parents often had more of an instructional tone to them. Parents were told what to do and usually given few, if any, alternatives for how to approach many parenting situations. Parenting methods that strayed from the norm were considered heretic and treated with suspicion.

Current parenting resources, however, highlight a variety of parenting styles and it is ultimately up to parents to choose elements that fit their family's values. Some present a more authoritarian philosophy—"do it because I said so"—while others describe a more relaxed, "laissez-faire" approach—"do it if it seems right for you." Still others fall somewhere within those extremes focusing on the parent-child relationship as a give-and-take relationship, the parent being teacher and facilitator, but neither dictatorial nor permissive. Couples may reflect on the experiences they had as a child, and decide consciously to either reject or embrace the parenting style of their own parents. Additionally, couples observe other families and make mental notes about attitudes and practices with which they agree or disagree.

New and prospective parents may believe that adopting one of these styles is a decision they can make later on when their child becomes a toddler and discipline becomes more of an issue. However, as couples peruse parenting resources, they will quickly discover that these "objective" resources sometimes contain subtle parenting styles. For example, some resources spell out parenting methods to help a baby go to sleep, other resources deplore these methods. Some resources describe ways to instill discipline in a newborn by adjusting the newborn to the parents' existing lifestyle and schedule. Other resources state parents are better able to make adjustments and should allow their newborn to dictate the parents' schedule until the newborn is better adjusted to their environment. Even authorities from seemingly similar religious perspectives may differ in their suggestions of how parents should raise their baby. From the moment a baby enters into their world, parents discover that they must make some fast all-important choices. "What kind of parenting style should we adopt?"

This is a weighty decision that should ideally be made upon close personal introspection, open dialogue and communication with one's partner, and while getting to know one's baby. However, with sleep and time at a minimum, and couple's and baby's needs at a premium, new parents often struggle through this process. However, this should not imply that if parents do make a choice, then they are stuck with that particular parenting style. Every baby is different, every family situation is different. Parents will find that there is a smorgasbord of parenting options that is available to them, and they should feel free to try any combination that works for their family and child.

Our research then, being based on objective standards, evaluates the quality of the information presented in these various resources and not the parenting style. Consequently, parents have the opportunity to objectively preview different parenting styles as they make their personal choices. Through our research, we have also highlighted some excellent general resources that offer such strategies as questions, exercises, affirmations, and narratives to help new families clarify their individual and collective values.

During our investigation, we also found resources that focused specifically on the individual needs of new fathers, new mothers, and siblings. To help in this process, we have recommended resources in this chapter to assist parents as they tackle issues such as:

- Fatherhood
- Motherhood
- Parent-To-Parent Support & Advice
- Sibling Relations

## Fatherhood

One of the gifts of becoming a father is getting the chance to revisit childhood yet another time. Of course, along with that newfound joy is the awesome responsibility involved with raising one's child to become an independent contributing member of society. A baby's entry into the world often invites change—some of it planned, much of it unplanned. And change can evoke panic when it seems as if all that was stable and predictable about daily life is now questioned.

New fathers often go through a birthing process themselves. Emotionally, they may become entangled between the intensive needs of their partner and the immediate needs of their baby. Financially, a new father might be facing new pressures such as how to adapt a two-income household into a one-income household if his partner decides not to return to work after maternity leave but instead stay home with their new baby. Simultaneously, however, many new dads themselves rethink priorities trying to figure out how they can best combine work, business travel, and home life. Socially, new fathers often must adapt to a new family lifestyle relinquishing some of their prior personal activities in order to attend to their family's needs. Some fathers also choose to become "stay-at-home dads" further adding to their sense of social isolation. Spiritually, new fathers begin to explore ways to impact their child's development and future prospects. Physically, well, no one gets enough sleep to survive those first few weeks or months of seemingly non-stop baby care.

Pregnancy, childbirth, breastfeeding, taking care of baby . . . what can a father do? Plenty. Although many aspects of having a baby may appear to be concerns facing a mother, many studies have shown the importance of a father's involvement with his child from the moment a baby is conceived through her formative years. To assist fathers in this birthing process, we discovered numerous resources focused on the needs and concerns of new fathers. Resources we have recommended in this section highlight ways to not only take care of your new baby, but also how to tackle other challenges throughout their childhood such as discipline and safety. Ways to prepare for your child's future, whether it be financially, academically, or spiritually, are also considerations in many of these resources. Some discuss the emotions that surface for new fathers, and offer suggestions for how to cope with the confusion as you adapt to new changes in your marriage and family life.

## Motherhood

The "baby blues," postpartum depression, lifestyle changes, and that tiny baby constantly crying for attention and nourishment . . . it's enough to make a woman wonder if she is up to the challenge of becoming a parent. After childbirth, many women are faced with not only caring for a newborn, but also figuring out how to take care of themselves, often with little outside help and usually without enough sleep to sustain them. Physically and emotionally, many women become drained. Hormonal shifts add to this exhaustion creating a sense of depression—"the blues"—in 50 to 80 percent of women who have just given birth. Some new mothers—10 to 20 percent—often experience more severe bouts of negative feelings, which can lead to further psychological and emotional problems.

Becoming a mother may seem at times to be a double-edged sword. On the one hand, there is that delightful beautiful new baby looking at you, memorizing every detail of your face to commit it to memory. The next moment, that same baby seems unrelenting in his demands upon you and sometimes nothing you do seems to satisfy him. Feelings of inadequacy creep in to many new mothers' psyche which when coupled with feelings of being isolated from the "real world" can leave one to question one's abilities and resolve.

To add to this dilemma, many new mothers go through an identity crisis. For example, working women can get caught up in the "Superwoman" syndrome. With maternity leave usually being six weeks long and with many women returning to work after maternity leave expires, some women stretch themselves thinly trying to do it all and do it all well. They struggle to balance work life, home life, and their marriages while at the same time they often have not fully regained their physical well-being from childbirth. New mothers, who previously worked but decide later to become "stay-at-home moms," may find themselves isolated from their prior, often work-related, friendships and question who they are and what they are accomplishing.

Numerous resources have been developed to help women understand the changes that occur when they become mothers. Many resources offer tips on how to deal with the realities of motherhood while appreciating that certain "myths" such as having the perfect delivery, perfect baby, perfect family life, etc. can be misleading. Some focus particularly on the postpartum period while others highlight ways to integrate a baby or child into one's lifestyle. Becoming a mother is not only a wonderful process but also an enlightening one. Using the resources we recommend should ease this process for you and your family and help you master this challenge.

## Parent-To-Parent Support & Advice

New parents find themselves barraged by well-meaning advice from others, whether it be their own parents, friends, health care providers, childcare providers, or whomever else they meet as they go about their daily activities. Just as new parents get a handle on one aspect of parenting, another opinion comes along to disrupt their newfound confidence. In frustration, they may then turn to the "experts." But even the experts can not always agree. Being forced to evaluate the relative quality of all this advice and information can cause consternation at a time when new parents just want to simplify their rapidly changing lifestyle.

Eventually, many parents realize that the best advice comes from the real experts—other parents who have asked the same questions and faced similar decisions. Being able to discuss options and weigh alternatives with others can help alleviate parenting stress. Other parents who have dealt with the same problems or who have tried various parenting "strategies" can be one of the best resources to give new parents the support and help they hunger for.

Through the advent of modern technology, numerous Internet websites and online services have sprung up to address new parents' needs to converse with others. Parent forums are available to help parents can read others' point of view on a variety of topics, offer their own opinions, and simply feel more connected and part of the "real world." Here, parents can also ask questions, reply to others' concerns, or simply just chat about any parenting topic. And, most important, they can "get together" any time, day or night. If parents are awake for their baby's feeding during the night, they may get "online" and find another parent out there who can offer them the support and reassurance they need.

In the pages that follow, we have recommended a few Internet websites and online services that cater to new parents' needs. Also be sure to check out our recommendations in Chapter Four—"All-Inclusive Overviews About Parenting." Many of the Internet resources we have recommended there also contain chat rooms where parents can have "live" conversations with others at any time to get support and advice.

## Sibling Relations

As parents introduce a new baby or child into the family, new questions arise. Methods for helping children adjust to their new brother or sister vary from one child to the next and from one age group to the next. Parents wonder when they should start this adaptation process. They wonder how they will be able to handle the stress, how they should delegate responsibility for solving sibling problems, and how they can keep their sanity intact as concerns arise.

Some decisions regarding siblings can be made before a new baby is introduced into the family. For example, some resources discuss the advantages of spacing children's births two years apart. Other resources offer different rationale and recommend a greater age difference. Many resources on sibling relationships debate the pros and cons of when an older child should first meet their sibling—at birth, later at the hospital, or when their new brother or sister comes home. These resources also highlight ways to make this first meeting a positive one and help the older sibling feel included in the process.

When a new baby arrives and if an older sibling is ready for preschool or childcare, parents worry if separating the older child from the home will be a positive experience or merely contribute to their sense of displacement. Other concerns may arise later, such as what to do when siblings vie for parents' attention or force parents into the "fairness" game. Should parents step in, back off, or expect the older child to behave most responsibly? Whether children must face having to share their parents with other children through birth, remarriage, adoption, or foster care, we have recommended some resources in the pages that follow. Parents will find that these resources offer great insights to help ease this adjustment for children and parents and make this transition a positive experience for all.

To help focus your search for answers, we have divided resources into these five categories:

Life as a new parent is certainly not lacking in advice or information. And it is certainly not lacking in challenges or change. One of the most enriching experiences though is working through those challenges and changes as a family finding out ways to meld each person's dreams and demands into a cohesive plan.

*"How many hopes and fears, how many ardent wishes and anxious apprehensions are twisted together in the threads that connect the parent with the child!"*

—Samuel G. Goodrich

**General Overviews**

# THE 7 HABITS OF HIGHLY EFFECTIVE FAMILIES
Building A Beautiful Family Culture In A Turbulent World

★★★★

## Recommended For:
Strengthening Your Family

## Description:
Covey's first "habit" urges family members to act based on principles and values rather than react based on emotion or circumstances. The second habit is to create a family mission statement. Habit Three suggests prioritizing family through regular family time and "one-on-one" time between family members. Habits Four through Six—termed root, the route and the fruit—are related. Habit Four is learning to create win-win situations instead of win-lose situations. This method is "the underlying motive, the nurturing attitude out of which understanding and synergy grow." The fifth habit is the route, or pathway, that this philosophy travels, from self-involvement to empathy and understanding others. Synergize, the fruit that is Habit Six, is the end result: Covey believes that two people working together can create something much better than the combination of the two working independently. The key to achieving synergy is to appreciate each other's differences. Habit Seven reminds the reader that everything worthwhile needs care and maintenance, including a healthy family.

## Evaluation:
In the first habit, the author offers that between a stimulus and a response lies freedom of choice. He describes four factors (self-awareness, conscience, imagination, and independent will) that illustrate the difference between "flying off the handle" and putting thought and consideration into one's response to a situation. A particularly important element of this to family is a sense of humor. Habit Two's mission statement exercise is not a simple matter of sitting down and writing out a few rote paragraphs. It requires deep reflection and communication between family members, making the process as important as the end result. The seventh habit talks about renewal—of self and of family. To prevent family "entropy", each member must engage in personal renewal by being healthy—physically, socially, mentally, and spiritually. The family as a whole also must be renewed by spending time together, engaging in family traditions, and including extended family members. While this may seem daunting, Covey gives crystal clear explanations of his concepts and suggests creative and unique tools to develop them. Some tools may seem a little goofy, but done in the spirit of fun can become memorable, valuable parts of the process.

## Where To Find/Buy:
Bookstores, libraries, or order direct by calling Franklin Covey at (800) 372-6839, through Fax at (801) 496-4252, or at 2200 West Parkway Boulevard, Salt Lake City, UT 84119-2331. An abridged audiotape version (90 minutes, 1997) is also available for $17.95 (ISBN No. 1883219965.)

**Overall Rating**
★★★★
Tried and true habits which emphasize bonding, respect, and clarifying priorities

**Design, Ease Of Use**
★★★★
Crystal clear explanation of concepts; tools and exercises for all ages

1–4 Stars

**Author:**
Steven R. Covey

Steven R. Covey is an internationally respected authority on leadership, a family expert, teacher, and organizational consultant. He is a husband, father, and grandfather whose family lives in Utah.

**Publisher:**
Franklin Covey/Golden Books

**Edition:**
1997

**Price:**
$15.00

**Pages/Run Time:**
390

**ISBN:**
0307440850

**Media:**
Book

**Principal Subject:**
Strengthening Your Family

**Secondary Subject:**
General Overview

**Age Group:**
Infants & Toddlers (0–3)

II. Strengthening Your Family

## Overall Rating
★★★★
Insightful and practical guide to help parents develop their own parenting philosophy

## Design, Ease Of Use
★★★★
Intimidating at first due to its wealth of information but it drives like an automatic car

1–4 Stars

## Author:
Laura Davis and Janis Keyser

Laura Davis is the mother of a preschooler and stepmother of a teenager. She has written three previous books. Janis Keyser is a parenting educator and program director. She has conducted workshops and facilitated parenting classes for 20 years.

## Publisher:
Broadway Books
(Bantam Doubleday Dell)

## Edition:
1997

## Price:
$20.00

## Pages/Run Time:
426

## ISBN:
0553067508

## Media:
Book

## Principal Subject:
Strengthening Your Family

## Secondary Subject:
General Overview

## Age Group:
Infants & Toddlers (0–3)

General Overviews

# BECOMING THE PARENT YOU WANT TO BE
## A Sourcebook Of Strategies For The First Five Years

## Recommended For:
Strengthening Your Family

## Description:
There are six parts to this guidebook. Part One contains nine chapters which detail the nine principles that lay down the authors' parenting foundation. Developing a vision, cultivating optimism, learning to value struggle, and teaching children to feel safe are four examples of these nine principles. Part Two deals with children's feelings. Four chapters offer information on how to respond to crying, tantrums, fears, helping your child deal with separation, and more. Part Three focuses on children's bodies: healthy eating, toilet training, sexual explorations, and sleep. Part Four contains four chapters dealing with difficult behavior, such as testing limits and negotiating conflicts. The five chapters in Part Five speak to social learning and play, while Part Six discusses issues inherent to family relationships. Subjects such as building strong sibling relationships, and parenting with a partner are addressed. Highlighted sections throughout the book offer additional insights on the subtopics. An 11-page index follows the final chapter.

## Evaluation:
Simply stated, this is a superb guidebook. It answers questions all parents have as well as those they've been afraid to ask or haven't even thought of yet. The authors have done an extraordinary job of taking a straightforward approach in helping parents become all they can be. This practical resource speaks respectfully to all types of families—stepparents, single parents, foster parents, gay and lesbian parents, and others. The book is inspiring and enlightening—a confident source that will afford parents in-depth suggestions and reliable advice. This reference also demonstrates a wide range of solutions to problems that arise in the raising of babies, toddlers and preschoolers; most often these tips are given with compassion, humor, and warmth. Parents will feel at ease discovering their own parenting philosophy while incorporating new strategies from this 426-page guidebook. The place for this reference is in every home where there are small children.

## Where To Find/Buy:
Bookstores and libraries.

**General Overviews**

# THE INTENTIONAL FAMILY
How To Build Family Ties In Our Modern World

**Recommended For:**
Strengthening Your Family

## Description:

"The intentional family is one whose members create a working plan for maintaining and building family ties," says the author. That is accomplished, he says, by creating and maintaining family rituals. "Family rituals are repeated and coordinated activities that have significance for the family." Part One describes what the author calls an intentional family. Part Two discusses family rituals of connection, such as family meals, morning time and going-to-bed time, going out and going away, and couple rituals. Part Three addresses family rituals of celebration and community, such as honorary days (birthdays, anniversaries, Mother's Day), Thanksgiving, Christmas, community and religious rituals, and rituals of passage (weddings and funerals). Part Four gives instruction on becoming a more intentional family, including traditional family units, single-parent, and blended families. First-person examples illustrate particular points.

## Evaluation:

As we look back on our past, some of our fondest memories are likely to involve the rituals that revolved around our loved ones. The goal of this book is to show how to transform family routines into rituals, gifting each family member with predictability, connection, identity, and a way to enact values. The author reasonably says rituals should be flexible enough to actually work and be effective. Those that offer no joy or pleasure should be exchanged for others that do. Creating ritual need not be complicated. Something as simple as sitting down every morning with your family for breakfast or greeting your spouse at the door at the end of the day can be meaningful rituals. Rituals happen in three phases, the author asserts: the transition phase, the enactment phase, and the exit phase. The transition phase is a "call to ritual" and is the transition between everyday life and the ritual. The enactment phase is the ritual, and the exit phase is the transition back to everyday life. The Intentional Family offers thought-provoking suggestions and positive encouragement for any family who seeks to become stronger through the ritual process, no matter how busy that family may be.

## Where To Find/Buy:
Bookstores and libraries.

---

**Overall Rating**
★★★★
Good ideas any family can implement

**Design, Ease Of Use**
★★★★
Table of contents & headings clearly describe content; strong index

1–4 Stars

**Author:**
William J. Doherty, PhD

William J. Doherty, PhD, is a practicing therapist and director of the Marriage and Family Therapy program at the University of Minnesota. Described as one of the leading family therapists in the country, he lives with his family in Minnesota.

**Publisher:**
Addison-Wesley Publishing Company

**Edition:**
1997

**Price:**
$22.00

**Pages/Run Time:**
221

**ISBN:**
0201694662

**Media:**
Book

**Principal Subject:**
Strengthening Your Family

**Secondary Subject:**
General Overview

**Age Group:**
Infants & Toddlers (0–3)

## Overall Rating
★★★★
Excellent companion to positive discipline focusing on emotions underlying behavior

## Design, Ease Of Use
★★★
Easily read, but should be read cover to cover; self-tests given; numerous anecdotes

1–4 Stars

## Author:
John Gottman, PhD, with Joan DeClaire

Gottman is a professor of psychology at the University of Washington. Since 1979 he has held a National Institute of Mental Health Research Scientist Award. DeClaire is a senior editor for Microsoft's Pregnancy and Childcare, an on-line consumer health-info service.

## Publisher:
Simon & Schuster

## Edition:
1997

## Price:
$22.00

## Pages/Run Time:
239

## ISBN:
0684801302

## Media:
Book

## Principal Subject:
Strengthening Your Family

## Secondary Subject:
General Overview

## Age Group:
Infants & Toddlers (0–3)

General Overviews

# THE HEART OF PARENTING
How To Raise An Emotionally Intelligent Child

**Recommended For:**
Strengthening Your Family

## Description:
Gottman coins the term "Emotion Coaching" to describe his five-step process of teaching children how to understand and manage their emotions. This 239-page guide is divided into seven chapters with an appendix of recommended children's books on emotions, a notes section, and an index. Chapter One outlines the benefits of using Emotion Coaching along with details of Gottman's study (two ten-year studies of 120+ families). Chapter Two describes four different parenting styles (dismissing, disapproval, laissez-faire, emotion coaching) and their responses to children's emotions; an 81 item self-test is provided to determine your parenting style. The five key steps of Emotion Coaching are outlined in Chapter Three. Chapter Four presents some strategies to deal with possible communication blocks between parent and child. Chapter Five discusses marriage, divorce, and children's emotions. "The Father's Crucial Role" is outlined in Chapter Six and how to continue Emotional Coaching as your child grows is the topic of Chapter Seven.

## Evaluation:
Defining emotional intelligence as being able to "concentrate better, have better peer relationships, higher academic achievement, and good health," Gottman's study doesn't focus on how to teach children to behave. It doesn't teach parents how to discipline. Instead, Emotion Coaching may help lead some parents to more constructive ways of dealing with emotional outbursts from their child and open better lines of communication. With numerous personal and professional anecdotes, Gottman explains the five steps: become aware of the child's emotion, recognize the emotion as a chance for intimacy and teaching, listen empathetically and validate the child's feelings, help the child label the emotion, and set limits while problem-solving. Bordering sometimes on the edge of psycho-babble, nonetheless, Gottman's message is well-founded. Providing evidence of how emotional intelligence can affect children's school performance, their physiological responses to stress, and the ability to withstand difficult social situations in middle childhood, this process may supply added strategies for dealing with children's behavior and emotions.

## Where To Find/Buy:
Bookstores and libraries. An abridged audiotape version (3 hours, 1997) of this book is also available for $17.95 (ISBN No. 1559274352).

**General Overviews**

# PARENTING AN ONLY CHILD
The Joys And Challenges Of Raising Your One And Only

**Recommended For:**
Strengthening Your Family

**Special Resource For:**
Parenting an only child

## Description:
Three parts and 12 chapters comprise this 239-page resource focusing on the needs of only children and their parents. Part One—"Considering the Only Child"—traces circumstances that currently lead to "the trend toward one." The other three chapters in this part debunk the myths associated with being an only child, describe the decisions and dilemmas "threesomes" face, and offer suggestions for how to be a single parent of an only child. Part Two presents advice for how to parent an only child beginning with "working attitudes" (moderation, not focusing on oneness, etc.), and then offering specific behaviors, expectations, and how to involve onlies with others. Part Three supports a families' decision not to have additional children with advice on how to deal with challenges from grandparents, other families, your spouse, and your only child. Also discussed are "future issues" such as wills, guardianship, developing support systems, and more. The book concludes with summary advice and quotes from only children.

## Evaluation:
Based upon input from over 200 people who discussed the merits and drawbacks of raising or being a single child, this resource does an excellent job of supporting those families who are "threesomes." In particular, parents will find Chapter Two ("debunking the myths") not only helpful as parents defend their choice, but also reassuring that they made the right decision. By giving parents concrete advice as found in Chapters Five through Eight, parents can also look toward relieving the anxieties that often stem from these myths. This resource is not based on "numbers or statistics" but the author admits that "opinions and emotions are plentiful." The only families we found not represented in this guide were those who had little other choice than to have one. Much of the author's discussion focused on those families who, for personal, work-related, or lifestyle issues, chose to have only one child. Supportive, informative, and reassuring, this resource will prove useful to parents who face the decision of whether or not to expand their "threesome" family.

## Where To Find/Buy:
Bookstores and libraries.

**Overall Rating**
★★★★
Traces decline of the multi-child household, along with practicalities of raising onlies

**Design, Ease Of Use**
★★★
Must be read cover to cover, but easily read; detailed table of contents; no index

1–4 Stars

**Author:**
Susan Newman

Newman is a contributing editor to *Working Parents* and *Mothers Today* magazines, and writes regularly for national magazines on parenting and related topics. She is also the author of three highly acclaimed books for children and teenagers.

**Publisher:**
Main Street Books (Doubleday/Bantam Doubleday Dell)

**Edition:**
1990

**Price:**
$12.95

**Pages/Run Time:**
239

**ISBN:**
0385249640

**Media:**
Book

**Principal Subject:**
Strengthening Your Family

**Secondary Subject:**
General Overview

**Age Group:**
Infants & Toddlers (0–3)

**★★★★**

## Overall Rating
★★★★

Supportive, useful as a measuring stick for the family to identify its positive qualities

## Design, Ease Of Use
★★★

Explicit table of contents; tiny print, but good headings and use of bullets, quotes, etc.

1–4 Stars

## Author:
Dolores Curran

Dolores Curran is an educator, noted columnist, international lecturer, family specialist, widely read writer and parent. She has a weekly syndicated column, "Talks with Parents" and has received two honorary doctorates. She resides in Colorado.

## Publisher:
Ballantine Books
(Random House)

## Edition:
1983

## Price:
$5.99

## Pages/Run Time:
322

## ISBN:
0345317505

## Media:
Book

## Principal Subject:
Strengthening Your Family

## Secondary Subject:
General Overview

## Age Group:
Infants & Toddlers (0–3)

## General Overviews

# TRAITS OF A HEALTHY FAMILY
### Fifteen Traits Commonly Found In Healthy Families By Those Who Work With Them

### Recommended For:
Strengthening Your Family

### Description:
This resource, winner of the Christopher Award for affirmation of the highest values of the human spirit, focuses on the regeneration of enduring family values. It contains 322 pages, 14 chapters, and describes the 15 major traits of a healthy family. These traits are based upon results from surveys (56 items) returned from 551 professionals in five fields (education, church, health, family counseling, and voluntary organizations) in which they were to choose 15 traits they considered to be evidence of a healthy family. The author's purpose was twofold: to give parents positive criteria from which to evaluate themselves, and to force institutions to scrutinize their policies as to whether they encourage or cripple those family strengths. Some of these 15 traits include effective communication, trust, respect, a sense of play and humor, balanced interactions with one another, a sense of right and wrong, family rituals and traditions, shared religion, respect of personal privacy, services to the community, and more. A chapter-by-chapter notes section, an additional resource list, and a comprehensive index conclude the book.

### Evaluation:
This is a positive and upbeat book focusing on what's good about families. The author spent 18 months researching the subject and has presented it in a well-written, thought-provoking format. Her intent was to counteract the negative focus used in looking at the problems of today's family and instead aims to look at family strengths. She, however, warns about families' tendencies to compare themselves with the "legendary perfect family" and suggests instead that these 15 traits should be used as an "invitation to . . . focus upon their own family's health by becoming aware of . . . and studying the hallmarks of these traits." Parents will find the material well-supported by research and professionals alike, and useful in a "self-help" context. First person experiences, as well as shared letters and surveys, help convey and identify aspired family traits as a way for families to scrutinize their own policies and behaviors. While not necessarily easily read, it is an inspiring resource meant to be read cover-to-cover. This is an interesting, useful resource that will be well worth families' time.

### Where To Find/Buy:
Bookstores, libraries, or order direct by calling (800) 733-3000.

**General Overviews**

# WHAT EVERY BABY KNOWS

★★★

## Description:

This resource takes the reader through the lives of five families. The book is divided into five major sections, each of which reflect the family histories and then delve into each family's core. Part One is about the Cotton family (who have twins) with information concerning their quiet child/active child, a section about sibling rivalry, and discipline within this family. Part Two focuses on the Mazza family, their separation and divorce, and the sleep problems they have had with their child. Part Three is about the Considine family, questions they have about their child's crying, the feelings of their middle child, and concerns about a non-walking child. Part Four follows the Sheehan-Weber family with issues involving early learning, stressful situations, and self-esteem. The final section, Part Five, is about the Schwartz family, their new baby, and their expectations. Part Six outlines the family systems theory underlying the work of Brazelton's Child Development Unit and the link between the five families in this book and the "brand of behavioral pediatrics" developed in the Unit's program.

## Evaluation:

This book contains some very valuable, timeless information. It is a well-written book, with clear, concise information set in a question-answer format making it a very enjoyable reading experience. The content is thorough and does a fine job of yielding to the old textbook-type format without being aloof. Parents are given the rare opportunity of following five families through their parenting struggles, enabling the reader to more closely identify and relate to specific questions they may share with the sample families. Brazelton provides sensitive answers with appropriate developmental background information. He carefully dissects each family's issues and concerns, then allows the reader to share in his follow-up when he revisits them and sees "where they are now." There are many black and white photographs throughout this resource which help to illustrate the subject matter; content is well-supported by research with a clear bibliography and index concluding the guide. Add this book to your family library for professional advice on parenting with a personal flavor.

## Where To Find/Buy:

Bookstores and libraries.

**Overall Rating**
★★★
Unique approach; although written some time ago, basic information still prevails

**Design, Ease Of Use**
★★★★
Clear and concise; question-answer format makes for untiring reading; consistent format

1–4 Stars

**Author:**
T. Berry Brazelton, MD

Dr. Brazelton, one of the most-renowned pediatricians, is a Professor of Pediatrics at Harvard Medical School, as well as chief of the Child Development Unit at Boston Children's Hospital. He is also a political advocate for families and has a TV show.

**Publisher:**
Ballantine Books
(Random House)

**Edition:**
1987

**Price:**
$11.00

**Pages/Run Time:**
272

**ISBN:**
0345344553

**Media:**
Book

**Principal Subject:**
Strengthening Your Family

**Secondary Subject:**
General Overview

**Age Group:**
Infants & Toddlers (0–3)

II. Strengthening Your Family

## General Overviews

★★★

### Overall Rating
★★★
Well-researched, intriguing look at the emerging field of ethnopediatrics

### Design, Ease Of Use
★★★
Attractive; information is dense yet well-written and readable

1–4 Stars

### Author:
Meredith F. Small

Small is a professor of anthropology at Cornell University. She is author of *Female Choices: Sexual Behavior of Female Primates* and *What's Love Got to Do with It? The Evolution of Human Mating*.

### Publisher:
Anchor Books
(Bantam Doubleday Dell Publishing Group)

### Edition:
1998

### Price:
$24.95

### Pages/Run Time:
292

### ISBN:
0385482574

### Media:
Book

### Principal Subject:
Strengthening Your Family

### Secondary Subject:
General Overview

### Age Group:
Infants (0–1)

# OUR BABIES, OURSELVES
How Biology And Culture Shape The Way We Parent

### Description:
Our Babies, Ourselves is presented as "the first book to explore to what extent the way we parent our infants is based on our biological needs and to what extent it is based on culture—and the startling consequences ignoring nature's imperatives can have on the well-being of our children." Small's 292-page book is laid out in seven chapters: "The Evolution of Babies"; "The Anthropology of Parenting" (description of the concept of ethnopediatrics); "Other Parents, Other Ways" (comparisons of various societies and how their societal impacts and is impacted by parenting styles); "A Reasonable Sleep" (an examination of infant sleep patterns and sleep locations); "Crybaby" (description of "infant state" including crying, temperament, etc.); "Food for Thought" (breastfeeding, bottlefeeding); and "Unpacking the Caretaking Package" (how to navigate the parenting choices available and "weigh a series of trade-offs"). A center section of photographs illustrates varying cultural baby-rearing styles. Also included are extensive note, reference, and index sections.

### Evaluation:
Small combines her years of experience in cultural anthropology with the new science of ethnopediatrics to study "why we parent our children the way that we do." By comparing parenting styles across cultural boundaries, from the most primitive to the most sophisticated, Small seeks to cut through cultural ethnocentricity to find out which baby-rearing practices offer the most benefits to infants and their newly formed families. "Each culture, and often each family, offers advice and directives on the right and wrong way to raise and care for infants, from feeding, interaction, and emotional support to mandating what is normal in terms of infant sleeping, crying, and more. Yet scientists are finding that . . . the right way to parent our children is often based on nothing more than cultural tradition—and may even run counter to a baby's biological needs." Small concludes that cultural practices such as nestling a child to sleep with her parents, allowing her to feed on demand, and spending most of his time in tactile contact with his mother and others are examples of cultural choices that actually benefit a baby's physical health and psychological development. The text is a bit dense, but it packs within it quite a lot of interesting knowledge.

### Where To Find/Buy:
Bookstores and libraries.

**General Overviews**

# ARE OUR KIDS ALL RIGHT?
Answers To The Tough Questions About Child Care Today

★★★

### Description:

This 372-page guide consists of two main parts with ten chapters. Part One offers results from various research studies. Topics discussed include: the problems associated with the various types of childcare available, the day care debate (daycare vs. mother care, daycare and behavior problems, etc.), parental attachment, the realities of parental/family leave, and how a parent's work life affects the lives of their children. Part Two—"Growing Children: A Practical Guide"—focuses on childcare and how it affects babies' development, how to choose the right care for children, how to meet the needs of young children, and what to consider when seeking care for school age children; interview questions and problem checklists are also given. Each chapter concludes with a summary of the material presented. A "Notes" section is included offering a chapter-by-chapter cross-reference. A 14-page bibliography is included along with an index.

### Evaluation:

This guide exposes the many pitfalls of our current childcare system and attempts to allay parental fears by offering answers to their questions based on research studies. This book neatly cites child development research and examines several issues that are controversial depending on one's point of view—the correlation between how much parents work and its effect on their children, the effect of childcare on children at various ages, and the correlation of good/bad childcare and school/life performance. The book concludes with pointedly making the statement that the present system of childcare in America today is abominable and change should be a priority. While a rather depressing dissertation, this interesting book should prove useful in opening adults' eyes for the betterment of our children. While not easy reading and not well-organized, this guide should be reviewed by all parents facing the childcare situation before they give birth to their child.

### Where To Find/Buy:
Bookstores and libraries.

**Overall Rating**
★★★
Informative resource coupling research studies with suggestions on finding quality care

**Design, Ease Of Use**
★
Broad, non-specific table of contents; not easily read or cross-referenced

1–4 Stars

**Author:**
Susan B. Dynerman

Susan B. Dynerman, a journalist and speech writer, has previously worked in corporate communications as an executive. She and her husband live in Washington, D.C. with their two sons.

**Publisher:**
Peterson's

**Edition:**
1994

**Price:**
$19.95

**Pages/Run Time:**
372

**ISBN:**
1560793341

**Media:**
Book

**Principal Subject:**
Strengthening Your Family

**Secondary Subject:**
General Overview

**Age Group:**
Infants & Toddlers (0–3)

II. Strengthening Your Family

## Overall Rating
★★
Interesting tools to create discussion between parent and child; narrow focus

## Design, Ease Of Use
★★★
Nice combination of italicized child and parent anecdotes; best read cover-to-cover

1–4 Stars

## Author:
Mimi Doe with Marsha Walch, PhD

Mimi Doe is a Harvard graduate, award-winning television producer, and cofounder of a multimedia company that develops children's programming. Marsha Walch, PhD, is a psychotherapist, a clinical consultant, and the mother of Mimi Doe.

## Publisher:
HarperPerennial (HarperCollins)

## Edition:
1998

## Price:
$13.00

## Pages/Run Time:
378

## ISBN:
0060952415

## Media:
Book

## Principal Subject:
Strengthening Your Family

## Secondary Subject:
General Overview

## Age Group:
Infants & Toddlers (0–3)

General Overviews

# 10 PRINCIPLES FOR SPIRITUAL PARENTING
Nurturing Your Child's Soul

## Description:
The authors write ten chapters which mirror their "ten principles." Chapters are entitled: "Know God Cares for You"; "Trust and Teach That All Life Is Connected and Has a Purpose"; "Listen to Your Child"; "Words Are Important, Use Them with Care"; "Allow and Encourage Dreams, Wishes, Hopes"; "Add Magic to the Ordinary"; "Create a Flexible Structure"; "Be a Positive Mirror for Your Child"; "Release the Struggle"; and "Make Each Day a New Beginning." The Introduction explains how to use the *Ten Principles for Spiritual Parenting*. Each chapter offers techniques, ideas, and tools to explain and practice each principle. At the end of each chapter are affirmations for both parent (an "Insight Building Exercise") and the child ("Children's Guided Journey"). These affirmations are provided to reinforce the understanding and use of each principle as well as improve visualization and insight. The last tool provided in each chapter is a "Check-In" question for parents and children.

## Evaluation:
The authors' thesis is that all children are born with a sense of the spiritual and an innate sense of wonder, and that parents must nurture those senses so they are never lost. Focused more on spirituality than on the practice of any specific religion, the principles within this book, while not exclusively Christian, assume that the God is a loving one. While the authors discuss ways to include God in a child's teachings, they also include in their descriptions any deity that the reader would choose to worship. The authors believe in and give evidence of prayer, faith, and ways to accept God's love which they suggest should be taught and modeled to children each day. In addition, imagination, structure, role-modeling, and language are provided as aids in reinforcing children's spirituality—means which may prove useful and inviting to many parents of toddlers and preschoolers. In addition, the exercises at the end of each chapter can provide impetus for wonderful discussions between parent and child. The appeal of this book, however, would be greater for parents who place a higher value on bringing forth a child's spirit or soul rather than those whose values include specific religious principles and practices.

## Where To Find/Buy:
Bookstores and libraries.

**General Overviews**

# THE EARLIEST RELATIONSHIP
Parent, Infants, And The Drama Of Early Attachment

★ ★

## Description:

This 250-page book is written for professionals from a variety of disciplines with the goal of alerting these professionals to the need for care of the parent and child as a unit. The authors say that professionals who care for infants can benefit from knowledge of parental emotions and conflicts that affect the parent-child bond. "A baby cannot exist alone, but is essentially part of a relationship." The book's 31 chapters go into detail on the aspects of this relationship. The book is broken into five parts tracing the evolution of attachment from "Pregnancy: The Birth of Attachment," "The Newborn as Participant," and "Observing Early Interaction" to "Imaginary Interactions" and ". . . A Complementary Approach to Infant Attachment." Subtopics covered include: the "prehistory of attachment," assessing the newborn, early interactions and observations, giving meaning to infant behavior, projection, assessing "imaginary interactions," assessing interaction, and more. The book ends with nine case studies and interventions used to assist in healing the parent-child bond. A ten-page reference list and an index are included.

## Evaluation:

This book is a fascinating look at the work that has been done on developmental observation; it also reflects the progress made in the holistic treatment of the parent and child. Well-organized and well-written, this book informs the reader thoroughly in each stage, so that even someone who has not had an education in psychology can understand the terminology, findings, and conclusions. That said, it is still not a "light" book. This book is targeted at various professionals—pediatricians, nurses, psychoanalysts, social workers, etc. The authors highlight an infant's normal development and point out that anxieties and ambivalences are the fuels that drive growth, and should not be singled out; normal development and pathology intermingle all the time and should be a part of any assessment. At the same time, the crises of parenthood generate a need for parents to learn and self-correct, so they can adapt. Professionals aware of this relationship can offer support and insight that will positively assist the parent-child bond. The reader will find that this book sheds light on these insights in a very informative way.

## Where To Find/Buy:

Bookstores and libraries.

---

**Overall Rating**
★★
Strong plea for professionals working with parents to care for parents & child as a unit

**Design, Ease Of Use**
★★★
Clear, well-organized; textbook structure and jargon may turn some off

1–4 Stars

**Author:**
T. Berry Brazelton, MD and Bertrand G. Cramer, MD

T. Berry Brazelton, MD, is an internationally known pediatrician, an advocate for children, and the author of many best-selling books. Bertrand G. Cramer, MD is Professor of Psychiatry at the University of Geneva, Switzerland and a practicing psychoanalyst.

**Publisher:**
Addison-Wesley Publishing (Merloyd Lawrence)

**Edition:**
1990

**Price:**
$12.00

**Pages/Run Time:**
251

**ISBN:**
0201567644

**Media:**
Book

---

**Principal Subject:**
Strengthening Your Family

**Secondary Subject:**
General Overview

**Age Group:**
Infants (0–1)

II. Strengthening Your Family

## Overall Rating
★★
Good explanation of this parenting style; too many scare tactics, some inaccuracies

## Design, Ease Of Use
★★★
Chapters are explained and organized well; language is easy to understand

1–4 Stars

## Author:
Tammy Frissell-Deppe

Tammy Frissell-Deppe is a third generation Attachment Parent and a strong believer and advocate for this style of parenting. She is the mother of two, raising her family according to the principles of Attachment Parenting.

## Publisher:
JED Publishing

## Edition:
1998

## Price:
$10.95

## Pages/Run Time:
173

## ISBN:
0966634144

## Media:
Book

## Principal Subject:
Strengthening Your Family

## Secondary Subject:
General Overview

## Age Group:
Infants & Toddlers (0–3)

General Overviews

# EVERY PARENT'S GUIDE TO ATTACHMENT PARENTING
## Getting Back To Basic Instincts!

## Description:
In Chapter One—"What is Attachment Parenting?"—The author outlines the five basic aspects of attachment parenting: responding to baby's cues, breastfeeding, "wearing" baby, using a family bed, and gentle discipline. The advantages of this parenting style, along with answers to common questions, also are included in Chapter One. Chapter Two, "Natural Birth and Bonding," discusses birth plans and options. Crying and breastfeeding on demand are discussed in Chapter Three—"Responding to Baby's Clues." The benefits of breastfeeding are explained in Chapter Four, "Breastfeeding-Breast is best!" along with answers to commonly asked questions. Chapter Five—"Babywearing"—explains the benefits of constantly carrying or holding the baby. Chapter Six—"The Family Bed"—explains the philosophy and gives advice on letting baby and toddler sleep with parents. Spanking is discouraged and alternative methods (time-out, diversions, etc.), are explained in Chapter Seven, "Gentle Discipline." In Chapter Eight—"Non-circumcision"—the author outlines her belief in the negative impacts of circumcision. Support groups, websites, mailing lists, are more are listed in Chapter Nine.

## Evaluation:
In our society, attachment parenting, which attends to a child's every emotional and physical need, is often perceived as "spoiling." That is misguided, says the author. "A child cries to fulfill a need, not to 'control' or 'manipulate' the parent." The author encourages parents to question and challenge a health care provider's advice when their instincts tell them otherwise. This is particularly valuable advice for parents, especially new parents, who often feel unsure about what they are doing and accept "the experts'" suggestions. The downside of this book is that not all of the information is accurate. For instance, the author equates the terms "midwife" and "doula." Also, scare tactics are used to convince the reader that attachment parenting alone is the best parenting method. This is evident especially in the chapters on babywearing ("Produce a smarter child-wear him!" and "By not wearing your baby, you are setting him up for negative behavior and making it more difficult for him to adjust to the environment.") and non-circumcision (as the baby is "strapped down like an animal and mutilated . . ." and "the pain from the circumcised penis is mentally scarring children for months . . . some for life." Good as a primer to determine if this parenting style fits your family, but caution is also advised.

## Where To Find/Buy:
Bookstores, libraries, or order direct by calling (978) 452-2364, or by contacting JED Publishing at P.O. Box 339, Dracut, MA 01826-0339.

**General Overviews**

# JOHN ROSEMOND'S SIX POINT PLAN FOR RAISING HAPPY, HEALTHY CHILDREN

## Description:

Each of the six points in the author's plan is outlined in its own chapter. Point One is entitled, "The Parent-Centered Family." Point Two is "The Voice of Authority." Point Three is "The Roots of Responsibility." "The Fruits of Frustration" is the fourth point. Point Five is "Toys and Play: The Right Stuff," and Point Six is "Television and Children: More than Meets the Eye." In the first section of this book, the author describes the foundation for his philosophy. A recap of the six points is summarized in the last section, entitled "Read This Last!" In each chapter, there are sections that address issues relative to that subject. For example the chapter on authority addresses family government, respect, and parental power. The chapter on responsibility talks about behavior, reward, and making amends. The chapter on frustration discusses tantrums and saying "no." Each chapter has a question and answer section regarding typical questions relating to the issue of that chapter.

## Evaluation:

If one can get past the author's sometimes harsh, tell-it-like-it-is attitude, his theory is presented with conviction. Rosemond believes that, with the evolution of child-raising "experts," people have given up their own instincts for whatever theory a particular expert happened to be extolling. "The ultimate purpose of parenting is to help our children out of our lives," he says. More gently said, the purpose of parents, he believes, is to teach children the tools they will need to successfully fly the nest. Rosemond's plan to accomplish that includes a return "to a more traditional, commonsense vision of childrearing." He directs the reader to put their marriage first, expect children to obey, expect and enable them to contribute to the family, give them everything they need, and give them a conservative amount of what they want. His most controversial statement may be that since World War II, he believes families have become child-centered instead of marriage-centered; children have become more important than the parents, which in turn has created self-centered and difficult children. For those parents who desire a more traditional, "father knows best" method of parenting, this book is the one.

## Where To Find/Buy:

Bookstores and libraries. An abridged audiotape version (1998) of this book is also available for $16.95 (ISBN No.1565112652).

---

**Overall Rating**
★★
Author's tell-it-like-it is style will appeal to more traditional parenting styles

**Design, Ease Of Use**
★★★
Fairly good organization of topics; attempted humor fails to appeal

1–4 Stars

**Author:**
John K. Rosemond

John Rosemond is a family psychologist and member of the teaching faculty of a local hospital. He writes a syndicated parenting column, is a featured writer for *Better Homes & Gardens*, and has authored other parenting books. He is a parent of two children.

**Publisher:**
Andrews and McMeel

**Edition:**
1989

**Price:**
$8.95

**Pages/Run Time:**
193

**ISBN:**
0836228065

**Media:**
Book

---

**Principal Subject:**
Strengthening Your Family

**Secondary Subject:**
General Overview

**Age Group:**
Infants & Toddlers (0–3)

II. Strengthening Your Family

★★

**Overall Rating**
★★
Interesting theories, but author offers unnecessary sales pitch for therapy

**Design, Ease Of Use**
★★★
Organization is clear and understandable; headings are self-explanatory

1–4 Stars

**Author:**
Mary Pipher, PhD

Mary Pipher, PhD, is a psychologist in private practice in Lincoln, Nebraska. She has taught at the University of Nebraska and Nebraska Wesleyan University, has been a commentator for Nebraska Public Radio, and authored Hunger Pains and Reviving Ophelia.

**Publisher:**
Ballantine Books
(Random House)

**Edition:**
1996

**Price:**
$12.95

**Pages/Run Time:**
282

**ISBN:**
0345406036

**Media:**
Book

**Principal Subject:**
Strengthening Your Family

**Secondary Subject:**
General Overview

**Age Group:**
Infants & Toddlers (0–3)

## General Overviews

# THE SHELTER OF EACH OTHER
## Rebuilding Our Families

### Description:

The purpose of this book, Pipher says, is to encourage discussion about what families need, sympathize with families' efforts to survive a difficult era, and help readers address how culture affects family. In Part One, the author tells the story of two families, one in the 1930s and another in the 1990s. She then makes comparisons about family and life in the two eras and discusses the part community plays in the health of a family. The last two chapters of Part One discuss therapy and lists ten mistakes that therapists make. Part Two discusses three traits: character, will, and commitment, with a chapter devoted to each. Throughout, the author illustrates her points by describing situations she has experienced as a therapist. Part Three offers solutions. Seven items are listed as strategies for protecting families, including time, celebrations, and connections. Families must make connections to one another, community, nature, and other aspects of life, she says. Each section has its own introduction.

### Evaluation:

The author makes a fair comparison of the two eras by addressing the good and bad in both. But, she argues, people earlier in the century were more sure of what their problems were. Threats to the family during that time period were related to physical survival: food, shelter, and warmth. Consequently, the family banded together to fight the problems they faced. Contrast that with today's society, in which neighbors often don't know each other and community ties are lost. Then, unfortunately, the last two chapters in Part One become primarily a sales pitch for family therapy. In Part Two, the author tells stories of modern families struggling with the issues of the times. The dynamics of the families that she highlights is varied, including a range of racial and religious groups, as well as "traditional" two-parent households. Of the three chapters in Part Two, one states its focus is on character, but actually turns out to be a discussion of self-esteem. One chapter purports to focus on will, but is a dialogue about the lack of values in today's young adults. The last chapter is on commitment. The author's solution to these problems, as offered in Part Three, are not necessarily unique or innovative, but offer good reminders of what sometimes gets lost in the everyday shuffle within families.

### Where To Find/Buy:

Bookstores and libraries.

**General Overviews**

# DR. MOM'S PARENTING GUIDE
Commonsense Guidance For The Life Of Your Child

## Description:

Written for those parents who feel "underprepared for parenthood and disillusioned with the on-the-job training approach to raising children," this 336-page guide offers Neifert's personal and professional childrearing knowledge and philosophies. Divided into ten chapters, the book begins by highlighting the pressures parents of today face along with how to cope with "The Myth of the Superparent" and how to enhance a child's self-esteem. Four chapters focus on specific challenges to parenting, such as raising siblings, behavior and discipline, instilling values, and the impact of divorce on children. One chapter offers suggestions for "enriching your family life" by preserving and creating family traditions, and through including a pet into your household. Neifert's husband penned a chapter and discusses "the stress of parenthood" and ways to manage it. The final chapter focuses on the "emotional roller coaster" of parenting and discusses issues such as disappointment, loss, unmet expectations, extreme adversity, and more. An appendix provides a script for a relaxation technique and an 18-page index concludes the book.

## Evaluation:

A satisfied reader familiar with Marianne Neifert's earlier book, Dr. Mom, will be disappointed with this resource. Her views expounded upon here make for good discussions, if parents are simply looking for arenas to develop their own parenting philosophy. But one won't find specifics here to help in dealing with sibling squabbles, misbehavior, or other challenges. An exception to this critique is the chapter entitled "You and Your Child's Self-Esteem." Many books have been written on the subject and the term has been thrown around without much direct advice; Neifert, however, manages to sum up the essential points here in easily digested chunks. Parents should peruse this one at the bookstore. If they like Dr. Mom's writing style and tone, then they need to check into her earlier book before spending time and money on this one.

## Where To Find/Buy:

Bookstores and libraries.

---

★★

**Overall Rating**
★★
Presents author's philosophy more than fact; disappointing compared to an earlier book

**Design, Ease Of Use**
★★
Good index, but a vague table of contents and chapter subheadings

1–4 Stars

**Author:**
Marianne Neifert, MD

Neifert is a pediatrician and associate clinical professor of pediatrics at the University of Colorado Health Sciences Center, as well as the mother of five children. She is a frequent lecturer and writes a column for *Parenting* and *Baby Talk* magazines.

**Publisher:**
Plume (Dutton Signet/Penguin Books USA)

**Edition:**
1996

**Price:**
$10.95

**Pages/Run Time:**
336

**ISBN:**
0452268648

**Media:**
Book

**Principal Subject:**
Strengthening Your Family

**Secondary Subject:**
General Overview

**Age Group:**
Infants & Toddlers (0–3)

II. Strengthening Your Family

★★

**Overall Rating**
★★
Too outdated to be of much use to busy parents trying to combine work and home life

**Design, Ease Of Use**
★★
Difficult to read, unclear on helpful solutions, rambling text

1–4 Stars

**Author:**
T. Berry Brazelton, MD

T. Berry Brazelton, MD is Associate Professor of Pediatrics at Harvard Medical School and Chief of the Child Development Unit at the Boston Children's Hospital Medical Center. Dr. Brazelton is considered a leading authority on child development.

**Publisher:**
Addison-Wesley Publishing (A Merloyd Lawrence Book)

**Edition:**
2nd (1985)

**Price:**
$13.00

**Pages/Run Time:**
197

**ISBN:**
0201632713

**Media:**
Book

**Principal Subject:**
Strengthening Your Family

**Secondary Subject:**
General Overview

**Age Group:**
Infants & Toddlers (0–3)

General Overviews

# WORKING AND CARING

**Description:**

Dr. Brazelton, in the beginning of this book, describes the conflicts working mothers face when torn between their beliefs in women's rights to experience the satisfaction of working, and their love and intense attachment to their babies. Here, he tries to address a woman's feeling of being split apart and ways to heal them. This is done by pointing out that the ambivalence a woman feels toward returning to her job generates new energy as she discovers new abilities. The big questions are when to return to work, how to share the care, and how to handle the development hurdles of normal childhood when caring for children is not your only job—issues that confront all parents, whatever their circumstances. By following the lives of three families (working professionals, a single parent, and a couple in which the father must be away for long stretches of time) through the first year of their new baby's life, he illustrates the challenges these families faced, and how these families managed to adjust. The center of his advice is to save some energy at the end of the day for the family's physical and emotional needs.

**Evaluation:**

In this book, Brazelton does a credible job of emphasizing that it is not just women's dilemma about how to combine work and home life. "The problem in a working family is that no one is there all the time to care for the children." To reflect men's changing roles in terms of fathering, men also need to take steps to further their nurturing abilities, say the author. The main problems of this book center on its presentation. It tends to ramble between the narratives on the families and Brazelton's interjected, sometimes distracting, comments. The type used in printing this book is also a negative, i.e. it is too small for easy reading, leaving one feeling cramped. Also, the book needs to be updated regarding the facts and statistics quoted concerning working parents. While this book is filled with experienced insights on the issues involved with returning to work after having a baby, there are other better books currently available today to meet working parents' needs.

**Where To Find/Buy:**
Bookstores and libraries.

**General Overviews**

# THE 10 GREATEST GIFTS I GIVE MY CHILDREN
Parenting From The Heart

## Description:

This book begins with three short sections on the purpose of the "10 gifts," the author's personal family history and experiences, and the benefits of using the five tools; the five parenting tools—forward focus, messages, teach, listen, and model—are described in Chapters One through Five. "Parenting from the Heart" (Chapter Six) pulls together the five tools. Chapters 7 through 15 explain each of the author's "gifts" which are: feeling fully, self-esteem, compassion, balance, humor, communication, abundance, integrity and responsibility, and conscious choice. Chapter 16 describes a recipe for partnership. Following Chapter 16 is a section that talks about solving societal problems from a "bottom-up" perspective, beginning with one parent at a time, one family at a time. The author uses many real-life stories and experiences to illustrate his methods and philosophy. Chapters on each gift consist of an explanation of what the gift is, story examples of when it is used and when it is not used, and descriptions of how the five tools can play a part in giving that gift.

## Evaluation:

The author states that "The 10 Greatest Gifts process provides a way to rediscover and realize those dreams [for the family] again-but with a much different twist," and that ". . . using these tools dramatically reduces episodes of acting up and acting out." All five of the tools are a process of simply remembering to look at experiences and situations from the positive perspective instead of the negative. It is such a simple, well-worn piece of advice that many parents take it for granted or forget to heed its wisdom. The author attempts to teach the reader to structure communication with children so that it doesn't focus on what children can't or don't do. Surprisingly, the reader will find that the author provides too many stories of parents' experiences with their children. The author validly uses these stories to explain how to use the tools and give the gifts, however the reader would benefit from more direct advice on how to handle various situations. In fact, there is no real instruction on how to give the gifts that are described in the later chapters. The author has some good ideas about healthy communication with children, but the presentation does not teach the reader how to use those methods.

## Where To Find/Buy:

Bookstores and libraries.

---

**Overall Rating**
★★
Presents valuable tools and "gifts" to give children, but needs much clarification

**Design, Ease Of Use**
★
Information within the chapters needs further clarification

1–4 Stars

**Author:**
Steven W. Vannoy

**Publisher:**
Fireside Book
(Simon & Schuster)

**Edition:**
1994

**Price:**
$12.00

**Pages/Run Time:**
271

**ISBN:**
0671502271

**Media:**
Book

---

**Principal Subject:**
Strengthening Your Family

**Secondary Subject:**
General Overview

**Age Group:**
Infants & Toddlers (0–3)

II. Strengthening Your Family

General Overviews

**Overall Rating**
★★
One person's reflections on how to parent presented in a day-to-day format

**Design, Ease Of Use**
★
Rambling format (no day-to-day continuity of topic); no index or table of contents

1–4 Stars

**Author:**
John Rosemond

John Rosemond is a family psychologist and director of the Center for Affirmative Parenting (CAP) in Gastonia, North Carolina. CAP is a national organization whose purpose is to provide families with advice and guidance in the raising of their children.

**Publisher:**
Andrews and McMeel (Universal Press Syndicate)

**Edition:**
1997

**Price:**
$14.95

**Pages/Run Time:**
368

**ISBN:**
0836204999

**Media:**
Book

**Principal Subject:**
Strengthening Your Family

**Secondary Subject:**
General Overview

**Age Group:**
Infants & Toddlers (0–3)

# BECAUSE I SAID SO!
## 366 Insightful And Thought-Provoking Reflections On Parenting And Family Life

### Description:
Rosemond, the director of the Center for Affirmative Parenting (North Carolina), has reprinted in this book 366 excerpts from his various books, newspaper columns, and magazine articles plus some new writings. Each reflection contained in this 368-page book is dated so the reader can begin at any point. Rosemond's intent is to "give parents daily doses of food for thought concerning children . . . that will hopefully help readers become . . . more grounded in . . . common sense concerning children and their upbringing." Using his autocratic family as an example in which the parents are "benevolent dictators," Rosemond expands upon his ideas of what's best for children. He insists that parents can encourage children to ask questions, but parents must make the final decisions, and offer restrictions in order to protect and guide children. He believes that "properly administered spankings can be . . . of inestimable value in the rearing of certain children." Topics range from the parents' role to the children's role, and more.

### Evaluation:
As evidenced by his introduction, Rosemond has a decidedly defensive posture when describing his parenting philosophy. Referring to mental health professionals as "the more helplessly humor-challenged of the bunch," he then proceeds to explain how American families have gotten off-track because of them in terms of their child rearing principles. The rest of his book then contains his advice on how to get back on-track. With a format and tone similar to one of his other written cries for attention, this book at least contains more detail in the daily entries. Whereas Rosemond's *Daily Guide to Parenting* was far too succinct to really benefit those who agree with his parenting style, this guide is much more explanatory. Rosemond's philosophy is neither scientifically based nor research based but instead loosely based on Scripture (he rarely cites specific passages) and his own personal experience. Not for everyone, this book would only be wholly appreciated by those parents with like parenting styles.

### Where To Find/Buy:
Bookstores and libraries.

**General Overviews**

# A FAMILY OF VALUE

## Description:

This book offers three sections, entitled "Through the Looking Glass," "A Family of Value: Rearing 'Three Rs' Children," and "General Questions." The four chapters in the first section are entitled "Have We Hit Bottom Yet," "Sounds Good, but It Doesn't Work," "Why Our Schools Are Floundering," and "The Politics of Parenting." The Three "Rs" in Section Two, each with its own chapter, are respect, responsibility (discipline), and resourcefulness ("the can-do child"). In the introduction, the author provides extensive information regarding his philosophies, how they developed, and his personal background. Section One is primarily devoted to larger issues such as the nation's school systems, historical and psychological theories of child-rearing, cultural trends, and political positions regarding children and families. In the chapter regarding respect, the author asserts that the single best thing a parent can do is make his or her marriage the first priority. "Resourcefulness" advocates turning off the television and video games, and helping the child develop hobbies. The last section offers questions and answers regarding a wide range of issues.

## Evaluation:

The author states immediately that he is a heretic within his profession, and that his views on child-rearing and family life are considered psychologically incorrect—"they rock the boat, upset the apple cart." He then continues by restating and trying to legitimize our ancestors' beliefs, values, attitudes, and practices; Rosemond believes that the old parenting styles, pre-1960, are the only effective styles. Those readers who consider themselves liberal, or even middle-of-the road, would probably take offense at Rosemond's hostile attack against anything not considered highly conservative. In his introduction, he states that the "American family is in a state of deepening crisis" and lists his reasons for this crisis-state: no-fault divorce, single parenthood, homosexuality, school sex education, and "radical feminists." All are evidenced, he says, by rising rates of violent juvenile crime, unmarried teen births, teen suicide, teenage depression, and declining SAT scores. The author promotes his belief then that a child must be taught the three "Rs" of respect, responsibility and resourcefulness, all of which are highly admirable goals. Unfortunately, the author discredits himself through the hateful tone evidenced throughout his book. Most people won't get past such hatefulness to get to some of the genuinely valid points he makes.

## Where To Find/Buy:

Bookstores and libraries.

**Overall Rating**
★★
Valid concepts buried in controversial opinions, rather hostile tone

**Design, Ease Of Use**
★
Chapter titles aren't clear as to content; discussions roam throughout the book

1–4 Stars

**Author:**
John Rosemond

John Rosemond is a family psychologist, columnist, radio talk-show host, and author. He is the director of the Center for Affirmative Parenting, which provides resources to parents, schools, and professionals.

**Publisher:**
Andrews and McMeel (Universal Press Syndicate)

**Edition:**
1995

**Price:**
$12.95

**Pages/Run Time:**
306

**ISBN:**
0836205057

**Media:**
Book

**Principal Subject:**
Strengthening Your Family

**Secondary Subject:**
General Overview

**Age Group:**
Infants & Toddlers (0–3)

II. Strengthening Your Family

## General Overviews

# GIVING THE LOVE THAT HEALS
## A Guide For Parents

**Overall Rating**
★★
Too wordy without providing particularly clear concepts and solutions

**Design, Ease Of Use**
★
Unclear organization within the chapters; ideas discussed at random

1–4 Stars

**Author:**
Harville Hendrix, PhD and Helen Hunt, MA

Hendrix and Hunt are a married couple writing from his 35 years of experience as a family therapist, her experience as an activist in women's issues, and their collective experience raising six children.

**Publisher:**
Simon and Schuster
Pocket Books

**Edition:**
1997

**Price:**
$14.00

**Pages/Run Time:**
357

**ISBN:**
0671793993

**Media:**
Book

**Principal Subject:**
Strengthening Your Family

**Secondary Subject:**
General Overview

**Age Group:**
Infants & Toddlers (0–3)

### Description:

Hendrix and Hunt describe their theory of Imago Relationship Therapy and "conscious marriage," and then apply it to parenting. Imago Relationship Therapy is "the science of patterns in marriage and parenting." A Conscious Parent is one who is aware of a child's developmental stages, attuned to the child's unique personality and temperament, and interactive with the child rather than reactive. Conscious Parents also understand why they react the way they do and change it if necessary. Parenting styles, labeled as "maximizer" or "minimizer," and their effects on a child are explored. For instance, a maximizer parent will be dependent, exaggerated, compulsive, and directed outward. In contrast, the minimizer parent tends to be a loner, rigid, independent, self-absorbed, and directed inward. As a solution to parenting shortfalls, the author suggests dialogue with a child that involves mirroring, validating, and empathizing. The first three sections explore the concept of connection, what it is, how it can be ruptured, and how it can be restored. The fourth section describes children's developmental stages. Sections Five and Six illustrate application of conscious parenting.

### Evaluation:

The foundation of the authors' theory is that when a child is wounded in childhood, that child will pass on the same wounds to his or her children. This may seem obvious to most readers, but the authors' exhaustively delve into the emotional aspects of this theory. To accept the author's theories, one has to ignore its psycho-babble tone. Hendrix originally developed his version of this theory during his work as a couples' therapist encouraging couples to heal each other. In this book, the authors state, "The sense in which parenting can be healing is that parents restore their wholeness when they stretch to meet the needs of their children at precisely those stages at which their own development has been incomplete." While some may balk at consciously subjecting their children to being a tool for a parent's own healing, the rest of the book doesn't explore this concept. Instead, it teaches a reader to get to know his or her child as an independent person, separate from the parent, and to interact with his or her child instead of reacting only to the child's words and actions. Unfortunately, these concepts are not expressed as clearly as they could be, and a reader is sometimes left to guess at the intent and meaning of the message, no matter how potentially helpful.

### Where To Find/Buy:

Bookstores and Libraries. An abridged audiotape version (1997) is also available for $18.00 (ISBN No. 0671577530).

**General Overviews**

# THE SEVEN SPIRITUAL LAWS FOR PARENTS
Guiding Your Children To Success And Fulfillment

★★

## Description:

Chopra's philosophy, based on a 5,000 year old system of mind/body medicine (Ayurvedic principles), embodies the belief that parents want their children to be successful and that the most direct way to success is through spirit. Success depends on what you are and not on what you do, states Chopra. He emphasizes that parents mistakenly confuse success with materialistic accomplishments. After exploring the topic of spirituality in Part One of his 156-page book, Chopra then discusses "the journey of spirit" which is based on living in harmony with natural law. He states the seven "laws" as detailed in his book *The Seven Spiritual Laws of Success*, and then restates them in less abstract terms for children (ex: "everything is possible," "if you want to get something, give it," "you are here for a reason," etc.); brief overviews are given for developmental stages and ages (birth to 15 years old). In Part Two, each law is outlined and then assigned a day of the week on which parents and children practice these spiritual skills.

## Evaluation:

This book was written in response to pleas from parents who had read Chopra's book *The Seven Spiritual Laws of Success* and desired to translate these lessons to their children. Parents sold on Chopra's beliefs will no doubt find this book helpful. Crossing most conventional western religions, Chopra creates visions of an ideal world with his approach toward spirituality. A lot of information about how to raise children spiritually is tendered here but few concrete suggestions; parents trying to bring spirituality down to earth for their child will need to hunt a bit. Parents need to read this resource cover to cover several times to best comprehend Chopra's generalities. Written in a heavy text style, it is somewhat random and repetitive at times. Many of the suggestions are geared more for parents of school age children (six and up) with some input for parents of younger children. On the plus side, earmarking given days of the week to practice spirituality will give many Chopra followers some concrete tools from which to work.

## Where To Find/Buy:

Bookstores and libraries. An abridged audiotape version (90 minutes; 1997; ISBN No. 0679460411) of this book is also available for $14.00 by calling (800) 726-0600.

**Overall Rating**
★★
Offers a spiritual base for some parents or excursion for others of western religions

**Design, Ease Of Use**
★
Heavy text style that must be read cover to cover; each "law" includes a synopsis

1–4 Stars

**Author:**
Deepak Chopra, MD
Chopra, who has practiced endocrinology since 1971, is the former chief of staff of New England Memorial Hospital in Stoneham, Massachusetts. He is also the president of the American Association for Ayurvedic Medicine. He is the author of 19 books.

**Publisher:**
Harmony Books (Crown Publishers/Random House)

**Edition:**
1997

**Price:**
$16.95

**Pages/Run Time:**
156

**ISBN:**
060960077X

**Media:**
Book

**Principal Subject:**
Strengthening Your Family

**Secondary Subject:**
General Overview

**Age Group:**
Toddlers (1–3)

II. Strengthening Your Family

General Overviews

# YOUR BABY & YOUR WORK
## Balancing Your Life

**Overall Rating**

★

Addresses the many ways of returning to work, but light treatment of childcare options

**Design, Ease Of Use**

★★★

Bulleted and blocks of highlights; great parent quotes; light on forms, checklists, etc.

1–4 Stars

**Author:**

Teresa Wilson

Wilson, a postnatal counselor for the National Childbirth Trust (NCT), has written about pregnancy and early childhood issues, and has been a full-time, stay-at-home mother, worked part time, and worked full time.

**Publisher:**

Fisher Books

**Edition:**

1997

**Price:**

$12.95

**Pages/Run Time:**

180

**ISBN:**

1555611265

**Media:**

Book

**Principal Subject:**

Strengthening Your Family

**Secondary Subject:**

General Overview

**Age Group:**

Infants (0–1)

## Description:

The author of this 180-page guide states that her aim is to "reflect the many ways of working that now exist and the kinds of childcare you can choose." Including numerous quotes from working parents, the book is divided into 11 chapters with a conclusion, list of resources, and an index. The author explores issues such as why women return to work, how they feel about returning, how they balance their work and home life, how mothers and fathers juggle their roles as a family, and more. Six chapters discuss the various types of childcare available—family daycare homes, preschools, workplace childcare centers, nannies, au pairs, informal childcare (neighbors, friends, relatives), after-school options, and other support care (postpartum doulas, mother's helper). Each chapter lists the benefits derived from that kind of care, the problems, how to find quality care, and more. Also presented are viewpoints from the childcare providers about the benefits and problems for each of these childcare options. The final chapter focuses on how mothers can continue to breastfeed when they return to work.

## Evaluation:

Parents using this book will get great advice on how to assuage their feelings of guilt about returning to work but they will get less direct advice on how to get childcare. The author includes numerous parent anecdotes to illustrate her points, the main one being that being a working parent is a challenge, a balancing act in which women and men work to resolve all their family's needs while enjoying a role in the workplace. Wilson states that if parents understand all of their options for both work-related and child-related issues, then they can strike this balance more successfully, hence the reason for this book. The issues related to returning to work are treated in-depth here, but less so are the issues related to childcare. Parents will get an overview of each option but nothing in detail. Interview questions, for example, are given for hiring a nanny, but none for the other available options. Many other resources include various checklists, forms for checking references, forms for applicants, etc. that help busy parents stay organized and prepared. Parents can use this resource to assuage feelings of guilt but they may well want to use other resources for finding quality childcare.

## Where To Find/Buy:

Bookstores and libraries.

**General Overviews**

# DAILY GUIDE TO PARENTING

## Description:

Rosemond offers 365 "nuggets of . . . parenting wisdom" within the confines of a 4" x 5 1/2" spiral bound flip book. Each page is dated for use throughout a year and includes one of Rosemond's opinions on a myriad of subjects. It is intended to be used for inspiration and thought-provoking, so parents can "stay the course through the inevitable ups and downs of parenthood." Advice sometimes flows from one day to the next along a given subject. Topics Rosemond expounds upon include: the child's place in the family ("Children show respect for parents by obeying them"), the parents' role ("Children need a lot of supervision, but not a lot of attention"; "Limit your child's inclusion in adult activities, and limit your involvement in your child's activities"), discipline ("It's possible to spank a child properly and have it accomplish something . . . lots of parents make a sorry mess of it"), and more. There are no illustrations, no index, and no table of contents.

## Evaluation:

Rosemond converts will enjoy getting their memories refreshed on a daily basis as they flip to yet another one of his pearls of wisdom. But parents looking for tried-and-true methods and concrete examples will definitely need to look elsewhere. At times his messages even contradict each other leaving the reader wondering if his belief system is as firmly founded as he would lead us to believe. For example, he states (July 30) that: "The young child must be convinced of his parents' ability to provide for and protect him under any and all circumstances." Then on the flip-side (June 3), he states that "When parents make a child's life into a bowl of cherries, the child will almost certainly, as an adult, be forever in the pits." If parents want opinions, they need to look to other sources that are more consistent.

## Where To Find/Buy:

Bookstores and libraries.

---

**Overall Rating**

★

Just one man's opinions; parents will certainly get the feeling he thinks highly of them

**Design, Ease Of Use**

★

Can't refer back to a "nugget"; helpful if organized in themes with an overall content page

1–4 Stars

**Author:**

John Rosemond

Rosemond, a family psychologist, is director of the Center for Affirmative Parenting, a national parent resource center offering seminars and educational materials to those who work with families. He also has a nationally-syndicated parenting column.

**Publisher:**

Thoughtful Books/Sta-Kris

**Edition:**

1994

**Price:**

$8.50

**ISBN:**

1882835441

**Media:**

Book

---

**Principal Subject:**

Strengthening Your Family

**Secondary Subject:**

General Overview

**Age Group:**

Infants & Toddlers (0–3)

II. Strengthening Your Family

**Overall Rating**

★

An interesting concept buried in a regurgitation of scientific studies

**Design, Ease Of Use**

★

Chapter and section organization make no sense; intense jargon throughout

1–4 Stars

**Author:**

Judith Rich Harris

Judith Rich Harris is a former writer of college textbooks on child development. She lives in New Jersey with her husband.

**Publisher:**

The Free Press
(Simon & Schuster)

**Edition:**

1998

**Price:**

$26.00

**Pages/Run Time:**

462

**ISBN:**

0684844095

**Media:**

Book

**Principal Subject:**

Strengthening Your Family

**Secondary Subject:**

General Overview

**Age Group:**

Infants & Toddlers (0–3)

General Overviews

# THE NURTURE ASSUMPTION
## Why Children Turn Out The Way They Do

**Description:**

The author of this book asserts that a child's personality is developed primarily from experiences outside the home, specifically their interaction with peers, and parents have little influence on what sort of people their children will become. In 15 chapters, Harris offers counsel on what a parent can and cannot do to produce a happy, well-behaved, and self-confident child. In the beginning chapters of the book, the author explores the history and misconceptions of the "nature vs. nurture" theories. She argues that "nurture" is not the same as environment. Other chapters illustrate the concept that each of us is a stew of personalities, offers information about child rearing in different cultures and times, discusses being part of a group and group socialization, including the effects of culture, gender differences, dysfunctional families, and problem kids. Chapter 14 offers suggestions of what a parent can do to develop a happy child. The author cites many references and studies as background for her theory. Appendix One addresses personality and birth order, and Appendix Two addresses ways to test theories of child development.

**Evaluation:**

The reader needs two things before opening this book: a solid knowledge of scientific concepts—including experimental techniques, genetics, and the science of psychology—and a lot of time. The premise of the book is an interesting one. "Children are born with certain characteristics," the author says. "Their genes predispose them to develop a certain kind of personality. But the environment can change them. Not 'nurture'—not the environment their parents provide—but the outside-the-home environment, the environment they share with their peers." Unfortunately, the author's point gets lost in recitation after recitation of studies, scientific and psychological theories, and even literary works. She manages to tear down every philosophy of child development that has evolved over the past hundred years, and her points sometimes conflict. For example, in one section of the book, she asserts that a child with certain genes will be predisposed to a certain personality. In another, she states that a child's inherited genes do not necessarily mean that the child will inherit a parent's characteristics. There may be some validity buried in the studies, but overall, it's disappointing that the author's provocative message will be lost to most who are not child development specialists or scientific theorists.

**Where To Find/Buy:**

Bookstores and libraries.

# CRIB NOTES FOR THE FIRST YEAR OF FATHERHOOD
## A Survival Guide For New Fathers

**Recommended For:**
Strengthening Your Family

### Description:

De Morier aims to offer a comprehensive guide for new fathers on a variety of topics in his ten chapter, 178-page book. Included is an index, and each chapter concludes by offering a resource list and De Morier's "crib notes" of advice. The author says in his introduction, "I hope you will find it to be a light, informative view of what happens when you become a father. The goal is to give you ideas about what to expect and what to prepare for, and to direct you to resources that will make the change easier to bear and more enjoyable." In meeting those goals, the author has included chapters on topics such as: helping out the new mom, getting organized, safety in the home, and expectations on the part of the new parents and others. Separate chapters focus on financial concerns, such as debt, budgeting, saving and investing, as well as buying a home. As an interactive bonus, there are worksheets throughout, especially in the financial sections. Many firsthand experiences are recounted by the author about his wife and two young sons. Humor is used as a medium to keep the reader entertained while providing information.

### Evaluation:

Finally, a how-to book that is fun to read! From beginning to end, the author, a master humorist as evidenced by this book, has managed to provide the perfect mix of entertaining reading and plenty of practical advice. For example, he states in his introduction that he and his wife obviously "had too much disposable time and money on our hands, and too many hours of REM sleep each night. Because suddenly, we were trying to have children." The "About the Author" section is written from his three-year old son's perspective— "Our father is a writer and lecturer, although the idea of someone actually paying him to talk is completely beyond [us]." As entertaining as the book is, it also provides a comprehensive overview of what men may expect and plan for when becoming a new parent. The information provided is more realistic than idealistic, although some information (feeding baby solid foods at three months) is not recommended. The chapters are divided into well-planned topic areas, then further divided. Topics include everything from babyproofing the home and pampering the new mom to financial planning. A great primer for any man (or woman) expecting a first child, it provides details without drowning the reader in technicalities.

### Where To Find/Buy:

Bookstores, libraries, or order direct by calling (800) 544-8207.

**Overall Rating**
★★★★
Perfect mix of humor and practical, realistic information and advice

**Design, Ease Of Use**
★★★★
Well thought-out topics and sections, with lots of handy worksheets and lists

1–4 Stars

**Author:**
Everett De Morier

De Morier conducts a series of adult education workshops. He lives in Vestal, New York, with his wife Debbie, and their two sons, Nicholas and Alexander. He also is the author of *Crib Notes for the First Year of Marriage: A Survival Guide for Newlyweds*.

**Publisher:**
Fairview Press

**Edition:**
1998

**Price:**
$14.95

**Pages/Run Time:**
178

**ISBN:**
1577490738

**Media:**
Book

**Principal Subject:**
Strengthening Your Family

**Secondary Subject:**
Fatherhood

**Age Group:**
Infants (0–1)

★★★★

## Overall Rating
★★★★
Will instill confidence in fathers to help them define their roles within the family

## Design, Ease Of Use
★★★★
Succinct; detailed table of contents, subheadings within chapters; whimsical drawings

1–4 Stars

## Author:
S. Adams Sullivan

Sullivan, a writer, illustrator, and artist, works at home allowing him to spend long hours with his children, sharing projects and pleasures, many of which found their way into this book. He is also the author of *The Quality Time Almanac*.

## Publisher:
Main Street Books (Doubleday/Bantam Doubleday Dell)

## Edition:
2nd (1992)

## Price:
$17.95

## Pages/Run Time:
391

## ISBN:
0385426259

## Media:
Book

## Principal Subject:
Strengthening Your Family

## Secondary Subject:
Fatherhood

## Age Group:
Infants & Toddlers (0–3)

# THE FATHER'S ALMANAC

### Recommended For:
Strengthening Your Family

## Description:
Published originally in 1980 to invoke an argument for "involved fatherhood," this revision notes changes in the role fathers play nowadays. This 391-page book is separated into 12 chapters, about 30 pages each. Chapter topics focus on: pregnancy and childbirth, baby care, fathers' jobs, family issues (working, stay-at-home, divorce, siblings, etc.), "providing" (childcare, safety, insurance, fix-it, etc.), daily events (baths, bedtime, reading, etc.), outings and special events, teaching and discipline, learning and playing with kids (games, activities,), working with kids ("handyman's helper," cooking, etc.), and "keeping a record" (photographing, videotaping, etc.). The table of contents lists major subtopics within chapters and bold headings are used for further divisions. The author has included his own black line illustrations throughout along with photographs of fathers with their children to introduce each chapter. A 16-page index completes the book along with a reference section to further reading.

## Evaluation:
What a perfect addition to the family library! Sullivan offers fathers the chance to see themselves as more than "babysitters," more than a "breadwinner," more than a stand-in for mom. By presenting common hurdles and problems that fathers face and offering bite-size tidbits of advice to help fathers deal with those problems, the author has accomplished what he set out to do: instill confidence in fathers so they will be and stay involved. From instructions for how to make a teepee to how to deal with absences due to business trips, this guide offers succinct and well-constructed tips for making fatherhood an enjoyable experience. The author's illustrations are charming, but not sickeningly cute. The only area that is treated lightly concerns that of child development. Fathers will need other resources to supplement this topic. Focused on the questions, needs, and abilities of fathers, mothers, however, will also benefit from its content. This resource deserves a real place of honor within the family home.

## Where To Find/Buy:
Bookstores and libraries.

**Fatherhood**

# NEW FATHER BOOK

**Recommended For:**
Strengthening Your Family

## Description:

The authors, collectively the fathers of five children, have put together a book that covers childhood from pregnancy through a child's early years. The first portion tackles the issue of what it takes to be a good dad. Other topics in this 96-page book include pregnancy, birth, the first two weeks, the first year, and the toddler and preschool years. The appendix is written especially for moms. It addresses five myths between mothers and fathers, such as "Household duties should be shared 50-50," and offers six tips for a mother to use when dealing with a new father, such as "Don't 'rescue' your husband." Every chapter offers many sidebars and lists, such as "10 Ways to Make Time for Your Children," "What's a Man To Do?" (when mom's in labor), and "Eagle's Eye View of Your Baby's First Year." The authors use firsthand experiences to illustrate their subjects. The last chapter addresses issues faced by fathers who adopt, are divorced, widowed, or single parents, as well as those who are stepfathers. A comprehensive index is included at the end of the book.

## Evaluation:

This book's success rests heavily on the authors' experience as fathers. While light on technical information, the book's greatest assets are the real-life tips, tricks and strategies the authors have learned and incorporated throughout. The text is not overloaded with medical information; there's just enough to inform. The book's other great strength is that on almost every page there is a sidebar discussion, chart, or list to highlight or supplement the topic being addressed. Chapter One asks—and answers—the question, "What makes a good dad?" It makes a good argument for a model of fatherhood that includes a supportive partnership with the mom and deep involvement in the child's life. Advice offered includes real-life information, for example, "Ideas and techniques that sounded great in (childbirth) class may be worthless during the real event. The key is to be flexible and improvise." Horn and Rosenberg stress the importance of prioritizing responsibilities. This book, while geared a little toward the "white-collar" professional, is a good resource for helpful information on pregnancy, childbirth, and child care.

## Where To Find/Buy:

Bookstores and libraries.

**Overall Rating**
★★★★
Excellent real-life advice from experienced fathers, light on technical information

**Design, Ease Of Use**
★★★★
Great to thumb through for information on-the-spot; many useful sidebar articles

1–4 Stars

**Author:**
Wade F. Horn, PhD, and Jeffrey Rosenberg, MSW

Horn is a clinical child psychologist who has held a number of private and public positions focusing on children's issues. He is the father of two teenage girls. Rosenberg is a father of three, including two-year old twins.

**Publisher:**
Better Homes and Gardens Books (Meredith Books)

**Edition:**
1998

**Price:**
$9.95

**Pages/Run Time:**
96

**ISBN:**
069620617X

**Media:**
Book

**Principal Subject:**
Strengthening Your Family

**Secondary Subject:**
Fatherhood

**Age Group:**
Infants & Toddlers (0–3)

II. Strengthening Your Family

**Fatherhood**

II. Strengthening Your Family

## Overall Rating
★★★★
Tools, suggested resources to inspire positive fathering

## Design, Ease Of Use
★★★
Clear paths, complete information; bulletin boards relatively inactive

1–4 Stars

## Publisher:
The National Center For Fathering

## Media:
Internet

## Principal Subject:
Strengthening Your Family

## Secondary Subject:
Fatherhood

## Age Group:
Infants & Toddlers (0–3)

# NATIONAL CENTER FOR FATHERING

**Recommended For:**
Strengthening Your Family

## Description:
The National Center For Fathering is an organization whose mission is "to inspire and equip men to be better fathers." It was formed 1990 by Ken Canfield, PhD, in response to "the dramatic trend toward fatherlessness." The center conducts research on fathers and fathering in order to develop practical resources which prepare and support dads for fathering. Its staff includes researchers, writers, speakers, and seminar instructors. Its goal is to become America's leading resource for fathers. It offers a nationwide radio program, a quarterly magazine, seminars and small group materials, a Life Course of Fathering curricula, and support for initiatives and lobbying efforts to strengthen fathers and their families. Its website offers Practical Tips/Hot Topics, a bookstore, a Fathering Hall of Fame where visitors can add tributes to their fathers, interactive activities with other fathers, subscriptions and access to fathering research, bulletin boards, and links. Included is information on a range of topics and fathering situations, including adoptive fathers, stepparents, single dads, surrogate fathers, and dads who travel, as well as information about every age child.

## Evaluation:
More than 27 million, or 39 percent of all U.S. children, now live apart from their father, according to statistics quoted at this website. In a typical year, more than one-third of these children won't even see their father. "Fathers leave an indelible mark on their children and society," Ken Canfield states. "We must encourage, equip, and support dads as they become the true heroes of the coming generation." This all is accomplished at this website which succeeds at combining straight talk, empathy, and education without demeaning the role of the father. The information presented is concise and direct, the topics are on-target for most fathers' concerns, and humorous interludes such as "The Top 10 Things Not To Do At Your Child's Performance" help alleviate those sometimes intense fathering moments. Disappointing at this site was the low-level involvement within the bulletin boards, perhaps best illustrating the author's suggestion that fathers need to better support one another in their efforts. Linking each "Hot Topic" to related books, tapes, and other resources succeeds in making parenting information accessible to busy dads. This site seeks to be a positive voice and role-model for fathers. It succeeds on most counts.

## Where To Find/Buy:
On the Internet using the URL: http://fathers.com

**Fatherhood**

# THE NEW FATHER
A Dad's Guide To The First Year

★★★★

**Recommended For:**
Strengthening Your Family

## Description:

This book is comprised of 13 chapters: the first on baby's first week and the remaining on months one through twelve. Each chapter is divided into three major sections: "What's Going on With Baby" (an overview of the four major areas of baby development—physical, intellectual, verbal, and emotional/social), "What You're Going Through," and "You and Your Baby" (tools to use to bond with baby). Some chapters also include a section on "Family Matters" which is a discussion about a various issues that impact the family as a whole, such as crying, family finances, and finding childcare. Sidebars and charts are included to supplement a discussion with additional information. Developmental milestones are listed in "What's Going On With Baby," and advice is tucked into "You and Your Baby." Some of the issues addressed in the third section and the "Family Matters" section include bonding with baby, life insurance, resuming sex with one's partner, striking a balance between work and family, feeling isolated from other men, discipline, and other issues.

## Evaluation:

This isn't the resource to use if an expectant father or new father is looking for all there is to know about taking care of baby. For example, dad can't, in a crisis, go to the chapter on feeding to find out quickly what to do. Other baby care books are better for that information. This book lends itself to being more of a resource that should be used before baby arrives and as a reminder throughout baby's first year of how he or she develops. However, the author wisely states that this book's primary focus "is on how fathers develop" rather than baby's development. Brott's tone offers "just the facts" with little embellishment, which may be an advantage to many readers. There is some humor, but the focus is on presenting information, not entertaining the reader. The sections in each chapter on baby development are presented as simple lists. "What You're Going Through" addresses special topics (SIDS, helping mother, etc.) and offers, in a non-threatening manner, empathy and advice for the different emotions, questions, and worries a father may experience regardless of the baby's age. As a suggested companion to books on baby care, moms will want to be sure to read this book too if they want to know what Dad is likely thinking and feeling.

## Where To Find/Buy:

Bookstores and libraries.

---

**Overall Rating**
★★★★
Interesting perspective of what the new father experiences

**Design, Ease Of Use**
★★★
Clearly organized, easily digested; however contents are sometimes too vague

1–4 Stars

**Author:**
Armin A. Brott

Brott has authored *The Expectant Father: Facts, Tips, and Advice for Dads-To-Be* and has also written for *BabyTalk* magazine, *The New York Times*, *Newsweek*, the *Washington Post*, and other parenting publications. He hosts a radio show on parenting in the San Francisco Bay area.

**Publisher:**
Abbeville Press
(Abbeville Publishing Group)

**Edition:**
1997

**Price:**
$10.95

**Pages/Run Time:**
239

**ISBN:**
0789202751

**Media:**
Book

**Principal Subject:**
Strengthening Your Family

**Secondary Subject:**
Fatherhood

**Age Group:**
Infants (0–1)

II. Strengthening Your Family

**Fatherhood**

# THE JOY OF FATHERHOOD
## The First Twelve Months

**Recommended For:**
Strengthening Your Family

## Description:

Written "by a man for men," this 228-page book aims to provide new fathers with information on the possible emotions, thoughts, and behaviors that they may experience. With the exception of the first chapter which deals with labor, delivery, and the postpartum period, the book includes twelve other chapters divided month-by-month for a baby's life from birth to 12 months of age. The author uses a consistent format for each of these chapters with subheadings highlighting: what's new with baby, "focus," what's new with mom, what's new with dad, "being there for your baby," and growing together (a one paragraph summary of the chapter's important points). Icons are used in the margins to mark each of these sections. The focus sections contain how-to instructions, questions and answers, clinical information, and advice on topics that concern new fathers, such as colic, getting in shape, anger management, how to maintain relationships with friends, and more. Each chapter includes a Q & A segment and various tips are offered in the margins. An appendix gives information about common childhood ailments.

## Evaluation:

The consistent format works well here making it a breeze for busy dads to find information. New fathers will also appreciate the focus sections as they wrestle with practical concerns such as safety issues, saving money for baby, and other topics. "I've tried to address not only the basics—what to expect each month, how to interact with your baby—but also the conflicting emotions you, as a man, might be experiencing and the complexities of maintaining a healthy relationship with your partner." Consequently, Goldman's book contains an excellent mix of basic how-to information (diapering baby, holding baby, feeding baby), discussions about the emotions that family members may be experiencing, and practical matters such as finance and planning. The organization of this book makes it one of the easiest to read and use by being divided into age categories, and further divided into standard topics that are relevant to each month. Chapters are written succinctly, knowing that a new father hasn't much time to sit down and read. Almost every page contains a small sidebar "tip" of information that isn't always found in other similar resources. The one chapter on childbirth shouldn't be all the information a new father relies on, however, if a new dad had to select one book, this would be a very good choice.

## Where To Find/Buy:

Bookstores, libraries, or order direct by calling (916) 632-4400 or by contacting Prima Publishing at P. O. Box 1260, Rocklin, CA 95677.

---

**★★★★**

**Overall Rating**
★★★★
Good succinct advice and info for men wrestling with emotional aspects of fatherhood

**Design, Ease Of Use**
★★
Consistent chapter format, but icons are annoying; photographs would be a nice addition

1–4 Stars

**Author:**
Marcus Jacob Goldman, MD

Goldman trained in general psychiatry at Harvard Medical School where he also completed the Gaughan Fellowship in forensic psychiatry. He has taught psychiatry and behavioral health at Harvard and currently practices geriatric psychiatry.

**Publisher:**
Prima Publishing

**Edition:**
1997

**Price:**
$15.00

**Pages/Run Time:**
228

**ISBN:**
0761504524

**Media:**
Book

**Principal Subject:**
Strengthening Your Family

**Secondary Subject:**
Fatherhood

**Age Group:**
Infants (0–1)

**Fatherhood**

# KEYS TO BECOMING A FATHER

★★★

### Description:

The stated theme of this book is that, as more fathers are becoming involved in child care, the father's relationship with his child is different than a mother's (but equally important). Sears' guide addresses the concerns that fathers face as they take on new roles with their children. Sears shares "uniquely male nurturing tips" that he himself has learned through fathering eight children. There are 36 "Keys" in this 152-page book, all of which are listed in the table of contents; these topics usually are covered in two to three pages. Topics include the following: fathering during pregnancy, fathering with a newborn, how to handle a fussy baby, relationships with your wife, how to juggle career and parenthood, helping your son or daughter develop healthy masculinity or femininity, being a single father, playing with your baby (three months intervals to one year), disciplining your baby/child (increments from birth), and fathering older children (one to three years old, three to six years old, six to 11 years old, teenager). A question and answer section is supplied at the end of the book listing ten questions posed from fathers and Sears' responses.

### Evaluation:

This book is not simply for fathers. Mothers, by reading this book, can get a better idea how (and why) fathers respond differently to their children. Sears speaks quite candidly about mistakes he has made, revelations he has gleaned, and the great joys and satisfactions he has received from his experiences as a father. No doubt any father will appreciate Sears' candor and feel supported without being babied—no psycho-babble here. The book's short, concise "Keys," although not written in great depth, offer just enough for busy fathers who might be reluctant to sit down and read a book on parenting. Although some of Sears' suggestions, such as working at home, easing back on work demands, etc., may not work with many fathers' careers, he does offer many thoughts on how to juggle fatherhood and careers; these tips are useful for working mothers too. His section on being a single father, however, seems weak; also, tips on how to be a "house husband/father" are missing. Hopefully these areas will be strengthened in future editions.

### Where To Find/Buy:

Bookstores and libraries.

---

**Overall Rating**
★★★
"Sound bites" of advice offering 36 tips on concerns new dads may have

**Design, Ease Of Use**
★★★★
All topics—"Keys"—listed in table of contents; short, concise text for busy dads

1–4 Stars

**Author:**
William Sears, MD

Sears, "one of America's most renowned pediatricians," has been in practice for 20 years and authored 10 books. Currently, he's a clinical assistant professor of pediatrics at USC School of Medicine.

**Publisher:**
Barron's Educational Series

**Edition:**
1991

**Price:**
$6.95

**Pages/Run Time:**
152

**ISBN:**
0812045416

**Media:**
Book

**Principal Subject:**
Strengthening Your Family

**Secondary Subject:**
Fatherhood

**Age Group:**
Infants & Toddlers (0–3)

II. Strengthening Your Family

**★★★**

**Overall Rating**
★★★
Reference manual on almost all aspects of being a father

**Design, Ease Of Use**
★★★
Subject information is provided in an easy to understand, lighthearted manner

1–4 Stars

**Author:**
Kevin Nelson

Kevin Nelson is a journalist and the author of twelve books. This is his first book on fatherhood. He is the father of two children, and his wife is expecting their third.

**Publisher:**
Contemporary Books (NTC/Contemporary Publishing Group)

**Edition:**
1998

**Price:**
$16.95

**Pages/Run Time:**
319

**ISBN:**
0809229633

**Media:**
Book

**Principal Subject:**
Strengthening Your Family

**Secondary Subject:**
Fatherhood

**Age Group:**
Infants & Toddlers (0–3)

**Fatherhood**

# THE DADDY GUIDE
Real-Life Advice And Tips From Over 250 Dads And Other Experts

## Description:
The 28 chapters in this book cover a myriad of parenting topics. Chapter topics on caring for baby include advice and inspirations on becoming a father, coaching during childbirth, finding childcare and preschools, activities to do with kids, feeding baby, diapering, discipline, and more. The author also discusses personal concerns of fathers such as combining careers and family, insurance, cars, sports, marital relationships, finances, saving for college, spirituality, business travel, and other areas. In the development of this book, the author interviewed more than 250 experts in parenting and fathering. These experts' advice and experiences are peppered throughout the book. Each chapter includes a question-and-answer section as well as a section that discusses the topic from the perspective of the subject-matter expert. Chapters are generally four to eight pages long and are further divided into subtopics and sections. At the end of each chapter, the author lists resources for additional information.

## Evaluation:
In this book, the author attempts to cover just about everything regarding parenting from a father's perspective. He doesn't quite make it, but almost. For example, little reference is made to breastfeeding even though fathers need support too in this area. Nelson even addresses a few things patently unrelated to becoming a father; is an entire chapter on selecting cars really necessary? Readers will note that very little of the meat-and-potato part of the book is actually written by the author. The author's role is to simply introduce the chapter, concept, or topic discussion. He then relies on interviews with experts to provide the information. Because the scope of this book is so extensive, one wouldn't want to try to read it in one sitting, or even two. It is more of a reference manual to have on hand when needed. The reader won't get a heavy dose of history, statistics, background, or theory on any particular subject. Nelson presents just the basic facts in a lighthearted, easy-to-read manner. This book would benefit any father, new or somewhat seasoned, but should be supplemented with more in-depth resources for particular subjects.

## Where To Find/Buy:
Bookstores and libraries.

**Fatherhood**

# SLOWLANE.COM
The Online Resource For Stay At Home Dads

### Description:
Slowlane.com is designed to provide support and information to stay-at-home dads. Its mission is to help dads connect with other dads, to compile a collection of online resources dealing with issues of fathering, family and being a stay-at-home dad, and to help support other not-for-profit websites for stay-at-home dads groups and organizations. Here you'll find research, an extensive collection of links, articles written by and for dads, comprehensive lists of kid-friendly home businesses, online chats and listserves, question and answer sections, and access to the At-Home Dad Handbook and Dad-to-Dad chapters.

### Evaluation:
First of all, Slowlane.com is, well, slow. That may give a dad the chance to grab a toddler out of the fishbowl while the page loads, but it may deter some from exploring this site in-depth. Patience, after all, knows only so many bounds. The site is, however, attractive and complete, with a sincere tone and information helpful to the community of stay-at-home fathers. Its extensive collection of links is particularly well-organized. Categories include single fathers, stay-at-home dad organizations, fathers and divorce, resources for fathers, personal stories, gay fathers, child-related sites, mothering sites, parenting sites, grandparents' resources, newspapers and magazines, international fathers, men's issues, and products by and for at-home dads. The articles presented, many written by Massey himself, are thoughtful and thought-provoking. The list of kid-friendly business ideas is appropriate for either mothers or parents searching for the economic ability to stay home with their children. This is a site designed to support a community of fathers and it accomplishes that goal admirably. There is little age-specific information here, however, so its appeal is a general one.

### Where To Find/Buy:
On the Internet using the URL: http://www.slowlane.com

**Overall Rating**
★★★
Sincere tone, strong sense of community and extensive links to other dad sites

**Design, Ease Of Use**
★★
Easy to navigate; some pages can't be printed

1–4 Stars

**Author:**
Jay Massey and Joe Martin, Jr.
Massey and Martin, both stay-at-home dads, host the Slowlane site. Slowlane is sponsored by Coco Design Associates as a service to the Stay-At-Home Dads' community.

**Media:**
Internet

**Principal Subject:**
Strengthening Your Family

**Secondary Subject:**
Fatherhood

**Age Group:**
Infants & Toddlers (0–3)

**Fatherhood**

## ★★★

**Overall Rating**
★★★
Much useful information, from the technical to the emotional

**Design, Ease Of Use**
★
Chapters are long, with not much to break them up

1–4 Stars

**Author:**
David Laskin

David Laskin is the father of three daughters, which include twin baby girls. He has written about infant development and many other topics in books and magazines.

**Publisher:**
Ballantine Books
(Random House)

**Edition:**
1990

**Price:**
$4.95

**Pages/Run Time:**
407

**ISBN:**
0345337077

**Media:**
Book

**Principal Subject:**
Strengthening Your Family

**Secondary Subject:**
Fatherhood

**Age Group:**
Infants (0–1)

# PARENTS™ BOOK FOR NEW FATHERS

### Description:

This book is an installment in the Parents™ Magazine Baby and Child Care Series. The author covers the process of becoming a father from the decision to have a child, through birth and the first year. He also includes information for special situations, including adoptive and single fathers. At the end of the book are two appendices, one on infant development and the other a resource list that covers a range of pregnancy and baby-care topics. Four chapters in this 14 chapter book discuss basic pregnancy issues, from how to make a baby to the more technical issues of medical problems that can occur during pregnancy. In addition to technical medical information, the author covers what emotions a father-to-be can expect to feel, how to handle worries about the baby, and what possible changes may occur in a new father's relationship with his wife. Other chapters include information regarding the birthing process, the first few weeks of a newborn's life, establishing new family routines, the difficulties of being a parent, bonding and playing with a baby, and providing adequate child care.

### Evaluation:

While this book is a wealth of information on almost every topic imaginable, the format leaves a little to be desired. The layout is that of a paperback novel, with few visual breaks. It is best suited for a reader who wants extremely comprehensive, detailed information, and has the time and stamina to read the book cover to cover, or at least chapter by chapter. It is not a book to thumb through while looking for specific information. The author uses testimony from other fathers to illustrate the topics. Chapter Three begins similar to a course on Health 101: How to Make a Baby, and ends with the various stages of fetal development. Obviously, this book is meant for an expectant father who begins knowing nothing and wants to know everything. In that, the author does well in covering the range of information from the technical to the emotional. Unexpectedly, Chapter 11 is a delightful chapter on bonding and playing with baby, and Chapter Ten takes a realistic look at the frustrations and stresses of becoming a parent. This book is a dry read, but offers well the "nuts and bolts" of pregnancy and baby care.

### Where To Find/Buy:

Bookstores and libraries.

II. Strengthening Your Family

**Fatherhood**

# A DAD'S GUIDE TO THE TODDLER YEARS

★ ★

### Description:

This book addresses all aspects of toddlerhood, from age 12 months to 36 months. The chapters are divided into age categories, in three month increments, i.e. 12 to 15 months, 15 to 18 months, etc. Each of the eight chapters focuses on a particular issue prevalent to that developmental stage. Like its companion book on baby's first year, each chapter of this book is divided into sections called "What's Going On with the Baby," "What You're Going Through," "You and Your Baby," and "Family Matters." In What's Going On with the Baby, the author describes the baby's physical, intellectual, verbal, and emotional/social development at this stage. What You're Going Through describes what a typical father experiences during this developmental stage. You and Your Baby ties the first two sections of the book together by describing ways child and father can interact. Family Matters addresses those topics that do not directly affect interaction between dad and baby, but are relevant to the family nonetheless, such as finances, family planning, nutrition, physicians, and more.

### Evaluation:

The author says this book, as are his others, is more about the father's development and growth over this time period than the child's. He uses humor to make the book less textbookish, but his primary goal is educating, not entertaining, the reader. Throughout, the author addresses topics of relevance to the parent of a toddler, regardless of age. Unfortunately, because the book is divided by age category, a father of a 20-month old might not find the information he needs on involving the baby in group activities because it isn't addressed until the chapter on toddlers from 30 to 33 months. The contents page should, but doesn't, include descriptions of issues addressed in each chapter. A father would be better served by reading the entire book at once, instead of relying only on reading the portion that pertains to his child's age. A number of the topics the author addresses are about "play." Although the author, in his introduction, states that a father will have to get his "exhaustive study of child development" from another source, it seems as if this author believes that a father's primary role is in spending time playing with his child. Good as a beginning primer, other resources would help fill in the gaps left by reading this book alone.

### Where To Find/Buy:

Bookstores, libraries, or order direct by calling (800) ARTBOOK.

**Overall Rating**
★★
Information is accurate, but content lacks depth—many issues are glossed over

**Design, Ease Of Use**
★★
Good chapter bullets, but content is badly organized, inadequate table of contents

1–4 Stars

**Author:**
Armin A. Brott

Armin Brott is the author of *The Expectant Father: Facts, Tips, and Advice for Dads-to-Be* and *The New Father: A Dad's Guide to the First Year.* He is a contributing writer to many newspapers and parenting magazines and hosts a weekly parenting radio show.

**Publisher:**
Abbeville Press

**Edition:**
1998

**Price:**
$15.95

**Pages/Run Time:**
223

**ISBN:**
0789204800

**Media:**
Book

**Principal Subject:**
Strengthening Your Family

**Secondary Subject:**
Fatherhood

**Age Group:**
Toddlers (1–3)

## Overall Rating
★★

Light reading of topics well worth consideration, might put off some reluctant new dads

## Design, Ease Of Use
★★

A quick and easy read with one page inspirational quotes; advertising in back distracts

1–4 Stars

## Author:
Jeanne Murphy

Murphy says that the suggestions made in this book are opinions which are true to the best of her knowledge. A parent herself, Murphy has also written a three book series entitled *Baby Tips for New Moms.*

## Publisher:
Fisher Books

## Edition:
1998

## Price:
$6.95

## Pages/Run Time:
135

## ISBN:
1555611699

## Media:
Book

## Principal Subject:
Strengthening Your Family

## Secondary Subject:
Fatherhood

## Age Group:
Infants (0–1)

**Fatherhood**

# BABY TIPS FOR NEW DADS
Baby's First Year

## Description:
This book is written for first time fathers who have yet to understand the possible effects that parenting can have on the marriage relationship. Before the book begins, Murphy gives notice that, "The suggestions made in this book are opinions and are not meant to supersede a doctor's recommendations." Nevertheless, the book does not particularly address medical issues. Instead, each page is a message or quote provided to offer teachings about new life situations (challenges) that arrive with the baby. Chapter topics include "Hormones and How to Handle Them," "The Monumentally Sensitive Issue of Weight," "What to Do and Say," "What Absolutely Not to Do and Say," and "Other General Survival Tips." In these passages, the demands of parenthood are described from the mother's point-of-view. The reader is told, for example, that "Being a good dad and husband isn't the result of a gene. It's the result of commitment." This book also contains the following: an index, a contest, a very brief first year interest/activity summary, a guide to resource organizations, catalog information, and coupons.

## Evaluation:
At first glance, this book seems to display the attitude that the mother will typically give it her all to meet her baby's needs, while the father may have a tendency to be a bit more selfish. Taken too literally this book could be discouraging to the reader, but Murphy's writing style is very lighthearted and easily considered by the reader. On the whole, the book conveys many of the new transitions and demands put upon the mother who is having her first child. Sometimes the scenario is a bit exaggerated (for example the chapter on "Hormones and How to Handle Them"), but the reader is entertained and gets the message. The reader is encouraged to resist putting his own needs first ("Remember: In the back of your wife's mind, she is probably thinking, 'One baby is enough,' so don't act like a baby . . .") and asked to give 100 percent ("It's better to give your wife a reason to say 'thank you' than it is for you to find a way to say 'I'm sorry.'"). This book provides good medicine for late-blooming fathers.

## Where To Find/Buy:
Bookstores and libraries.

**Fatherhood**

# FATHERS & BABIES
How Babies Grow And What They Need From You, From Birth To 18 Months

★ ★

## Description:
This 1993 step-by-step manual aims to "teach both practical skills and child development theory." It includes five major sections with a preceding introduction. Chapter One includes information and advice on newborns: feeding, how to handle and soothe an infant, bathing, changing diapers, and more are covered. Chapter Two discusses child care for infants one to six months. Sleeping and eating idiosyncrasies, discipline, dressing, bathing, some developmental milestones, and other topics are contained in this section. Chapters Three, Four, and Five cover similar topics of infant care but in a progressive age-specific format from six to nine months, nine to 12 months, and 12 to 18 months of age, respectively. Additional information and advice is provided on the following topics: beginning walking, shyness, first words, safety and childproofing, how to keep your patience, toilet training, activities to do with your child, infant toys, birthday parties, recipes, and more. There is no index.

## Evaluation:
This is a well-intentioned guide targeting an audience (fathers) who might appreciate concise information. However, much more depth could have been added to this resource without sacrificing brevity. Lightly touching on just the very basics, this book gives fathers a sampling of what its like to be a primary care provider. The problem is that, in so doing, it sometimes delivers the message to the reader in dumb-downed fashion—"If your baby likes to poke, watch out for your eyes." Other examples include how to determine when a child is able to sit so that the father no longer needs to prop them up or how to change a baby at someone else's house. The author does provide some helpful advice and information, such as offering baby a toy to play with while changing their diaper, ways to babyproof the home, and fun activities and games. The book is written in a humorous vein, with extensive use of black and white line illustrations. Worth the read? Other resources serve fathers' needs better. Use them instead.

## Where To Find/Buy:
Bookstores and libraries.

**Overall Rating**
★★
Too concise and hodgepodge—fathers are capable of assimilating more in-depth info

**Design, Ease Of Use**
★
Index would have contributed immensely; no detailed help from table of contents

1–4 Stars

**Author:**
Jean Marzollo
Jean Marzollo graduated from the University of Connecticut and the Harvard Graduate School of Education. She previously has written parenting articles for such magazines as Scholastic's *Let's Find Out*, *Parents Magazine*, *Family Circle*, and *Working Mother*.

**Publisher:**
HarperPerennial (HarperCollins)

**Edition:**
1993

**Price:**
$12.50

**Pages/Run Time:**
235

**ISBN:**
0060969083

**Media:**
Book

**Principal Subject:**
Strengthening Your Family

**Secondary Subject:**
Fatherhood

**Age Group:**
Infants & Toddlers (0–3)

II. Strengthening Your Family

**Overall Rating**
★★★★
Most comprehensive guide to dealing with and understanding postpartum "blues"

**Design, Ease Of Use**
★★★★
Summaries given before each chapter, numerous case examples, checklists, etc.

1–4 Stars

**Author:**
Ann Dunnewold, PhD and Diane G. Sanford, PhD

Dunnewold, a psychologist, specializes in women's mental health issues, including prenatal and postpartum adjustment, pregnancy loss, infertility, and PMS. Sanford, a psychologist, educator, and mother, is nationally recognized for the treatment of postpartum disorders.

**Publisher:**
New Harbinger Publications

**Edition:**
1994

**Price:**
$13.95

**Pages/Run Time:**
275

**ISBN:**
1879237806

**Media:**
Book

**Principal Subject:**
Strengthening Your Family

**Secondary Subject:**
Motherhood

**Age Group:**
Infants (0–1)

# POSTPARTUM SURVIVAL GUIDE

**Recommended For:**
Strengthening Your Family

**Description:**
As the authors of this 275-page self-help book state, "This book was written to let you know that having a baby is a tough adjustment: feeling lost or down or nervous is completely understandable." Citing research that says 50 to 80 percent of all new mothers experience the "blues" with 10 to 20 percent experiencing long-lasting negative feelings, this book delves into postpartum depression, how to take care of yourself, and ways to cope. A continuum of reactions to new parenthood is the topic of Chapter Two including checklists, descriptions, and case examples for: normal postpartum depression, postpartum mania, postpartum panic, obsessive-compulsive reaction, and post-traumatic stress. Chapter Three focuses on biological, psychological, and relationship risk factors that can cause postpartum difficulties; questionnaires are provided. The next three chapters focus on how new parents can take care of themselves, including a chapter for "single mothers, older mothers, adoptive mothers, and families with infertility issues." Other chapters discuss professional help, prenatal planning tips to reduce postpartum feelings, and more.

**Evaluation:**
New mothers sometimes have difficulty with feelings of self-blame, disillusionment with motherhood, and isolation. Knowing you aren't alone and hoping that you'll eventually get beyond this period may help, but it isn't enough. Fortunately, this book takes you much further than the chapter provided in most childbirth books on the subject of postpartum "blues." New mothers will find tools and strategies within each chapter to help them manage their feelings and move forward. For example, if a mother is feeling overwhelmed or powerless, the authors suggest that she "single out one area in which [she does] have control, and in which [she is] accomplishing something . . . write this down on a notecard and post it . . . pat [her]self on the back . . . take things one day at a time. . . ." Another suggestion when a mother is feeling that her identity is lost is to think of herself as a pie chart with various segments such as mother, wife, teacher, etc.; while one segment at the moment is the largest, the rest are still there. If someone you know is suffering alone or needing emotional support after having a baby, do them a favor. Offer them an empathetic ear and this book.

**Where To Find/Buy:**
Bookstores and libraries.

**Motherhood**

# THIS ISN'T WHAT I EXPECTED
Recognizing And Recovering From Depression And Anxiety After Childbirth

**★★★★**

### Recommended For:
Strengthening Your Family

## Description:
Authors Kleiman and Raskin draw on their own experiences as medical professionals and mothers to discuss postpartum depression and related anxiety disorders triggered by pregnancy. As many as 30 percent of women experience some degree of post-pregnancy anxiety, the authors say, and their suffering too often is misunderstood. The book describes the syndrome of postpartum depression and includes checklists of both depression and panic disorders to allow readers to early on gauge their own level of concern. One chapter is written specifically for a woman's partner; another is devoted to helping mobilize support from a spouse, family and friends. The book also addresses unresolved issues with a woman's parents that may be affecting her sense of personal esteem as she struggles with postpartum depression. The authors also describe stages of recovery and common concerns that may emerge as a woman recovers. Included are a number of checklists and assessments, including the authors' own Raskin-Kleiman Postpartum Depression and Anxiety Assessment.

## Evaluation:
Readers will find solid information, reassurance and common sense here. The book's plain packaging may cause some bookstore browsers to pass it by, but that would be a mistake. Despite the unimaginative cover, the book presents 288 pages of straightforward information any woman suffering from a postpartum anxiety disorder can use immediately. Readers will learn the latest scientific theories about possible causes of postpartum anxieties and depression and when to seek emergency help. They'll discover how to get through the day when every hour seems impossible. "Get out of bed, even if you feel like you can't," is first on an empathetic list that also urges setting aside time for crying, if needed, and nurturing oneself. Quirky chapter titles, easy reading of on-target information, and patients' stories pull readers along. Who among us could pass up Chapter Five—"I'm Tired, Fat, Ugly, and Still Wearing My Nightgown at Noon"—which turns out to offer a new mother fighting depression dozens of ways to nurture herself even when she hasn't the energy to comb her hair. Self-help is the book's focus, and healthy self-empowerment is its aim making this one of the best for helping someone dealing with postpartum depression.

## Where To Find/Buy:
Bookstores and libraries.

**Overall Rating**
★★★★
Full of practical straightforward advice based on the authors' self-help program

**Design, Ease Of Use**
★★★★
Particularly approachable with bulleted lists, self-assessment questions, and more

1–4 Stars

**Author:**
Karen R. Kleiman, MSW and Valerie D. Raskin, MD

Kleiman, a licensed clinical social worker, is founder of the Postpartum Stress Center (Philadelphia). Raskin, a psychiatrist, was director of the Pregnancy and Postpartum Treatment program (Department of Psychiatry) at the University of IL College of Medicine.

**Publisher:**
Bantam Books (Bantam Doubleday Dell Publishing)

**Edition:**
1994

**Price:**
$12.95

**Pages/Run Time:**
297

**ISBN:**
0553370758

**Media:**
Book

**Principal Subject:**
Strengthening Your Family

**Secondary Subject:**
Motherhood

**Age Group:**
Infants (0–1)

II. Strengthening Your Family

II. Strengthening Your Family

**★★★★**

**Overall Rating**
★★★★
A beautiful, useful and compassionate book for surviving your first year as a mother

**Design, Ease Of Use**
★★★★
Clear color illustrations; highlighted inserts useful for self-help tips

1–4 Stars

**Author:**
Sheila Kitzinger

Sheila Kitzinger is the author of twenty-two books, including the bestselling *The Complete Book of Pregnancy and Childbirth*. She has an international reputation as a social anthropologist, researcher, and women's advocate on pregnancy.

**Publisher:**
Charles Scribner's Sons

**Edition:**
1994

**Price:**
$13.00

**Pages/Run Time:**
302

**ISBN:**
0684825201

**Media:**
Book

**Principal Subject:**
Strengthening Your Family

**Secondary Subject:**
Motherhood

**Age Group:**
Infants (0–1)

Motherhood

# THE YEAR AFTER CHILDBIRTH
Surviving And Enjoying The First Year Of Motherhood

**Recommended For:**
Strengthening Your Family

**Description:**

*The Year After Childbirth* is 302 pages long and divided into fourteen chapters. The book begins with an introductory overview of the challenges and changes a woman can expect to face in the coming year. Then each chapter takes a different aspect of a woman's experience and expands on it. The topics included are: how your body changes with childbirth, learning to enjoy your body again, movement and exercises, understanding the strains and possible damage to the pelvic floor, bladder and vagina and what to do about it, breastfeeding, nutrition, depression in mothers, recognizing the personality of your child, the development of father's feelings, changes to your identity and relationships, and information on resuming your sex life. The final chapter is titled "Coming up for Air" and focuses on what a new mother can do to care for herself amid the stresses of caring for another. This book includes a glossary of terms, reference notes, a list of "helpful organizations," and an index. This book is intended to be a practical tool for the potentially stressful first year of parenthood.

**Evaluation:**

This book is a must read for any first-time mother. Up-to-date and concise, it is also insightful and compassionate. Beginning with information from what is normal bleeding and what is not, to the physical maladies that linger after labor, this book offers complete support with clear advice of what a woman can do to help herself. Detailed information is provided on such things as: the pelvic-floor muscles; how to avoid surgeon-recommended "repairs;" problems inherent with episiotomies; and other information concerning why one may not want particular medical treatments. Other issues of motherhood, including depression and its causes, are also given thorough and up-to-date treatment. This work also contains a beautiful chapter on fatherhood. In short, the book addresses many more challenges than are reviewed here; and each is easily referenced, well-illustrated, and practical. A lovely book to look at as well as to read, this one will sit on the nightstand and be well-thumbed.

**Where To Find/Buy:**
Bookstores and libraries.

**Motherhood**

# CHILD OF MINE
Writers Talk About The First Year Of Motherhood

★★★

## Description:

Christina Baker Kline collected and edited a group of essays written by women who are both mothers and also published novelists, journalists, or essayists. In her introduction, the author states that she felt a desire to, "hear the truth about other women's mothering experiences," but few stories existed, which enhanced her feeling of isolation. Therefore, she asked "a diverse group of women from around the country to write personal narratives on a specific aspect of new motherhood that interests them." The essays in this book address a wide range of concerns, including body image, the mother/child bond, breastfeeding, and many other topics. The stories focus on motherhood experiences from before conception through the first year and are divided into three sections: anticipation, initiation, and "child of mine."

## Evaluation:

"The narratives would explore the powerful physical, intellectual, and emotional experiences that women go through as mothers," Kline explained. "I wanted women to reveal through writing those things they couldn't or wouldn't say aloud, to delve into and interpret what they were really feeling—and to put those thoughts and feelings out there for the rest of us to mull over, argue, or identify with." And these authors do, with fervor. The stories reflect a myriad of emotions regarding motherhood, from fear, ambivalence, and self-doubt to joy, anticipation, and hope. Each story is a poignant account of the author's experience with motherhood. As Kline intended, the stories allow a reader to identify with the entire range of emotions that a woman may experience, thereby dispelling feelings of isolation, uncertainty, and wondering if "there is anyone else out there that feels the way I do." Beautifully written and inspiring, this book would be a sigh of relief for any mother-to-be or new mother.

## Where To Find/Buy:

Bookstores and libraries.

**Overall Rating**
★★★
Thought-provoking stories that reflect real emotions of motherhood

**Design, Ease Of Use**
★★★★
Essays divided by topic into three areas; despite variety of authors, it is easily read

1–4 Stars

**Author:**
Christina Baker Kline

Christina Baker Kline is a novelist and nonfiction writer. She has taught creative writing at Yale, New York University, and the University of Virginia. She is a wife and mother of two sons.

**Publisher:**
Hyperion

**Edition:**
1997

**Price:**
$21.95

**Pages/Run Time:**
333

**ISBN:**
0786862335

**Media:**
Book

**Principal Subject:**
Strengthening Your Family

**Secondary Subject:**
Motherhood

**Age Group:**
Infants (0–1)

II. Strengthening Your Family

★★★

**Overall Rating**
★★★
An insightful guide to ways mothers can bond with their infants

**Design, Ease Of Use**
★★★
Quite readable and concise

1–4 Stars

**Author:**
Martha Sears, RN, with William Sears, MD

Martha Sears, RN, is a certified childbirth educator, breastfeeding consultant, and labor support expert. Together with her husband, William Sears, MD, a pediatrician, they have authored several books on parenting, including *The Birth Book* and *The Baby Book*.

**Publisher:**
Harvard Common Press

**Edition:**
1995

**Price:**
$7.95

**Pages/Run Time:**
117

**ISBN:**
1558320695

**Media:**
Book

**Principal Subject:**
Strengthening Your Family

**Secondary Subject:**
Motherhood

**Age Group:**
Infants (0–1)

**Motherhood**

# 25 THINGS EVERY NEW MOTHER SHOULD KNOW

## Description:

Written by two experts in the field of parenting and child care, this slim guide seeks to encompass the key elements of motherhood for first-time mothers. With conciseness as its goal, this book does not cover the practicalities of baby care, but chooses to focus on the transition into motherhood and effective parenting. The authors speak from both professional and personal experience as the parents of eight children in writing this book. The book's philosophical foundation is what the authors call "attachment parenting," which "includes closeness right from birth, responding sensitively to cries, babywearing, sharing sleep, and breastfeeding." It is the authors' belief that such parenting leads to the greatest closeness between mother and child as well as healthy, stable children. There are 25 separate sections to this book, each of which focuses on a separate parenting issue, such as breast/bottle-feeding, how to respond to the baby's crying, how to address baby's needs during the day and during the night, making the decision to stay home with the baby, learning to trust intuition and become the best "expert" on the baby's care, and more.

## Evaluation:

For mothers without much time to wade through the sheer volume of baby books out there, this little volume includes much sage advice about mothering. It wisely leaves the practicalities to other books in order to focus exclusively on the elements of successful mothering. This book represents a shift in parenting styles away from a model of strict, authoritarian parenting towards a style of parenting that believes a mother can interpret and respond to a baby's needs without fear of "spoiling" or "ruining" the child. The authors believe the closest attachment of an infant to her mother occurs through exclusive breastfeeding, immediately responding to a baby's cries, sharing sleeping arrangements in the early months, and being a full-time mother. Even if these ideas feel conflicting for some, this book can enrich every mother's perspective without dominating her own style of mothering.

## Where To Find/Buy:

Bookstores and libraries.

**Motherhood**

# LAUGHTER AND TEARS
## The Emotional Life Of New Mothers

### Description:

*Laughter And Tears* is a book on the new mother's postpartum period and baby's first year. This two part book ("Preparation" and "Being There") includes chapters on "Creating Your Circle of Support," "The Early Hours," "Transition Time: Six Weeks to Six Months," "Finally Feeling Like a Mom," and more. It is first and foremost a book on the postpartum period. The book explores many aspects of new motherhood, including physical, emotional, social, and medical aspects associated with being a new mother. A small section of the book discusses the roles of father, grandparents, extended family, and friends as well. The authors share experiences of many mothers, as well as fathers, to express the range of emotions during this time—from joy and satisfaction to resentment and depression. Breastfeeding, exercise, sleep deprivation, and relationship with one's partner are also discussed. Intermingled in the pages of this book is information about baby, including newborn care, developmental stages, and separation anxiety. A resource guide and an index are included at the back of the book.

### Evaluation:

This book's intent is largely for new parents, especially mothers, who desire more information about what a mother can expect within herself during the postpartum period. Although this book does contain some information about the growth and development of the new baby, parents looking for a book on baby's development will do better finding a different resource. *Laughter And Tears* reaches deep into the emotional realm, filling the gap left by the volumes of other "new parents and baby" type books that only briefly address the large and real needs of new mothers. The experiences the authors share of mothers and fathers present a sensitive look into this period and provide needed support for parents. The authors have done a fine job in addressing the range of emotions of new mothers. The resource guide provides a helpful list of other materials on the subject of the postpartum period and beyond. This book is probably best read cover to cover to obtain the continuity of information, as it does not work as well as a reference guide.

### Where To Find/Buy:

Bookstores and libraries.

---

**Overall Rating**
★★★
Good resource for exploring the array of emotions of new motherhood

**Design, Ease Of Use**
★★★
Best read cover to cover; good index for finding specific information

1–4 Stars

**Author:**
Elisabeth Bing and Libby Colman, PhD

Bing introduced American women to the Lamaze method of natural childbirth through her book *Six Practical Lessons For An Easier Childbirth*, and she has written many other books. Colman is a social psychologist and coauthor of *Pregnancy: The Psychological Experience.*

**Publisher:**
Henry Holt and Company

**Edition:**
1997

**Price:**
$16.95

**Pages/Run Time:**
276

**ISBN:**
0805041575

**Media:**
Book

**Principal Subject:**
Strengthening Your Family

**Secondary Subject:**
Motherhood

**Age Group:**
Infants (0–1)

II. Strengthening Your Family

★★★

**Overall Rating**
★★★
Excellent primer balances medical information, experience, and commonsense advice

**Design, Ease Of Use**
★★★
Short, concise chapters; bullets, boxed highlights, narratives; comprehensive index

1–4 Stars

**Author:**
Linda Sebastian

Sebastian is a psychiatric nurse with 25 years of experience. An Advanced Registered Nurse Practitioner, she provides outpatient therapy, medication management, and education for professionals about postpartum depression and anxiety.

**Publisher:**
Addicus Books

**Edition:**
1998

**Price:**
$12.95

**Pages/Run Time:**
129

**ISBN:**
1886039348

**Media:**
Book

**Principal Subject:**
Strengthening Your Family

**Secondary Subject:**
Motherhood

**Age Group:**
Infants (0–1)

Motherhood

# OVERCOMING POSTPARTUM DEPRESSION & ANXIETY

## Description:

The author uses her background as a nurse and psychotherapist, as well as her own firsthand experience, to provide information regarding postpartum mood disorders, an often misunderstood and seldom-discussed consequence of having children. "There was little discussion about the adjustment period following the birth and no mention of how devastating postpartum blues can be, let alone the possibility of more severe depression," she writes. These 129 pages include eight chapters, an appendix/resource list, a bibliography, and an index. Peppered throughout the book are firsthand accounts of women who have experienced different types of mood disorders. Discussions include the background and history of the study of postpartum mood disorders, the lack of awareness and information available to new mothers, risk factors, typical symptoms, and classification methods. Specific chapters are included which briefly discuss the different types of anxiety and depression along with a list of symptoms typically experienced in each disorder. The effects on the new baby and other family members, particularly spouses, also is addressed.

## Evaluation:

This book is a useful primer for those who may be experiencing a postpartum disorder and are seeking information about what is happening to them. Throughout, the author offers a good balance of medical explanation, experiential knowledge, and practical advice. Medical descriptions are clear and understandable to a lay person, thorough without being overwhelming. Descriptions are short and to the point, a bonus to someone who is suffering and seeks readily accessible information. The author addresses the importance of getting professional, medical help and does not downplay the potential seriousness of the problems. In addition, common sense self-help methods are included and serve as useful reminders to a woman who may need simple advice. A comprehensive index serves as a quick reference tool for finding specific information provided within the book. What makes this book stand out is that it covers a lot of useful information in a short time. Information is clear and succinct, making it a good starting point for anyone who is searching for a foundation of knowledge regarding postpartum mood disorders.

## Where To Find/Buy:

Bookstores, libraries, or order direct by calling (800) 352-2873.

**Motherhood**

# THE BIRTH OF A MOTHER
How The Motherhood Experiences Changes You Forever

### Description:

The authors state that "this book is about the inner, often most private experiences of becoming a mother." This book is divided into three parts according to three stages of the birth of a mother. Part One—"Preparing to Be a Mother"—deals with pregnancy and preparation of becoming a new mother, the transition period of giving birth, and self-fulfilling prophecies and new roles. Part Two is "A Mother is Born." The five chapters within the second section address the survival of baby, the responsibility of loving the new baby, and seeking affirmation. There is also a first person account of one mother's experience, and a diary of a new mother's transition with her baby. Part Three is entitled "A Mother Adapts." The last three chapters in this section address special needs babies, mother's career, and husbands and fathers. The purpose of this book is to explain how a woman's mindset changes as she experiences motherhood. The authors reinforce that it doesn't happen just at the birth of one's baby, but continues over the course of several months, beginning during the pregnancy and ending some months after the birth.

### Evaluation:

The focus of this book is on the "motherhood mindset," how it is unique yet universal, and includes all the values, sensitivities, and preferences each person possesses. It is the authors' contention that a woman who has become a mother has undergone a fundamental change in her mindset. The authors further believe that the mindset is what organizes our mental lives and makes us coherent individuals. Unfortunately, the authors fail to make it clear what this mindset actually encompasses. Sometimes they describe what simply sounds like personality, but not quite. Sometimes it seems as if they describe the mothering instinct, but then leave the reader thinking it is more than that. Reading the authors' descriptions, any mother would immediately identify with the concept, even though it is a little bit hazy. However, even without clearly defining this change in mindset, the authors do a good job of describing some of the effects caused by this change as well as how it impacts a woman's life. Focusing solely on the emotional possibilities of a woman who is about to become, or has just recently become, a new mother, this book will help identify the phases a mother may pass through on her road to motherhood.

### Where To Find/Buy:

Bookstores and libraries.

---

**Overall Rating**
★★★
Specialized focus written with sensitivity and insightfulness

**Design, Ease Of Use**
★★
Organization could be a little more specific to the content

1–4 Stars

**Author:**
Daniel Stern, MD, Nadia Bruschweiler-Stern, MD, and Alison Freeland

Daniel Stern is a professor of psychology at the University of Geneva, adjunct professor at the University Medical Center-New York Hospital, and an expert in the mother-infant relationship. Nadia Bruschweiler-Stern is a pediatrician and child psychiatrist. Alison Freeland is a freelance writer, author, and reporter for Vermont Public Radio.

**Publisher:**
BasicBooks (Perseus Books, LLC)

**Edition:**
1998

**Price:**
$23.00

**Pages/Run Time:**
246

**ISBN:**
0465016219

**Media:**
Book

---

**Principal Subject:**
Strengthening Your Family

**Secondary Subject:**
Motherhood

**Age Group:**
Infants & Toddlers (0–3)

★★★

**Overall Rating**
★★★
Conversational, humorous tone gives frank, practical advice focusing on the mom

**Design, Ease Of Use**
★★
Nothing fancy, basic organization, easy to read

1–4 Stars

**Author:**
Vicki Iovine

Iovine, a mother of four, writes an advice column for *Child* magazine entitled "Girlfriend to Girlfriend." She has been on the *Today* show, *Oprah*, and CNN. She has law degrees, and has been a *Playboy* centerfold, TV producer, and radio talk show host.

**Publisher:**
Perigee Books (The Berkley Publishing Group/Penguin Putnam)

**Edition:**
1997

**Price:**
$12.00

**Pages/Run Time:**
272

**ISBN:**
0339523308

**Media:**
Book

**Principal Subject:**
Strengthening Your Family

**Secondary Subject:**
Motherhood

**Age Group:**
Infants (0–1)

Motherhood

# THE GIRLFRIENDS' GUIDE TO SURVIVING THE FIRST YEAR OF MOTHERHOOD

## Description:

The author of this book focuses on the care of the mother during the first year of baby's existence. She educates a brand new mother by explaining several key concepts, such as what to expect from the hospital stay and what is needed for the trip home (carseat, pain medication, self-control, confidence). In Chapter Three, the author suggests the new mom do a head-to-toe assessment of the toll that pregnancy and birth have taken. The emotional highs of motherhood are described in Chapter Four, in which the author goes into the pleasantries of poo-poo and the plain fact that one's baby is better than anyone else's, or anyone else (including dad). On the flipside, the emotional lows are described in the chapter following in which five myths and truths about postpartum depression are described. Changing relationships between the new mother and her own mother, the in-laws, friends, moms and dads, and any other important relationship are explained. Body changes (both temporary and permanent), sleep (or lack thereof), keeping healthy, going back to work, and having the second baby are topics covered in subsequent chapters.

## Evaluation:

In this book, directed at new mothers, the author views a woman's new lifestyle in the context of how it has differed from the old. She doesn't explain how to diaper. She doesn't compare the pros and cons of breastfeeding versus formula/bottlefeeding, and she doesn't say a mother should discipline this way or that. What this book does do is slap you in the face with the cold, hard realities that becoming a mother means no more sleeping in, leaking everywhere, and realizing that sex, for a while anyway, becomes nonexistent. Iovine suggests that "when in doubt about the baby's well-being, read Dr. Spock or Dr. Brazelton, but when in doubt about your own well-being, read" this book. All of this information manages to be conveyed with a sense of humor in the attitude of "we women have to stick together." Without any formal training, all of Iovine's advice and information comes straight from her own experiences. Thus some readers may find their experiences to be somewhat different. The best thing about this book is the reminder for any new mom to relax and take care of herself, which is something that can easily get lost in the excitement of the new baby.

## Where To Find/Buy:

Bookstores and libraries.

**Motherhood**

# I WISH SOMEONE HAD TOLD ME
A Realistic Guide To Early Motherhood

★★★

## Description:

In this book, the author interviewed more than 60 new mothers about their experiences with a variety motherhood issues. The information is presented in a series of ideal statements and their correlating facts. Chapter One is about the realities of labor. Chapter Two addresses the expectations of having a "perfect" baby. Recovery from the birth process and all the changes that a woman's body goes through are explained in Chapter Three. In Chapter Four, a woman's mental and emotional ups and downs are discussed. Chapter Five moves into the area of parenting styles, and whether to rely on books versus instinct. Chapters Six and Seven are about feeding and sleeping, respectively. Chapters Eight and Nine talk about the effect of a new baby on the marriage relationship and the new mother's relationship with her own mother. Going back to work and finding good childcare are the topics of Chapters 10 and 11. Chapter 12 sums it all up in a discussion about being a good mother.

## Evaluation:

The author attempts in *I Wish Someone Had Told Me* "to capture the sort of comfort I got from talking to other new mothers about what we were going through." As many new mother swill attest, there is a shortage of books and information that tell it like it is. Here, interview material is used to demonstrate how many different ways there are of approaching subjects that are typically controversial, emotional, or problematic—"becoming a mother makes you feel so much closer to your own mother." The information provided was not used to form any type of theory or parenting philosophy, but simply to provide anecdotal experiences. The author hopes in doing so to debunk the myth of Superwoman and thus discontinue deflating the self-confidence of new mothers who are trying to live up to that standard. In each chapter, the author provides real-life stories, a few statistics and studies, and recommended resources for finding further information. Her message is simply this: childbirth is tough, motherhood is tough, it's never as easy as it sounds, and it is always worth it.

## Where To Find/Buy:

Bookstores and libraries.

**Overall Rating**
★★★
Reassuring belief that a variety of situations can be normal

**Design, Ease Of Use**
★★
Ideal and fact format is a bit cumbersome

1–4 Stars

**Author:**
Nina Barrett

**Publisher:**
Academy Chicago Publishers

**Edition:**
2nd (1997)

**Price:**
$14.00

**Pages/Run Time:**
237

**ISBN:**
0897334426

**Media:**
Book

**Principal Subject:**
Strengthening Your Family

**Secondary Subject:**
Motherhood

**Age Group:**
Infants (0–1)

**★ ★**

**Overall Rating**
★★
Promotes a natural lifestyle, with comprehensive information on breastfeeding

**Design, Ease Of Use**
★★★
Good layout, easy to read; many illustrations

1–4 Stars

**Author:**
Robin Lim

Lim, the mother of five, has written for *Mothering* magazine and many local publications in her home state of Hawaii.

**Publisher:**
Celestial Arts

**Edition:**
1991

**Price:**
$14.95

**Pages/Run Time:**
308

**ISBN:**
0890875901

**Media:**
Book

**Principal Subject:**
Strengthening Your Family

**Secondary Subject:**
Motherhood

**Age Group:**
Infants & Toddlers (0–3)

**Motherhood**

# AFTER THE BABY'S BIRTH . . . A WOMAN'S WAY TO WELLNESS
A Complete Guide For Postpartum Women

**Description:**

This book is intended as a guide for postpartum women, written from the author's perspective and experience as a mother of five children. Chapters describe the physical and psychological phases a woman may experience during the postpartum period, from birth through year four. There are four main parts to this 308-page resource. Within Parts One and Two are sections which cover breastfeeding and breast care, postpartum pelvic health, and toning exercises for the postpartum mother. Other sections address such issues as health care, exercises, infections, and the return to sexual activity. An exercise section to help a woman tone and stretch her body includes explanations and drawings for illustrative purposes. Part Three—the health section—includes chapters on healing touch, Eastern philosophies of women's health, and the Ayurvedic lifestyle. The last part of the book includes information and shared stories regarding various "issues of the heart," including bonding, postpartum blues, single mothers, and children who have died.

**Evaluation:**

The author, a mother of several children, uses her experiences from the traditions of her home in Hawaii along with a lifestyle that leans more toward the organic. Although there is much useful information regarding breastfeeding and general health, it is important for the reader to keep in mind that the author writes mainly from her own perspective, without taking into account much individuality between women. The tone in several parts of the book seems to dictate to a woman what to feel. The discussions regarding postpartum pelvic health and toning exercises are especially useful. Additionally, the breastfeeding and breast care section covers every aspect of the topic including the physiology behind lactation. The book is comprehensive and informative. The chapter on the Ayurvedic lifestyle is interesting, but seems best suited for another book. This book offers some practical advice along with moral support and encouragement to a postpartum woman. It would be especially useful to women who practice or desire a more natural lifestyle.

**Where To Find/Buy:**

Bookstores and libraries.

**Motherhood**

# MOTHERING THE NEW MOTHER
Your Postpartum Resource Companion

★★

## Description:

This book is about the care and comfort necessary for new mothers. The author asserts that American society expects the transition to new motherhood to be accomplished effortlessly and without support when, in reality, many new mothers feel overwhelmed by the life changing experience of giving birth. Many wide-ranging issues are covered in the book's nine chapters: realistic expectations of a new mother's feelings after childbirth, postpartum rituals in different cultures, support and assistance during the postpartum weeks, breastfeeding, postpartum depression, returning to work, staying at home, and helping siblings deal with a newborn. Resources are listed at the end of each chapter, rather than at the end of the book. First-person experiences and testimony illustrate the author's points. The author, who compiled her information in part by collecting questionnaires from new mothers, discusses in depth the concept of a doula, or a mother's helper. Advice on "creating a postpartum plan" is offered in the final chapter in which the author assists the reader in creating a support network using worksheets and checklists.

## Evaluation:

There is much attention given to background, personal testimonials, and history of the various subjects the author addresses. However, the "practical, useful" information is wisely separated from the main body of the text by the use of sidebars, so that the reader can choose what level of information to focus on. Chapters also are divided into short, relevant subsections. The detail the author provides is quite comprehensive, although not concise, and fairly easy to understand. Some may find that there are too many statistics and too much history given without enough practical, working knowledge provided. This book's most valuable asset for new mothers and fathers is the resource list at the end of each chapter. Each entry includes contact information along with detailed descriptions of what the resource includes. These resources, however, will be more beneficial to those who desire and have the time to coordinate background information with practical how-tos. This resource is better suited for those who support postpartum mothers; those wanting more immediate help may need to rely on other more succinct resources.

## Where To Find/Buy:

Bookstores and libraries.

**Overall Rating**
★★
Much background on various topics, balanced with useful, practical information

**Design, Ease Of Use**
★★★
Wordy at times, but excellent resource lists are provided at the end of each chapter

1–4 Stars

**Author:**
Sally Placksin

Placksin has written, produced, and narrated many national radio programs, including the documentary "Mothering the New Mother" for National Public Radio's Horizons series. She has received various grants and awards and is the mother of two children.

**Publisher:**
Newmarket Press

**Edition:**
1994

**Price:**
$15.95

**Pages/Run Time:**
328

**ISBN:**
1557041784

**Media:**
Book

**Principal Subject:**
Strengthening Your Family

**Secondary Subject:**
Motherhood

**Age Group:**
Infants (0–1)

II. Strengthening Your Family

**Overall Rating**
★★
Informative, intense, a bit vague at times due to the subjective nature of the illness

**Design, Ease Of Use**
★★★
Numerous narratives from mothers; chapters are well-organized, well-indexed

1–4 Stars

**Author:**
Sharon L. Roan

Roan is a journalist and a mother. She has received many awards for her research, and she is the personal health columnist for the *Los Angeles Times*.

**Publisher:**
Adams Media

**Edition:**
1997

**Price:**
$9.95

**Pages/Run Time:**
246

**ISBN:**
1558507655

**Media:**
Book

**Principal Subject:**
Strengthening Your Family

**Secondary Subject:**
Motherhood

**Age Group:**
Infants (0–1)

## Motherhood

# POSTPARTUM DEPRESSION
### Every Woman's Guide To Diagnosis, Treatment, & Prevention

### Description:

Roan has not herself experienced postpartum depression (PPD), but she has been both personally and professionally affected by it. As a newspaper reporter, she came to know a woman who killed her infant while suffering postpartum psychosis. Within her personal social circle, half suffered postpartum depression to the point that it "shattered" lives. Roan believes that many women (and others in their life) are caught unaware and unprepared to deal with postpartum depression. Within this resource's 246 pages, Roan offers "information and solutions these women need, through the advice of the top experts in the field and the personal experiences of dozens of women who have recovered from this postpartum illness." In the first half of the book, the reader is educated about depression in general, and postpartum in particular. Throughout the book, there is an emphasis on private/nonprofessional measures to help the PPD sufferer; professional interventions are also highlighted. The book acknowledges some ramifications for the entire family of a PPD sufferer. An eight-page "Resource" guide, bibliography, and more are also given.

### Evaluation:

This book conveys the harsh realities of PPD; it would most likely be too overwhelming for any reader who is already a victim. But for others (a pregnant women, a friend, a spouse, an in-law, etc.) who want to gain an understanding of the topic, this book will offer insight. While Roan does state that a minority of women suffer from PPD, she describes so many severe situations that the reader may feel threatened. Roan's findings may be accurate, but it may unnecessarily alarm prospective mothers believing that this condition will virtually happen to them after their baby is born. More unsettling is Roan's assertion that this is not a condition fully understood, easily treatable, or completely acknowledged within the medical community. Roan does provide a useful resource guide to help the reader obtain help for an individual situation. Readers will find comfort in the author's thrust to the reader to understand as much as possible about PPD, accept the reality, look for treatment if need be, and offer support for those suffering from PPD.

### Where To Find/Buy:

Bookstores, libraries, or order direct by calling (800) 872-5627 or (617) 767-8100.

**Motherhood**

# COMPOSING MYSELF
A Journey Through Postpartum Depression

### Description:
Shaw says, "It seems paradoxical to say that my writing has been, in some way, close to a scream. Not that it is one, but that it's been trying to make sense of what it was that took me beyond words." Shaw begins her personal narrative story by describing her relationship and life with her husband around the time their first daughter was born. Life during this time was harmonious. Then, within ten days of giving birth to her second daughter, life became miserable and confusing. The remainder of this book ponders Shaw's personal feelings and experiences relating to her severe postpartum depression. She was hospitalized, given ECT (electroconvulsive therapy), medications, and assigned psychiatrists. Professionals encouraged Shaw to try to forget the experience, yet she wanted to reach an understanding and requested referral to a psychologist. Eventually, she used her inheritance to fund private counseling. Both her writing and her counseling have brought her some peace, or as she states, "Nevertheless it has been by way of words—my words—that I have gradually taken hold of my life."

### Evaluation:
Presenting a unique view of the topic of postpartum depression (PPD), this is the story of Shaw's personal journey. Readers drawn to this book because of an interest in learning about PPD will fully realize the author's message that help is not readily available, and that there is no easy cure. Because Shaw details both of her pregnancies, it may seem clear to PPD information seekers that she experienced extreme depression by apparent chance. Shaw conveys on nearly every page that, at least in her case, the most effective treatment was introspection/psychotherapy. Although Shaw's depression was triggered by the birth of her second child, this story focuses less on pregnancy, instead emphasizing honestly knowing oneself through all of one's life experiences. This story is embellished with imagery and sensory detail which help to translate the tremendous sadness, emptiness, and aloneness that Shaw had to work through. For those who would prefer to read a personal narrative of PPD rather than a more medically-based description and treatment of PPD, this book will offer insight and a possible course of action. Others may feel more comfort in a resource that offers narrative stories and more easily accessed information.

### Where To Find/Buy:
Bookstores and libraries.

---

**Overall Rating**
★★
Personal journal of one woman's struggle with PPD and possible treatments

**Design, Ease Of Use**
★★
Reads as a novel, a relatively chronological introspective; no cross-referencing or index

1–4 Stars

**Author:**
Fiona Shaw

Shaw suffered one year of postpartum depression which forced her and her infant into hospital care. She lives in northern England and is now working on her first novel.

**Publisher:**
Steerforth Press

**Edition:**
1998

**Price:**
$24.00

**Pages/Run Time:**
210

**ISBN:**
1883642973

**Media:**
Book

---

**Principal Subject:**
Strengthening Your Family

**Secondary Subject:**
Motherhood

**Age Group:**
Infants (0–1)

II. Strengthening Your Family

**Overall Rating**

★★

Useful for those considering hormone therapy

**Design, Ease Of Use**

★★

Clearly presented, numerous personal stories provided; tone somewhat formal and aloof

1–4 Stars

**Author:**

Katharina Dalton with Wendy M. Holton

Dalton is an international authority on premenstrual syndrome and postnatal depression (PND). She is also a pioneer of hormone therapy.

**Publisher:**

Oxford University Press

**Edition:**

3rd (1996)

**Price:**

$15.95

**Pages/Run Time:**

206

**ISBN:**

0192861859

**Media:**

Book

**Principal Subject:**

Strengthening Your Family

**Secondary Subject:**

Motherhood

**Age Group:**

Infants (0–1)

**Motherhood**

# DEPRESSION AFTER CHILDBIRTH

How To Recognize, Treat, And Prevent Postnatal Depression

## Description:

In the introduction, postnatal depression (PND) is defined as "the first occurrence of psychiatric symptoms severe enough to require medical help occurring after childbirth and before the return of menstruation." Dalton stresses early identification of symptoms, including anticipation of and preparation for PND before a baby is born. Based on her area of expertise, Dalton emphasizes treatment of PND through the use of hormone therapy. The book begins by explaining the role of hormones in the body. Then, several chapters detail symptoms of PND: "The Blues," "Black Depression," "Endless Exhaustion," "Irrational Irritability," "Not Tonight, Darling," "Psychosis," and "Infanticide and Homicide." While Dalton distinguishes between the "blues," "depression," and "premenstrual syndrome," she relates each one as a hormonal condition. Interspersed amid the medical teachings, the reader will find quotes from individual sufferers. The book concludes with an explanation of the hormonal treatments that are available, along with placing responsibility on professionals and nonprofessionals to identify when a woman needs treatment for PND.

## Evaluation:

While acknowledging that there can be psychological factors, Dalton expresses faith in hormone therapy to successfully treat PND. The opening discussions of hormones and their role in the body is educational for the reader; the graphs and charts included here are effective, as are illustrations in a later chapter correlating PND and PMS. The author's historical overview and discussion on mental illness and PND helps the reader to understand the experts' scheme for the understanding and treatment of PND. While this book offers good insight into the topic of PND and how it can be treated with hormone therapy, there is only limited mention of other treatment possibilities. Also, even though personal quotes are inserted throughout the text, there is a rather formal and professional tone to this book which may deter some readers. Considering that this book was originally published in England, many of the "Useful Addresses" and "Further Reading" listings are also to be found outside of the USA. Primarily useful for those considering hormone therapy, others interested in a discussion of other possible treatments will need further back-up resources.

## Where To Find/Buy:

Bookstores, libraries, or order direct by contacting Oxford University Press, Inc., 200 Madison Avenue, New York, NY 10016.

**Motherhood**

# SHOULDN'T I BE HAPPY?

## Description:

Misri has written this 340-page book as a resource for mothers and their network of supporters. Following the birth of her first son, Misri was supported in her postpartum period by Indian tradition. At that time, her mother and a family assistant came from India for six months to nurture mother and baby. In contrast, Misri points out that in the industrialized West, we should consider giving "distinct recognition and support to women in the postpartum period." To that end, this book considers many possible problems of the postpartum period (psychological, medical, and obstetrical) as well as some specific events (miscarriage, fetal abnormalities, congenital defects, death, depression and mood disorders, breastfeeding and psychiatric illness, and marital upset). Misri fears that, and offers her rationale why, many suffer in silence. While the general focus of the book is based on psychiatric counseling, alternatives such as medications and electroconvulsive treatment are also considered in Part Two—"Getting Professional Help." Along with her insights, patients' stories are included throughout the book.

## Evaluation:

As with many books available on "emotional problems of pregnant and postpartum women," this book was written to help the reader acknowledge, accept, and cope with postpartum depression (PPD). As described in the book's title, Misri gives some good rationale to illustrate the cultural and individual motives for denying postpartum problems rather than dealing with them. Her book describes how closely the mother's self-perception and consequent emotional state are connected to her perceived success or failure as a mother. She does a fine job at outlining the varying emotional problems of pregnant and postpartum women. However, the patient stories she includes do not particularly convey the intensity of those emotions or personal struggles; they tend to serve as mere illustrations of psychological influences and the effects they can impart. Misri also makes certain judgements about mothers that appear biased and not well-founded, especially in regards to breastfeeding. No resource list is included to connect the reader with a professional who might help. This book was clearly written from a psychiatric point-of-view and adheres to that reference point throughout the book.

## Where To Find/Buy:

Bookstores and libraries.

---

**Overall Rating**

★

Information does not come across as particularly solid, influential, or stimulating

**Design, Ease Of Use**

★★

Logical organization with Q and A segments, personal stories; rather clinical tone

1–4 Stars

**Author:**

Shaila Misri, MD

Misri (mother of two) is a clinical professor of psychiatry and obstetrics/gynecology at the University of British Columbia (Vancouver, Canada). She also serves as the Director of the Reproductive Psychiatry Program at St. Paul's Hospital.

**Publisher:**

The Free Press
(Simon & Schuster)

**Edition:**

1995

**Price:**

$23.00

**Pages/Run Time:**

340

**ISBN:**

002921405X

**Media:**

Book

**Principal Subject:**

Strengthening Your Family

**Secondary Subject:**

Motherhood

**Age Group:**

Infants (0–1)

Motherhood

**Overall Rating**

★

An autobiographical nonfiction book written by a whiny parent

**Design, Ease Of Use**

★

Written in a story format; no index is included; chapter titles are extremely vague

1–4 Stars

**Author:**
Patricia Hart Clifford

Patricia Hart Clifford is an author and a mother.

**Publisher:**
Paulist Press

**Edition:**
1990

**Price:**
$5.95

**Pages/Run Time:**
98

**ISBN:**
0809131927

**Media:**
Book

**Principal Subject:**
Strengthening Your Family

**Secondary Subject:**
Motherhood

**Age Group:**
Infants & Toddlers (0–3)

# TERRIBLE ANGEL
## Surviving The First Five Years Of Motherhood

### Description:

This 98-page non-fiction book is the story of a mother and her experiences in the first five years of raising her child. The book traces the phases of the author's relationship with her daughter. There are ten chapters, followed by a list of references. Some of the references include works by M. Scott Peck, T. Berry Brazelton, Abraham Maslow, and Betty Friedan, to name a few. The resources are frequently quoted as supportive passages to the author's topics. *Terrible Angel* weaves a Christian theme throughout. Other chapters illustrate this through their titles: "Creation," "Incarnation," "The Questions of Job," "The Sins of the Mother," and "Exodus." The book's intended audience are new mothers emerging from a conventional lifestyle, perhaps previously as a professional, and now placed into a motherhood role.

### Evaluation:

Patricia Hart Clifford's book about her metamorphosis into the role of motherhood discusses various aspects of how having a child can disturb a woman's professional life, "upsetting the family balance and cluttering the house with cribs, playpens and disposable diapers." It is about the "uprooting" of her "conventional life" to raise her newborn daughter. The book's main focus is on the author's coping abilities. It is a somewhat depressing book in that the author discusses all of the "sacrifices" and "stress" she has had to deal as the result of having to make changes to accommodate the needs of her baby. She talks little of the small joys of parenthood. The author admits her limitations. She doesn't know what to expect from children, but accepts the fact that her child forces her to see what she must change about herself. But largely, the book carries a "woe-is-me" theme. The book is predominately "I-centered." Look for this in the "Never mind" section of your bookstore.

### Where To Find/Buy:

Bookstores and libraries.

# MOMS ONLINE (AOL)
## A Home For Moms In Cyberspace

**Recommended For:**
Strengthening Your Family

## Description:

Found on AOL using the Keyword: Mom's Online. Several options are available at Moms Online's homepage, "A home for Moms in cyberspace." "Chat" and "Message Boards" offer forums for moms to discuss parenting issues. The "Daily Alexander" is a running chronicle about raising a four-year old boy and a baby girl, and being a working mom (Dad contributes an article on Wednesdays). The "Daily Sphinx" is a daily game of three questions related to maternal trivia. "Hot Tips" consists of contributions from moms on various subjects ranging from choosing a pediatrician to limiting TV-time. "Weekly Magazine" features a new mom in "Mom of the Week," along with her perspectives in raising children, strengths, and weaknesses, etc. It also offers essays written by various moms, "The Guidance Council," crafts, and articles on various other topics. Other links include a weekly poll, an advice link called "Ask the Pros," and "The Baby Namer." Two other major links are "The Daily Dish," an index of recipes and kitchen tips submitted by moms, and "Time Out, The Virtual Spa for Moms," which includes "comfort corners," humor, and creative projects. A "Teen Center" is available for parents with teens as well as "Homeschooling Center."

## Evaluation:

This website's strength lies in its unusual format—its use of journals, articles, and submissions from moms. Trust is placed in moms as experts, a refreshing stance for moms who often feel defeated, overly advised, or powerless. Moms are invited to chat with one another, discuss issues, offer "hot tips," submit articles, nominate moms for "Mom of the Week," ask questions, and offer feedback to the site, making this an inviting place to air frustrations and voice celebrations. Moms can even find a link pertinent for their needs, when it is time to take a brief mental break from life as a parent. A database of recipes and kitchen tips submitted by moms is available for any occasion, even those quick, low-fat, recipes with few ingredients that all hurried moms love to have on hand. Reading the ongoing saga of life with a four-year old and a baby, and how one family works through its problems makes this website come alive. What one will not find here are hard facts or objective information; parents will need to find that information elsewhere. However, Moms Online is a friendly, fun, and supportive home for moms needing a lift in their day.

## Where To Find/Buy:

Found on AOL using the Keyword: "Mom's Online"; also found on the Internet at the URL: http//www.momsonline.com/

**Overall Rating**
★★★★
An active community of moms, packed with useful and fun information

**Design, Ease Of Use**
★★★
Novel use of journaling and essays by moms; easy-to-follow layout

1–4 Stars

**Media:**
Online Service

**Principal Subject:**
Strengthening Your Family

**Secondary Subject:**
Parent-To-Parent Support & Advice

**Age Group:**
Infants & Toddlers (0–3)

II. Strengthening Your Family

**★★★★**

### Overall Rating
★★★★
An active community of moms, packed with useful and fun information

### Design, Ease Of Use
★★★
Novel use of journaling and essays by moms; easy-to-follow layout

1–4 Stars

### Media:
Internet

### Principal Subject:
Strengthening Your Family

### Secondary Subject:
Parent-To-Parent Support & Advice

### Age Group:
Infants & Toddlers (0–3)

**Parent-To-Parent Support & Advice**

# MOMS ONLINE (INTERNET)
## A Home For Moms In Cyberspace

### Recommended For:
Strengthening Your Family

### Description:
Fourteen options are available at Moms Online's homepage, "A home for Moms in cyberspace." "Chat" and "Message Boards" offer forums for moms to discuss parenting issues. The "Daily Alexander" is a running chronicle about raising a four-year-old boy and a baby girl, and being a working mom (Dad contributes an article on Wednesdays). The "Daily Sphinx" is a daily game of three questions related to maternal trivia. "Hot Tips" consists of contributions from moms on various subjects ranging from choosing a pediatrician to limiting TV-time. "Weekly Magazine" features a new mom in "Mom of the Week," along with her perspectives in raising children, strengths, and weaknesses, etc. It also offers essays written by various moms, "The Guidance Council," crafts, and articles on various other topics. Other links include a weekly poll, an advice link called "Ask the Pros," and "The Baby Namer." Two other major links are "The Daily Dish," an index of recipes and kitchen tips submitted by moms, and "Time Out, The Virtual Spa for Moms," which includes "comfort corners," humor, and creative projects.

### Evaluation:
This website's strength lies in its unusual format—its use of journals, articles, and submissions from moms. Trust is placed in moms as experts, a refreshing stance for moms who often feel defeated, overly advised, or powerless. Moms are invited to chat with one another, discuss issues, offer "hot tips," submit articles, nominate moms for "Mom of the Week," ask questions, and offer feedback to the site, making this an inviting place to air frustrations and voice celebrations. Moms can even find a link pertinent for their needs, when it is time to take a brief mental break from life as a parent. A database of recipes and kitchen tips submitted by moms is available for any occasion, even those quick, low-fat, recipes with few ingredients that all hurried moms love to have on hand. Reading the ongoing saga of life with a four-year old and a baby, and how one family works through its problems makes this website come alive. What one will not find here are hard facts or objective information; parents will need to find that information elsewhere. However, Moms Online is a friendly, fun, and supportive home for moms in cyberspace.

### Where To Find/Buy:
On the Internet at the URL: http://www.momsonline.com/

**Parent-To-Parent Support & Advice**

# A CURE FOR THE GROWLY BUGS
And Other Tried-And-True Tips For Moms

★★

## Description:

Compiled by the author for MOPS, (Mothers of Preschoolers), this 109-page book is a collection of "advice, tips, and tidbits" for parents of young children. MOPS is an organization for mothers to share their concerns, explore areas of creativity, and learn ways to prepare for the responsibilities of family and community. This book is divided into 11 chapters. At the beginning of each chapter is a short story which sets the stage for the activities, games, and ideas which follow. There is advice such as giving time warnings—"Five minutes until bath time"—and safety tips, like teaching your child to "stand on the yellow parking line or 'safety spot'" while you load the car. Material lists for doing household chores, easy-to-mix "recipes" for making homemade baby wipes, window washing solution, and more are also included. One of the chapters, "Doings with Dad," offers suggestions for how dads can interact with toddlers—"take one child out to breakfast each Saturday." Related resources are also listed at the end of the book.

## Evaluation:

MOPS has managed to compile a wealth of "snippets," without overpowering the reader, in a handy pocket-size guidebook. Although it is based on Christian principles, it doesn't come across as overbearing or preachy. In it the reader finds things to do with toddlers on road trips, improving a child's character, striving for consistency in parenting, and suggestions for mom's timeouts, (catnaps, spending guiltless time with friends, ways to take care of herself, etc.). Advice on soothing remedies for when one's child has the chicken pox and methods for pain-free splinter removal are events everyone will appreciate help with. The book, however, doesn't have an index, which makes searching for specific subjects difficult, especially since the chapter titles are rather vague—"Keeping House," "In the Kitchen." Also, the book itself is disorganized and the reader needs to wade through it to find desired information.

## Where To Find/Buy:

Bookstores and libraries, or contact MOPS International at (303) 733-5353 or toll free at (800) 929-1287.

**Overall Rating**
★★
Useful hodgepodge of advice from making memories to playtime to housecleaning

**Design, Ease Of Use**
★
Without an index or a descriptive table of contents, you will most likely get lost

1–4 Stars

**Author:**
Mary Beth Lagerborg
Mary Beth Lagerborg is publishing coordinator for MOPS (Mothers of Preschoolers) International. She has also coauthored other books. She and her husband have three sons.

**Publisher:**
Zondervan Publishing House (HarperCollins Publishers)

**Edition:**
1997

**Price:**
$6.99

**Pages/Run Time:**
109

**ISBN:**
0310211352

**Media:**
Book

**Principal Subject:**
Strengthening Your Family

**Secondary Subject:**
Parent-To-Parent Support & Advice

**Age Group:**
Infants & Toddlers (0–3)

II. Strengthening Your Family

**Overall Rating**

★

Offers only email connections for stay-at-home, attachment parenting moms and dads

**Design, Ease Of Use**

★

Once you're connected, you're barraged with email; email offers no clues as to topics

1–4 Stars

**Media:**
Internet

**Principal Subject:**
Strengthening Your Family

**Secondary Subject:**
Parent-To-Parent Support & Advice

**Age Group:**
Infants (0–1)

# ATTACHMENT & BONDING

### Description:

This website states that it is a "support and information forum for full time moms or dads parenting in ways that promote attachment between parent and child." The homepage simply is a registration for a visitor to sign onto an e-mail mailing list. When a member posts an email message, it goes to the 300 other members of the email list. The site lists topics that are open for discussion: gentle pregnancy and birth, breastfeeding, delaying solids, extended breastfeeding, child-led weaning, family bed, baby-wearing and more. Topics not supported also are listed, such as: forced weaning, sleep training, spanking, etc. The site states that it does not endorse any particular medical approach, but instead supports attachment and bonding. Members subscribing to the SAH-AP (stay-at-home/attached parent) list are invited to voice concerns, ask questions and share the joys of being a stay-at-home parent. The method of subscribing is explained at the site, along with a description of what one will receive. The site offers links to another sites for information on FAQs and other resources.

### Evaluation:

As an experiment, one of the reviewers for this book subscribed to this website's list. She immediately began receiving an endless stream of email (over 300!) before she got off the list. Email "conversations" ranged from "what do you look like?" to "do swings in parks promote detachment?" to "what do I bring for treats to my La Leche League meeting?" In our effort to unsubscribe from the mailing list, we contacted the webmaster/creator at the email address given if "you have any questions or problems." After several weeks we still had not been contacted by the webmaster/creator. If one wants to eavesdrop or partake in casual conversation with other stay-at-home parents, there are other parenting sites that support attachment parenting and offer more directed/moderated forums.

### Where To Find/Buy:

On the Internet at the URL: http://www.kjsl.com/sah-ap

**Parent-To-Parent Support & Advice**

# THE MOMMY TIMES
Dedicated To Preserving The Sanity Of Moms Everywhere

### Description:

The Mommy Times website, also billed as "The Mom to Mom Support Community on the Web," established itself first as a publication in 1992 and as a website in 1995. Registration is required to access the site's features, which include the following: "Mommye-mail," "Mommy-to-Mommy," and back issues of "The Mommy Times." The site hosts articles, and questions and answers "written for moms by moms . . . everything from pregnancy and puberty and many topics in between." Through "Mommye-mail," moms may quickly post messages to one another. "Mommy-to-Mommy" offers a chance for moms to create new topics, post a question and read others' responses, or read archives of past questions and answers. Past issues of "The Mommy Times" may be accessed either through the website (from the October/November 1996 issue forward). The current online issue of "The Mommy Times" (November/December 1998) includes 12 articles on topics such as the holidays, life with twins, toys for less, and consumer product tips.

### Evaluation:

Many websites have been developed to support the needs of busy moms who want to communicate with others in a convenient manner with no time constraints. This site, however, lacks substance, has no direction, and is more frustrating than it is supportive. Question and answer forums are inviting, but without a helpful structure. For example, if one wants to read others' concerns and feedback regarding bedtime rituals, she needs to scroll through endless pages of posted topic headings to find the appropriate ones. What would be extremely helpful here is some categorization, e.g. "Bedtime Rituals." Also, if a mother wants to respond to a question or topic posted in the "Mommy-to-Mommy" archive, she must create a topic in the new section (since the archive is closed to responses), recap the question, and then add her response. It would be helpful to have an index of topics from past issues, so that a visitor looking for specific information could find it easily. If a mom has the time, this site is a mildly amusing place to check into routinely, but all in all, busy moms could well be spending their precious time elsewhere.

### Where To Find/Buy:

On the Internet at the URL: http://www.mommytimes.com/

---

**Overall Rating**
★
This site lacks substance and direction

**Design, Ease Of Use**
★
Must register to use site's features; past Q & A topics can't be easily accessed/ retrieved

1–4 Stars

**Media:**
Internet

**Principal Subject:**
Strengthening Your Family

**Secondary Subject:**
Parent-To-Parent Support & Advice

**Age Group:**
Infants & Toddlers (0–3)

II. Strengthening Your Family

★★★★

**Overall Rating**
★★★★
Excellent examples and professional advice for parents working through sibling rivalry

**Design, Ease Of Use**
★★★★
Flows well, recap summary at end of tape; good mix of parent stories and professional advice

1–4 Stars

**Publisher:**
Skydance Productions

**Edition:**
1994

**Price:**
$24.98

**Media:**
Videotape

**Principal Subject:**
Strengthening Your Family

**Secondary Subject:**
Sibling Relations

**Age Group:**
Toddlers (1–3)

# THOSE BABY BLUES
A Parent's Guide To Helping Your Child Adjust To The New Baby

**Recommended For:**
Strengthening Your Family

**Special Resource For:**
Helping both a parent and a child adjust to a new sibling (using companion videotapes)

## Description:

Reported by Marcia Ladendorff (board member of the Childbirth Education Association), this 30 minute videotape offers both family stories and professional advice (Dr. Brenda Wade, psychologist and contributor for "Good Morning America"; Dr. Glen Aylward, professor of child and family psychology). Designed to "help you consider the situations you'll face before you're in the thick of things," this tape focuses on an older sibling's reactions to a new sibling. Discussions include changes in behavior, throwing tantrums, aggression, hidden hostility, regression, "nothing's wrong," withdrawal, and depression. Family stories are relayed with film footage showing sibling interactions. Each professional's perspective and advice is offered on how to handle given situations. Emphasis is on parents knowing their child's personality and ways to help them cope, acknowledging their feelings, noting and rewarding positive behavior, and more. A complimentary videotape for siblings—"Oh, Baby"—accompanies this one and is specifically intended "to trigger discussion in a more removed, less threatening context."

## Evaluation:

Parents who are either wrestling with how to help an older sibling adjust to the birth of a baby, or parents who are already "in the thick of things," will be pleased with the information and support in this tape. Seeing family members' interactions directly coupled with the professionals' advice works extremely well here. Responses of an older child are addressed along with an understanding of their response in adult terms. For example, Wade draws a comparison between an older sibling's feelings when parents bring a new baby home to having one's spouse bring home a new wife, saying "Isn't she cute? She's so little . . . You'll grow to really like having her around." Free-flowing at times, the video neatly recaps all major points at the end offering a list and brief overview of warning signs, what to do for your child depending on their personality, and other major tips. Also provided is a list of organizations for further information; one organization offers information about classes for older siblings. We highly recommend parents invest their time and money in this resource. They'll walk away refreshed.

## Where To Find/Buy:

Bookstores, libraries, videotape dealers, or order direct by calling AMR at (877) 99VIDEO. Orders can also be taken online by AMR at http://www.amr1.com.

**Sibling Relations**

# LOVING EACH ONE BEST
## A Caring And Practical Approach To Raising Siblings

★★★★

### Recommended For:
Strengthening Your Family

### Description:
With ten chapters, three appendices, and an index, this 210-page resource contains advice for parents as they cope with sibling conflicts, handle the ensuing stress, and adjust their lifestyle to the addition of a new sibling. Chapters One and Two contain information about what to expect before and after parents give birth to baby number two. The stress involved with being a full-time mother, the roles fathers play, and ways to relieve stress are explored in Chapter Three. Some of the topics discussed in Chapters Four through Seven include sibling conflicts, fairness and jealousies, recognizing the differences between children, and what parents can do when they feel angry about parenting. Chapter Eight offers interviews with children as they tell their side of the story. The final Chapters, Nine and Ten, suggest ways to approach daily life in an upbeat manner by savoring the "lovely moments" and good times that family life can provide. The appendixes offer a reading list along with parent and child questionnaires used in writing this book.

### Evaluation:
With humor and insight, this book uses a compassionate, caring approach to raising siblings. This easily read reference is based on the author's parenting workshops throughout the U.S. and includes advice from real parents who have survived the "aggravating and mystifying aspects of raising more than one child." Whereas most books dealing with sibling relationships are primarily child-centered, this book also focuses on the adults involved thus offering parents a refreshing new perspective. With a thoughtful and reassuring tone, the author details how many parents cope with the stresses involved with having a new sibling. Many parents will feel relieved that their silent thoughts, fears, and feelings are echoed here. Useful examples of positive and negative parent-child dialogues are presented along with bulleted tips, numerous suggestions, and chapter wrap-ups. With no heavy text or tables to wade through, this book should be required reading for worried parents bringing home baby number two.

### Where To Find/Buy:
Bookstores and libraries.

**Overall Rating**
★★★★
Provides excellent advice and information and is very supportive of parents' needs

**Design, Ease Of Use**
★★★
Small print, but good spacing; bolder highlights would make it more user-friendly

1–4 Stars

**Author:**
Nancy Samalin with Catherine Whitney

Nancy Samalin, a parenting expert, has written several other books. She is a consulting editor and columnist for *Parents* magazine, and is director of Parent Guidance Workshops which are known throughout the United States and abroad.

**Publisher:**
Bantam Books
(Bantam Doubleday Dell)

**Edition:**
1996

**Price:**
$12.95

**Pages/Run Time:**
210

**ISBN:**
0553378341

**Media:**
Book

**Principal Subject:**
Strengthening Your Family

**Secondary Subject:**
Sibling Relations

**Age Group:**
Toddlers (1–3)

II. Strengthening Your Family

**Overall Rating**
★★★★
Script examples, cartoons, and anecdotes are major conveyance of authors' advice

**Design, Ease Of Use**
★★★
Easy read; text has a tendency to ramble at times

1–4 Stars

**Author:**
Adele Faber and Elaine Mazlish

Adele Faber and Elaine Mazlish are noted for their work in adult-child communication. Both are sought after for their lectures and group workshop programs. They live in Long Island, New York. Each of them has three grown children.

**Publisher:**
Avon Books
(Hearst Corporation)

**Edition:**
2nd (1998)

**Price:**
$12.00

**Pages/Run Time:**
250

**ISBN:**
0380799006

**Media:**
Book

**Principal Subject:**
Strengthening Your Family

**Secondary Subject:**
Sibling Relations

**Age Group:**
Toddlers (1–3)

# SIBLINGS WITHOUT RIVALRY
How To Help Your Children Live Together So You Can Live Too

**Recommended For:**
Strengthening Your Family

**Description:**

Consisting of eight chapters, this 250-page resource focuses on strategies parents can use when intervening in sibling rivalries. Chapter One illustrates the past and present relationship of a brother and sister presented in a story format. Chapter Two focuses on expressing feelings and explores inner negative feelings. Chapters Three and Four deal with equality and comparisons between siblings. Chapter Five addresses sibling roles and how to avoid locking children into descriptive stereotypes ("messy," "clean," etc.). Chapter Six explains how to successfully intervene in conflicts and Chapter Seven contains advice on "making peace" with sibling relationships in one's past. Chapter Eight, new to this edition, highlights parents' stories that illustrate how they coped and encouraged appropriate behaviors between brothers and sisters; also given are expectations for children who are home alone due to their parents' employment. Charts, reminders, comic strip Dos and Don'ts, and Q & As are presented in many chapters. An index is also given.

**Evaluation:**

This book was first published ten years ago and it became a bestseller almost immediately. Now, after ten years of communicating with parents through letters, TV and radio talk shows, the same authors have released a tenth anniversary edition of their book with the addition of several new chapters. A large part of this resource continues to be based upon the authors' combined experiences with their own families and with those who participated in their workshops. In fact, the reader has the sensation of being in a workshop through this book, learning from the expertise of the authors and fellow participants. As such, stories make up much of this book's content. And, like a workshop, the story telling is dynamic and somewhat disorganized. So, if one is looking for clear answers to specific questions bolstered by a great, organized layout, this is not the resource. But if the reader wishes to have the sense that he/she is a fellow seeker with other parents who are tackling one of the toughest problems parents have to handle and that this is done in the midst of story telling and anecdotes, this is an appropriate resource.

**Where To Find/Buy:**
Bookstores and libraries.

**Sibling Relations**

# WELCOMING YOUR SECOND BABY

★★★

### Description:

Six questions, separated and explained in six chapters, make up this 99-page reference on welcoming a second baby into your home. Chapters One through Three contain information to help parents best prepare their child for the birth of a new baby, ways to help them adjust to mom's absence while in the hospital, and options to consider when deciding whether or not children should be present at the birth of the new baby. Chapters Four through Six discuss how parents can keep their older child from feeling left out, how to help them accept the new baby, and ways to help their child handle special circumstances, such as adoption or Cesarean birth. Throughout each chapter are additional resources, (descriptions of books, videos, etc. for children, divided by age groups and topic; self-help groups; etc.), tips ("Prepare postcards or notes to mail your child from the hospital"), and highlighted blocks of quotes from parents offering their personal stories, experiences, and words of encouragement. An index completes the book.

### Evaluation:

This resource strives to put parents at ease struggling with such concerns as whether or not they will love their second child as much as their first, feeling "disloyal" to their firstborn, and wondering if their second child will be a competitor for their attention and love. Giving advice and suggestions to help prepare parents and their child for the new arrival, the author has collected ideas and presented them in a concise, matter-of-fact format for quick-fix solutions. Interspersed throughout each paragraph are tons of additional age-appropriate resources, with information on where to buy them (when available). This guide is unique and very easy to read in its no-nonsense, bulleted note format, a quality that a busy parent in the throes of their pregnancy will appreciate. The table of contents is adequate and the index does a fine job as back-up. Parents may spend some time searching for specific topics, but the hunt will be well worth it.

### Where To Find/Buy:

Bookstores and libraries, or order direct from Practical Parenting at (800) 255-3379.

---

**Overall Rating**
★★★
Noteworthy collection of helpful tips and advice

**Design, Ease Of Use**
★★★★
Highlighted blocks of parent anecdotes; bulleted tips; clear topic and subtopic headings

1–4 Stars

**Author:**
Vicki Lansky

Vicki Lansky has authored over 25 books, and is well-known for her column in *Family Circle* magazine and *Sesame Street Parents' Guide Magazine*. She has also appeared on national TV shows like *Donahue*, *Oprah*, and *Today*.

**Publisher:**
The Book Peddlers

**Edition:**
3rd (1995)

**Price:**
$6.95

**Pages/Run Time:**
99

**ISBN:**
916773124

**Media:**
Book

---

**Principal Subject:**
Strengthening Your Family

**Secondary Subject:**
Sibling Relations

**Age Group:**
Toddlers (1–3)

II. Strengthening Your Family

**★★**

## Overall Rating
★★
Helpful for understanding sibling dynamics, less useful for how to deal with rivalry

## Design, Ease Of Use
★★★★
Clear, well-organized, well-referenced and indexed

1–4 Stars

## Author:
Judy Dunn

Judy Dunn is an international authority on childhood development, Distinguished Professor of Human Development at Pennsylvania State University, and also the recent recipient of a Guggenheim Fellowship. She has done extensive research in the field of sibling relations.

## Publisher:
Fawcett Columbine Book (Ballantine Books/Random House)

## Edition:
1995

## Price:
$10.00

## Pages/Run Time:
217

## ISBN:
0449906450

## Media:
Book

## Principal Subject:
Strengthening Your Family

## Secondary Subject:
Sibling Relations

## Age Group:
Toddlers (1–3)

**Sibling Relations**

# FROM ONE CHILD TO TWO
What To Expect, How To Cope, And How To Enjoy Your Growing Family

## Description:
This 217-page guide contains three main sections with twelve chapters. The first two years of caring for two children, second pregnancies, how to prepare for the arrival of a second child, coming home from the hospital, the evolving sibling relationship, and more are all discussed in Part One's 7 chapters. Part Two contains two chapters. Sibling conflicts and competition, as well as violence and anger that arise in families are addressed. Part Three offers three chapters. These contain information about the differences between children, information about twins and siblings, and what to expect in terms of children's behavior in the coming years. Each chapter concludes with a summary of bulleted tips. An Appendix listing organizations, a one-page bibliography, and a comprehensive index complete the book. The suggestions contained within the book are based upon the author's personal experience (twins and toddler under the age of 18 months) and 15 years of observing family and sibling relationships.

## Evaluation:
If the reader's fears center on whether their older child can adjust to a new sibling, then this resource is worth checking into. This book's strength lies in the extensive observational research done by the author culminating in this book and others. It offers practical suggestions and advice on introducing a second child into the family. Parental burnout, the father's changing role, coping with the changing demands of a marriage, and ways of juggling schedules are just some of the issues addressed. Parents often wonder if they'll be able to love the second child just as much as the first without taking anything from the first. This book answers such concerns as these in a direct, reassuring, and practical manner. The summary at the end of each chapter with bulleted tips is quite helpful. The index is very extensive making up for the lack of bolder subheadings within the book. Coupled with other resources that offer more in-depth strategies for handling sibling rivalry, this book will prove an indispensable guide.

## Where To Find/Buy:
Bookstores and libraries.

**Sibling Relations**

# SURVIVING SIBLING RIVALRY
## Helping Brothers And Sisters Get Along

★ ★

## Description:

One in a series entitled *Lee Canter's Effective Parenting Books*, this 48-page guide is all about warding off sibling conflicts. The book is divided into 10 sections, beginning with questions and answers that parents most often ask. Some of these concern issues such as: jealousy, being fair, and establishing family rules. Sections following include information on why siblings argue and fight, how to create a positive environment, ways to prevent conflicts, and what do to when children continue to fight. The remaining sections suggest ways to resolve continuing problems and how to speak to your child so they will listen. There are interactive worksheets, such as a "Family Rules" chart, a "Cooperation Station" chart, a "Colossal Cooperation Award," and a "Sibling Contract" that are to be used in conjunction with the authors' suggestions within the sections. The book closes with the "Top 10 'Sibling Rivalry' Reminders" consisting of guidelines to help put sibling conflicts into perspective. This book does not contain an index.

## Evaluation:

For parents at their wits' end with sibling squabbles and who are seeking a quick-fix, this positive book might offer welcome relief. It describes ways that families can cope with everyday stresses and it offers advice on how to keep conflicts to a minimum. The book seeks to help parents understand why conflicts evolve and what they might do to avoid ensuing confrontations. It also provides reassurance that sibling rivalry can be constructive and, as the authors state, siblings should be given the chance to work things out first before parental intervention. Several highlighted asides offer insight and advice on ways to create a positive environment. This guide offers good conflict management tools for parents through a role-play format with a stated "solution" following each proposed problem; verbal cues are provided for parents in most cases. Although the information here is given in concise "bits," parents will find it is worth a measure of their time.

## Where To Find/Buy:

Bookstores and libraries, or order direct by calling (800) 262-4347 or (310) 395-3221.

**Overall Rating**
★★
At times too concise; but provides good information especially for busy parents

**Design, Ease Of Use**
★★★★
Easy read despite not having an index; sibling contracts, charts, & awards provided

1–4 Stars

**Author:**
Lee Canter and Marlene Canter
Lee and Marlene Canter are from the educational consulting firm Lee Canter & Associates. They are nationally renowned for their work in parenting and education.

**Publisher:**
Lee Canter & Associates

**Edition:**
1993

**Price:**
$5.95

**Pages/Run Time:**
48

**ISBN:**
0939007770

**Media:**
Book

**Principal Subject:**
Strengthening Your Family

**Secondary Subject:**
Sibling Relations

**Age Group:**
Toddlers (1–3)

II. Strengthening Your Family

# AND BABY MAKES FOUR
Welcoming A Second Child Into The Family

**Overall Rating**
★★
Most information is too basic, too few innovative suggestions

**Design, Ease Of Use**
★★
Contents are very well defined, but the layout is uninteresting

1–4 Stars

**Author:**
Hilory Wagner

Hilory Wagner is the author of *The New Parents Sourcebook*. She also writes for *Parenting, Parents, Child*, and *Baby Talk* magazines. She is a mother of two children.

**Publisher:**
Avon Books

**Edition:**
1998

**Price:**
$12.00

**Pages/Run Time:**
205

**ISBN:**
0380795051

**Media:**
Book

**Principal Subject:**
Strengthening Your Family

**Secondary Subject:**
Sibling Relations

**Age Group:**
Infants & Toddlers (0–3)

## Description:

This book is divided into three parts. Part One addresses "Planning For Two." This part of the book discusses topics such as the changes a family will go through when deciding to have a second child, whether the family is ready for a second child, and how to help a child become a sibling. Part Two—"Pregnancy and Preparation"—addresses topics such as pregnancy the second time around, being pregnant and a mom, and preparing a child for the birth of a brother or sister. Part Three—"Your New Family"—helps the reader plan and know what to expect when coming home with the second baby, how to cope with new sibling problems, ways to deal with two children instead of one, and how to keep in touch with one's mate. This book makes extensive use of first-person accounts as examples of specific situations that each chapter's topic addresses. Suggested reading lists for various family members, contact information to various organizations, and products and references to other works are provided throughout. The author often uses her own experiences with her two children as examples of problems that may arise in a family that has or is planning to have a second child.

## Evaluation:

The author's goal is for this book become a source for "dozens of tips and practical advice that might help ease this bumpy road ahead of you." For the most part, she succeeds. Still, Part One is a waste of time. The considerations that she suggests a family must take into account are so basic that they don't need an entire section of a book. These include, for example, financial considerations, effects to career and travel/leisure plans, family expectations, and personal ideals of the "perfect family." Chapter Six in Part Two—"Sibling Prep 101"—does offer many tips on how to help a child adjust to a pending new brother or sister. The author's tips aren't ground breaking nor innovative, but she does offer some practical information, such as what age a child understands the concept of pregnancy or what may "Your New Family"—offers a mix of pertinent information any mother should know regarding the sibling adjustments. Chapter Nine—"Stepping Up to Siblinghood"—is also a jackpot of information. Throughout the book, the author uses a friendly, "I know how you must feel" tone that can be comforting to some, annoying to others. Offering some good basic advice, this resource, however, is best complimented by other guides.

## Where To Find/Buy:

Bookstores and libraries.

**Sibling Relations**

# SIBLING RIVALRY
The Healthy Parenting Series

### Description:

Presented by "noted therapists and authors" Jean Rosenbaum and Veryl Rosenbaum, this 28-minute videotape is part of The Healthy Parenting series and focuses on sibling relations. Consisting of family interviews, parent stories, and interjections by the therapists, this video outlines various responses an older sibling may have to a new sibling. Reactions discussed include general reactions ("attention getting devices"—obnoxious noises, loud talking, hyperactivity, etc.), aggressive behaviors (hitting, excessive fawning, etc.), and regression (acting infant-like). Suggestions for how to handle negative sibling rivalry include: allowing the older child to express his negative feelings without fear of disapproval, inviting story-telling and drawings of the family as techniques for ridding aggression, encouraging opportunities for the older child to play with his peers, giving the older child special time with one or both parents, allowing the older child to participate with taking care of the infant, and more.

### Evaluation:

A simplistic message using amateurish production techniques are the only way to best describe this tape. Parents want to know how to avoid sibling rivalry to begin with or they want some real answers to some real situations. The majority of the time spent on this tape, however, focused on one specific strategy (drawings by the child) credited by the therapist as the best way for ridding aggression. However, how many parents are trained to analyze children's drawings and the underlying emotions embedded within them? Other answers were far too obvious and simplistic. The narrator's first summary point was that an older child should feel loved and not be made to feel left out . . . pretty obvious. The narrator's second summary point was that an older child should be encouraged to express their feelings . . . again fairly obvious. Not quite as obvious is the narrator's third and final summary point that "the situation invariably resolves itself." Parents can more effectively resolve family squabbles by checking into better resources.

### Where To Find/Buy:

Bookstores, libraries, videotape dealers, or order direct by calling VIDEO 11 at (800) 471-4109 or AMR at (877) 99VIDEO. Orders can also be taken online by AMR at http://www.amr1.com.

---

**Overall Rating**
★
Simplistic answers (and reliance on a professional technique) to multi-faceted problems

**Design, Ease Of Use**
★
Amateurish quality; parent interview format doesn't work due to lack of solid advice

1–4 Stars

**Publisher:**
JVM Productions

**Price:**
$19.98

**Media:**
Videotape

**Principal Subject:**
Strengthening Your Family

**Secondary Subject:**
Sibling Relations

**Age Group:**
Toddlers (1–3)

II. Strengthening Your Family

# CHAPTER FOUR—ALL-INCLUSIVE RESOURCES ABOUT PARENTING

Watching a newborn baby gaze with wonder at his or her parents' face for the first time, and watching new parents smile and coo in return, illustrates the wonder and joy of becoming a parent. It is hard to imagine that in just a few short years, that same baby will become the star player on the softball team, or the waltzing flower in the ballet recital, or the child at the dinner table who talks about what homework they must do that night and what they learned at school that day. Parenting decisions will evolve from "How do I take care of him?" to "How do I teach him to take care of himself?" A parent's concern will also evolve from "How do I hold her?" to "How do I let her go?" Those first few days, weeks, and months of a baby's life are intensified by the worries, joys, and trial-and-error involved with becoming a parent. Learning on the job, minute by minute and day by day, results in pride and exhilaration, as well as great concern and exhaustion.

As daunting as this process of learning may seem, any new parent will attest to the fact that there are plenty of answers available . . . everyone's answers! From the moment their child is born, advice begins pouring in. How do new inexperienced parents drink from this well of information and separate the good tips from the not-so-good tips? In search of answers, parents may turn to the bookstore's vast array of parenting resources only to discover yet another question—"How do we choose the best resource to guide us as we guide our child?"

The heart of parenting is guidance—each child guides their parents and each parent guides their child. Parents are constantly observing how other adults and children respond to each other and in the process reject some approaches while embracing others. During these observations, parents compare their child to others' children. Through it all, parents ask themselves "Is our child developing correctly? Are we doing things right?"

Every child is unique and every child's growth pattern and responses will vary even within the same family. Their development relies on the interplay of various factors, including their biological heredity, their social environment, and their experiences within the family. What works for one child, will not always work for another. The learning curve never remains constant but continues to change. "What do we do now?"

Keeping all these issues and questions in mind, parents need a resource that can become their 24 hour companion to explain what to expect as their child grows, inform them of their available choices, and assuage their worries. Most of all, parents need reassurance that they are doing their best and are doing a great job. They need a resource that will educate them about options, possibilities, and consequences. In other words, parents need an "all-inclusive" manual or resource. But what type of information should be present to make this a worthwhile investment of time and money?

As we developed this guidebook, we looked for resources that would offer parents a full perspective of child development, children's growth and learning issues, and basic child care. Since effective parenting often does not rely on one authority's opinion, all-inclusive resources should strive to remain objective, allowing parents to understand other parenting styles while developing and refining their own. Most new parents will most likely combine elements of their own personality, beliefs, and experiences to create an environment that works best for them and their child.

We have identified some of the best all-inclusive resources available in the following pages. These resources will address topics ranging from how to diaper your newborn to how to encourage your toddler's need for independence to how to prepare your preschooler for kindergarten. You'll find advice and information on how to take care of your baby and young child through illnesses, injuries, and emergencies, along with how to nurture their development with activities, experiences, and appropriate parental responses. Please take the time to carefully read our full-page review of each recommended resource, so that you can choose those that are best for you.

Parenting offers rewards, gifts, and riches that absolutely nothing else in life can bring. Becoming a parent allows you to experience the magic of being the center of your child's universe, revisit your own childhood again through the eyes of your own child, and discover your world in new and glorious ways.

*"Children are our most valuable natural resource."*

—Herbert Clark Hoover

★★★★

**Overall Rating**
★★★★
Comprehensive guide to children's physical, emotional, social and cognitive growth

**Design, Ease Of Use**
★★★★
Clear, concise, well-illustrated, and direct; excellent index

1–4 Stars

**Author:**
Steven P. Shelov, MD, FAAP

The Feeling Fine Programs and the American Academy of Pediatrics, an organization of 45,000 pediatricians dedicated to the health, safety, and well-being of infants, children, adolescents, and young adults, developed this book as the first of a three part series.

**Publisher:**
Bantam Books

**Edition:**
2nd (1993)

**Price:**
$17.95

**Pages/Run Time:**
670

**ISBN:**
0553371843

**Media:**
Book

**Principal Subject:**
All-Inclusive Overview

**Age Group:**
Infants & Toddlers (0–3)

# CARING FOR YOUR BABY AND YOUNG CHILD
Birth To Age 5

**Recommended For:**
All-Inclusive Overview

## Description:

This 670-page reference book contains advice from the American Academy of Pediatrics and is broken into two parts. The first part contains advice on basic care from infancy through age five, along with guidelines and milestones for physical, emotional, social, and cognitive growth. Early chapters address such issues as: preparing for a new baby, birth and the moments after (in a hospital), basic infant care, and the basics of feeding a baby. In Chapters 5–12, advice is grouped by age and stage, i.e. newborn, the first month, one month through three months, four months to seven months, eight months to twelve months, the second year, the third year, the fourth, and the fifth year. Each of these groupings address growth and development, basic care, family, health watch, safety check, immunizations, and more. A chapter each is devoted to how to keep your child safe and how deal with part-time childcare issues. The second part of the book, with "guide words" at the top of the page, is a medical reference guide for child-related topics (behavior, eyes, skin, etc.). A great many illustrations, information boxes, and tables are given.

## Evaluation:

The American Academy of Pediatrics sponsored this book with contributions from 70+ "pediatric specialists and a six-member AAP editorial review board," making it a baseline standard for child care and pediatric medical information in America today. Beautifully illustrated and nicely designed for readability, this book has all the touches that publishers use to make a book easy to look at and digest. Where other books take a question and answer approach to providing information, this book lines up its topics and hands out advice in a straightforward and authoritative manner. In this way, it covers the same information as similar books on this topic, but seems to do it in a much more readable and inviting way. If one is making a choice on a first year baby book, this may well be *the* book.

## Where To Find/Buy:

Bookstores and libraries.

# THE FOCUS ON THE FAMILY COMPLETE BOOK OF BABY AND CHILD CARE
From Pre-birth Through The Teen Years

★★★★

## Recommended For:
All-Inclusive Overview

## Special Resource For:
Christian perspectives on child care, child development, and parenting choices

## Description:
This book is divided into 14 chapters, which address a child's growth and care at different ages, and 18 sections or "Special Concerns" that deal with specific issues. The book is divided into two sections. The first offers a chronological tour of a child's life. The second is a health care reference. Preparing for parenthood is the focus of Chapters One through Three. The remaining chapters are divided into the following age categories: the first three months (in two parts), three to six months, six to 12 months, 12 to 24 Months, two-year-olds, three and four-year-olds, ages five through 11, the adolescent years (in two parts). The last chapter discusses ways to instill values and virtues in the next generation. Some of the topics addressed in the "Special Concerns" sections include: the adopted child, birth defects, postpartum depression, childhood fever, caregivers, eating disorders, education, and divorce; the pages are outlined in blue for easy reference. Charts, graphs, definitions, illustrations, and resource listings are provided throughout. A reference section on illnesses and a separate section on medical emergencies are provided as well.

## Evaluation:
This book is an example of the childcare books on the market that are encyclopedic in magnitude, but this one has a twist. The writers provide not only a thoroughly complete body of information about child care and children's development, but weave Christian viewpoints and the Christian belief system throughout. The authors do an excellent job of presenting the pros and cons of various Christian perspectives while not emphasizing any one style in particular. The information provided is solidly founded in common childcare methodology and scientific facts. There are many drawings and photographs to illustrate concepts being discussed. Charts, lists, and sidebar articles help further supplement the information. This is not a book to sit down and read in a few evenings. It is a reference manual meant to be kept on hand for a lifetime. Or at least until the next edition. The authors manage to successfully meld the scientific and the spiritual. If parents do not consider themselves to be especially religious or spiritual in the Christian belief, there is still much information to be gained here, and readers will not get the feeling they are being solicited.

## Where To Find/Buy:
Bookstores and libraries.

**Overall Rating**
★★★★
Reference book on all aspects of child care, with a Christian emphasis

**Design, Ease Of Use**
★★★★
Exceptional organization, info is thoughtful, and thorough

1–4 Stars

**Author:**
Paul C. Reisser, MD

**Publisher:**
Tyndale House Publishers

**Edition:**
1997

**Price:**
$29.99

**Pages/Run Time:**
887

**ISBN:**
084230889X

**Media:**
Book

**Principal Subject:**
All-Inclusive Overview

**Age Group:**
Infants & Toddlers (0–3)

★★★★

**Overall Rating**
★★★★
This resource offers fundamental information with a positive approach

**Design, Ease Of Use**
★★★★
Sidebar tips, numerous black and white photos; extensive resource and bibliography section

1–4 Stars

**Author:**
Pamela Patrick Novotny

Pamela Patrick Novotny is a journalist whose work has appeared in many magazines and newspapers. She currently teaches writing at the University of Colorado. She is the parent of five children, two of which are twins.

**Publisher:**
Crown Trade Paperbacks (Crown Books)

**Edition:**
2nd (1994)

**Price:**
$16.00

**Pages/Run Time:**
324

**ISBN:**
0517880717

**Media:**
Book

**Principal Subject:**
All-Inclusive Overview

**Age Group:**
Infants & Toddlers (0–3)

# THE JOY OF TWINS AND OTHER MULTIPLE BIRTHS
Having, Raising, And Loving Babies Who Arrive In Groups

**Recommended For:**
All-Inclusive Overview

**Special Resource For:**
Parenting twins or multiples

**Description:**
The author states that this 324-page resource grew out of her belief that "twinship is a gift: to parents who can learn they are far more capable that they ever dreamed. . . ." There are 12 chapters in this parenting guide. Chapter One explains how multiple births occur, while Chapter Two discusses how parents can understand and take care of themselves and their babies after birth. Chapters Three and Four offer the "how-tos and whys" of feeding, and developing attitudes and routines through the first year. The next four chapters include information on mother care, family adjustments, going back to work, and language ability. Developing a sense of identity is the focus of Chapter Nine. A quick-reference list is offered in Chapter Ten. Chapter 11 deals with premature births, and Chapter 12 offers tips on how to deal with more than two babies. A reader questionnaire, a list of resources, a bibliography, and an index complete the book. Sidebar tips are given in bold, along with numerous black and white photographs throughout.

**Evaluation:**
This book strives to offer a realistic and positive outlook to parents of multiples. This guide, taking a look at the most "recent research," shows parents options they may not have considered in raising their children. Myths about having multiples are dispelled throughout this resource helping parents cope with the advice and comments of others. The book is meant to be used as a "browse through" to fetch useful ideas when parents don't really have time to sit down and read. The index is extensive allowing for easy access to specific topics. There is an incredible eight-page bibliography, and the "Resources" section lists: useful organizations for parents of multiples; information sources for childbirth, infant and new mother care; parent and marriage support groups; baby equipment; and additional periodicals and publications. While this guide does not spend too much energy on any one topic, it touches on the important primary issues, mainly parenting twins. As a quick reference, this book offers a good deal of information and support.

**Where To Find/Buy:**
Bookstores and libraries.

# THE PORTABLE PEDIATRICIAN FOR PARENTS

★★★★

**Recommended For:**

All-Inclusive Overview

## Description:

Reflecting recommendations from professional organizations (American Academy of Pediatrics, American Academy of Pediatric Dentistry, etc.) and child development researchers (Burton L. White, Erik Erickson, Jean Piaget, etc.), this 502-page resource offers a month-to-month guide to children's physical and behavioral development from birth to five years of age. Part I encompasses most of the book and discusses "The Well Child." The 11 chapters within this part focus on a given age range; topics that are discussed within each chapter include: a narrative description of the age group, separation issues, setting limits, health and illness, day to day issues (developmental milestones, sleep, growth, teeth, feeding and nutrition, activities, etc.), "windows of opportunity," and more. Part II focuses on "frightening behaviors" (fever, inconsolable crying, etc.), first aid, and bodily ailments. Part III offers six essays from a pediatric's point of view. Part IV offers pediatric "Handouts" designed to alleviate disagreements between parents, relatives, and caregivers. Part V is a glossary of medical terms. A 17-page index is also provided.

## Evaluation:

By using her background as a pediatrician coupled with studies by well-known child development researchers, Dr. Laura Walther Nathanson allows parents to see growth and changes from the child's point of view. She then strongly encourages parents to view their child's pediatrician as a team player who should be interested in informing, but not advising, parents. With her experience of over "100,000 office visits and more than twice as many phone calls," she is able to give detailed, age appropriate information regarding medical and developmental questions. And, if the reader is still in doubt, she encourages them to seek professional advice. This resource, then, is a most unusual book—parents won't find many better resources available that offer a variety of professionals' advice and suggestions in one neat affordable package.

## Where To Find/Buy:

Bookstores and libraries.

---

**Overall Rating**
★★★★
This complete guide includes advice from child development experts & professionals

**Design, Ease Of Use**
★★★★
Side tabs for each age group; extensive index; reader friendly

1–4 Stars

**Author:**
Laura Walther Nathanson, MD, FAAP

Nathanson, MD, is board Certified in Pediatrics and Peri-Neonatology. She earned her BA from Harvard and her MD from Tufts Medical School. She has handled over 100,000 office visits, more than twice as many phone calls, and says she still hears something new.

**Publisher:**
HarperPerennial (HarperCollins)

**Edition:**
1994

**Price:**
$20.00

**Pages/Run Time:**
502

**ISBN:**
0062731769

**Media:**
Book

**Principal Subject:**
All-Inclusive Overview

**Age Group:**
Infants & Toddlers (0–3)

★★★★

## Overall Rating
★★★★

A superb, answer-all resource to your child from 13 months to 36 months

## Design, Ease Of Use
★★★★

Thoughtfully laced out and comprehensive; 2 column narrative and Q & A format

1–4 Stars

## Author:
Arlene Eisenberg, Heidi E. Murkoff, Sandee E. Hathaway, BSN

Arlene Eisenberg, Heidi E. Murkoff, and Sandee E. Hathaway have co-authored three previous books on child care.

## Publisher:
Workman Publishing

## Edition:
1996

## Price:
$15.95

## ISBN:
0894809946

## Media:
Book

## Principal Subject:
All-Inclusive Overview

## Age Group:
Toddlers (1–3)

# WHAT TO EXPECT THE TODDLER YEARS

## Recommended For:
All-Inclusive Overview

## Description:
Beginning with the 13th month, and progressing through the 36th month of a child's life, this four part guidebook contains over 900 pages of information for parents of toddlers. Part One has sixteen chapters that offer advice and suggestions on topics such as child development, setting limits, communicating with your child, encouraging imagination, and more. Each chapter has four subtitles—"What Your Toddler May Be Doing Now," "What You May Be Concerned About," "What's Important to Know," and "What's Important For Your Toddler to Know." Part Two covers the care of a toddler, addressing such issues as nutrition, health concerns, toilet learning, and the special needs child. Part Three defines the toddler interaction within the family including siblings and childcare. Part Four includes common home remedies, height and weight charts, and "Best-odds Recipes," to name a few references. Descriptive diagrams and tips are interspersed throughout the manual. There is an extensive 19-page index.

## Evaluation:
What a great reference! This guide has information on nearly every phase of a child, from age one to three years of age, and then some. It is well written, easy-to-use, and has a comfortable, user-friendly format. The information is impartial and thorough. This is truly an all-inclusive guide, even addressing cholesterol levels in children. The table of contents is extensive and progressive. Readers will find there is information on: caregivers and siblings; on treating toddler injuries; keeping worrying in perspective; and more. This book's valuable advice will take a parent through their child's adolescent years as well with such advice as poison control, preventing the spread of illnesses, appendicitis warnings, and herbal remedies. This book's forte definitely lies in preparing parents to understand the needs, behavior, and development of their children while offering hundreds of suggestions on their care, guidance, and management. This a priceless "find."

## Where To Find/Buy:
Bookstores and libraries.

# PARENT SOUP

**Recommended For:**
All-Inclusive Overview

## Description:

Parent Soup, a member of the iVillage, offers many links on its website homepage. "Soup specials" include features such as child and senior care directories, chats with Random House children's authors, parental "survival kits," a children's resume maker, child development profiles, baby name finder, a book club, and a shopping service. Parent Soup offers e-communities from those considering pregnancy to those who are parents of teens. A daily parent poll seeks visitors' opinions, and the site offers a selection of daily chats and message boards. A guided tour helps a visitor learn what is available. A roster of experts offers information on early education, family counseling, child development, health and pediatrics, breastfeeding, and summer camps. Guest experts add additional voices. Other resources include Community Challenges, a community discussion of a monthly parenting challenge, iBaby, a baby needs store, a library, an online guide, and an archive of parenting news stories.

## Evaluation:

Refill your tea cup, pull your chair closer to the computer screen, and prepare to spend some time at this website. Anyone with a child of any age—parent, grandparent, family member, or interested friend—will find more to do here than there is time to experience in one sitting. The decision will be where to start. The site features areas for everyone from expectant parents to parents of teens. The homepage itself offers a wealth of other informational services and entrances to discussions of individual topics. Discussion chats change daily, and special chats are scheduled with professionals in any number of fields. Information is updated continually, and topics range from the humorous which encourage the child in us all (The Whine Cellar) to the useful (Bedwetting). Site organization is energizing, attractive, and a little messy. You're sure to wander off the path, following one nugget or another, so be sure you know your way home. Program Director Susan Hahn says this is "a place to share the funny moments and everyday delights that are part of being a parent. It is a place to enrich our lives." It certainly is.

## Where To Find/Buy:

On the Internet at the URL: http://www.parentsoup.com

★★★★

**Overall Rating**
★★★★
Attractive, well-designed, unbelievably comprehensive

**Design, Ease Of Use**
★★★
Lots of information in an easy-to-navigate format; can get lost at times in the layers

1–4 Stars

**Author:**
Parent Soup is one of two parenting web sites included in the iVillage community of web sites.

**Publisher:**
iVillage Inc.

**Media:**
Internet

**Principal Subject:**
All-Inclusive Overview

**Age Group:**
Infants (0–1)

II. All-Inclusive Resources About Parenting

★★★

**Overall Rating**
★★★
The "bible" for those who enjoy a philosophy of non-authoritarian parenting

**Design, Ease Of Use**
★★★★
Anecdotes interspersed throughout; table of contents lists subtopics; extensive index

1–4 Stars

**Author:**
William Sears, MD & Martha Sears, RN

Sears, "one of America's most renowned pediatricians," has been in practice for 20 years and authored 10 books. Currently, he's a clinical assistant professor of pediatrics at USC School of Medicine. His wife is a childbirth educator, registered nurse, & breastfeeding consultant.

**Publisher:**
Little, Brown and Company

**Edition:**
1993

**Price:**
$21.95

**Pages/Run Time:**
689

**ISBN:**
0316779059

**Media:**
Book

**Principal Subject:**
All-Inclusive Overview

**Age Group:**
Infants & Toddlers (0–3)

# THE BABY BOOK
Everything You Need To Know About Your Baby—From Birth To Age Two

## Description:

Pediatric specialists and parents of eight, Sears and his wife present their parenting philosophy as it relates to the practice of raising children in this 689-page, 28 chapter book. Detailing a parenting style called "attachment parenting" in Chapter 1, Sears uses this as a foundation for the remainder of the book. You will find five parts to this book focusing on topics for parents of newborns through age two. These five parts deal with "Baby-Care Basics" (giving birth through the early weeks); "Infant Feeding and Nutrition" (breastfeeding, bottlefeeding, solid foods, toddler feeding); "Contemporary Parenting" ("babywearing," nighttime parenting, parenting the "fussy or colicky baby," working outside your home); "Infant Development and Behavior" (0–6 months, 6–12 months, the second year, toddler behaviors, toilet training); and "Keeping Your Baby Safe and Healthy" (baby-proofing, checkups, immunizations, medicines, self-help home care, lifesaving procedures, and first aid). Personal anecdotes from their own children as well as patients are used by the authors for illustration purposes throughout the text.

## Evaluation:

A conscientious new parent has zillions of nagging questions, e.g. "should I let my baby cry or should I pick her up? Should I let my baby sleep with me or should he sleep alone? Should I breastfeed my baby or bottlefeed?" Different experts answer these questions in different ways since there are several schools of thought and differing philosophies about raising a child. The Searses describe "attachment parenting" here as one in which parents use five "tools" to "get connected to [their] baby which include connecting early with one's baby, reading and responding to her/his cues, breastfeeding, 'wearing' the baby, and sharing sleep with one's baby." This book, then, is for those who believe that a baby who forms a strong attachment to their caretakers (trusting them to fulfill all his or her emotional, social and physical needs) will feel secure and self-confident. Whether one buys into Sears' parenting style or not, their medical advice and behavioral descriptions are universally useful, in particular their section on how to handle a baby with colic. Some of their medical information (immunizations in particular), however, needs to be updated.

## Where To Find/Buy:

Bookstores and libraries.

# COMPLETE BABY AND CHILD CARE

★★★

## Description:

This 352-page reference contains six major chapters. Chapter 1 contains behavior and health information about newborn babies. The second chapter deals with a child's everyday care including their environment, feeding, dressing, bathing, crying/comforting, and sleeping. Children's development (physical, speech and language, and mental), teeth, vision, hearing, and social behavior are a few of the topics in Chapter Three. The fourth chapter focuses on family life and discusses such topics as organization, separation and divorce, and multiple births. Children with special needs are addressed in Chapter Five, and the final chapter contains information about medicine and health care. Each topic is separated into four age groups (young baby, older baby, toddler, and preschool child), with color-coded bands given to access key information for each gender and age group. Illustrations and photographs guide parents through suggested routines. The book includes a first aid section, contact info for organizations, and an index.

## Evaluation:

The word for this visually appealing book is simply, "WOW!" Case studies, tips, extensive illustrations, and graphs are just the tip of the iceberg in describing this very well-presented guide. The book has made every effort to touch all aspects of child care, and has done an excellent job, although some updating needs to be done in terms of immunizations. The information is intelligent, with in-depth advice on topics as diverse as bathing a baby, to coping with disorders such as epilepsy and dyslexia. Special panels on the side of the page highlight and explain the differences in caring for and the differences in development between boys and girls in many areas. Case studies provide new insights, while medical facts help answer common parental questions. New parents will find Dr. Stoppard's commonsense approach informing, reassuring, and inspiring. This guide's index, while somewhat brief, includes boldly highlighted topics along with related subtopics for easy access. In short, this is a wonderful book, thoughtfully constructed, offering valuable information in a sensitive, compassionate, while professional, manner.

## Where To Find/Buy:

Bookstores and libraries.

**Overall Rating**
★★★
Great all-inclusive guide; immunizations discussion needs updating

**Design, Ease Of Use**
★★★★
500+ color photographs, drawings, graphs, & charts; color coding makes for easy access

1–4 Stars

**Author:**
Miriam Stoppard, MD
Miriam Stoppard, MD, is the author of many bestselling books on pregnancy and childcare.

**Publisher:**
Dorling Kindersley (Carroll & Brown Limited)

**Edition:**
1995

**Price:**
$29.95

**Pages/Run Time:**
352

**ISBN:**
1564588505

**Media:**
Book

**Principal Subject:**
All-Inclusive Overview

**Age Group:**
Infants & Toddlers (0–3)

★★★

**Overall Rating**
★★★
Good basic coverage of all childhood and parenting topics presented in a succinct manner

**Design, Ease Of Use**
★★★★
Very well-organized with 2 table of contents, extensive index, icons of various tips, etc.

1–4 Stars

**Author:**
Keith Boyd, MD, and Kevin Osborn

Boyd is the directory of the combined Pediatrics and Medicine Residency Program at the Rush-Presbyterian-St. Luke's Medical Center in Chicago. He is the father of three sons. Osborn, author of 36+ books for both adults and children, is the father of three children.

**Publisher:**
Alpha Books (Macmillan General Reference/Simon and Schuster Macmillan)

**Edition:**
1997

**Price:**
$16.95

**Pages/Run Time:**
345

**ISBN:**
0028617339

**Media:**
Book

**Principal Subject:**
All-Inclusive Overview

**Age Group:**
Infants & Toddlers (0–3)

# THE COMPLETE IDIOT'S GUIDE TO PARENTING A PRESCHOOLER AND TODDLER, TOO

## Description:

This book's intent is to present parents with an "operator's manual" offering information about children's developmental stages along with warnings about potential parenting challenges and discussions about parenting issues. Divided into four parts and 26 chapters, this 345-page book includes two table of contents (one, at a glance; the other, a detailed listing), a 15-page index, and an appendix of parenting resources. Parts are divided by age ranges—the early toddler (13–24 months), "the terrific, terrible twos" (25–36 months), the three-year-old, and the four-year-old. Each part has various chapters that address parental challenges during that stage along with discussions of children's physical, mental, and emotional development, health and safety issues, and more. Summaries of what is discussed in each chapter are given both at the beginning and end of each chapter. Also provided throughout are icons highlighting parenting anecdotes, tips, safety warnings, myths, and observations.

## Evaluation:

Busy parents wishing succinct answers in a well-organized format will find this book warrants their time and attention. It is extremely reader-friendly, offering basic development information and tips, advice, and reassurances for parents as they grow with their child. Parents will find the book very well laid-out with bold headings, inset colored blocks of suggestions, and an extensively cross-referenced index. Additionally, the inclusion of two table of contents makes information readily accessible; major topics are presented in the "Contents at a Glance," and page-by-page details are listed in the second table of contents. Many areas, however, are treated lightly—discipline, sibling relations, toilet training, and activities to do with children to name a few. In trying to cover (almost) too much ground, this resource has a tendency to include generalizations in many areas while spending considerable more time in some. Other resources focus more on a child's developmental and behavioral changes. Parents interested in more in-depth coverage in these areas need to check into other all-inclusive resources instead.

## Where To Find/Buy:

Bookstores and libraries.

# THE GIRLFRIENDS' GUIDE TO TODDLERS

A Survival Manual To The "Terrible Twos" (And Ones And Threes) From The First Step, The First Potty And The First Word ("No") To The Last Blankie

★★★

## Description:

"We don't go in any sort of chronological or developmental order, but rather from hot topic to hot topic," the author explains. Rather, Iovine suggests that the reader go directly to the part of the book that addresses his or her particular crisis of the moment. "Top Ten" lists on toddler myths, toddler lessons, and other toddler issues are peppered throughout the book. Each of the eleven chapters addresses one particular "toddler issue" that a parent may face. Chapter titles include "The Social Life of Toddlers," "The Comfort Zone," "Eating (Or Not)," "Discipline," "The Potty," "Sleepy Time," "Fashion," "Toddlers and Babies," "School Days, School Days" and "More Than a Mommy." Interspersed are additional lists of things for parents to do when their toddler drives them nuts and things they'll miss most about toddlers. Chapter One—"Who Are These People, Anyway?"— Gives an overview of the toddler in general. It discusses developmental stages of a one to three year old, babyproofing, and typical toddler behavior. Tips are provided throughout pertinent to each chapter's topic.

## Evaluation:

This book, the author says, "is a handbook designed to quickly and efficiently deal with many of the issues and concerns that you will have over the next couple of years" and that "we give it to you straight, fast and funny." The humorous tone is set from the beginning by the "Top Ten Toddler Myths." Iovine succeeds in providing advice that is practical and to-the-point. The wisdom imparted in each chapter suggests that parents should lighten up, that if they love their children and try to be the best parent possible, things will turn out fine. Serious behavior problems are not addressed in this book, which is limited to the everyday worries of eating, sleeping, pottying, and playing. Because she recognizes that most parents of toddlers have precious little time, the author doesn't require the reader to read the entire book from start to finish. In fact, she wisely suggests that the reader only read what is necessary to the situation. In the last chapter—"More Than a Mommy"—the author urges her mother readers to take time out for themselves, nurture their marriages, expect changes, and have confidence that, most of all, things get better. While that may sound like a dispirited approach to parenting a toddler, any parent of a two year old will know and grow to appreciate what she means by reading her book.

## Where To Find/Buy:

Bookstores and libraries.

**Overall Rating**
★★★
Humorous and fun to read; simple wisdom

**Design, Ease Of Use**
★★★★
Chapters arranged by "problem" for easy access to information

1–4 Stars

**Author:**
Vicki Iovine

Vicki Iovine is the mother of four children. She is also a monthly columnist for *Child* magazine and a regular contributor to *Redbook*. She has been featured on *Oprah*, *Today*, and *The View*.

**Publisher:**
Perigee (The Berkley Publishing Group/Penguin Putnam)

**Edition:**
1999

**Price:**
$12.00

**Pages/Run Time:**
271

**ISBN:**
039952438X

**Media:**
Book

**Principal Subject:**
All-Inclusive Overview

**Age Group:**
Toddlers (1–3)

II. All-Inclusive Resources About Parenting

★★★

**Overall Rating**
★★★
Extremely detailed information on the basics of baby care

**Design, Ease Of Use**
★★★★
Organized chapter subjects, many color photographs, lists, and charts

1–4 Stars

**Author:**
Dagmar Von Cramm and Eberhard Schmidt, MD

Von Cramm, a writer specializing in nutrition and children's topics, is author of two other books and is the mother of three. Schmidt, father of four, is a member of the National Commission on Breastfeeding and Nutritional Committee of the German Society of Pediatric Medicine.

**Publisher:**
Barron's

**Edition:**
2nd (1997)

**Price:**
$16.95

**Pages/Run Time:**
287

**ISBN:**
0812097785

**Media:**
Book

**Principal Subject:**
All-Inclusive Overview

**Age Group:**
Infants (0–1)

# OUR BABY: THE FIRST YEAR

## Description:

Front and back covers are a chart outlining baby's development, health, feeding, and "you and your family" from birth to 12 months. Sections include preparing for baby, the first week at home, care and handling, feeding, development, health, and other topics. Colored sidebars of related information are included throughout the book. The first section gives an overview of baby life and baby care in the first week, including feeding, medical examinations, visitors, diapering, umbilical cord care, bathing, and care of nails, ears, eyes, nose and teeth. The feeding section begins with breastfeeding instruction, tips, and alternatives. Information on weaning, baby food comparisons, and guidelines follow. In the section entitled "Becoming a Family," the author touches on a variety of subjects, such as the father's role, private time for parents, siblings and grandparents, mother's physical care, and other topics. The development section divides information into three age groups: one to four months, four to eight months, and eight to 12 months. Preventative health care, illnesses, vaccinations, and an alphabetical listing of common illnesses are also discussed.

## Evaluation:

For a book that focuses solely on this age group, it is exceptional in its ease of use, and clearly defined and illustrated information. This book does not examine and address pregnancy itself, but recommends a few things that can be done prior to and in preparation for baby's arrival. It doesn't cover every possible situation, but focuses on the basics: care, feeding, diapering, development, and health. The information provided is complete in many aspects. For example, the section on diapering gives a full explanation of all the different diapering options, including how to diaper using different methods (with photographs), costs of each option, and cleaning. Recipes and meal plans, exercises for Mom to get back into shape, and relaxation techniques are a few of the "extras" found here that are missing from most books on baby care. The abundance of color photos used in this book to teach methods and illustrate points make it stand out. The last chapter on organization and checklists is especially helpful. Great as a primer for basic baby care and understanding baby's growth, this resource will offer parents terrific visuals to help address their needs.

## Where To Find/Buy:

Bookstores and libraries.

# DR. SPOCK'S BABY AND CHILD CARE
The One Essential Parenting Book

★★★

## Description:

Dr. Spock and Dr. Rothenberg together have created a sixth edition of the well-known Dr. Spock Baby and Child Care Book. This 832-page book is written in short numbered sections of about a page each. Each numbered entry covers a single aspect of child care. Sections are grouped into subject categories such as: the role of the parents, equipment and clothing, medical and nursing care, infant feeding, breastfeeding, bottlefeeding, daily care, problems of infancy, managing young children, age related issues (from birth to adolescence), child development, illness, special situations, and many more subjects. Although information is provided from the perspective of the authors, two persons with documented authority and experience on the subject, it is written in a first person format. The clear intent of this book is to provide factual and supportive information for first-time parents so they can handle the huge learning curve they need to climb in order to become well-informed parents.

## Evaluation:

Spock's reassuring voice may be just the one a new parent needs to hear in order to claim some personal control over a new and occasionally anxious situation. Parents face a world offering various opinions on what a parent should or should not do, what is good and what is not good for the child. This book attempts to provide a balanced and experienced perspective in a positive and succinct way. The scope of this book is massive; every possible topic appears to be touched on at least briefly. The style of writing is authoritative, yet done in a gentle and inviting manner, allowing the reader to reflect on all possible options and not feel that it must be done "the Dr. Spock way." For the most part, the organization of the book is clear and easily referenced. While not the kind of book one sits down to read straight through, each section is written in an interesting and factual way. Some sections definitely need updating due to latest findings (SIDS, immunizations, etc.); other sections reflect the author's opinion (sometimes inconsistent with current scientific fact), but generally the book seems fresh and relevant whether your child is six days or six years old.

## Where To Find/Buy:
Bookstores and libraries.

**Overall Rating**
★★★
Comprehensive, balanced, supportive; needs updating re: SIDS, immunizations, etc.

**Design, Ease Of Use**
★★★
Easy to read, easy to reference; unclear as to why sections are numbered

1–4 Stars

**Author:**
Benjamin Spock, MD, and Michael B. Rothenberg, MD

Benjamin Spock, MD, practiced pediatrics in New York City from 1933 to 1947. Then he became a medical teacher and researcher. Michael B. Rothenberg, M.D., is a pediatrician and child psychiatrist who had combined these two fields in his work since 1957.

**Publisher:**
Pocket Books
(Simon & Schuster)

**Edition:**
6th (1992)

**Price:**
$7.99

**Pages/Run Time:**
832

**ISBN:**
0671760602

**Media:**
Book

**Principal Subject:**
All-Inclusive Overview

**Age Group:**
Infants & Toddlers (0–3)

★★★

## Overall Rating
★★★
Comprehensive, but best for parents of older kids; customized searches, active "Boards"

## Design, Ease Of Use
★★★
Commercialism abounds; easily navigated, well-organized site; book reprinted online

1–4 Stars

## Media:
Internet

## Principal Subject:
All-Inclusive Overview

## Age Group:
Infants & Toddlers (0–3)

# FAMILY.COM
Disney.Com

## Description:
Coordinated with Disney, this site covers a range of family related information including activities, education, parenting, shopping, and cooking. Options available at the homepage allow a visitor to choose one of those categories or select an article from "current feature," which, at this visit, discussed healthy snacks, whining, parenting an only child, and activities, such as making puppets and snowmen. There are more than a few search engines included at this website: one to search any topic, one to search meals and recipes by ingredient, and one to search a visitor's geographic area for local information on family activities. In the "Activities" section, a visitor can choose from several feature articles or search for an activity by indicating a topic and an age group. In "Education," one can again choose from a number of articles or search through the archives using the same criteria. Other sections of the website that use that format include the food and parenting sections. Bulletin boards are available on many topics, which are categorized into sections such as "All About You," "Family Ties," and many more.

## Evaluation:
This site looks just like a slick magazine cover, overwhelming the senses and with abundant commercialism. However, unusual to this site are the vast number of customized searches available and the reprints from respected authorities' books. Whether parents require a check-off list for evaluating preschools, need support for their parenting decisions, or want a quick activity for their three year old on a snowy day, they will find it here. Parents looking for others to share ideas and tips with will find the "Boards" to be a well-organized feature. Topics are arranged under the same headings as the site's homepage, with multiple subtopics found under each, and age ranges can be chosen. A novel feature to this segment is that visitors can specify that they want to read only the most current postings or include those more than a year old. This saves busy parents from wasted time and effort responding to chats that are no longer current. One won't find a lot of technical advice about heavy parenting issues or how to take care of a newborn at this site. This site, while comprehensive, is better suited for parents of toddlers, preschoolers, and older children.

## Where To Find/Buy:
On the Internet at the URL: http://family.go.com

# KIDSOURCE ONLINE

## Description:

This online community, created by a group of parents with varied backgrounds, aims to find "the best of the healthcare and education information . . . and deliver it . . . in new and innovative ways. . . ." General options on the site's homepage offer various articles under the headings of "Education," "Health," "Recreation," "Parenting," "Guide to Best Software," "New Products," and more. Specific options address four age groups—newborns, toddlers, preschoolers, and K–12. Within these categories are subtopic headings that lead to links on topics such as safety, specific areas (education, health, growth & development, parenting, etc.), online forums, websites, and other related areas. Also listed within these categories are articles categorized by what's new, recent recalls, and product information. Brief descriptions of these articles are offered. Most of the articles within this website are ranked using a five star system, with five stars being "best, in depth and most helpful overall." A list of articles is then presented, along with a brief synopsis of the article's contents and its rating; generally, articles average two to three pages.

## Evaluation:

This well-organized site hosts unusual contributors—the U.S. Department of Education, child-related organizations (child abuse consortia, etc.) and associations (learning disabilities), among others. The articles' succinct nature, positive tone, and friendly voice easily can be handled by any busy parent. Rating the articles presents yet another convenient way to ease up on the plethora of articles that face a parent interested in getting some new information and advice. Graphics are absent from the site intentionally, say the creators, because "most of (the) visiting parents do not have time to wait for extensive graphics to download"; the site will upgrade its design as parents upgrade their systems. The general discussion forums are well-organized and titled. Unfortunately, the age specific forums were cumbersome, simply consisting of a running list of titles; subject groupings would be more helpful. This site is a good informational site; other sites, however, provide better opportunities for discussions and chats with other parents.

## Where To Find/Buy:

On the Internet at the URL: http://www.kidsource.com/

**Overall Rating**
★★★
Unusual contributors, succinct articles make research an easy and interesting task

**Design, Ease Of Use**
★★★
Graphics are absent; articles are cross-referenced and rated according to a 5 star system

1–4 Stars

**Media:**
Internet

**Principal Subject:**
All-Inclusive Overview

**Age Group:**
Infants & Toddlers (0–3)

★★★

## Overall Rating
★★★
Unique approach invites parents to develop their own style while relaying others' tips

## Design, Ease Of Use
★★★
Use the table of contents and index to guide you; could use bolder headings and graphics

1–4 Stars

## Author:
Linda Albi, Deborah Johnson, Debra Catlin, Donna Florien Deurloo, and Sheryll Greatwood

Linda Albi, Deborah Johnson, Debra Catlin, Donna Florien Deurloo, and Sheryll Greatwood are mothers of twins and members of the same support group.

## Publisher:
Fireside (Simon & Schuster)

## Edition:
1993

## Price:
$14.00

## Pages/Run Time:
414

## ISBN:
067172357X

## Media:
Book

## Principal Subject:
All-Inclusive Overview

## Age Group:
Infants & Toddlers (0–3)

# MOTHERING TWINS
## From Hearing The News To Beyond The Terrible Twos

## Description:
This guide's 15 chapters focus on having and caring for twins. Chapter One begins with parents' revelation when they find out they are carrying twins and continues with what to expect. Chapters Two through Four take parents through the birthing experience including information on what to expect and focusing on the possibility of having premature twins. Chapters Six through Nine show parents how to establish a support system, locate childcare, and help older siblings adjust. Chapters 11 and 12 speak to the "couple relationship" and how to find time to regenerate oneself. Chapters 5, 10, 13, and 14 discuss the development of twins from the first six months through preschool. Chapter 15 is dedicated to the father's perspective of life with twins. An epilogue of the authors' final thoughts and reflections follows this final chapter. A resource directory is given supplying contact information for organizations, support groups, and more. A suggested reading list and a nine-page index are also provided.

## Evaluation:
Offering a variety of personal narratives and "it worked for me" solutions, this 414-page guide is a unique approach to the caring for twins. Emphasizing individuality and adaptability, the authors seek to encourage mothers to develop their own parenting approach based on what's best for themselves and their children. This is a wonderful book full of insight and practical tips. Of special note is Chapter 15: five fathers of twins (the authors' husbands) give their touching and sensitive perspectives on what it's like to have twins. Parents of twins will find this to be a well-written guide—relaxed, but comprehensive. Neither dictating nor forcing solutions, the authors merely express suggestions and advice from their own experiences. Parents of twins will find this very thoughtful book to be both interesting and informative from all five points of view. This resource has managed to cover a lot of ground, while being careful not to omit the essentials.

## Where To Find/Buy:
Bookstores and libraries.

# WHAT TO EXPECT THE FIRST YEAR
The Comprehensive Guide That Clearly Explains Everything Parents Need To Know About The First Year With A New Baby

★★★

## Description:

*What to Expect the First Year* is arranged in a textbook-like fashion. The Table of Contents illustrates the details to be found in this 671-page book, with an outline type format on what is to be found within. Part One addresses the infant's first year. The facts on such topics as bottle vs. breastfeeding, along with recommended equipment for either, is coupled with the emotional concerns of impending parenthood. Each chapter covers issues for each month of the baby's life. What the baby may be doing, what to expect from the monthly checkup, feeding issues, normal parental concerns for this stage, and "what's important to know" are included. Part Two—"Of Special Concern"—addresses special interest areas (summer clothing and winter concerns), common baby illnesses, first aid, adoption, and more. Supportive information is also provided on babies with problems, including references on the most common birth disorders. The last five chapters in this part deal with emotional and lifestyle adjustments. Part Three is a collection of recipes and common home remedies as well as a table on common childhood illnesses.

## Evaluation:

Reading this book is like reading a user friendly encyclopedia. Throughout, it sounds like advice from an experienced mother/nurse down the street who can be counted on to know exactly what to expect from the baby at whatever stage of his/her development, and how to do whatever needs to be done. It is light on illustrations, but made readable by frequent sub-heading breaks in the two-column text which insert questions and answers on child care issues. One example of this is the question on vegetarian diet, with a parent questioning whether a strict vegetarian diet provides enough nutrition. The answers are given in bulleted paragraphs, each with a different possible solution to the question depending on the age of the infant. This approach is used throughout the book. As a general reference this book is comprehensive; its information is mainstream with a friendly supportive tone and generous safety and medical tips.

## Where To Find/Buy:

Bookstores and libraries.

**Overall Rating**
★★★
A massive amount of information conveyed in a question and answer format

**Design, Ease Of Use**
★★★
Easy to reference, easy to read

1–4 Stars

**Author:**
Arlene Eisenberg, Heidi E. Murkoff, Sandee E. Hathaway, BSN.

Arlene Eisenberg, Heidi E. Murkoff, and Sandee e. Hathaway, BSN are the authors of the bestselling *What To Expect* series.

**Publisher:**
Workman Publishing

**Edition:**
2nd (1996)

**Price:**
$22.00

**Pages/Run Time:**
671

**ISBN:**
1563058766

**Media:**
Book

**Principal Subject:**
All-Inclusive Overview

**Age Group:**
Infants (0–1)

★★★

**Overall Rating**
★★★
Concise, sensitive "operations manual" for arriving home with the new baby

**Design, Ease Of Use**
★★★
Well drawn illustrations, helpful charts and index

1–4 Stars

**Author:**
Linda Todd, MPH

Linda Todd, MPH is coordinator of prenatal education at Fairview Riverside Medical Center in Minneapolis. She has been a faculty member for the International Childbirth Education Association's workshops and is the author of *Labor and Birth: A Guide for You.*

**Publisher:**
Harvard Common Press

**Edition:**
1993

**Price:**
$6.95

**Pages/Run Time:**
134

**ISBN:**
1558320547

**Media:**
Book

**Principal Subject:**
All-Inclusive Overview

**Age Group:**
Infants (0–1)

# YOU AND YOUR NEWBORN BABY
## A Guide To The First Months After Birth

**Description:**

Written by a childbirth educator with 25 years of experience, this book reflects a growing desire on the part of participants in her childbirth classes to focus on what one is to expect after the birth. Consequently, it offers ideas on things one can do to make the time after birth easier. The book consists of three major parts: "The Newborn Mother," "The Newborn Baby" and "The Newborn Family." The "Newborn Mother" addresses questions about how the mother can take care of herself physically and emotionally before and after the birth. "The Newborn Baby" focuses on the health care of the baby, her/his development of sensory and motor skills, and basics regarding feeding, bathing and diapering. The final part—"The Newborn Family"—encourages the family to keep their relationships strong with the birth of a new family member. Special attention is given in this section to the "postpartum father" and to other children in the family.

**Evaluation:**

In the United States, where nearly 99 percent of women give birth in hospitals, the time that a mother and her baby remain in the hospital after the birth continues to shrink. In fact, by the year 2000, discharge from the hospital within 24 hours of the birth will probably become the norm. Such a continuing trend challenges the family of the newborn as they alone face the postpartum experience, cut off from trained personnel who, in many other countries, are there to teach parenting skills, assess the mother's and baby's health, and provide moral support. This book, then, is meant to fill in that gap. Its tone is that of a well educated, sensitive, reassuring professional who is vicariously there to help the family who feels so happy, but also overwhelmed and disorientated, as they walk into their home with a new child. Along with its encouraging and sensitive tone, the book is filled with well-drawn illustrations regarding breastfeeding, diaper changing, swaddling, etc. If one is desperately searching for a no-panic "operations manual" to substitute for the caregiver who will not be there, this short, easy to read book may fit the bill.

**Where To Find/Buy:**
Bookstores and libraries.

# YOUR BABY & CHILD
From Birth To Age Five

★★★

## Description:

This third revised edition of Leach's book incorporates the "latest research and thinking on child development and learning, and reflects the realities of today's . . . new approaches to parenting." Leach is also known for her TV series under the same title—"Your Baby & Child." This 559-page resource is divided up into five sections which include information on newborns, babies in their first six months, older babies (from six months to one year), toddlers (one year to two and a half), and young children (from two and a half to five years). Each section includes characteristics for each age group, such as feeding/eating and growing, teeth and teething, everyday care, excreting, sleeping, and crying and comforting. Some sections also contain material on the senses, muscles, eyesight and hearing, listening and speaking skills, and playing and learning/thinking skills. The book is written in a text format with italic side bar headings, full color illustrations, charts, and highlighted question and answer sections. An index concludes the book.

## Evaluation:

If parents want a book that covers nearly every aspect of child care in terms of an older baby's development through the age of five, this book is a great choice. This resource provides parents and caregivers with the information they need to truly understand and enhance their child's growth. However, parents of newborns will find their questions answered, but in a rather clinical manner; advice on breastfeeding is adequate but not definitive, and is sometimes derogatory. For example, in describing benefits of bottlefeeding, Leach states that it "let[s] you off the intense (and sometimes uncomfortable) physical and emotional involvement with your baby that establishing breast-feeding requires." Different to this version is the absence of a medical section. Instead, it has been replaced by tinted text sections offering parent's point of views on various subjects. While not necessarily reflecting the author's opinion, these opinions may open up debate issues as parents strengthen their beliefs—for example, "any toddler who bites . . . should be bitten . . . back." New questions have been added along with notes on hazards and safety guidelines. This book's advice sometimes reflects the author's perspective, but on the whole it is well-researched.

## Where To Find/Buy:

Bookstores and libraries.

---

**Overall Rating**
★★★
Focuses more on caring for the older baby through age five; some info on newborn care

**Design, Ease Of Use**
★★★
Compact print difficult to read; consistent format; numerous color photos and charts

1–4 Stars

**Author:**
Penelope Leach, PhD

Leach, with a PhD in psychology, is a Fellow of the British Psychological Society and a founding member of the UK branch of the World Association for Infant Mental Health. She is a leading authority and advocate in the field of child development and care.

**Publisher:**
Alfred A. Knopf
(Random House)

**Edition:**
3rd (1997)

**Price:**
$20.00

**Pages/Run Time:**
559

**ISBN:**
0375700005

**Media:**
Book

**Principal Subject:**
All-Inclusive Overview

**Age Group:**
Infants & Toddlers (0–3)

II. All-Inclusive Resources About Parenting

★★★

**Overall Rating**
★★★
Author's approach presents facts, disputes myths, so parents can be decision-makers

**Design, Ease Of Use**
★★
Vague table of contents; good headings within book; book's size & weight cumbersome

1–4 Stars

**Author:**
Marianne Egeland Neifert, MD, with Anne Price and Nancy Dana

Neifert is an award-winning pediatrician, professor of pediatrics, and mother of five children.

**Publisher:**
Signet (Dutton Signet/Penguin Books)

**Edition:**
1986

**Price:**
$6.99

**Pages/Run Time:**
529

**ISBN:**
0451163117

**Media:**
Book

**Principal Subject:**
All-Inclusive Overview

**Age Group:**
Infants & Toddlers (0–3)

# DR. MOM
## A Guide To Baby And Child Care

### Description:

Neifert coined the name "Dr. Mom" because she believes strongly in "the importance of nurturing new parents, in order to bring to blossom their long-term competency." Her 529-page book is divided into 17 chapters. The first three focus on preparation for parenthood from making the decision to giving birth to outfitting the nursery. Chapters Four through Six center on newborn and infant care. Children's development (birth to age five) is discussed in Chapter Seven. Chapter Nine offers ten pages of information on "toilet learning." Chapter Eight—"The Challenge of Parenting"—addresses discipline choices, while Chapter Ten focuses on understanding various behaviors (tantrums, biting, pacifiers, etc.). The next three chapters offer information on caring for a sick child, dealing with illnesses and disorders (80 pages), and what to do in an emergency. The pros, the cons, and feedback on "contemporary concerns" (sexual abuse, kidnapping, the family bed, breastfeeding in public, etc.) are presented in Chapter 14. The last three chapters deal with parenting styles and family strategies (nonsexist, working parents, single families, divorce, etc.).

### Evaluation:

Neifert does a fine job of commingling her personal experiences as the mother of five with her professional aspiration to nurture new parents by "acknowledging their good intentions and sound intuition . . . supplying them with factual information . . . (so that they can) meet their children's needs. . . ." Throughout her book, she grants parents the privilege of making their own decisions on parenting issues. Some resources do a better job dealing with topics such as toilet training/learning, discipline, and behavior. Neifert's book does a better job at examining the various sides of "hot" issues today such as the family bed, nursing in public places, and more. Some information is outdated due to the book's copyright so, as always, parents should check with their baby's doctor before making certain decisions. The book's size is awkward; hopefully future editions will be a larger format with fewer pages making it easier to hold and read. The section on illnesses/disorders is well-done and comparable to that found in better resources. Not recommended for use on its own, this book would be a welcome companion to another more inclusive resource.

### Where To Find/Buy:

Bookstores, libraries, or order direct by contacting Penguin USA at P.O. Box 999, Dept. #17109, Bergenfield, NJ 07621.

# PARENTTIME

★★★

## Description:

Access to this site's features can begin with either selecting a child's age range or a topic-driven department for specific information. Age range choices include pregnancy, baby, toddler, preschool, and school-age. "Departments" feature many articles and sub-articles focusing on a child's growth and health concerns, issues for parents, finances, "Parenting A to Z," a "Pregnancy Primer," celebrity parents, fun and games, and more. The age range selection takes a visitor to age-appropriate features, "This Week's Feature," "Expert," and "Boards and Chats." The Table of Contents lists all of the site's articles and information, organized into topics: Parent Time Specials, Travel, Fun & Games, Health Guide (which includes a medical encyclopedia and a first aid resource), Parenting A to Z, Parent Talk, Pregnancy Primer, and Expert Advice. This site is owned by Time Inc. and Proctor & Gamble Productions, with references including links to other publications such as *Money*, *Time* and *People* magazines, Dr. Ruth Westheimer, and *Parenting* and *BabyTalk* magazines.

## Evaluation:

Once a visitor finds his or her way through the maze of commercialism, product ads, and company promotions to arrive at the Table of Contents, a wealth of information is available to answer most questions and address most concerns. The pages specialized for particular age ranges offer helpful, if limited, tips and advice. Boards and chat rooms discuss topics pertaining to that age range. "Ask an Expert," the question and answer section, and experts' perspectives on topical parenting issues are features not be missed. The Health Guide's encyclopedia of medical terms and first aid (help in treating emergencies) are especially useful resources to have readily available. The site's archived articles—primarily reprints from *Parenting* magazine—cover a wide variety of parenting topics, from the technical to the supportive to the whimsical (sending an e-card in the Fun and Games department). This website even covers financial situations that parents (or others) may face, such as buying a home; some information is in the format of links to other websites. Another particular plus—a project planner that offers easy craft projects for each month. Once one learns the route, time spent at this site will definitely be worthwhile.

## Where To Find/Buy:

On the Internet at the URL: http://www.pathfinder.com/ParentTime/ homepage/homepage.all.html

---

**Overall Rating**
★★★
Access to abundant info, discussions on selected topics

**Design, Ease Of Use**
★★
Most info is buried deep, but fairly well-categorized, graphics slow down the process

1–4 Stars

**Media:**
Internet

**Principal Subject:**
All-Inclusive Overview

**Age Group:**
Infants & Toddlers (0–3)

II. All-Inclusive Resources About Parenting

**★★**

**Overall Rating**
★★
Lots of info and resources given to cover topics of pregnancy through early child care

**Design, Ease Of Use**
★★★★
Numerous quotes from families of multiples; detailed table of contents and index

1–4 Stars

**Author:**
Betty Rothbart, MSW

Betty Rothbart is a psychiatric social worker. She is currently a science and health writer, educator, and trainer of teachers for the New York City Board of Education. She is also an adjunct professor at the Bank Street College of Education.

**Publisher:**
Hearst Books
(William Morrow)

**Edition:**
1994

**Price:**
$12.00

**Pages/Run Time:**
383

**ISBN:**
0688116426

**Media:**
Book

**Principal Subject:**
All-Inclusive Overview

**Age Group:**
Infants & Toddlers (0–3)

# MULTIPLE BLESSINGS
From Pregnancy Through Childhood, A Guide For Parents Of Twins, Triplets, Or More

**Description:**

This guidebook is divided into four sections. The first section is about pregnancy and includes such topics as the delivery, planning for your multiples' births, premature babies and coping with the loss of a child. Section Two's focus is on "Life with Multiples," dealing with the parent partnership and expectations, naming your babies, breastfeeding, and the logistics of caring for multiples. It also includes advice on how to select a pediatrician and helping siblings to adjust. Section Three offers advice on enlisting help and support, finding babysitters, and a discussion of Mothers of Twins Clubs and a listing of other resources. The final section speaks to the parenting challenges and joys. One-on-one time, overcoming favoritism, bonding, handling stress, and making comparisons are just a few of the subtopics in this section. The appendices include a glossary of terms, additional resources, a bibliography, and a listing of books for children about twins and triplets. An index is also included.

**Evaluation:**

Using quotes from interviews with the family of multiples, this 383-page book offers advice and suggestions on raising twins, triplets, and more. A large section of the book deals, in general, with the birthing/delivery aspect, followed by broad-based blanketed advice on what parents might expect life to be with multiples. One valuable section in Part Two is "Multiple Feats: The Logistics of Caring for Multiples." Some of the subtopics in this section include how to bathe babies; deal with mealtime, scheduling and routines; toilet training; and record keeping. "Parenting Challenges and Joys," Section Four, contains good material (handling stress, giving equal love, avoiding typecasting, etc.), but otherwise seems a rather random array of issues. The resource section includes periodicals, organizations, and mail-order buying information for parents of multiples. There are, however, more comprehensive books on multiples than this one.

**Where To Find/Buy:**
Bookstores and libraries.

# THE NATIONAL PARENTING CENTER

★★

## Description:

Programmed and hosted by ParentsPlace.com, The National Parenting Center (TNPC) was founded in July 1989 to provide parents "with comprehensive and responsible guidance from nine of the world's most renowned child-rearing authorities. . . ." Features at the homepage include articles, a mall, chat facilities, and a daily feature. Articles, presented through the "ParenTalk Newsletter," are written by the panel of parenting authorities (bios include a psychologist, pediatrician, parenting authors, and more). Information is grouped by the following categories: pregnancy, newborns, infancy, toddler, preschool, preteens, and adolescence; various subcategories then are presented, along with the respective author. Articles typically range from half a page to one-page in length. "Chat" leads a visitor to ParentsPlace.com's discussion rooms with 100+ topics that are divided into categories. TNPC's "Mall/Shopping Center" houses award-winning products from the group's Seal of Approval program. Products are organized by age groups and can be purchased online.

## Evaluation:

Visitors to this site will be initially impressed by the discussion forums available here. The topics are more numerous than most other sites, they're clearly labeled for access, and the participants are active. At the "Mall," the lists of toys, books, music, furniture, and other child-related products are, of course, limited to those that were tested by the group's volunteers. It would be helpful to know what products overall were evaluated. For example, is a particular product not a "quality" product or has it simply not been tested by the parent judges? The articles were adequate, but just that and nothing more. The advice given is succinct, albeit a bit too brief to be of any real help to a struggling parent. In one instance, helpful hints for "Terrible Twos" invite the parent to remember the author's five rules to "escape toddlerhood in one piece." Such directions are rather negative and simplistic. Visitors are likely to miss the Q & A information archives available at other sites. Other sites, as well, provide more in-depth follow-through and situational help than this one.

## Where To Find/Buy:

On the Internet at the URL: http://www.tnpc.com/ or by calling (800) 753-6667

---

**Overall Rating**
★★
Information and advice from "authorities" rather succinct; shopping and chats good

**Design, Ease Of Use**
★★★★
Good graphics in their "mall," easily navigated, well-organized headings

1–4 Stars

**Media:**
Internet

**Principal Subject:**
All-Inclusive Overview

**Age Group:**
Infants & Toddlers (0–3)

**★★**

## Overall Rating
★★
Excellent advice, but geared more toward parents of toddlers and preschoolers

## Design, Ease Of Use
★★★★
Detailed table of contents introduces a clearly written, bulleted, and highlighted text

1–4 Stars

## Author:
Vicki Lansky

Vicki Lansky has authored over 25 books, and is well-known for her column in *Family Circle* magazine and *Sesame Street Parents' Guide Magazine*. She has also appeared on national TV shows like *Donahue*, *Oprah*, and *Today*.

## Publisher:
Meadowbrook Press
(Simon & Schuster)

## Edition:
3rd (1992)

## Price:
$8.00

## Pages/Run Time:
186

## ISBN:
0671792059

## Media:
Book

## Principal Subject:
All-Inclusive Overview

## Age Group:
Infants & Toddlers (0–3)

# PRACTICAL PARENTING TIPS
Over 1,500 Helpful Hints For The First Five Years

## Description:

This 186-page resource, in its third edition, is separated into eight major sections. The first section, "New Baby Care," includes information on such topics as Cesarean deliveries, what to do if your baby cries, diapering, and working moms. The second section focuses on the "basics" in caring for your child. Some topics that are discussed here include feeding, clothing, and sleeping issues for babies, toddlers, and young children. Section Three deals with hygiene and health. Cleanliness, dental care, first aid, encouraging good habits, illnesses, and toilet training are a few of the topics addressed. Section Four focuses on childproofing and safety. Section Five offers advice and suggestions on manners, tantrums, sibling rivalry, kicking habits, fears, and developing self-esteem. Family heritage and traveling with family are addressed in Sections Six and Seven. The final section includes seasonal fun for both inside and outdoors, arts and crafts, encouraging reading, and preparing a child for school. An index is also provided.

## Evaluation:

This book is more a rescue guide than simply a guide with helpful hints. With over 1,500 ideas for making a parent's life easier, here is a cure-all for everything from how to remove gum from hair to advice such as draping a towel over the top of the bathroom door to keep your child from locking himself inside. This guide covers a wide variety of topics in a progressive and logical manner. However, it focuses primarily on taking care of older children, principally preschoolers. Included in the book's hints are the best shared experiences, recipes, and tips from other parents. Bold subheadings and bulleted sections make this resource easy and quick to use. The author uses a relaxed, comfortable writing style while offering a variety of suggestions from which parents may choose. Comical illustrations add to the book's humor. The author has taken care to make sure that new ideas (400) have been incorporated in this revised edition and that former material has been updated to accommodate current lifestyles and parenting information. Parents of older children will find this book is worth buying, however, parents of newborns looking for tips and suggestions on baby care will find other resources better suit their needs.

## Where To Find/Buy:

Bookstores and libraries, or order direct by calling (800) 338-2232 or (612) 930-1100. FAX orders may be placed at (612) 930-1940.

# KEYS TO PARENTING YOUR ONE-YEAR-OLD

★★

## Description:

This 154-page resource, one in Barron's Parenting Keys series, focuses on questions and answers for parents of one-year-old children. The table of contents is divided into three parts. Included is information on growth, developmental differences in personality, and common behavior issues. Part One discusses how one-year-olds grow and change. Part Two highlights temperamental style with topics such as adaptability, attention span, sensitivity, and more. Part Three addresses toddler behavior with three subsections. Section One deals with family interactions. Some issues in this section include tantrums, separating from parents, and clinging to parents. Section Two deals with getting along with others; sharing, biting, and choosing childcare are also included. Section Three discusses a one-year-old's habits with topics such as drinking from a bottle, breastfeeding, head banging, and more. A question and answer section, glossary of terms, and a list of suggested resources and readings are also included.

## Evaluation:

This is a great resource for parents anxious to learn about the changes their child will experience as they learn to communicate, adapt to new situations, and grow in the first year of their life. The book is easy to follow with a simple table of contents and a reliable index. Some of the issues specific to one-year-olds include toilet training readiness, sensitivity, tantrums, and "loveys." Intelligently interpreted, this guide addresses some of the more popular parenting questions, such as "How can I break her of the bottle habit?" There are ten questions included from parents which the author, a pediatric nurse practitioner, answers authoritatively, but with compassion. The suggested reading and resources section is an added bonus. Although the information is worthy, parents will most likely want more advice and depth in certain areas. Look elsewhere for a more comprehensive resource to take home and study.

## Where To Find/Buy:

Bookstores and libraries.

**Overall Rating**
★★
Good resource for pinpointing basic issues involved with raising a beginning toddler

**Design, Ease Of Use**
★★★
Well-orchestrated layout with bulleted highlights; no photos or illustrations

1–4 Stars

**Author:**
Meg Zweiback, RN, MPH, CPNP

Meg Zweiback is a pediatric nurse practitioner and an associate clinical professor at the University of California in San Francisco.

**Publisher:**
Barron's

**Edition:**
1992

**Price:**
$5.95

**ISBN:**
0812047729

**Media:**
Book

**Principal Subject:**
All-Inclusive Overview

**Age Group:**
Toddlers (1–3)

★★

**Overall Rating**
★★
Basic no-nonsense approach to understanding a two-year-old's development and growth

**Design, Ease Of Use**
★★★
Detailed table of contents and index useful; no graphics to break up the text's monotony

1–4 Stars

**Author:**
Meg Zweiback, RN, MPH, CPNP

Meg Zweiback is Associate Clinical Professor at the University of California, San Francisco's Department of Family Health Care Nursing.

**Publisher:**
Barron's Educational Series

**Edition:**
1993

**Price:**
$6.95

**ISBN:**
0812014162

**Media:**
Book

**Principal Subject:**
All-Inclusive Overview

**Age Group:**
Toddlers (1–3)

# KEYS TO PARENTING YOUR TWO-YEAR-OLD

## Description:

This 166-page book is one in a series of guidebooks offering advice on parenting toddlers, specifically, two-year-olds. The contents is separated into three parts. Part One discusses how two-year-olds develop and change. Becoming independent, language development, feeding, sleep, toilet training, and discipline are some of the subtopics. Part Two focuses on the variety of two-year-olds' temperament. Their ability to adapt, their moods, attention span, distractibility, and sensitivity are some of the issues explained. The final section, Part Three, focuses on "Behavior and Misbehavior"; areas highlighted include temper tantrums, communication, social development, siblings and other children, anger and aggression, and demand for attention. Following Part Three is a dedicated question and answer section. The ten questions range from dealing with picky eaters to time-out to television usage. A list of suggested reading and materials is also provided along with a glossary of seven terms and an index.

## Evaluation:

This reference strives to help parents of two-year-olds cope with raising their child in an often demanding modern time where parents often have little outside support. The author embraces the positive aspects of living with a two-year-old by dispelling the myth of the "terrible twos" and explaining their personalities so parents will better understand how to "enjoy the challenges." She offers parents suggestions on how to set realistic expectations and advice on how to cope with potential behavior problems. Helpful keys are provided in Part One describing a toddler's development and how it affects his/her behavior in his daily activities—sleeping, feeding, toileting, and discipline. This book has a comfortable layout with an easy-to-read style. The information is worthy, but leaves one with a sense of wanting more advice and depth on the subject matter. Parents will find they need to look elsewhere for a more comprehensive resource to add to their parenting library.

## Where To Find/Buy:

Bookstores and libraries.

# PARENTSPLACE.COM

## Description:

This site is a member of the iVillage community of websites. ParentsPlace's goals are to connect visitors with one another and with various support agencies and associations, to "provide a unique shopping site on the web," to provide a forum for all parents, and to make enough money to allow the site's hosts to continue to work at home while parenting their son. Subsections include Fertility, Health, Stages, Family, Work, Fun, Experts, Shop, Chats, Boards, and Tools. Much of the site's information is directed to pregnancy and newborn concerns, however a search for "toddler" yielded almost 2,000 references, including Feeding Guidelines for Toddlers, Toddler Birthday Bash, Breastfeeding Past One Year, Power Bars for Toddlers, and Welcome to the Scribbling Stage. Inside many subsections, one can select an age range for additional age-appropriate activities and information. A variety of chat room discussions and message boards are offered on selected topics. Subject experts host pages that allow visitors to submit questions; a selection of past Q and As are also given. The site also offers a free weekly email newsletter and a selection of email postcards.

## Evaluation:

ParentsPlace.com is a joyful, colorful website engagingly presented and packed with educational, informational, and interesting topic discussions and activities. Although the site itself is strong enough to warrant a recommendation to any parent of small children, its offerings for toddlers is sporadic. Most of the toddler-specific information is housed within the Q and As from ParentsPlace's panel of experts. Beyond that, the site lacks depth concerning information on toddlers. For example, inside the "fun" section, visitors may select an age range and categories that include books, videos and music, toys and software, and more. Yet there are no videos or music listed in the toddler section, no toys or software, and the book section combines infant and toddler selections. Even more confusing, under "travel," are listed directions for making glitter play dough and a related recipe for "silly slime." Not many parents would agree that making slime is a good activity to make in the back seat of the family car while traveling. In general, the ParentsPlace site remains a worthwhile stop. Its potential, however, which is showcased in its pregnancy-related sections, has not been reached when it comes to toddlers.

## Where To Find/Buy:

On the Internet at the URL: http://www.parentsplace.com/pregnancy/

---

★★

**Overall Rating**
★★
Highly qualified expert advice; toddler-specific offerings thinner than expected

**Design, Ease Of Use**
★★★
Expertly designed with clear pathways between topics and selections

1–4 Stars

**Author:**
ParentsPlace.com began three years ago as a home-based business of two parents who wanted to find a way to stay home with their newborn son. Since then, ParentsPlace.com has grown to become an award-winning site gaining recognition throughout the Internet.

**Publisher:**
iVillage

**Media:**
Internet

**Principal Subject:**
All-Inclusive Overview

**Age Group:**
Infants & Toddlers (0–3)

II. All-Inclusive Resources About Parenting

★★

**Overall Rating**
★★
Intriguing concept for raising a baby that is more "hands-off" than usual

**Design, Ease Of Use**
★★★
Chapters and sections give clear, brief descriptions of how to apply principles

1–4 Stars

**Author:**
Magda Gerber and Allison Johnson

Magda Gerber is the founder and director of Resources for Infant Educarers (RIE). She lectures and conducts workshops for parents and professionals, and has created a series of instructional videos. Allison Johnson is a freelance writer.

**Publisher:**
John Wiley & Sons

**Edition:**
1998

**Price:**
$14.95

**Pages/Run Time:**
236

**ISBN:**
0471178837

**Media:**
Book

**Principal Subject:**
All-Inclusive Overview

**Age Group:**
Infants & Toddlers (0–3)

# YOUR SELF CONFIDENT BABY
How To Encourage Your Child's Natural Abilities—From The Very Start

## Description:
This book is written about the Resources for Infant Educarers (RIE) approach to parenting. The author founded this organization to help ". . . parents and children from birth to twenty-four months learn to treat each other with respect." The three sections of the book are entitled: "How RIE Can Benefit Your Baby"; "Your Baby at the Beginning of Life: From Birth to Your Baby's First Steps"; and "As Your Child Grows: Toddlerhood and Its Challenges." Section One contains two chapters on the basic principles and history of RIE. The second section takes a look at how to apply RIE basic principles in everyday situations and at the early developmental stages a child goes through. It contains five chapters regarding the newborn baby, newborn parents, the first months with baby, selecting the right childcare, and baby becoming mobile. Section Three discusses all aspects of toddlerhood, including separation, play, safety, tantrums, bedtime, and teething. The author illustrates how the RIE philosophy can be practically applied by describing a typical evening and bedtime routine. Throughout the book are comments, stories, and anecdotes from families who have worked with the RIE principles.

## Evaluation:
In her introduction, Gerber states that, "If you treat your child respectfully from birth, he may have a better chance of gaining confidence and developing good judgment." This respectful approach make parents' lives easier and more predictable, she says. "If we refrain from teaching them, they learn from experience." The author's concept of respect includes setting, and enforcing, boundaries for the child and the parent. The parents' needs are an equal part of the equation, not lesser than the child's needs. The author states that the parent should, without expectations, let the child develop at her own pace, realize her resourcefulness, and take pride in her accomplishments. A heavy emphasis is placed on observing the child and learning from those observations. In this age of hands-on parenting, this approach emphasizes that the parents remain "hands-off." That doesn't mean ignoring the child, however. Parents remain in the scene but as observers only. When a situation arises in which the child needs parental involvement, the parent should observe the child and assess what the child's actual needs are at the moment. This philosophy goes so far as to discourage parents from such actions as rocking a baby to sleep and using infant seats which may seem extreme to some parents.

## Where To Find/Buy:
Bookstores and libraries.

# 1, 2, 3 . . . THE TODDLER YEARS
## A Practical Guide For Parents & Caregivers

★ ★

## Description:

Part One of this book, comprised of 18 chapters, is entitled, "Respect for Toddlers. What Does This Mean and How Can We Make It Work?" Chapters address issues such as independence, feelings, boundaries and limits, learning, time with parents, planning ahead, sleep, fighting, tantrums, toilet learning, sex roles, eating, new siblings, and being in public. Part Two of the book—"Successful Parenting"—focuses more on the parents. Chapter topics include learning from others, trusting in yourself, taking care of yourself, keeping your child safe, asking for help, feelings of guilt, and enjoying your child. Part Three deals exclusively with finding and keeping quality childcare. This book is based on the work at the Toddler Care Center in Santa Cruz, California, which is founded on the Resources for Infant Educarers (RIE) philosophy of parenting and childcare. This philosophy requires respect for the child, treating each child as a special individual, giving children the opportunity to grow and learn at their own pace, and allowing them freedom to create and master their own challenges.

## Evaluation:

The author states that the Toddler Care Center's philosophy "focuses on the development and communication of genuine respect for each toddler." This is a "how-to" book, not one on theory. Its goal is to help parents make the most of the toddler years. Most of the techniques in the book focus on talking with the child, explaining what the adult is going to do, is doing, or has done. When a child becomes upset, the parent acknowledges and explains those feelings to the child. If a child is throwing a tantrum, the parent explains why certain behavior is needed and offers choices to the child to help her cooperate. A lot of the problems that face parents with a toddler are answered by the solution of distraction. For example, if two children are fighting over the same toy, one can be distracted with another toy. If a child refuses to engage in a particular action, the parent is encouraged to talk to the child about the situation and present some sort of distraction to get the child's mind off what they were fighting for in the first place. These may seem a bit deceptive, but most parents know distraction is a valid and valued tool to get children to cooperate willingly, and this resource outlines many ways to make distraction successful.

## Where To Find/Buy:

Bookstores, libraries, or order direct by calling (408) 476-4120.

---

**Overall Rating**
★★
Information is marginally interesting, methods could be more clear

**Design, Ease Of Use**
★★
Chapter organization is average, language is easy to read

1–4 Stars

**Author:**
Irene Van der Zande

Irene Van der Zande holds a degree in psychology, spent two years as a VISTA volunteer, and five years as executive director of the Volunteer Bureau of Santa Cruz County. She currently is principal partner of Comprehensive Consulting and is the mother of two.

**Publisher:**
Santa Cruz Toddler Care Center

**Edition:**
2nd (1995)

**Price:**
$11.95

**Pages/Run Time:**
184

**ISBN:**
0940953234

**Media:**
Book

---

**Principal Subject:**
All-Inclusive Overview

**Age Group:**
Toddlers (1–3)

**★★**

**Overall Rating**
★★
Includes info about product recalls; good list of "family fun" links

**Design, Ease Of Use**
★★
Layout clear and easy to navigate

1–4 Stars

**Media:**
Internet

**Principal Subject:**
All-Inclusive Overview

**Age Group:**
Infants & Toddlers (0–3)

# BABY BAG
The In-Site To Parenting

## Description:

Website departments at Baby Bag Online include parenting information, health and safety, feeding and nutrition, family fun, cook's corner, reviews of products, books and videos, business and job opportunities, childcare, and selected yellow pages. Interactive features focus on online shopping, nine categories of bulletin boards, and "ask the professional," in which parents may submit questions to a pharmacist, a childbirth educator, a midwife, and the owner of a homebased business. The site's homepage provides information about current product recalls and safety information, as well as access to a selection of children's stories. Bulletin boards are available on specific topics: product reviews, parents over 30, at-home moms, working parents, single parents, feeding, expectant parents, and parents under 30. Features and articles for parents include topics such as "parents are a child's first teacher," "a grandparents' guide for family nurturing and safety," "preventing dehydration in children," "facts about media violence and effects on the American family," and an extensive list of parenting tips offered by parents.

## Evaluation:

Baby Bag Online offers two particular strengths: online shopping and tips for parents by parents. If a parent enjoys the convenience of online shopping, this site offers items from booster seats and lead detection kits to furniture and toddlers' swim diapers and goggles. Its "helpful hints" section provides a staggeringly long list of tips on anything a parent would want to know, along with many they've never thought of before. A recipe for homemade baby wipes or a teething biscuit recipe? This is the place. Want to know how to entertain a toddler or how to handle a toddler while shopping? This section has some ideas. While there isn't as much toddler-specific information as one might like, Baby Bag Online offers arts and craft projects suitable for this age group, as well as an extremely interesting list of "family fun" links, guaranteed to transport visitors to interesting and unusual cyber-destinations.

## Where To Find/Buy:

On the Internet at the URL: http://www.babybag.com/

# GETTING ORGANIZED FOR YOUR NEW BABY
## A Checklist And Planner For Busy Parents-To-Be

★★

### Description:

A wife and mother of two has compiled numerous check-off lists, fill-in-the-blank forms, outlines, graphs, charts, and more to "make your pregnancy preparations as simple and convenient as possible." Her 175-page planner is organized in two ways—information given by topic and then subsequently by trimester. The ten topic chapters consist of the following: planning for a baby (plotting menstrual cycles, basal body temps), prenatal planning (selecting caregiver and birthsite, morning sickness, etc.), mother's needs (clothing, meds, manicures, etc.), baby's needs (breast- vs. bottle-feeding), family members and household needs (siblings, duties, shopping, menus, etc.), financial planning (budgets, insurance, investments), celebrations (showers, religious ceremonies), day care and babysitters, final countdown (labor, going home), and postpartum considerations (support systems). A second and separate table of contents lists organizers based upon trimester with pages listed for cross-referencing. Each page within the text is also labeled by trimester to establish a reference point.

### Evaluation:

The reader of this resource will find list upon list, chart upon chart, and more organizer tools than she/he ever dreamed of. Due to the wide number and variety of topics, one list or another is bound to be a helpful tool to "getting organized" during pregnancy. Readers will note the author's disclaimer: "each pregnancy is unique and the lists presented in this book are offered only as guidelines to help one organized." Consequently, the reader must think through the purpose and value of each particular list as he/she uses it. In this way the reader will not fall prey to ONLY relying on the author's list. Also, some lists appear to be superfluous and/or intimidating to most first-time parents. Truly, there is a need to get organized for the delightful, traumatic entry of a new person into one's life. But there is also the learning involved by living through this experience which too many lists and organization can too overly anticipate, such that the event becomes more a project than a mystery to be experienced. The book's central image is a very busy mother orchestrating all, but such an emphasis seems to ignore the evolving role of fathers both before and following the birth. If one lives for checking off lists and filling in charts, this resource will be a help.

### Where To Find/Buy:

Bookstores and libraries, or order direct by calling (800) 338-2232.

**Overall Rating**

★★

Those who like lists will love this; otherwise, too many lists, too much time involved

**Design, Ease Of Use**

★★

Two separate table of contents organize information by topic and by trimester; no index

1–4 Stars

**Author:**

Maureen Bard

Bard is a wife, a mother of two, and a career woman who lives in Indianapolis and is a faculty member at Indiana State University.

**Publisher:**

Meadowbrook Press

**Edition:**

2nd (1995)

**Price:**

$9.00

**Pages/Run Time:**

175

**ISBN:**

0881662429

**Media:**

Book

**Principal Subject:**

All-Inclusive Overview

**Age Group:**

Infants (0–1)

II. All-Inclusive Resources About Parenting

★★

**Overall Rating**
★★
In-depth full-text papers on numerous, but scattered, parenting topics

**Design, Ease Of Use**
★★
Much information provided here; gateways to other related sites

1–4 Stars

**Media:**
Internet

**Principal Subject:**
All-Inclusive Overview

**Age Group:**
Infants & Toddlers (0–3)

# NATIONAL PARENT INFORMATION NETWORK

## Description:

The National Parent Information Network is a project sponsored by two clearinghouses of information: the ERIC Clearinghouse on Urban Education at Teachers College, Columbia University, New York City, and the ERIC Clearinghouse on Elementary and Early Childhood Education at the University of Illinois at Urbana-Champaign. The network's purpose is to provide information to parents and to those who work with parents, and to foster the exchange of parenting materials. The NPIN website offers a variety of academic papers and research findings about many aspects of parenthood along with links to dozens of parenting-related websites and publications. It also provides a portal to the AskERIC website, an Internet-based information service for educators, parents, and others hosted by the two sponsoring university programs. AskERIC includes an email question-answering service and the AskERIC Virtual Library.

## Evaluation:

Here parents, educators, grandparents, and others who care about the welfare of children and families will find the latest academic research and full-text papers on parenting and families. Examples include: in the Parents and Families in Society section, "Centered on Families: Parenting Adolescents"; in the Child Care section, "Making Child Care Work for Everyone"; in the Parents and Schools as Partners section, "Building Parent-Teacher Partnerships"; and in the Early Childhood Learning section, "Discussing the News with 3- to 7-Year Olds: What To Do?" The topics offer a depth and breadth not often targeted toward strengthening the future of families. Access to the research alone, including the AskERIC opportunity to have personal parenting questions answered directly by researchers and educators, is worth the visit to this site.

## Where To Find/Buy:

On the Internet using the URL: http://ericps.ed.uiuc.edu/npin

# PAMPERS PARENTING INSTITUTE
Expert Advice For Caring Parents

★★

### Description:

This site is also dubbed "Total Baby Care: Newborn to Toddler." The homepage focuses on five main areas: "House Call," "Well Baby," "Healthy Baby Skin," "Pampers Diapers," and "Ask our Experts." T. Berry Brazelton, a pediatrician, offers advice, encouragement, and information about your child's development in "House Call." You may select your baby's age (newborn, three weeks, six weeks, etc., to three years) and interest area (feeding, sleeping, communication, cognitive, motor skills, etc.). "Well Baby" includes a comprehensive encyclopedia of child care information provided by Suzanne Dixon, MD, a pediatrician; various ages again can be selected along with interest areas. Caring for your baby's skin, from cord care to rashes and sunburn, is the focus of "Healthy Baby Skin," written by Alfred Lane, M.D., a pediatric dermatologist. Diapering and product information is included in "Pampers Diapers." "Ask our Experts" is just what the title implies—a list of frequently asked questions and their answers on topics such as development, behavior, sleep, feeding, and health. Visitors can submit questions and receive replies by email.

### Evaluation:

For those who enjoy T. Berry Brazelton and his perspectives, this site likely will prove disappointing. The information included within his segment is dry and barely covers the subject matter. His advice reads like "sound bites," lacking the usual warmth and compassion evidenced by "What Every Baby Knows," his television program. The site asks the visitor to select the child's age and choose an interest area; information is displayed and can then be browsed or printed. The developmental information in "Well Baby" is well laid out and easily can be read in a sitting. The information offered in this section is general in nature and offers guidelines to babycare in the various age groups. For instance, a sample menu is offered in the "feeding" section, according to age. The "House Call" section of the site answers questions and addresses problems regarding the same topics and age groups as "Well Baby." Together, the two sections of this website complement each other; one offers general information and the other answers specific questions about specific issues. Overall, this site is best when combined with other sources.

### Where To Find/Buy:

On the Internet at the URL: http://www.totalbabycare.com/

**Overall Rating**
★★
Information dry but adequate; Brazelton fans most likely will be disappointed here

**Design, Ease Of Use**
★★
Navigation design is average

1–4 Stars

**Publisher:**
Procter & Gamble

**Media:**
Internet

**Principal Subject:**
All-Inclusive Overview

**Age Group:**
Infants (0–1)

**★★**

### Overall Rating
★★
Summary information from other references, websites; unclear as to the source at times

### Design, Ease Of Use
★★
Improved site design, but can sometimes get lost, no site map; concise info is rather dry

1–4 Stars

### Media:
Internet

### Principal Subject:
All-Inclusive Overview

### Age Group:
Infants & Toddlers (0–3)

# PARENTING OF BABIES AND TODDLERS
Your Mining Co. Guide

## Description:
An at-home mother who studied child development, psychology, and other areas developed this site—one of The Mining Co.'s family of websites—to offer support and information on the issues facing parents of toddlers and babies. The homepage offers "Net Links" on various topics such as: answers from experts, baby care, baby's first year, child health and nutrition, early learning, etc. Topics are listed alphabetically. Each topic is a compilation of other resources' highlights (mainly print references), or a connection to other websites, or both; a one sentence summary of each resource is provided so parents will know the gist of what is included. The site's homepage also includes articles "In The Spotlight" consisting of the creator/author's newest features; drug addicted babies, crib to bed transition and one-income living were among topics spotlighted at the time of our visit. A chat room, bulletin boards and a newsletter are also provided. General topics are listed to one side of the page for reference. Feature articles are centered on the page, and the alphabetical listing of the articles is accessed on the right side of the page.

## Evaluation:
Once parents get to the information offered here, they'll find that the site does an acceptable job of presenting the major points concerning most parenting issues. Unfortunately, the source of the information at times is unclear and the visitor can only be confused at times regarding what he/she is reading—is it the creator's opinion, recaps from other sites, or references to other printed resources? This needs to be made more clear. Also, the online newsletter can only be accessed through a subscription, although past issues are readily available. The topics in those issues, however, should be indexed for easy search. The layout of this website is simple and effective. Easy navigation on the homepage consists of a list of general topics that are addressed. The available articles are alphabetized, but could be categorized. Despite the easy navigation, the content of the information tends to leave one wanting more information. Parents need to check out more solid resources.

## Where To Find/Buy:
On the Internet at the URL: http://babyparenting.miningco.com

# PARENTING YOUR TODDLER
The Expert's Guide To The Tough And Tender Years

## Description:
The Barnard College Center program, an organization with which one of the authors is affiliated, is based on the philosophy of Jean Piaget, who believed that children best learn through their own active exploration, with little interference from adults. In this book, the reader will find "both our philosophy and practical, hands-on recommendations about toddler issues such as toilet training, eating, sleeping, setting limits, playdates, preparing child for a new baby, separating, and becoming an individual." Additional chapters focus on siblings, caregivers, family vacations, potty training, temper tantrums, and other issues. Each of the 16 chapters contains subsections that address specific concerns of each topic. For example, the chapter on sleeping covers issues such as the bedtime routine, nighttime waking, nightmares, naps, the family bed, and other related issues. Throughout the book there are helpful lists, such as the signs of readiness for potty training. Question and answer sections also are included periodically throughout the book.

## Evaluation:
The authors say that the purpose of this book is to offer "not only step-by-step guidelines, but also helpful ways of talking to your toddler and understanding how to promote her independence and confidence." Basic themes throughout the book include: following the toddler's lead by not giving suggestions or changing what he's interested in, setting limits to make her feel safe, and understanding and articulating what he feels. The authors consider these concepts the foundation for raising a healthy child, and offer simple explanations of what to do in certain situations, such as when a child screams in a public place. Few books go into much detail about sibling interactions; this is an exception. Two particularly helpful chapters are those on preparing the toddler for a new baby and helping the toddler deal with a younger sibling. Advice is matter-of-fact and grounded in common practice. While this is an adequate source for basic information, the authors do not take any risks or offer any new, creative information that can't be found elsewhere, an approach that could have set this book apart.

## Where To Find/Buy:
Bookstores and libraries.

---

**Overall Rating**
★★
Descriptions and advice are clear, but offer relatively uncreative solutions

**Design, Ease Of Use**
★★
Chapter subjects are straightforward without frills

1–4 Stars

**Author:**
Patricia Henderson Shimm and Kate Ballen

Patricia Henderson Shimm has directed the Barnard College Center for Toddler Development for 20 years. Kate Ballen is an associate editor at Fortune magazine.

**Publisher:**
Perseus Books

**Edition:**
1995

**Price:**
$12.00

**Pages/Run Time:**
227

**ISBN:**
020162298X

**Media:**
Book

---

**Principal Subject:**
All-Inclusive Overview

**Age Group:**
Toddlers (1–3)

II. All-Inclusive Resources About Parenting

## Overall Rating
★★
Good information, but it's tough to wade through the material to get to the specifics

## Design, Ease Of Use
★
Desperately needs an index to cross-reference a clumsy table of contents

1–4 Stars

## Author:
Robin Goldstein with Janet Gallant

Robin Goldstein, MA, is a parenting consultant and educator. She has taught college courses on child development and helps preschools plan and improve their programs. She writes a newspaper column on child rearing.

## Publisher:
Penguin Books

## Edition:
1990

## Price:
$7.95

## Pages/Run Time:
267

## ISBN:
0140133453

## Media:
Book

## Principal Subject:
All-Inclusive Overview

## Age Group:
Infants & Toddlers (0–3)

# EVERYDAY PARENTING
## The First Five Years

## Description:
This ten-chapter book includes the following issues: dependency; sleeping; eating; independence; setting limits; children's thinking; fear and imagination; toys, play, and socializing; being nice; and caretakers and preschools. There is no index, but instead the subtopics are listed in the table of contents under the ten chapter topics. This 267-page book is based upon the author's newspaper column on child rearing and its aim is to answer the questions that parents most often asked her. Within each chapter there are approximately six to twelve subtopics, some in a question and answer format, such as, "Why Is My Child Afraid of Santa Claus?" Other topics include questions about spanking, falls and accidents, taking a child to the dentist, and how to know when a child is ready for kindergarten. Over 90 questions are addressed in the book. This book does not offer parents a "comprehensive look at theory" but instead is designed to "offer practical advice on the specific issues of child rearing."

## Evaluation:
By answering common questions parents ask about raising children, this book is a somewhat useful and practical guide for parents. It offers a basic understanding of a child's social, intellectual, and emotional needs but in a limited sense. It is not comprehensive, but instead takes a rather relaxed and random approach. An index would have been beneficial to this guide. This way parents, interested in "practical advice" on a given topic, could more easily locate the information especially if it is included in several chapters. The articles deal generally with children from infancy to five years of age. The book, by grouping this wide age range and not breaking the topics up by age group, makes it less desirable and less usable. For example, in selecting a caregiver, the needs of parents of infants will be different from those of preschoolers, but the information in the book is not easily differentiated. Such broad blanket suggestions may well confuse parents who are seeking more age-specific advice. This is a lukewarm reference; parents can do better.

## Where To Find/Buy:
Bookstores and libraries, or order direct by calling (800) 253-6476.

# HOW TO PARENT
The Indispensable Guide To Your Child's Formative Years

★★

## Description:

This book is composed of 14 chapters in 444 pages. Chapter One begins with information on mothers: their feelings, adjustments to being a mom, and a description of children's early stages of development. Chapter Two takes the reader into the world of infants, from birth to twelve months of age, and is divided into three month segments. General information on toddlers can be found in Chapter Three, while Chapters Four and Five further explore this stage in terms of a child's "first adolescence." Here the author discusses topics such as feelings, temper tantrums, toilet training, play, and more. Chapters Six and Seven address the preschool years with topics such as impulses, peers, sexuality, choosing preschools and kindergarten, and more. Chapters Eight and Nine focus on discipline. Violence and its influence in the media and children's toys can be found in Chapter Ten. The remaining chapters (11–13) discuss ways parents can teach their child (language, reading, math, etc.) and how to select toys and books for children. A summary of the guide's major points is included in Chapter 14. There is no index; the author states, it was "meant to be read as a unified whole."

**Author:**
Dr. Fitzhugh Dodson

Fitzhugh Dodson, PhD has more
than twenty years of professional
work, both as a psychologist and
an educator. He has appeared on
TV and radio show, and lectures
throughout the U.S. Dodson is an
honors graduate of John Hopkins
and Yale universities.

## Evaluation:

The author has purposefully not included an index. His intention is that if readers can't look up specific topics, they will then need to read the entire guide and will gain a better understanding of the whole development process. This is not, however, convenient or user-friendly for those who have read the whole book and are trying to relocate information. Much useful information is given, but some information is bent towards the author's strong opinion. This is evidenced especially in his advice regarding breastfeeding and teaching preschoolers; the author believes there is no scientific evidence that breastfeeding is better physically for the baby than bottlefeeding; he also believes children should be taught some skills (math, reading, etc.) before their school years begin. Some strong sweeping generalizations are included, such as "the new mother's whole life now seems to revolve around this little baby . . . and frankly she resents this." Since the book's 1970 copyright date, more current information about parenting has come to light. Unless parents know what to weed out, they would be best advised to look for more updated material.

**Publisher:**
Signet (Penguin Group/
Penguin USA)

**Edition:**
1970

**Price:**
$6.99

**Pages/Run Time:**
444

**ISBN:**
0451156250

**Media:**
Book

**Principal Subject:**
All-Inclusive Overview

**Age Group:**
Infants & Toddlers (0–3)

## Where To Find/Buy:

Bookstore, libraries, or order direct by contacting Penguin USA at P.O. Box 999, Dept. #17109, Bergenfield, New Jersey 07621, or by calling (800) 253-6476.

**★★**

**Overall Rating**
★★
Excellent graphics, much opportunity for visitor participation

**Design, Ease Of Use**
★
Horribly disorganized, information not worth the effort needed to find it

1–4 Stars

**Media:**
Internet

**Principal Subject:**
All-Inclusive Overview

**Age Group:**
Infants & Toddlers (0–3)

# PARENTHOODWEB

## Description:
Various options are available at this website's homepage. Visitors can gain quick access to spotlighted topical questions, participate in a quick poll to express an opinion on a given subject, review "facts and figures" (news abstracts), and note the latest product recall notices. Also available are birth announcements, greeting cards, and links to other parenting sites. The visitor to this site can offer her/his opinion on pregnancy and parenting issues. Articles focusing on pregnancy, labor, childcare, and parenting issues are available throughout the website. Many articles are linked to other websites. Additional resources are listed and a weekly newsletter is available through email. Various areas allow you to either ask questions of experts (their bios are given) or read their responses to others' questions. Links to topics include shopping, pregnancy, recipes, sleep, names, safety, chat rooms, and boards. Graphics, photos, and illustrations of particular issues are woven throughout.

## Evaluation:
Good luck to any visitor trying to find a way around this navigational nightmare. This site is so disorganized that it distracts, even discourages, a visitor from taking the time to unearth valuable information. Much of this site offers parents chances to be heard and to hear others; this certainly will fill a need for parents at home looking for others' feedback. The homepage offers many links to articles and information, none of it organized in any recognizable manner. The information available needs to be categorized in age groups or main issues. On the positive side, this site offers good opportunities for a visitor to participate in polls, chat areas, and message boards. The graphics are excellent. For example, in the Pregnancy section, photographs of fetal ultrasounds are better than those found in most doctors' offices. Also available in the same section are a series of charts that detail fetal growth in each month of pregnancy, supplemented by detailed illustrations. Overall, however, this site offers nothing that one can't find elsewhere with much less effort and confusion.

## Where To Find/Buy:
On the Internet at the URL: http://www.parenthoodweb.com/

# THE CYBERMOM DOT COM

### Description:
Developed by a husband-and-wife team with advertising backgrounds, this site's "floor plan" is laid out to reflect the rooms in a home. The Library offers a parenting resource section; the Study encompasses work, careers, daycare, and other topics; the Powder Room offers health and beauty information; the Guest Room presents features from guest experts; the Kitchen offers recipes and household hints; the Playroom includes "everything about the kids, toys, homework, software and the Web," and the Family Room houses reviews, draft ideas, and stories. Other features include "best birthday gift ideas," The CyberMom's 100 Best Children's Books, parenting Tip of the Day, shopping online, parenting chat boards, opportunities for live chats, and horoscopes.

### Evaluation:
Parents looking for a break from parent-intensive sites will find The CyberMom Dot Com may be worth a quick visit. Its goal is to provide a well-rounded offering of home, personal, and parenting activities and information. In that, it succeeds well enough. Information presented here is for parents of children of all ages. The parent library section on toddlers offers information on 30 topics with an extensive list of articles; each section includes additional tips and list of resources. Unfortunately, there is no indication of where the information comes from. Articles lack documentation, so visitors are left to either believe willy-nilly anything that is presented there or attempt to sort out for themselves if the information is valid or has value. Chat boards on topics such as eating concerns and potty training are active. The most distressing aspect of the site, however, is its heavy commercial tone. While not sponsored by a company, the site's authors have taken the use of site banners and web advertisements to a new high—or low. And infuriatingly, it seems the ads are the fastest to draw, so you're left staring at the advertisement while the rest of the page leisurely loads. Overall, The CyberMom Dot Com probably is worth a quick visit, but don't bother to bookmark it.

### Where To Find/Buy:
On the Internet at the URL: http://www.TheCyberMom.com/

**Overall Rating**
★
Heavy commercialism; sources of information not documented

**Design, Ease Of Use**
★★★
"Floor plan" layout attractive and easy to navigate

1–4 Stars

**Media:**
Internet

**Principal Subject:**
All-Inclusive Overview

**Age Group:**
Infants & Toddlers (0–3)

II. All-Inclusive Resources About Parenting

**Overall Rating**
★
Methods founded in
questionable assumptions

**Design, Ease Of Use**
★★★
Succinct information provided
in an organized manner;
negativistic in tone

1–4 Stars

**Author:**
Gary Ezzo and Robert
Buchnam, MD

Gary Ezzo is a graduate of
Theology and executive director
of Growing Families International.
He and his wife have co-authored
parent curriculums. Dr. Robert
Buchnam is a pediatrician in the
Denver area.

**Publisher:**
Multnomah Books
(Questar Publishers)

**Edition:**
1995

**Price:**
$9.99

**Pages/Run Time:**
134

**ISBN:**
0880708077

**Media:**
Book

**Principal Subject:**
All-Inclusive Overview

**Age Group:**
Infants & Toddlers (0–3)

# ON BECOMING BABYWISE, BOOK TWO
Parenting Your Pre-Toddler Five To Fifteen Months

## Description:
This book builds upon Ezzo's previous book, On Becoming Babywise, and readers are encouraged to become familiar with its principles. There are seven brief chapters in this book, and three appendices. The first chapter—"Back to the Basics"—reviews the three foundations of the author's philosophy including the importance of prioritizing marriage, recognizing the dangers of child-centered parenting, and knowing how to avoid extremism in the parenting process. Chapter Two—"Moral Foundations"—discusses growth and learning. In the third chapter—"Mealtime Activities"—the authors describe weaning and appropriate foods for pre-toddlers. The fourth chapter on "Highchair Manners" uses this setting as the backdrop for discipline and behavior training. "Waketime Activities" are discussed in Chapter Five. Those activities include the use of a playpen, time with family members, and free playtime. The authors offer "Some Thoughts about Discipline" in Chapter Six. Finally, Chapter Seven focuses on "Nap and Sleeptime Activities." Child language development, teaching sign language, and potty training are explained in the three appendices.

## Evaluation:
The authors state that, "The moral training of a child is the foundation of his or her upbringing . . . the result being a child who is healthy, happy, and relationally secure throughout life." This assumes a simplistic cause-effect view that being moral guarantees happiness. If only life were that easy. While many would agree that morality training should be a vital part of every child's upbringing, and will definitely put a child on a path leading to lifelong happiness, it should not be relied upon as the sole source of finding happiness. Many other factors may enter into that equation. Another major doubt that arises from reading this book is the authors' contention that children of this age range are willfully disobedient. Their methods of discipline (verbal reprimand, using the crib for isolating the baby or child, losing a privilege or toy, swatting the baby or child's hand) then are based on this assumption, lending a negativistic tone to the authors' discussion. While it is always appropriate to set boundaries for children, at this age those boundaries are primarily set for the child's safety, while still providing them with an opportunity to learn, experiment, and grow. Readers will find other resources suit their needs better than this one.

## Where To Find/Buy:
Bookstores and libraries.

# THE BABY JOURNAL
## Your Weekly Guide To Baby's First Year

### Description:

The companion book to *The Maternal Journal*, this resource "is designed to provide you with an enriched experience of your baby's first year of life." Accompanied by color illustrations, *The Baby Journal* provides developmental milestones, facts, tips, and selected information about one's baby from his/her first month through the fourteenth. Presented in a wall-calendar style, it also has a little space (about 1" x 1") for making notes about the baby from day to day. Special highlighted tips (roughly half a page) include information on giving massage to one's baby, skin care, bathtime, getting more sleep for the parent and the baby, exercise tips for mothers, introducing solid foods, babyproofing one's home, emergencies/first aid, playtime, weaning, choosing toys, avoiding gender stereotypes when choosing toys, and interacting with one's child.

### Evaluation:

As this "journal" aims more at entertainment than information, an introduction warns the reader that it is "by no means intended to be a comprehensive encyclopedia of all existing data on raising children." With that in mind, potential consumers must weigh this book's value against the more extensive information the same money would purchase in another resource. Advice offered here is really on the slim side. Additionally, there is hardly any space for mothers to actually write notes or journal entries, an activity that many parents may find useful and cathartic. The illustrations are amusing, and it makes a colorful wall-hanging. But parents should save their dollars and buy either a real journal with adequate space, a good book on baby care, or even a nature/art calendar that your baby will enjoy looking at too.

### Where To Find/Buy:

Bookstores and libraries, or order direct by calling (800) 338-2232.

---

**Overall Rating**
★
Entertaining but not really informative

**Design, Ease Of Use**
★★
Some useful tips and amusing color illustrations

1–4 Stars

**Author:**
Matthew Bennett

**Publisher:**
Meadowbrook Press

**Edition:**
1992

**Price:**
$10.00

**ISBN:**
0671867776

**Media:**
Book

**Principal Subject:**
All-Inclusive Overview

**Age Group:**
Infants (0–1)

**Overall Rating**
★
Watch for hidden commercials; subtly encourages use of Enfamil® baby formula

**Design, Ease Of Use**
★★
Easy to navigate

1–4 Stars

**Media:**
Internet

**Principal Subject:**
All-Inclusive Overview

**Age Group:**
Infants & Toddlers (0–3)

# MOMNESS CENTER

**Description:**

The Momness Center web site is sponsored by Mead Johnson, makers of the Enfamil® family of baby formulas. Its goal is to be "the place for information and inspiration for moms and moms-to-be. "The homepage offers a number of selections, including "Baby Care," a collection of guides for the new mother, from breastfeeding to daycare; "As Your Baby Grows," a month by month account of fetal development from conception to the first few weeks after birth; "Chronicle of a New Mom," the personal story of one new mother; and "Beautiful Mom . . . and Mom-to-be," which offers information on the physiological changes during pregnancy, wardrobe tips for pregnant women, and "thoughts from the online community on what makes motherhood beautiful." A fifth selection, "Baby 123" invites visitors to join the site's online club and receive special product offers and discounts. The site also offers archived informational material on everything from a list of what to pack for the hospital to "Help! My Baby is Turning Into a Toddler," FAQs, and links.

**Evaluation:**

This is an attractive and well-designed site full of helpful basic information. It also is a website that requires a strong caution. It is sponsored by Mead Johnson, the makers of the Enfamil® family of baby formulas. While the site includes sections that discuss why breastfeeding is best for baby and mother with tips on successful breastfeeding, breast care, and expressing and storing mother's milk, it includes many other references that suggest, incorrectly, that most breastfeeding women will want to rely to some extent on commercial infant formulas. The wording is subtle and, while it may be unintentional, it also is obvious. Example: a large subheading is entitled "When You Need to Supplement," instead of "If You Need to Supplement." That section then proceeds to say that "almost every nursing mother will need (ed: not choose) to supplement her baby with bottled breast milk or an infant formula." Another section contains wording that suggests Enfamil® formulas are almost identical to breast milk. Inaccuracies such as these mar an otherwise enjoyable site and lend worry that inexperienced parents will accept these statements as fact, when more accurate and supportive information about breastfeeding and its benefits is available elsewhere.

**Where To Find/Buy:**

On the Internet at http://www.womenslink.com/momness/index.htm

# TODDLER TAMING
## A Survival Guide For Parents

### Description:

The purpose of this book, according to the author, is to ". . . give some practical, commonsense advice, boost parents' self-confidence, and make them feel happier and more in control." All aspects of raising a toddler are included in this book. Some of the 20-chapter topics include: developmental stages of a toddler, normal and abnormal behavior, making life easier, tantrums, sleep problems, diet, fears, and many others. The last few chapters address such issues as toddler education, working mothers, single parents, grandparents, the handicapped toddler, and common toddler illnesses. Within each chapter, subtopics are described. For example, the chapter on discipline addresses different methods of discipline, from spanking to negotiation. The author categorizes the types of attention that parents give their children and calls them Grade A attention (the best attention a parent can give), Grade B attention, on down to Grade Z attention (the worst, no attention at all). Tantrums, the author believes, are manifested in many forms and he offers suggestions on how to deal with them. Examples and stories are given throughout to illustrate a particular subject.

### Evaluation:

The overall tone of this book seems to encourage the parent not to worry as the author reminds the parent that most behavior, especially difficult behavior, is normal, just relax. An admirable message, and one of the very few positive things that can be said about this book. In the first few chapters, as the author discusses developmental stages and general toddler behaviors, it seems as if he addresses the child only when he or she is being troublesome. No child—even an active toddler—is difficult all the time. One of the few truly helpful chapters is on feeding. The author's philosophy is that a child should not be forced to eat when he or she doesn't want to, which seems to be something most parents forget, even in our enlightened times. A child should be encouraged to eat with the family, but not forced to "finish his plate," the author suggests. While Green manages to touch on just about every possible topic, the advice is quite ordinary and at times too simplistic. For example, ". . . young children tend to feel much more secure when they live in an environment that has structure and clearly defined limits." Overall, the information offered in this book is no more unique than that contained in hundreds of other toddler advice books, and there are many that are much better.

### Where To Find/Buy:

Bookstores and libraries.

---

**Overall Rating**
★
Bland information that can be better found elsewhere

**Design, Ease Of Use**
★★
Organization within the chapters is adequate; chapter organization is random

1–4 Stars

**Author:**
Dr. Christopher Green

Dr. Christopher Green is a renowned pediatrician and was the head of the Child Development Unit at the Royal Alexandra Hospital for Children in Australia. He also is author of Dr. Greens Baby Book and Understanding A.D.H.D..

**Publisher:**
Fawcett Columbine (Ballantine Books/Random House)

**Edition:**
1984

**Price:**
$11.95

**Pages/Run Time:**
224

**ISBN:**
0449901556

**Media:**
Book

**Principal Subject:**
All-Inclusive Overview

**Age Group:**
Toddlers (1–3)

II. All-Inclusive Resources About Parenting

## Overall Rating
★

Another parenting theory, this one based on 1950s Re-evaluation Counseling

## Design, Ease Of Use
★

Unfriendly, impersonal tone with language too dense to read easily

1–4 Stars

## Author:
Aletha J. Solter, PhD

Dr. Aletha Solter is a developmental psychologist who studied with Dr. Jean Piaget. She has been working with parents since 1978 and conducts workshops. She is the mother of two children.

## Publisher:
Shining Star Press

## Edition:
1994

## Price:
$11.95

## Pages/Run Time:
271

## ISBN:
0961307307

## Media:
Book

## Principal Subject:
All-Inclusive Overview

## Age Group:
Infants (0–1)

# THE AWARE BABY
## A New Approach To Parenting

## Description:
In this book, the author seeks to teach the reader to understand baby's emotional needs. Chapter One of this book is entitled "Beginning: Letting Your Baby Feel Loved" and addresses bonding, the birth experience, and holding the new baby. In Chapter Two "Crying: Letting Your Baby Release Tension"—the author goes into detail about baby's crying. Chapter titles are as follows: "Sleep: Letting Your Baby Rest"; "Food: Letting Your Baby Nourish Himself"; "Play: Letting Your Baby Learn"; "Conflicts: Letting Your Baby Feel Respected"; and "Attachment: Letting Your Baby Feel Safe." At the end of each chapter, the author includes a series of exercises to help parents enhance their personal strengths and overcome any weaknesses. The exercises and philosophies in this book are loosely based on the Re-evaluation Counseling theory developed in the 1950s, in which adults relearn the ability to express intense emotions (crying, laughing, shaking, and raging) in order to heal themselves of past hurtful experiences.

## Evaluation:
The author begins by presenting the "four basic assumptions concerning human nature" that underlie the ideas in this book. He believes that human beings are born knowing what they need for optimal development, that they are born with the potential for both good and bad behavior, that experiences in life can have a profound and lasting effect on feelings and behavior patterns, and that effects of traumatic experiences are reversible. The author uses this platform then to teach the reader how best to develop a child's emotional stability. Unfortunately, the author's message is completely lost in this dry and humorless textbook. Included are many recitations of studies on the emotional development of babies, a fascinating subject whose effect here is to simply bore the reader. The language is unnecessarily technical for the target audience. For example, a table that describes a baby's negative behavior and possible cause is called, "Examples of Common Control Patterns in Babies and Their Possible Origins." Also, the author works on the premise that many of an infant or toddler's cries are due to the mourning of a past hurt, as opposed to expressing a current need. With a cornucopia of books available today on "how to raise a healthy and happy baby," this comes across as just another theory.

## Where To Find/Buy:
Bookstores and libraries.

# THE BABY AND CHILD PLACE

## Description:

Various options are presented at this site's homepage. Pertinent topics are entitled: "Passionate About Parenting," "On the Fire," "Net Nurse," "Your Section: Parents' Articles and Comments," along with online baby pictures. Visitors may view photos or submit their own baby's picture. "Passionate About Parenting" is a new feature to this site in which an author writes weekly on a given topic. One recent example is "Quality and Quantity," a half-page of advice to parents about giving time to their child, written by the editor/publisher of Nurturing Magazine. "On the Fire" offers one the chance to submit questions and responses, or read responses to questions already posed to the site; currently seven questions are listed. "Net Nurse" offers advice about common questions parents might have concerning their child, such as "What is that stuff in my baby's eyes?" written by a nurse with a disclaimer to seek medical attention if symptoms arise. "Your Section . . ." includes advice and suggestions by parents on various subjects ranging from eating dinner to discipline to teething.

## Evaluation:

This site dreams of being a place "where parents can go to find everything they want to help care for their children." That dream has not, as yet, been accomplished. Due to its amateurish layout and content, visitors to this site will spend far more time figuring out where they're going and what they're reading than the resulting material is worth. Even if the site improves its design in the future, there isn't much content to hold it together. This site desperately needs direction, purpose, and an underlying premise. Parents want sincere answers, not pat responses (on how to have a "healthy, happy and active baby": "while your baby is asleep for about 3–4 hours, you have all this time for yourself . . ."). Parents want helpful advice, not cliches ("One of the most important ways to be a good parent is to be there . . ."). In summary, parents will want to spend their precious time with other resources.

## Where To Find/Buy:

On the Internet at the URL: http://www.babyplace.com/

**Overall Rating**
★
This site lacks interest and purpose

**Design, Ease Of Use**
★
Amateurish layout is distracting, as are the typos; no graphics except for the logo

1–4 Stars

**Media:**
Internet

**Principal Subject:**
All-Inclusive Overview

**Age Group:**
Infants & Toddlers (0–3)

II. All-Inclusive Resources About Parenting

## Overall Rating
★

Very basic information; access to overall information limited based on registration data

## Design, Ease Of Use
★

Navigation frustrating at times; must register to use the site

1–4 Stars

**Publisher:**
women.com Network

**Media:**
Internet

**Principal Subject:**
All-Inclusive Overview

**Age Group:**
Infants & Toddlers (0–3)

# STORKSITE
The Premier Pregnancy And New Parenting Website

## Description:

StorkSite's goal is to "provide emotional and informational support in an interactive, community-based environment." A visitor must register to gain access to the site's free features, which include "The Front Porch," the "Stork Site Library," "The Storkzine," and "The Picket Fence." The Front Porch offers a personal due date ticker, suggested baby names, email notices, access to a reference library, chat rooms, Baby Grams and more. Baby Grams are one-page monthly descriptions of a baby's growth and development from early pregnancy to about 2 years of age. The Storkzine, the online magazine, offers various articles (typically one-page) on pregnancy, childbirth, and the first year; recent articles dealt with postpartum blues, hot spots to raise children, and myths regarding birth control pills. "Ask Tori R.N." is a Q & A forum for issues concerning pregnancy and childbirth. Users can access a glossary, name database, medical references, and more through The Stork Site Library. The Picket Fence, "the heart and soul of Stork Site's community," offers chat rooms, "Best Friends Forums," and other features.

## Evaluation:

This website offers little information on pregnancy, childbirth or baby care. Once a visitor has registered, information provided at various points is specific only to the biographical information submitted through the registration process. This limits the user to finding information that may be current to his or her situation, but doesn't allow a visitor to explore ideas or problems in general. The user is unable to access Baby Grams on older children (just those under 2 years old). Reference materials available through both The Storkzine and The Stork Site Library may be useful for some. Many of these references, however, are either too unwieldy (medical abstracts) or too brief to be relevant to many parents' needs. The Picket Fence may provide some emotional support; the Q & A forum provides interesting feedback, but it's one person's viewpoint, not a team that might offer varying points of view to consider. In short, a parent can look elsewhere for more comprehensive and user-friendly information.

## Where To Find/Buy:
On the Internet at the URL: http://www. storksite.com/index2.html

# SPECIAL
# RESOURCES
# FOR SPECIFIC
# PURPOSES

III

# Special Resources For Specific Purposes

During the course of our ongoing research, we have determined several other "views" of the resources we have reviewed. Each of the 12 resources listed in this section uniquely meets a specific purpose for various parenting circumstances. We have placed a short description of each here so you get a foretaste, and we have cross-referenced the full-page review on each so you can further review our descriptions and evaluations of the resource's contents.

These specific resources focus on:

- Nursing mothers who want to continue breastfeeding when they return to work
- Support and advice for parents who continue to nurse their child beyond one year
- The how-tos of infant care and development (using a videotape)
- The how-tos of infant care and development (using CD-ROM)
- Understanding a baby's development (using a videotape)
- Choosing a nanny as caregiver of your baby
- Parenting twins or multiples
- Parenting an only child
- Parenting a strong-willed child
- Christian perspectives on child care, child development, and parenting choices
- Correlating the latest in brain research with suggested advice for raising young children
- Helping both a parent and a child adjust to a new sibling (using companion videotapes)

Take some time to read the full descriptions and evaluations for each recommended resource carefully. We are certain that you will discover the right resources to best serve your family's needs.

## Nursing mothers who want to continue breastfeeding when they return to work

| | |
|---|---|
| **Title:** | **Nursing Mother, Working Mother** |
| **Subtitle:** | The Essential Guide For Breastfeeding And Staying Close To Your Baby After You Return To Work |
| **Author:** | Gale Pryor |
| **Overall Rating:** | ★★★★ |
| **Media Type:** | Book |
| **Short Description:** | Extending a section of her other book, Nursing Your Baby, Pryor discusses how to combine work and breastfeeding. Within this seven chapter book, the whys and hows of breastfeeding are given along with a plea to change workplace attitudes. Three chapters specifically focus on the transition from new motherhood to work including maternity leave, getting ready (supplies, finding care, etc.), and returning to work. |

■ **Read The Full Review Of This Resource On Page 38.**

## Support and advice for parents who continue to nurse their child beyond one year

| | |
|---|---|
| **Title:** | **Mothering Your Nursing Toddler** |
| **Author:** | Norma Jane Bumgarner |
| **Overall Rating:** | ★★★★ |
| **Media Type:** | Book |
| **Short Description:** | Believing that nursing plays a great role in a child's ability to grow up, Bumgarner focuses on the breastfeeding relationship in terms of the child's developmental needs. Advice and information is given on the "whys" of breastfeeding (for mother and for child), the "hows" of nursing (marital concerns, night nursing, mother's health, etc.), the changing dynamics of the breastfeeding relationship (to age four and beyond), and various ways to approach weaning. |

■ **Read The Full Review Of This Resource On Page 37.**

## The how-tos of infant care and development (using a videotape)

| | |
|---|---|
| **Title:** | **Baby Basics (Videotape)** |
| **Subtitle:** | The Complete Video Guide For New And Expectant Parents |
| **Overall Rating:** | ★★★★ |
| **Media Type:** | Videotape |
| **Short Description:** | Divided into eight "chapters," this 110 minute videotape focuses on the development and care of newborns and infants. Topics discussed include: the newborn's appearances, postpartum care of the mother, adjusting during the first days at home, daily care (bathing, diapering, dressing, and more), feeding (breastfeeding, bottlefeeding), health and safety, babies' cries, sleep patterns, and infants' growth and development. |

■ **Read The Full Review Of This Resource On Page 17.**

## The how-tos of infant care and development (using CD-ROM)

| | |
|---|---|
| **Title:** | **Your Pregnancy, Your Newborn** |
| **Subtitle:** | The Complete Guide For Expectant And New Mothers |
| **Overall Rating:** | ★★★★ |
| **Media Type:** | CD-ROM |
| **Short Description:** | Developed by the editors of PARENTING magazine, this CD-ROM focuses on pregnancy topics and a newborn baby's needs. Pregnancy issues include how to plan for pregnancy, a month-by-month description of pregnancy, and labor & delivery. Discussions about a newborn's care focus on the first few weeks and "Life With Baby." Advice is given on how to adapt to the changes, how to take care of a baby, and how to seek childcare. |

■ **Read The Full Review Of This Resource On Page 18.**

## Understanding a baby's development (using a videotape)

| | |
|---|---|
| **Title:** | **Touchpoints, Volume 2** |
| **Subtitle:** | The First Month Through The First Year |
| **Overall Rating:** | ★★★★ |
| **Media Type:** | Videotape |
| **Short Description:** | Brazelton's 45 minute videotape focuses on the emotional, cognitive, and motor development of babies from one month to 15 months. Five different families are showcased along with their frustrations, concerns, and joys. More than 15 "touchpoints" are illustrated and explained sequentially through the tape. Touchpoints are, as Brazelton defines them, "periods of time that precede a rapid growth in learning for both child and parent." |

■ **Read The Full Review Of This Resource On Page 99.**

## Choosing a nanny as caregiver of your baby

| | |
|---|---|
| **Title:** | **The Safe Nanny Handbook** |
| **Subtitle:** | Everything You Need To Know To Have Peace Of Mind When Your Child Is In Someone Else's Care |
| **Author:** | Peggy Robin |
| **Overall Rating:** | ★★★★ |
| **Media Type:** | Book |
| **Short Description:** | This book addresses the process for hiring a nanny, from the decision to hire a nanny through having to fire a nanny. Explanations are provided on hiring a nanny either through an agency or independently, the stages of the hiring process, and negotiating an agreement. Tips on how to handle a variety of common problems, sample employment agreements, and ways to train the nanny are included. |

■ **Read The Full Review Of This Resource On Page 52.**

## Parenting twins or multiples

| | |
|---|---|
| **Title:** | **The Joy Of Twins And Other Multiple Births** |
| **Subtitle:** | Having, Raising, And Loving Babies Who Arrive In Groups |
| **Author:** | Pamela Patrick Novotny |
| **Overall Rating:** | ★★★★ |
| **Media Type:** | Book |
| **Short Description:** | The author strives to offer "an upbeat, practical guide to raising and loving babies that arrive in groups of two or more." This book contains medical, psychological, and sociological findings on caring for two or more children simultaneously. Chapter topics include: the logistics of caring for multiples after birth, through their first year, and beyond; mother care; family adjustments; premature births; and more. |

■ **Read The Full Review Of This Resource On Page 274.**

## Parenting an only child

| | |
|---|---|
| **Title:** | **Parenting An Only Child** |
| **Subtitle:** | The Joys And Challenges Of Raising Your One And Only |
| **Author:** | Susan Newman |
| **Overall Rating:** | ★★★★ |
| **Media Type:** | Book |
| **Short Description:** | Divided into three parts, this guide focuses on the needs of only children and their parents. Myths are debunked, advice tendered on raising only children, and suggestions given for dealing with others' demands and questions. Compiled from the input, quotes, and anecdotal stories of over 200 people, this guide aims to support "threesome" families' decisions not to have additional children. Quotes from onlies are also given. |

■ **Read The Full Review Of This Resource On Page 207.**

## Parenting a strong-willed child

| | |
|---|---|
| **Title:** | **Parenting The Strong-Willed Child** |
| **Subtitle:** | The Clinically Proven Five-Week Program For Parents Of Two- To Six-Year-Olds |
| **Author:** | Rex Forehand, PhD and Nicholas Long, PhD |
| **Overall Rating:** | ★★★★ |
| **Media Type:** | Book |
| **Short Description:** | This book focuses on a program to help parents of strong-willed children find positive and manageable solutions to their children's difficult behavior. The four parts of this book highlight factors that cause and contribute to strong-willed behavior, techniques of the authors' five-week program, ways to develop a positive environment in the home, and how to deal with specific behavior problems (temper tantrums, aggression, etc.). |

■ **Read The Full Review Of This Resource On Page 158.**

## Christian perspectives on child care, child development, and parenting choices

| | |
|---|---|
| **Title:** | **The Focus On The Family Complete Book Of Baby And Child Care** |
| **Subtitle:** | From Pre-birth Through The Teen Years |
| **Author:** | Paul C. Reisser, MD |
| **Overall Rating:** | ★★★★ |
| **Media Type:** | Book |
| **Short Description:** | This book addresses a child's growth, development, and care at different ages from pre-birth through the adolescent years. Sections entitled "Special Concerns" deal with specific issues. All topics are addressed with a Christian perspective presenting the pros and cons of various Christian viewpoints. The book is divided into two sections, the first offers a chronological tour of a child's life, the second includes a health care reference. |

■ Read The Full Review Of This Resource On Page 273.

## Correlating the latest in brain research with suggested advice for raising young children

| | |
|---|---|
| **Title:** | **I Am Your Child** |
| **Overall Rating:** | ★★★★ |
| **Media Type:** | Internet |
| **Short Description:** | Supporting a national campaign "to make early childhood development a top priority for our nation," this website correlates the latest findings in brain research to the first three years of a child's development. Ten guidelines for raising children are offered, along with brain research data, details about child development from prenatal to age three, questions, answers and insight from "top experts" (Brazelton, Koop, etc.), and more. |

■ Read The Full Review Of This Resource On Page 96.

## Helping both a parent and a child adjust to a new sibling (using companion videotapes)

| | |
|---|---|
| **Title:** | **Those Baby Blues** |
| **Subtitle:** | A Parent's Guide To Helping Your Child Adjust To The New Baby |
| **Overall Rating:** | ★★★★ |
| **Media Type:** | Videotape |
| **Short Description:** | Combining family stories, footage of sibling interactions, and professional advice, this 30 minute videotape focuses on sibling rivalry. Discussions include changes in behavior, throwing tantrums, aggression, hidden hostility, regression, "nothing's wrong," depression, and withdrawal. Advice and tips are given for ways to handle each reaction and understand the child's behavior. A complimentary video for siblings is also provided. |

■ Read The Full Review Of This Resource On Page 262.

# Helpful
# Organizations

IV

# HELPFUL ORGANIZATIONS

Many of the resources we have reviewed include contact information on support groups, associations, and other organizations. On the pages that follow, we have listed a number of these organizations. They are grouped by the principal focus of their work as it relates to the chapters in this guidebook. You will find that many of these organizations can further refer you to other local, regional, or national organizations that may offer you additional benefits or aspects of support that meet your needs.

The support groups, associations, and other organizations which follow are listed alphabetically within the following topics and subtopics:

## General Information

### American Academy of Pediatrics

141 Northwest Point Blvd.
Elk Grove Village, IL 60007-1098

**Phone:** (847) 228-5005
**Fax:** (847) 228-5097

**Email:** kidsdocs@aap.org
**URL:** http://www.aap.org/

The American Academy of Pediatrics is an organization consisting of 55,000 primary care pediatricians, pediatric medical subspecialists, and pediatric surgical specialists dedicated to the health, safety, and well-being of infants, children, adolescents, and young adults. They provide information and publish free brochures for parents and professionals related to children's health issues.

### Center For Study Of Multiple Birth

33 East Superior Street
Chicago, IL 60611

**Phone:** (312) 266-9093
**Fax:** (312) 280-8500

**URL:** http://multiplebirth.com/

The CSMB's goal is to promote and advance the health of women and children, especially multiple birth children, through public service, education and research. The center offers printed information by mail upon request.

### Children's Defense Fund

25 E Street NW
Washington, DC 20001

**Phone:** (202) 628-8787

**Email:** cdfinfo@childrensdefense.org
**URL:** http://childrensdefense.org

Calling itself "America's strongest voice for children," the mission of the Children's Defense Fund is to "ensure every child a Healthy Start, a Head Start, a Fair Start, a Safe Start, and a Moral Start in life and successful passage to adulthood with the help of caring families and communities." Founded in 1973, the CDF is a private, nonprofit organization which pays particular attention to the needs of poor and minority children and those with disabilities. It offers advocacy, education, resource materials, and support to parents, parenting groups, educators, and others.

### Consumer Product Safety Commission

Publication Request
330 East-West Highway
Bethesda, MD

**Phone:** (800) 638-CPSC (2772)
**Fax:** (301) 504-0051

**URL:** http://www.cpsc.gov

This commission establishes and monitors safety standards for children's products, provides safety information, and maintains lists of recalled products.

## National Safe Kids Campaign (The)

111 Michigan Avenue, NW
Washington, DC 20010

**Phone:** (202) 662-0600

**URL:** http://www.safekids.org

This group provides publications on child safety and childproofing.

## Care—Breastfeeding

### Breastfeeding National Network (BNN) Medela, Inc.

P.O. Box 660 4610 Prime Parkway
McHenry, IL 60050-0660

**Phone:** (800) TELL-YOU (835-5968)
**URL:** http://www.medela.com

This manufacturer of breast pumps and breastfeeding support materials offers a list of local lactation consultants. You also can leave an email message at the company website and receive a personal email reply.

### Center For Breastfeeding Information

**Phone:** (847) 519-7730 x241

This center, part of La Leche League International, handles inquiries from health professionals, breastfeeding counselors, and researchers. It also offers a brochure for parents.

### Centers For Disease Control And Prevention Office of Public Inquiries

1600 Clifton Road NE
Atlanta, GA 30333

**Phone:** (800) 311-3435; pre-recorded
information line (404) 332-4555

This center offers advice regarding infectious diseases and breastfeeding.

### Denver Mothers' Milk Bank

Presbyterian/St. Luke's Medical Center
1719 East 19th Ave.
Denver, CO 80218

**Phone:** (303) 869-1888

This organization is the largest distributing milk bank in North America, providing screened and processed donor breast milk.

### International Lactation Consultants Association (ILCA)

4101 Lake Boone Trail, Suite 201
Raleigh, NC 27607-6518

**Phone:** (919) 787-5181

**Email:** ilca@erols.com
**URL:** http://www.ilca.org

This association can help women find a lactation consultant in their local area.

## La Leche League International, Inc. (LLLI)

1400 N. Meacham Road
P.O. Box 4079
Schaumberg, IL 60168-4079

**Phone:** (800) LALECHE, or (847) 519-7730

**Email:** lllhq@llli.org
**URL:** www.lallecheleague.org/

This organization provides information, support, and materials about breastfeeding. The 800 number is staffed by a volunteer La Leche League leader. The organization members also offer referrals to local La Leche League support groups.

### Mother's Help Line

924 C Calle Negocio
San Clemente, CA 92673

**Phone:** (800) 824-6351

This is sponsored by White River Concepts and offers free basic breastfeeding advice and care plans in English and in Spanish.

### Nursing Mothers Council, Inc.

2509 NE Thompson
Portland, OR 97212

P. O. Box 50063
Palo Alto, CA 94303

**Phone:** (503) 293-0661

**URL:** http://www.nursingmothers.org

This nonprofit, nonaffiliated organization aims to "help mothers enjoy a relaxed and happy feeding relationship with their baby" by providing breastfeeding information and support through chapters in various locations. This contact number reaches a referral message to a number of resources and information options.

## Care—Choosing A Caregiver

### American Council Of Nanny Schools

A-74 Delta College
University Center, MI 48740

**Phone:** (517) 686-9417

An information packet can be sent to families upon request.

### Au Pair Care/European Nanny Service

1 Post Street, Suite 700
San Francisco, CA 94104

**Phone:** (800) 428-7247, or (415) 434-8788

This service provides au pair referrals and connections for families. Their 12-month childcare and cultural exchange program matches families with screened foreign students 18 to 26 years of age. There is typically a six to eight week waiting period for families upon applying. Au pairs may work up to 45 hours a week with a maximum limit of 10 hours a day.

Families provide a stipend and room and board. The service's au pairs are not professional childcare professionals, but are trained in first aid and child development.

## Au Pair Exchange

161 6th Avenue
New York, NY 10013

**Phone:** (800) 287-2477

This cultural exchange program matches families with foreign students. Cost for hosting an au pair is $230 per week, and includes up to 45 hours flexible live-in childcare.

## Au Pair In America
## American Institute for Foreign Study

102 Greenwich Ave.
Greenwich, CT 06830

**Phone:** (800) 727-2437

This "largest and oldest au pair agency" offers opportunities for foreign students to work in American family homes. They also offer an international companion program during the summer months.

## Au Pair Programme USA

6965 Union Park Center, Suite 100
Salt Lake City, UT 84047

**Phone:** (800) 937-6264
**Fax:** (801) 255-7782

**Email:** jacque@app/childcrest.com

This agency was originally established as a nanny referral organization and served families for 15 years. Since 1989, they became one of six authorized agencies which bring au pairs into the US. There is a $280 application fee and a $4180 placement fee for their services, which includes the au pair's airfare, medical insurance, a counselor, visa work, and 32 hours of training. Students commit to one year of au pair service.

## Au Pair USA (Interexchange)

161 Sixth Ave.
New York, NY 10013

**Phone:** (800) 287-2477

**Email:** info@interexchange.org
**URL:** http://www.interexchange.org

This cultural exchange is a US designated program which welcomes au pairs, providing families with a year's worth of live-in childcare in exchange for room and board, a weekly stipend, and payment of up to $500 for the au pair's education. The family must engage the au pair as a member of the family. Au pairs are between 18 and 25 years of age, male or female, have at least one year of childcare experience and three references, have undergone background screening and criminal background check, participate in a three-day intensive program in which they are trained in CPR and child safety. One year of local support is also provided.

## Child Care Action Campaign

330 Seventh Ave., 17th Floor
New York, NY 10001

**Phone:** (212) 239-0138
**Fax:** (212) 268-6515

**Email:** hn5746@handsnet.org
**URL:** http://www.ccac.org

The Child Care Action Campaign is a national childcare advocacy organization which serves the general public, parents, government agencies, and the media. The organization sponsors an electronic discussion group called "Children, Youth and Families Forum" which provides information on childcare advocacy and current legislation. The discussion list email address is: HN0003@handsnet.org.

## Child Care Aware

1319 F St. NW, Suite 810
Washington, DC 20004

**Phone:** (800) 424-2246
**Fax:** (202) 393-1109

**Email:** hn6125@handsnet.org

Offering a "connection to good quality care sponsored by Cheerios," this organization's nationwide 1-800 number can refer parents to phone numbers of local childcare resources and referrals. Parents may also call Child Care Aware and request their free packet ($10 for pack of 100) of tip sheets for choosing quality childcare. This includes checklists to use for interviewing careproviders, advice on how to find quality childcare, information on accreditation of childcare centers and homes, and more. A list of their national non-profit partners and corporate sponsors is also available through their phone number.

## Euraupair Intercultural Child Care Program

**Phone:** (800) 713-2002 (West), (800) 901-2002 (East), (800) 960-9100 (Midwest), or (800) 618-2002 (South)

The Euraupair Intercultural Child Care Program is a non-profit, public benefit organization which is officially designated as an exchange visitor program by the United States Information Agency. This organization's au pairs consist of screened young adults between the ages of 18 and 26 who seek the opportunity to live with an American family, and help care for the family's children in exchange for the chance to learn more about our culture and language. The au pairs speak English, are "well educated, healthy, and willing to make a 12 month commitment to live as a member of an American family."

## International Nanny Association (The)

900 Haddon Ave., Suite 438
Collingswood, NJ 08108

**Phone:** (609) 858-0808
**Fax:** (609) 858-2519

**Email:** ina@nanny.org
**URL:** http://www.nanny.org/

Since 1986, the INA (a non-profit association) has served as a clearinghouse for information on the in-home childcare industry. The INA serves over 700 members who are committed to professional in-home childcare. Their membership is made up of nannies, nanny educators, nanny referral agency owners and personnel, and individuals who support the in-home childcare industry. Those members who join agree to abide by the association's recommended practices.

## National Association for Family Child Care (NAFCC)

206-6th Ave., Suite 900
Des Moines, IA 50309-4018

**Phone:** (515) 282-8192
**Fax:** (515) 282-9117

**Email:** nafcc@nafcc.org
**URL:** http://www.nafcc.org

A nationwide study of family daycare in 1978 recommended formation of the National Association for Family Day Care (NAFDC) in 1982. This was later reestablished in 1994 as the National Association for Family Child Care. This "national voice for family child care" provides technical assistance to family childcare associations. This assistance is provided through developing leadership and professionalism, addressing issues of diversity, and by promoting quality and professionalism through NAFCC's Family Child Care Accreditation.

## National Child Care Information Center

243 Church Street NW, 2nd floor
Vienna, VA 22180

**Phone:** (800) 616-2242
**Fax:** (800) 716-2242

**Email:** agoldste@nccic.org
**URL:** http://www.nccic.org

This is a clearinghouse for information on childcare. They disseminate information to anyone interested in finding out how to choose childcare—parents, national or local organizations, state agencies, employers, schools, media, journalists, etc. The center was established in the mid-1990s, and offers no endorsement of information they offer. If information is not available through the center, they will refer you to other organizations that might have that information.

## Growth & Learning

### American Academy Of Child And Adolescent Psychiatry (AACAP)

3615 Wisconsin Ave. NW
Washington, DC 20016-3007

**Phone:** (800) 333-7636, or (202) 966-7300

**URL:** http://www.aacap.org

The AACAP's mission statement is the "promotion of mentally healthy children, adolescents and families through research, training, advocacy, prevention, comprehensive diagnosis and treatment, peer support and collaboration." As a public service, they offer information—"Facts for Families"—and other resources to help parents understand the developmental, behavioral, and mental disorders which may affect children and adolescents.

### American Psychiatric Association

1400 K Street, NW
Washington, DC 20005

**Phone:** (202) 682-6000
**Fax:** (202) 682-6850

**Email:** apa@psych.org
**URL:** http://www.psych.org/

The American Psychiatric Association is a "medical specialty society recognized worldwide." Its members consist of 40,500 U.S. and international physicians who specialize in the diagnosis and treatment of mental and emotional illnesses and substance use disorders. The association also maintains "fact sheets" through their website which are geared for the public. Other publications are available for the public as well.

### American Psychological Association (APA)

750 First Street, NE
Washington, DC 20002

**Phone:** (202) 336-5500

**URL:** http://www.apa.org

The APA is the "largest scientific and professional organization representing psychology in the United States and is the world's largest association of psychologists." APA's membership consists of more than 159,000 researchers, educators, clinicians, consultants, and students.

### Arc (The)

National Headquarters
500 East Border Street, Suite 300
Arlington, TX 76010

**Phone:** (817) 261-6003
**Fax:** (817) 277-3491

**Email:** thearc@metronet.com
**URL:** http://www.thearc.org/

Formerly known as the Association for Retarded Citizens, this non-profit organization makes referrals to local chapters throughout the US. It provides parents with early intervention services for babies and toddlers in an effort to give them a head start through developing their motor skills, coordination, and recognition. This organization also offers free and low-cost brochures, booklets, and videos.

### Association For Childhood Education International (ACEI)

17904 Georgia Ave., Suite 215
Olney, MD 20832

**Phone:** (800) 423-3563

**URL:** http://www.udel.edu/bateman/acei

This association is dedicated to promoting the rights, education, and well-being of children (from infancy through early adolescence), as well as establishing high standards of preparation and professional growth for educators.

### Council For Exceptional Children

1920 Association Dr.
Reston, VA 22091-1589

**Phone:** (703) 620-3660
**Fax:** (703) 264-9494

**Email:** cec@cec.sped.org
**URL:** http://www.cec.sped.org

The CEC is the largest international professional organization dedicated to improving educational outcomes for individuals with exceptionalities, students with disabilities, and/or the gifted. The council sets professional standards, advocates for appropriate governmental policies, provides continual professional development, advocates for newly and historically underserved individuals with exceptionalities, and helps professionals obtain conditions and resources necessary for effective professional practice.

### ERIC Clearinghouse On Elementary And Early Childhood Education

51 Gerty Drive
Champaign, IL 61820-7469

**Phone:** (800) 583-4135, or (217) 333-1386

**Email:** ERICEECE@UIUC.edu
**URL:** http://npin.org

This clearinghouse consists of a large database of education, parenting, and education-related information all of which is in the public domain and can be reproduced for distribution. Much of the information is also available online through their affiliated website (National Parent Information Network) which offers two-page digests, a bi-monthly newsletter, and more. Specific topic searches can be requested by calling their 1-800 number or contacting them through their email address. Visitors will be provided with a list of citations (journals, books, teaching guides) pertaining to that subject.

### National Association For The Education Of Young Children (NAEYC)

1509 16th St. NW
Washington, DC 20036-1826

**Phone:** (800) 424-2460

**Email:** naeyc@naeyc.org
**URL:** http://www.naeyc.org

Founded in 1926, NAEYC is the nation's largest organization of early childhood professionals and others who are dedicated to improving the quality of early childhood education programs for children from birth through age eight. It includes a national network of more than 400 local, state, and regional early childhood organizations affiliated with NAEYC. NAEYC Affiliate Groups share and help to implement NAEYC's primary goals of improving professional practice and working conditions in early childhood education and building public understanding and support for high quality early childhood programs.

## Parent Support—General

### Family Resource Coalition Of America (FRCA)

20 N. Wacker Cr., Suite 1100
Chicago, IL 60605

**Phone:** (312) 338-0900
**Fax:** (312) 338-1522

**URL:** http://www.frca.org/

The FRCA works to strengthen and empower families and communities so that they can foster optimal development of children, youth, and adult family members. They believe in solving problems by preventing them. Their goal is to establish a society in which families, communities, government, social service institutions, and businesses work together to provide healthy, safe environments for children and families to live and work in. The coalition publishes and distributes resources for program providers and planners so they can develop and maintain quality family-supportive programs.

### National Depressive and Manic Depressive Association

730 N. Franklin, Suite 501
Chicago, IL 60610

**Phone:** (312) 642-0049

**URL:** http://www.ndmda.org/

This organization's goal is to educate families, patients, mental health professionals, and the general public concerning depressive and manic-depressive illness as treatable medical diseases. They hope to eliminate patient discrimination, bring about self-help for families and patients, and improve access to care.

## National Institute Of Mental Health

Public Inquiries
5600 Fishers Lane, Rm. 15-C-05
Rockville, MD 20857

**Phone:** (800) 421-4211, or (301) 443-2403

The National Institute of Mental Health offers public and professional education and research on a range of mental health disorders. Professionals and the general public may receive information about the institute's latest research of many disorders by calling its toll-free information line.

## Parents Without Partners (PWP)

401 N. Michigan Ave.
Chicago, IL 60611-4267

**Phone:** (800) 637-7974, or (312) 644-6610
**Fax:** (312) 321-5194

**Email:** pwp@sba.com
**URL:** http://www.parentswithoutpartners.org

Billed as "an international, non-profit, educational organization devoted to the interests of single parents and their children," this group was founded in 1957. Its intent is to provide single parents and their children with an opportunity to enhance personal growth, self-confidence, and sensitivity towards others through an environment of support, friendship, and the exchange of parenting techniques.

## Parent Support—Special Circumstances

## Federation For Children With Special Needs (FCSN)

1135 Tremont Street, Suite 420
Boston, MA 02120

**Phone:** (800) 331-0688 (in MA), or
(617) 236-7210

**Email:** fcsninfo@fcsn.org
**URL:** http://www.fcsn.org/

The Federation is a center for parents and parent organizations to work together on behalf of children with special needs and their families. Organized in 1975 as a coalition of parent groups representing children with a variety of disabilities, the Federation operates a Parent Center in Massachusetts which offers a variety of services to parents, parent groups, and others who are concerned with children with special needs.

## Federation Of Families For Children's Mental Health

1021 Prince Street
Alexandria, VA 22314-2971

**Phone:** (703) 684-7710

**URL:** http://www.ffcmh.org/

This federation is a national parent-run organization focused on the needs of children and youth with emotional, behavioral, or mental disorders and their families. Their focus is on family participation and support in care, and therefore, the Federation works to develop and implement policies, legislation, funding mechanisms, and service systems that utilize the strengths of families. A list of the federation's chapters, state organizations, and other contacts for support is also available.

## National Down's Syndrome Association

666 Broadway, Eighth Floor
New York, NY 10012

**Phone:** (212) 460-9330

**Email:** info@ndss.org
**URL:** http://www.ndss.org/

National organization that promotes research and public awareness of Down's syndrome. Also provides free printed information packets, video cassettes, and a directory and early intervention and parent support groups.

## National Mental Health Association

1021 Prince Street
Alexandria, VA 22314-2971

**Phone:** (800) 969-NMHA, or (703) 684-7722

**URL:** http://www.nmha.org/

This association provides information free of charge on various mental health topics, referral to mental health organizations or facility, and a directory of their nationwide network of mental health professionals.

## Parent Support—Child Abuse

## Child Welfare League Of America, Inc.

440 First St., NW, Suite 310
Washington, DC 20001-2085

**Phone:** (202) 638-2952
**Fax:** (202) 638-4004

**URL:** http://www.cwla.org

CWLA, "the nation's oldest and largest membership-based child welfare organization," is committed to promoting the well-being of children, youths, and their families, and protecting every child from harm. This association consists of almost 1,000 public and private nonprofit agencies that assist abused and neglected children and their families each year with a wide range of services.

## Childhelp, USA. (also known as National Child Abuse Hotline)

**Phone:** (800) 422-4453

By calling this hotline, parents may receive free literature on abuse-related issues, such as child abuse symptoms, definitions, and other

parenting issues. A videotape is also available entitled "Break the Silence" which cites statistics and ways to detect if a child has been abused.

## National Council On Child Abuse And Family Violence (NCCAFV)

1155 Connecticut Ave., NW, Suite 400
Washington, DC 20036

**Phone:** (202) 429-6695

**URL:** http://www.nccafv.org

The NCCAFV, in its second decade of service to all fifty states, Puerto Rico, and the US Virgin Islands, is a resource center on family violence prevention. NCCAFV's commitment is to intergenerational family violence prevention of child abuse, domestic violence (spouse/partner abuse), and elder abuse. The council provides public awareness and education materials, program and resource development consultation, and technical assistance and training in the US and internationally.

## Prevent Child Abuse America

P.O. Box 2866
Chicago, IL 60690

**Phone:** (312) 663-3520

**Email:** ncpca@childabuse.org
**URL:** http://www.childabuse.org

Formerly the National Committee to Prevent Child Abuse, Prevent Child Abuse America is a nationwide organization dedicated to preventing child abuse in all its forms. Established in 1979, they offer opportunities for prevention education, research, advocacy, and prevention programs on the state as well as the national level. Parenting tips and resources for children are available through their website.

## Parent Support—Twins, Multiples, Preemies

## Mothers of Supertwins (MOST)

P.O. Box 951
Brentwood, NY 11717

**Phone:** (516) 434-MOST

This national support network is for families who are expecting, or who are already the parents of, triplets or more. One of the organization's goals is to help families make informed decisions regarding their pregnancy and their children's development.

## National Organization Of Mothers Of Twins Clubs, Inc.

P.O. Box 23188
Albuquerque, NM 87192-1188

**Phone:** (800) 243-2276, or (505) 275-0955

**Email:** NOMOTC@aol.com
**URL:** http://www.nomotc.org/

This organization offers a complimentary brochure of helpful hints for parenting twins, as well as referrals to local support groups.

## Parent Care, Inc.

101-1/2 South Union Street
Alexandria, VA 22314-3323

9041 Colgate Street
Indianapolis, IN 46268

**Phone:** (in IN) (317) 872-9913

This coalition aims to support parents of premature babies by connecting them with their local support groups. They provide information, resources, and support, a quarterly newsletter, and issues papers which outline the concerns faced by parents of premature and high-risk infants. They also provide a handbook to help parents care for the preterm baby.

## Parents of Prematures (POP)

P.O. Box 3046
Kirkland, WA 98033

This nonprofit organization is run by parents who have experienced the birth of a premature child. They offer emotional support, a national newsletter, a baby book, and clothing patterns geared toward the premature infant.

## Triplet Connection

P. O. Box 99571
Stockton, CA 95209

**Phone:** (209) 474-0885
**Fax:** (209) 474-2233

**Email:** tc@tripletconnection.org

The Triplet Connection, a non-profit, tax exempt organization, is a "network of caring and sharing" for multiple-birth families. It provides vital information to families who are expecting triplets, quadruplets, quintuplets or more, as well as encouragement, resources, and networking opportunities for families who are parents of larger multiples.

## Twin Services

P. O. Box 10066
Berkeley, CA 94709

**Phone:** (510) 524-0863

**Email:** twinservices@juno.com

This nonprofit agency was founded in California in 1978 and is dedicated to providing resources and expertise for parents of multiples. They offer free over-the-phone counseling for parents, educators, and other professionals on issues such as pregnancy, parenting, and child development of multiple-birth children. They also offer their members a quarterly newsletter and an annual conference geared toward both parents and professionals. Send a SASE envelope for a list of their publications and services.

## Depression After Delivery (DAD)

P. O. Box 1282
Morrisville, PA 19067

**Phone:** (800) 944-4PPD (4773)

This national, nonprofit organization was the first group of its kind to offer information and support to women who suffer from pre- and postpartum mood disorders. It provide a packet of information with general information about pregnancy-related mood disorders, as well as referrals to support groups, professional organizations and volunteer contacts. Telephone answering service only; requests are answered by mail.

## Mothers At Home

8310-A Old Courthouse Rd.
Vienna, VA 22182

**Phone:** (800) 783-4666, or (703) 827-5903
**Fax:** (703) 790-8587

**Email:** mah@mah.org
**URL:** http://www.mah.org

Mothers At Home (MAH) is the nation's largest and oldest national nonprofit organization supporting mothers who have chosen, or would like to choose, to be at home to nurture their families. The group began in 1984 in an effort to address the lack of support for those who choose (or would like to choose) to be at home with their children. Mothers At Home also publishes a monthly journal entitled Welcome Home.

## Mothers' Home Business Network

P. O. Box 423
East Meadow, NY 11554

**Phone:** (516) 997-7394
**Fax:** (516) 997-0839

**Email:** momhomebiz@mhbn.com
**URL:** http://www.homeworkingmom.com/

Created in 1984, the Mothers' Home Business Network is the first and largest national organization to provide ideas, inspiration, and support for mothers who choose to work at home. A newsletter and other publications are available for members.

## National Association Of Mothers Centers

64 Division Avenue
Levittown, NY 11756

**Phone:** (800) 645-3828

This national network of support and resource groups for new parents can help connect you with a local support center or help you start your own.

## National Association of Postpartum Care Services (NAPCS)

**Phone:** (800) 45-DOULA (453-6852)

Founded in 1989, this is the first national organization of doula postpartum caregivers. NAPCS acts as a referral source for women looking for local service and for those women who wish to start a service. The toll-free number provides membership information and contact information for association services across the country.

## National Organization Of Single Mothers

P. O. Box 68
Midland, NC 28107-0068

**Phone:** (704) 888-KIDS
**Fax:** (704) 888-1752

**URL:** http://www.singlemothers.org

Created in 1991 in response to the needs of single mothers wishing advice and support, this organization also publishes a newsletter entitled SingleMOTHER. They will send free information upon receiving a postcard with your name, address, and request.

## National Women's Health Network

1325 G Street NW, Lower Level
Washington, DC 20005

**Phone:** (202) 347-1140

This advocacy group focuses on women's health issues and strives to educate people about women's health rights.

## Postpartum Stress Center (The)

1062 Lancaster Ave., Suite 18-D
Rosemont, PA 19010

**Phone:** (610) 525-7527

Started in 1987, this support and counseling service offers therapy and referrals to local support groups for couples, as well as a pregnancy support program to identify and support those women at risk for PPD or stress.

## Postpartum Support International (PSI)

927 N. Kellogg Avenue
Santa Barbara, CA 93111

**Phone:** (805) 967-7636

**Email:** thonikman@compuserve.com
**URL:** http://www.iup.edu/an/postpartum

International network of individuals and groups dedicated to increasing awareness about the emotional health of pregnant and postpartum women and their families. Organizational members and professionals receive access to an annual conference, a lending library, researchers and counselors. Parents and the general public receive telephone support and information, as well as referrals to books on the subject and local resources.

### Pregnancy and Postpartum Treatment Program (The)

Department of Psychiatry
University of Illinois at Chicago
912 South Wood Street
Chicago, IL 60612

**Phone:** (312) 996-2200

This outpatient treatment program offers parent-centered treatment and support for postpartum women. Services include mental health services, pregnancy planning for women who have experienced PPD before, consultation for breastfeeding mothers, risk assessment, family and marital therapy, support for new fathers, and more. Also available are referrals to community self-help programs, pediatric care, and parenting skills training.

### Single Mothers By Choice (SMC)

P. O. Box 1642, Gracie Square Station
New York, NY 10028

**Phone:** (212) 988-0993

**URL:** http://www3.parentsplace.com/readroom/smc/index.html

This national, non-profit organization was founded in 1981 by Jane Mattes, CSW and psychotherapist. Its members are devoted to providing information and support to single mothers, as well as those who are contemplating or trying to achieve single motherhood. Members of this organization receive SMC's quarterly newsletter.

### Women's Bureau

United States Department of Labor
Women's Bureau Clearing House
Box EX 200 Constitution Ave., NW
Washington, DC 20210

**Phone:** (800) 827-5335

**Email:** www.wb-wwc@dol.gov
**URL:** htttp://www.dol.gov/dol/wb/

This clearinghouse offers how-to brochures concerning women's workplace issues such as sexual discrimination, sexual harassment, the family and medical leave act, age and wage discrimination, and more.

# INDICES

V

# TITLE INDEX

# AUTHOR INDEX

# PUBLISHER INDEX

# MEDIA INDEX:

**Note**: This media index is created using the media reviewed. In a number of cases, resources are also available in other media formats (audiotape, videotape, etc.); the availability of these other formats is noted in the "Where To Find/Buy" section found in the full-page reviews of such resources.

## Book

★★ Good-Bye Diapers   191
★★ Guide To Baby Products   69
★★ How To Parent   307
★★ How To Read Your Child Like A Book   120
★★ The Infant & Toddler Handbook   153
★★ John Rosemond's Six Point Plan For Raising Happy, Healthy Children   215
★★ The Joyful Child   148
★★ Joyful Play With Toddlers   149
★★ Keys To Parenting Your One-Year-Old   295
★★ Keys To Parenting Your Two-Year-Old   296
★★ Making The "Terrible" Twos Terrific!   181
★★ More Games To Play With Toddlers   151
★★ Mothering The New Mother   251
★★ Multiple Blessings   292
★★ My Toddler   117
★★ No More Tantrums   179
★★ The Nursing Mother's Guide To Weaning   50
★★ Parenting Your Toddler   305
★★ Postpartum Depression   252
★★ Practical Parenting Tips   294
★★ Raising A Happy, Unspoiled Child   121
★★ Right From Birth   114
★★ The Seven Spiritual Laws For Parents   223
★★ The Shelter Of Each Other   216
★★ Sleeping Through The Night   85
★★ Surviving Sibling Rivalry   267
★★ Surviving Your Two-Year Old   122
★★ Toilet Training Without Tears   190
★★ The Well-Fed Baby   78
★★ Working And Caring   218
★★ Your Child At Play: 2 To 3 Years   118
★★ Your Child At Play: One To Two Years   115
★★ Your One-Year-Old   112
★★ Your Self Confident Baby   298
★ 365 Days Of Creative Play   157
★ 365 Food Kids Love To Eat   79
★ The Aware Baby   314
★ The Baby Journal   311
★ Childcare Kit   60
★ Choosing Your Children's Books   154
★ Daily Guide To Parenting   225
★ Dr. James Dobson On Parenting   182
★ The Good Nanny Book   61
★ Helping Your Child Sleep Through The Night   86
★ Madeleine's World   124

★ The Magic Years   125
★ The New Dare To Discipline   183
★ The Nurture Assumption   226
★ On Becoming Babywise, Book One   88
★ On Becoming Babywise, Book Two   310
★ Potty Training Your Baby   192
★ Preventive Parenting With Love, Encouragement, And Limits   184
★ Self-Esteem Activities   156
★ Shouldn't I Be Happy?   255
★ Solve Your Child's Sleep Problems   87
★ Terrible Angel   256
★ Toddler Taming   313
★ Toilet Learning   194
★ Toilet Training In Less Than A Day   193
★ Your Baby & Your Work   224

**Internet**

★★★★ I Am Your Child   96
★★★★ Moms Online (Internet)   258
★★★★ National Center For Fathering   230
★★★★ Parent Soup   277
★★★★ Zero To Three   104
★★★ American Academy Of Family Physicians   20
★★★ BabyCenter   22
★★★ Breastfeeding.com   44
★★★ Family.Com   284
★★★ iBaby.com   67
★★★ KidSource Online   285
★★★ ParentTime   291
★★★ ProMoM, Inc.   47
★★★ Slowlane.com   235
★★★ Time-In   171
★★★ Welcome To Cooking With Young Children   143
★★ Baby Bag   300
★★ Daycare Providers Home Page   152
★★ The Kidz Are People Too Page   25
★★ La Leche League International   51
★★ Medela   49
★★ National Parent Information Network   302
★★ The National Parenting Center   293
★★ Pampers Parenting Institute   303
★★ ParenthoodWeb   308
★★ Parenting Of Babies And Toddlers   304
★★ ParentsPlace.com   297

# SUBJECT INDEX
1–4 Stars (4 = Best)

# AGE GROUP INDEX

## All-Inclusive Overviews About Parenting

# About The Editor

**Julie Soto, MS**, is a Parent Educator, a Family Life specialist, and mother of two grown children. Julie's career includes over twenty years of experience in teaching parenting classes, teaching child development to college students, training professionals in the field of family support, designing parenting curriculum, and developing programs for families with young children. Since 1989, she has been Director of Parent Education at Bellevue Community College. Julie has presented parenting seminars locally in Washington and throughout the United States, with a recent focus on the subject of new brain research and its application to the first three years of a child's life. She is currently a member of the Family Resource Coalition of America, a member of the National Association for the Education of Young Children, a charter member of the Northwest Parent Education Network, and a member of the task force working on the new National Parent Education Network Organization. Her past professional appointments included Board member of the Family Resource Coalition of Washington State and President of the Organization for Parent Education in Washington Community and Technical Colleges. Julie is committed to empowering all families with the understanding that parenting is one of the most important jobs that one can have.

# About The Advisory Council

Resource Pathways would like to thank our Advisory Council for their contributions to this revised edition! Our Advisory Council includes professionals (who are in most cases parents too) that are involved with child development, child health concerns, and family well-being. In their professional and personal roles, our Advisory Council members are familiar with situations parents face and questions they ask. While each Council member has made suggestions and provided input incorporated into this edition, their support does not imply their endorsement of individual resource ratings and recommendations—those decisions are the sole responsibility of our editors.

**Michelle Barnea, RN, MS**, Educational Consultant, Dover, New Jersey

A Registered Nurse, Michelle Barnea attended Duke University where she received her BSN. At Bank Street Graduate School of Education, she then received her MS in Education specifically focused in Infant and Parent Development. A member of both the National Association for the Education of Young Children (NAEYC) and the Coalition of Infant and Toddler Educators (CITE), Ms. Barnea has been working with young children and families for more than 15 years as a nurse and Child Care Center Director in hospital, home, and center settings. She has also developed and taught an eight-week Parent Survival Skills course throughout New Jersey.

**Leah Bratton, MEd**, Early Childhood Coordinator, Windham County, Vermont

With an MEd in Early Childhood Education and Child Development, Leah Bratton has worked with children and families for more than 20 years. Currently she is the Early Childhood Coordinator for the home visiting program of Early Education Services (EES) which provides center-based and home-based child development and parent support services to families with children from birth to three years old in Windham County, Vermont. Prior to her work with EES, Ms. Bratton was co-director of Brattleboro Child Development Center, a NAEYC-accredited childcare center for children from three to twelve years old. She has also served on community and statewide planning groups and boards connected with education, child welfare, and other children's issues. Most recently, she has been part of her county's infant mental health planning group. In 1994, she received the VT Social and

Rehabilitation Services Children and Family Services Commissioner's Award for her role in child advocacy. She was also selected as the recipient of the Vermont AEYC 1998 Distinguished Service Award.

**Marianne Dambra, MS**, Parent/Community Involvement Coordinator, Early Childhood Education Consultant, Rochester, New York

Marianne Dambra works actively on advocacy issues with the Rochester Area Children's Collaborative, part of the local YWCA. Currently, Ms. Dambra is the Parent/Community Involvement Coordinator for the Volunteers of America of Western NY Child Care Center. She also serves on the Board of Directors for the New York State Association for the Education of Young Children (RAEYC), and she is a member of NAEYC. Ms. Dambra has taught toddlers, preschool, and kindergarten, and has been an educational director for childcare facilities. As a single mother of a six year old daughter, Brieanne, Ms. Dambra loves helping students and their parents learn more on the Internet as a volunteer for the Academic Assistance Center on America Online. With a degree in Teaching and Curriculum/Innovations in Education, she also enjoys sharing her experiences with parents and teachers through educational presentations which she offers nationally.

**Deborah K. Hall, FAAP, MD**, Pediatrician, Olympia, Washington

As a fellow of the American Academy of Pediatrics, Deborah Hall has had fifteen years in pediatric practice. She is currently focusing her efforts in the area of child abuse. This includes the diagnosis, treatment, and prevention of physical abuse, sexual abuse, and neglect of children. She is the Medical Director of the St. Peter Hospital Sexual Assault Clinic in Olympia, Washington.

**Kent S. Herbert, MD**, Family Practice Physician, Olympia, Washington

Currently a Family Practice Resident Physician at St. Peter Family Practice, Kent Herbert received his medical degree from the University of New Mexico. He also holds a Master of Arts in teaching degree from Lewis and Clark College. Before entering the field of medicine, Dr. Herbert taught high school science in Oregon for five years. Together with his wife, Tiffany (Herbert), he developed and taught a parenting class to high-risk new parents through the Maternity and Infant Care Program at the University of New Mexico. Most importantly, he is the parent of three children—Taylor (6), Mackenzie (5), and Matthew (5 months).

**Sandra L. Morris**, Early Childhood Consultant, Early Childhood Trainer, Missoula, Montana

With a BA in Elementary Education, Sandra Morris has been providing inservice training for childcare providers and other early childhood professionals for the past 11 years. Currently, she is Project Director for TIME (Training in a Manila Envelope: A Child Care Plus+ Outreach Project to Expand Care and Education Options for Young Children with Disabilities and Their Families), part of a federally funded program through the University of Montana at which Ms. Morris offers inservice training to childcare providers and other early childhood professionals. Her inservices are centered around issues of inclusion of children with disabilities and their families in early childhood settings. A childcare advocate, Ms. Morris is a member of NAEYC and the Council for Exceptional Children/Division for Early Childhood (CEC/DEC). Ms. Morris is the editor of an early childhood newsletter, and author or co-author of many publications including three books, several journal articles, a number of factsheets, and multiple inservice training curricula. She is the mother of four children, grandmother of three preschoolers, and has been a foster mother for newborns, a La Leche League leader, and respite coordinator for families of children with disabilities.

**Ginger Ramsden, MA**, Parent Educator, Child Development Specialist, Evansville, Indiana

A former kindergarten teacher and director of a childcare center, Ginger Ramsden has been a parent educator and professional child development specialist for early childhood education teachers and caregivers for over 30 years. For the last ten years, she has held her current position as Manager of Family, School, and Children's Programs at the University of Southern Indiana where she teaches early childhood courses, provides consulting for the design and start-up of new childcare centers, and facilitates community-based programs for parents, children, and educators. With an MA in Elementary Education, Ms. Ramden is a member of NAEYC and its Indiana affiliate, IAEYC, has served as a board member for the area 4C (Community Coordinated Child Care) for the past 15 years, is a board member of Indiana Association for School-Aged Child Care, and advocates for inclusive programs for children with disabilities through the Evansville ARC. Ms. Ramsden is the parent of two grown children, and along with her husband of 30 years, she is revisiting all of these parenting resources again to stay in tune with her eleven year old daughter.

**Mary Rolf**, Head Start Supervisor, Brandon, Minnesota

Since 1970, Mary Rolf has worked for Head Start at West Central Minnesota Communities Action, Inc. During her first three years, she set up and taught a home-based program in rural Douglas County. Later, she began as Education Coordinator and served as Handicap Coordinator as well. With a BS in Elementary Education, Ms. Rolf has been a member of the Minnesota Association for the Education of Young Children for most of her career. She is also a member of National Head Start Association, and Association for Childhood Education International. Ms. Rolf has also served on numerous county collaborative committees as well as regional committees concerned with early childhood issues.

**Dawn Rouse**, Director of Child Care, Somersworth Housing Authority, Somersworth Child Care Center, Somersworth, New Hampshire

After graduating from the University of Vermont with a BS in Education, Dawn Rouse found her true calling in caring for infants and toddlers. Published in such childcare professional journals as *Child Care Information Exchange*, and a very active speaker and presenter on infant and toddler education and parenting issues in the New England area, Ms. Rouse is passionate about quality care and education for infants, toddlers, and their families. As Adjunct Faculty at Hesser College, Chairperson of the Strafford County Child Care Association, and long-time member of NAEYC, Ms. Rouse shares her love of young children, her dedication to Early Childhood Education, and her knowledge and experience with families, staff, and students.

**Sally Sugarman, MS, CAS**, Professor of Childhood Studies, Bennington College, Bennington, Vermont

For the past 29 years and at present, Sally Sugarman has taught Childhood Studies at Bennington College in Bennington, Vermont. From 1970 to 1995, she was also the Director of the Bennington College Early Childhood Center. While she was Director, the Center had a strong parent program serving children and families of children from two to six years of age. Ms. Sugarman was on the Vermont State Board of Education from 1989 to 1997, and was chair from 1993 to 1997. The founding president of the Bennington County Child Care Associate, Ms. Sugarman was also active in the local Head Start Council for many years. She has an MS in Early Childhood Education from Bank Street College of Education, and a CAS in Educational Research from SUNY Albany.

**Kresha Warnock, MA**, Early Childhood Education Instructor and Consultant, Long Beach, California

With a Masters Degree in Early Childhood Education, Kresha Warnock currently teaches in the Child Development and Early Childhood Education department at Long Beach Community College. She also works with families as an Early Childhood Consultant. Ms. Warnock has been active in parent support groups and has worked with parents as a temperament specialist. A strong advocate for young children, she served as state chairman of the Utah Association for the Education of Young Children. Previously, Ms. Warnock taught preschool, directed a childcare center, and served as a trainer for childcare workers. She currently resides in Long Beach, California with her husband and two children.

# GUIDEBOOKS FOR LIFE'S BIG DECISIONS

For every important issue we face, there are resources that offer suggestions and help. Unfortunately, we don't always know much about the issue we've enountered and we don't know:

- Where to find these sources of information
- Much about their quality, value, or relevance

Resource Pathways guidebooks help those facing an important decision or challenging life-event by directing them to the information they need to understand the issues they face and make decisions with confidence. In every Resource Pathways guidebook:

- We **describe and evaluate virtually all quality resources** available in any media (books, the Internet, CD-ROMs, videotape, audiotape, and more).

- We **explain the issues** that are typically encountered in dealing with each subject, and **classify each resource** reviewed according to its primary focus.

- We **make a reasoned judgment** about the quality of each resource, give it a **rating**, and decide whether it should be **recommended**. We select only the best as "Recommended" (roughly 1 in 4).

- We **provide information on where to buy or how to access** each resource, including ISBN numbers for books and URL "addresses" for Internet websites.

- We **publish a new edition of each guidebook frequently**, with updated reviews and recommendations.

Those who turn to Resource Pathways guidebooks will be able to locate the resource they need, saving time, money, and frustration as they begin their research and learning process.

# LIFECYCLES SERIES

■ *". . . a calm and hope-filled guide . . ."*

*Anxiety & Depression:*
*The Best Resources To Help You Cope*

Editor: Rich Wemhoff, PhD
ISBN: 1-892148-09-9 (2nd Ed)
256 Pages (Available July, 1999)

■ *". . . an invaluable guide that will save time, emotional energy, and money . . ."*

*Divorce: The Best Resources To Help You Survive*

Editor: Rich Wemhoff, PhD
ISBN: 1-892148-00-5 (2nd Ed)
324 Pages

■ *". . . valuable and remarkable directory . . ."*

*Marriage: The Best Resources To Help Yours Thrive*

Editor: Rich Wemhoff, PhD
ISBN: 1-892148-05-6
256 Pages (Available April, 1999)

# PARENTING SERIES

■ *". . . an incredible resource guide . . ."*

*Raising Teenagers:*
*The Best Resources To Help Yours Succeed*

Editor: John Ganz, MC, EdD
ISBN: 1-892148-04-8
268 Pages

■ *"A comprehensive gem of a resource guide! . . . a great time-saver . . ."*

*Having Children: The Best Resources To Help You Prepare*

Editor: Anne Montgomery, MD, IBCLC, FAAFP
ISBN: 1-892148-06-4 (2nd Ed)
312 Pages (Available May, 1999)

■ *". . . exciting, comprehensive, and hands-on practical . . ."*

*Infants & Toddlers:*
*The Best Resources To Help You Parent*

Editor: Julie Soto, MS
ISBN: 1-892148-10-2 (2nd Ed)
390 Pages (Available August, 1999)

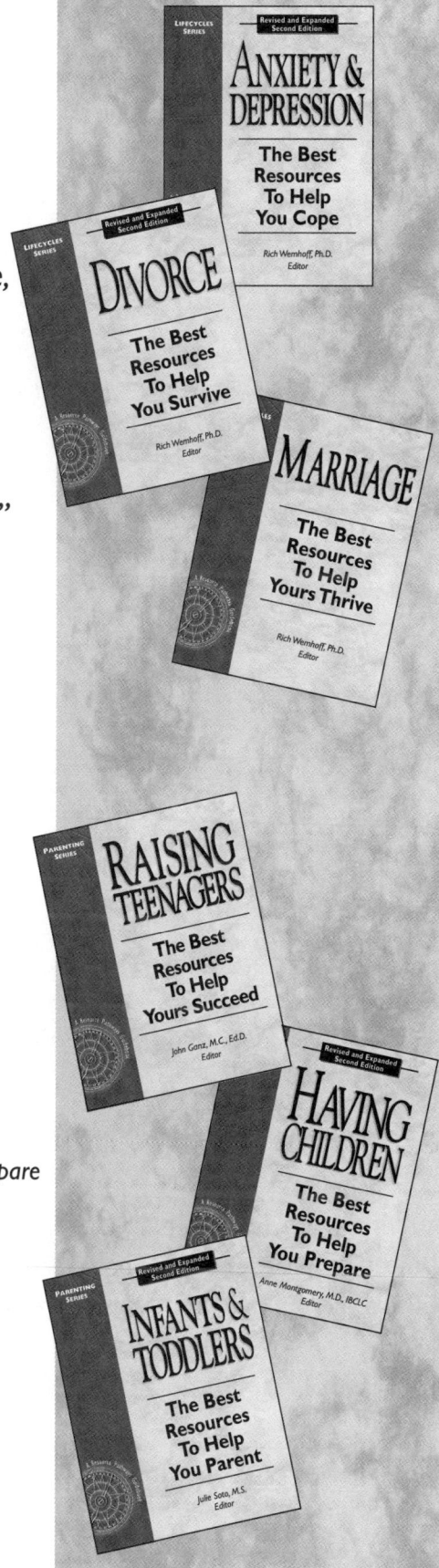

# HIGHER EDUCATION & CAREERS SERIES

■ *". . . quintessential guide to the guides . . ."*

*College Choice & Admissions:*
*The Best Resources To Help You Get In*

Editor: Dodge Johnson, PhD
ISBN: 0-9653424-9-2 (3rd Ed)
336 Pages

■ *". . . comprehensive . . . a real time and money saver . . ."*

*College Financial Aid:*
*The Best Resources To Help You Find The Money*

Editor: David Hoy
ISBN: 1-892148-01-3 (3rd Ed)
278 Pages

■ *". . . thorough, honest, and complete . . ."*

*Graduate School:*
*The Best Resources To Help You Choose, Get In, & Pay*

Editor: Jane Finkle, MS
ISBN: 0-9653424-7-6
278 Pages

■ *Career Transitions:*
*The Best Resources To Help You Advance*

Editor: Resource Pathways Editors
ISBN: 1-892148-08-0
256 Pages (Available June, 1999)

■ *". . . a clear and concise roadmap . . ."*

*Starting Your Career:*
*The Best Resources To Help You Find The Right Job*

Editor: Laura Praglin, PhD
ISBN: 1-892148-03-X
248 Pages

*Your favorite bookstore or library may order any of these guidebooks for you, or you can order direct, using the pre-paid postcards on the following pages.*

## ORDERING INFORMATION

**Order by phone:** 888-702-8882 (Toll-free 24/7)
**Order by fax:** 425-557-4366
**Order by mail:** Resource Pathways, Inc.
22525 SE 64th Place, Suite 253
Issaquah, WA 98027-5387

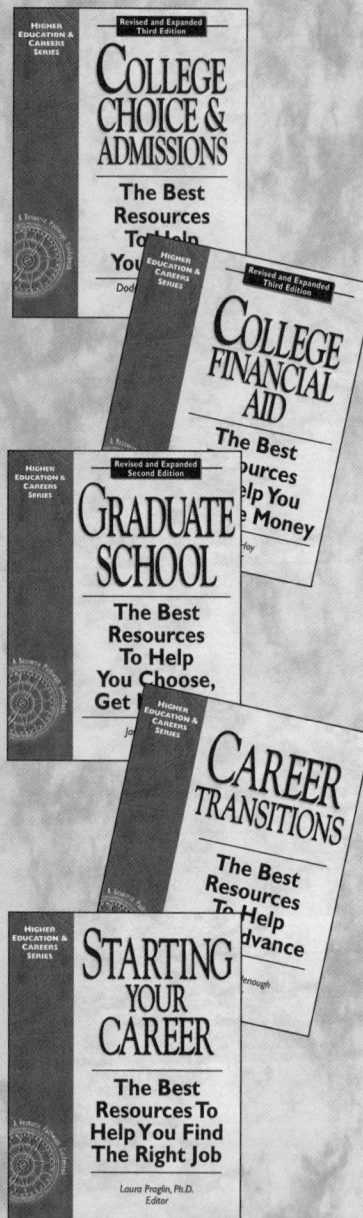

# ORDER FORM

| | |
|---|---|
| **Order by phone:** 888-702-8882 (Toll-free 24/7)<br>**Order by fax:** 425-557-4366 | **Order by mail:** Resource Pathways, Inc.<br>22525 SE 64th Place, Suite 253<br>Issaquah, WA 98027-5387 |

☐ *Anxiety & Depression:*
  *The Best Resources To Help You Cope*

☐ *Divorce: The Best Resources To Help You Survive*

☐ *Marriage: The Best Resources To Help Yours Thrive*

_____

☐ *Raising Teenagers:*
  *The Best Resources To Help Yours Succeed*

☐ *Having Children: The Best Resources To Help You Prepare*

☐ *Infants & Toddlers: The Best Resources To Help You Parent*

☐ *College Choice & Admissions:*
  *The Best Resources To Help You Get In*

☐ *College Financial Aid:*
  *The Best Resources To Help You Find The Money*

☐ *Graduate School:*
  *The Best Resources To Help You Choose, Get In, & Pay*

☐ *Career Transitions: The Best Resources To Help You Advance*

☐ *Starting Your Career:*
  *The Best Resources To Help You Find The Right Job*

_____ copies at $24.95 = _____

Shipping (USPS Priority Mail): $3.95 for first copy; $2.00/copy for additional copies

\+ Shipping & Handling = _____

We will include an invoice with your shipment

Total = _____

Name (please print) _____

Organization _____ Title _____

Address _____

City _____ State _____ Zip _____

Phone _____ Email _____

---

# ORDER FORM

| | |
|---|---|
| **Order by phone:** 888-702-8882 (Toll-free 24/7)<br>**Order by fax:** 425-557-4366 | **Order by mail:** Resource Pathways, Inc.<br>22525 SE 64th Place, Suite 253<br>Issaquah, WA 98027-5387 |

☐ *Anxiety & Depression:*
  *The Best Resources To Help You Cope*

☐ *Divorce: The Best Resources To Help You Survive*

☐ *Marriage: The Best Resources To Help Yours Thrive*

_____

☐ *Raising Teenagers:*
  *The Best Resources To Help Yours Succeed*

☐ *Having Children: The Best Resources To Help You Prepare*

☐ *Infants & Toddlers: The Best Resources To Help You Parent*

☐ *College Choice & Admissions:*
  *The Best Resources To Help You Get In*

☐ *College Financial Aid:*
  *The Best Resources To Help You Find The Money*

☐ *Graduate School:*
  *The Best Resources To Help You Choose, Get In, & Pay*

☐ *Career Transitions: The Best Resources To Help You Advance*

☐ *Starting Your Career:*
  *The Best Resources To Help You Find The Right Job*

_____ copies at $24.95 = _____

Shipping (USPS Priority Mail): $3.95 for first copy; $2.00/copy for additional copies

\+ Shipping & Handling = _____

We will include an invoice with your shipment

Total = _____

Name (please print) _____

Organization _____ Title _____

Address _____

City _____ State _____ Zip _____

Phone _____ Email _____

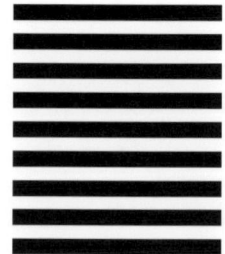

# BUSINESS REPLY MAIL
**FIRST-CLASS MAIL     PERMIT NO. 176     ISSAQUAH, WA**

POSTAGE WILL BE PAID BY ADDRESSEE

**RESOURCE PATHWAYS INC.**

**22525 SE 64TH PL STE 253**

**ISSAQUAH WA 98027-9939**

NO POSTAGE
NECESSARY
IF MAILED
IN THE
UNITED STATES

# BUSINESS REPLY MAIL
**FIRST-CLASS MAIL     PERMIT NO. 176     ISSAQUAH, WA**

POSTAGE WILL BE PAID BY ADDRESSEE

**RESOURCE PATHWAYS INC.**

**22525 SE 64TH PL STE 253**

**ISSAQUAH WA 98027-9939**

# DISCOUNTS AND SUBSCRIPTIONS FOR PROFESSIONALS

**Do you provide professional services to couples or families experiencing these life-events?**

If so, you should know that Resource Pathways offers very attractive discounts to professionals for subscriptions to current and new editions of any title.

**To obtain additional information or place an order, complete and return this postcard, or call 425-557-4382 (8-6 PST), or 888-702-8882 (Toll-free 24/7).**

Name (please print) _____

Organization _____ Title _____

Address _____

City _____ State _____ Zip _____

Phone _____ Email _____

# DISCOUNTS AND STANDING ORDERS FOR LIBRARIES

Resource Pathways' titles are distributed to libraries throughout North America by the National Book Network, through Ingram, Baker & Taylor, and many other regional wholesalers.

**You can order any of our titles through your usual wholesaler or distributor, or direct from the National Book Network:**

**National Book Network, Inc., 15200 NBN Way, Blue Ridge Summit, PA 17214
800-462-6420 / 800-338-4550 (fax)**

You can order directly from Resource Pathways at very attractive discounts, for both individual and standing orders.

**To obtain additional information or place an order, complete and return this postcard, or call 425-557-4382 (8-6 PST), or 888-702-8882 (Toll-free 24/7).**

Name (please print) _____

Organization _____ Title _____

Address _____

City _____ State _____ Zip _____

Phone _____ Email _____

# BUSINESS REPLY MAIL

FIRST-CLASS MAIL     PERMIT NO. 176     ISSAQUAH, WA

POSTAGE WILL BE PAID BY ADDRESSEE

**RESOURCE PATHWAYS INC.**

**22525 SE 64TH PL STE 253**

**ISSAQUAH WA 98027-9811**

NO POSTAGE
NECESSARY
IF MAILED
IN THE
UNITED STATES

# BUSINESS REPLY MAIL

FIRST-CLASS MAIL     PERMIT NO. 176     ISSAQUAH, WA

POSTAGE WILL BE PAID BY ADDRESSEE

**RESOURCE PATHWAYS INC.**

**22525 SE 64TH PL STE 253**

**ISSAQUAH WA 98027-9811**

NO POSTAGE
NECESSARY
IF MAILED
IN THE
UNITED STATES